D0845675

Tortillas for the Gods

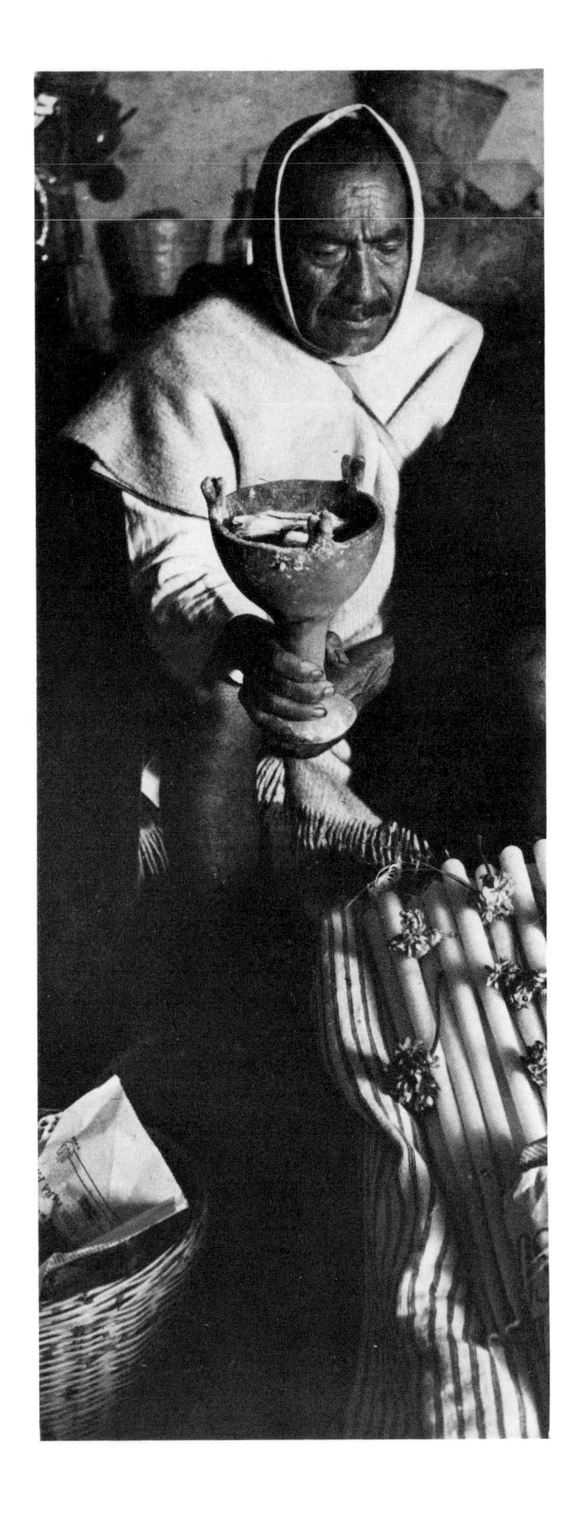

Evon Z. Vogt

Tortillas for the Gods

A Symbolic Analysis of Zinacanteco Rituals

HARVARD UNIVERSITY PRESS
Cambridge, Massachusetts, and London, England 1976

Printed in the United States of America

Library of Congress Cataloging in Publication Data

Vogt, Evon Zartman, 1918-
Tortillas for the gods.

Bibliography: p.
Includes index.
1. Tzotzil Indians—Rites and ceremonies.
2. Indians of Mexico—Rites and ceremonies.
3. Zinacantán, Mexico—Social life and customs.
4. Zinacantán, Mexico—Religion. I. Title.
F1221.T9V59 299'.7 75-28470
ISBN 0-674-89554-1

To the Memory of Alfonso Caso

Preface

THE RITUALS I describe and analyze in this book are performed in Zinacantan, a Tzotzil-speaking *municipio* (municipality) in the Highlands of Chiapas in southeastern Mexico. Tzotzil is a Mayan language, and Zinacantan is located near the western border of the contemporary Mayan Indian area of Mexico, Guatemala, and Belize.

My research there began in the summer of 1957, and, with the exception of 1966, I have returned each year, either during the summer months or during the fall or spring terms, for continuing field work. Since the 1957 beginning of the Harvard Chiapas Project, I have been accompanied by able students and younger colleagues who have pursued their own interests in studying various aspects of culture in Zinacantan, as well as in the neighboring Tzotzil-speaking municipios of Chamula, Huistán, and San Andrés Larrainzar and in the Spanish-speaking town of San Cristóbal Las Casas.

Field operations have alternated between our project headquarters in San Cristóbal Las Casas, where our informants could be offered hospitality and interviewed without the usual interruptions of Indian life, and the Tzotzil villages in the mountains where we have lived in Indian homes and participated in the daily and annual round of native life. When possible, the performances of ceremonials have been photographed and recorded with tape recorders. The photographs have later served to elicit additional data during the systematic interviewing. The tapes have been transcribed by informants whom we have taught to read and to write (and in several cases to type) in both Tzotzil and Spanish. The Harvard Chiapas Project and Zinacantan are described in detail in *Zinacantan: A Maya Community in the Highlands of Chiapas* (Vogt 1969).

From the outset I have been deeply interested in the ritual life of Zinacantan and have spent more field time concentrating on this topic than on any other aspect of the culture. Even so, this book does not attempt to describe and analyze all of the Zinacanteco rituals, a task that would require several volumes. Rather, I have here undertaken to cover only selected aspects of the ritual life. Apart from the length and complexity of a full inventory of the rituals, there are other reasons for this selectivity. I have, for example, omitted the Easter Season in the calendrical round simply because I have never managed to be in Zinacantan at Easter. (Some aspects of the Easter Season rituals are covered in Bricker 1973; additional details may be found in Early 1965.) The reader will also discover a gap when it comes to witchcraft rituals. Here again, my knowledge is still lacking compared to that of Francesco Pellizzi, who has studied witchcraft for several years and is currently writing on the subject. Further, it is worth noting that the Zinacanteco shamans regularly perform several types of complex curing ceremonies while I have (in Chapter 5) chosen to focus upon only one type. Since this ceremony is the longest and most complex, and incorporates most of the typical ritual procedures performed in the other ceremonies, I have decided to consider it a kind of "master" of the genre.

Acknowledgments

The Harvard Chiapas Project is sponsored by the Center for the Behavioral Sciences and the Peabody Museum of American Archeology and Ethnology at Harvard University, and by the Instituto Nacional Indigenista in Mexico. The research funds have been provided by the National Institute of Mental Health of the United States Public Health Service (Grants No. M-1929 and MH-02100); the Carnegie Corporation of New York under a grant (B-3204) for the Columbia-Cornell-Harvard-Illinois Summer Field Studies Program, which was later supported by the National Science Foundation (Division of Undergraduate Education and Science); the American Philosophical Society (Grant No. 2295); the Harvard University Summer School; and a Ford Foundation Grant-in-Aid. I have also received support from the National Science Foundation (GS-262, GS-976, GS-1524) to undertake an aerial survey of the Tzotzil and Tzeltal zone in the Highlands of Chiapas.

Over the years I have become obligated to many persons and institutions in the United States and Mexico for assistance of many types on the Project. At Harvard I have received strong support from the two sponsoring institutions of the Project, and I would like to express my gratitude to the Director of the Center for the Behavioral Sciences, Dr. E. L. Patullo, and to the Director of the Peabody Museum, Professor Stephen Williams. I have also had many stimulating conversations concerning the Project and our data with my colleagues, especially Professors Gordon R. Willey, David Maybury-Lewis, John B. Haviland, Jeremy A. Sabloff, Dr. H. E. D. Pollock, and Miss Tatiana Proskouriakoff.

In Mexico, I would first like to express my appreciation to the Instituto Nacional Indigenista from which I have received intellectual stimulation and logistic support, especially from the late Dr. Alfonso Caso, and from Dr. Gonzalo Aguirre Beltrán and Professor Alfonso Villa Rojas. I have also profited intellectually and logistically from the cooperation of the Instituto Nacional de Antropologıa e Historia, especially in contacts with Dr. Ignacio Bernal and Professor Fernando Cámara Barbachano, and from my association with Dr. Alberto Ruz Lhuillier, the Director of the

For ease in distinguishing them, Spanish words have been italicized at first mention; thereafter, they appear in regular type. Tzotzil words have been set in capital letters throughout, although family and given names and names of places found on Mexican maps have not. Whenever possible, English translations for Tzotzil or Spanish have been employed after first mention. For an understanding of the pronunciation of the Tzotzil words, see the list and description of Tzotzil phonemes in Appendix I.

Centro de Estudios Mayas of the Universidad Nacional Autónoma de Mexico.

In Chiapas, I have also had the good fortune to enjoy the support of the Governor, Dr. Manual Velasco Suárez, who has maintained an active interest in our Project and its publications; of Licenciado Angel Robles, the Director of the Office of Asuntos Indígenas of the state government of Chiapas, who has helped us in countless ways; of Sr. Leopoldo Velasco Robles, formerly Presidente Municipal of San Cristóbal, who has offered warm hospitality and close cooperation; and of Doña Gertrudis Duby Vda. de Blom, who maintains the famous Casa Blom with its magnificent library and research center. We are also indebted to the Bishop of the Diocese of San Cristóbal Las Casas, Samuel Ruiz García, and to Sr. Fernando Hernández Velasco, who have helped us on many occasions.

In Zinacantan we have deeply appreciated the hospitality and cooperation of many Indian families with whom we have been working all these years. I should especially mention Domingo de la Torre Pérez, José Hernández Pérez, Mariano Hernández Zárate, Andrés Gómez Rodríguez, José Pérez Nuh, Mariano Pérez ʔOkots, and Antonia González Pakanchil, and their families.

The assistance of my research assistants and secretaries over the years, especially Dolores Vidal, Sharon Latterman, and Suzanne Abel, in typing and assembling the manuscript is gratefully acknowledged. I am also indebted to Suzanne Abel and Elizabeth M. Dodd for their splendid editorial work in bringing the manuscript to completion. Ms. Abel has helped me rewrite many sections of the book during the past year; her skills in improving the style and the interpretations will, I am certain, be appreciated by the reader.

Maps were drawn by Samuel H. Bryant. The originals of the line drawings were done by Elizabeth M. Dodd, except for Figure 38 by Mary E. Scott, Figures 39 and 40 by Christopher R. Fletcher, and Figure 45 by B. N. Colby. Whitney Powell of the Peabody Museum produced the final drafts of all the figures.

The photographs were taken by Frank Cancian, except for Figures 10, 23, 41, and 48, which were taken by John D. Early. I appreciate their permission to use them.

I am grateful to my wife, Catherine C. Vogt, who continues to accompany me on my field trips to Chiapas and to provide warm hospitality at our field headquarters for field workers, Indian informants, visiting anthropologists, and friends. At Harvard she has also served as a research assistant, playing an important role in organizing data on the ceremonial life of Zinacantan.

The first draft of the manuscript of this volume was constructively reviewed by a number of my students and junior colleagues, especially Victoria Reifler Bricker, Frank Cancian, George and Jane Collier, Thomas Crump, James J. Fox, Gary H. Gossen, Carol J. Greenhouse, John B. Haviland, Eva Hunt, Robert M. Laughlin, Priscilla Rachun Linn, Francesco Pellizzi, Richard S. Price, Michelle and Renato Rosaldo, and Mary E. Scott. It required more than a year of hard work to respond to all of their comments and to make the necessary revisions, but I am certain the manuscript has been markedly improved as a result. The final version benefited from the sensitive editing of Mrs. Philip C. McLaughlin of Harvard University Press.

Finally, I would like to add that the Project would have been impossible without the remarkable work of my students and junior colleagues (see Appendix II) who have done field research with me in Chiapas.

E.Z.V.

Cambridge, Massachusetts
June 1975

Contents

FIGURES

TABLES

Tortillas for the Gods

I

Introduction

WHEN ZINACANTECOS LIGHT white wax candles at their mountain shrines, they say they are offering "tortillas" to their ancestral gods who live inside the mountains. They provide "cigarettes" in the form of smoke from burning copal incense. Cane liquor, poured on the ground, completes the meal.

The gods' meals are like those eaten by men. Or, as the Zinacantecos express it, men eat what the gods eat. For in the Zinacanteco perception of order in the universe, the ancestors provide the model for human life, they know best how to cultivate maize, build houses, herd sheep, weave clothing, deal with their kinsmen, and perform ceremonies. Communication with these ancestors (and the other gods populating the Zinacanteco world) is essential for the good life. Much of what can be described as Zinacanteco "religion" involves symbolic transactions between men and gods in intricate rituals that use metaphors to express and regenerate the basic principles of the Zinacanteco social and natural universe.

Some Problems in Decoding Ritual Symbols

Interpreting ritual is a maddening intellectual challenge when the members of a society are not so articulate as Victor Turner's Ndembu, or the Navaho among whom I worked before starting field research in Zinacantan. Native exegesis on the meaning of rituals (whether from laymen or specialists) is the most revealing source of information, either in the form of direct statements from informants or, more indirectly, from ritual prayers and songs, or myths. But when, as any Mesoamerican field worker knows all too well, the most common response of an informant asked why or what about a ritual is "it's the custom," then the discovery and interpretive procedures are long and involved indeed. Often, if not universally, much of what is orderly in a culture is covert, even unconscious and acquires meaning for the investigator only after repeated observations of the behavior. Years of observing highly repetitious rituals, of puzzling over recurring details of ritual paraphernalia, of keeping track of all the contexts in which ritual symbols are used, of studying the subtleties of the Tzotzil language, of reading Lévi-Strauss, Leach, Turner, Douglas, Geertz, and other colleagues for theoretical leads, of then coming back to informants with fresh questions often end in prying out highly pertinent native exegesis —an exegesis which often proves available to the investigator when the right questions can be asked. Sometimes the meanings behind a ritual turn out to be so simple and straightforward that I am astonished at not having perceived them years before; in other cases, they turn out to be subtle, complex, unexpected, and largely implicit.

For ten years I puzzled over why Zinacantecos setting out on a ceremonial circuit nearly always proceed counterclockwise from shrine to shrine. That this has been a Maya pattern since prehistoric times is well-recognized, but this tells nothing other than that the Mayas have always done it this way. I repeatedly questioned informants, only to elicit the usual "it's the custom." I tried out various hypotheses, including clues from nature—such as the apparent counterclockwise wheeling of the constellations around the polestar—as possible models for this regularity. This particular hypothesis elicited nothing of value from my informants; nor was it foolproof on its own, since dozens of tribal cultures in the Northern Hemisphere observe the same constellations moving in a counterclockwise direction every night, yet proceed clockwise in their ceremonial circuits. Finally, the breakthrough came in 1967-68 when one of my younger colleagues, Gary H. Gossen, was engaged in field research in the neighboring Tzotzil municipio of Chamula, where circuits are also counterclockwise. One day, standing in front of the church in the ceremonial center, he observed a procession of Chamula ritualists emerge from the church and proceed counterclockwise around the sacred atrium. It suddenly struck him that the explanation was probably as follows: when the ritualists face "sacred space" and set out to "enclose" it, they start by moving off *to the right*, thus creating the counterclockwise circuit.* Gossen had been interviewing about right and left-hand symbolism in Chamula, and had discovered the overwhelming importance of the BAZ'I K'OB (the "genuine" hand, as the right hand is called in Tzotzil). It seemed obvious that ritual processions would follow the principle of the primacy of the right hand over the left hand in initiating circuits (Gossen 1972). Subsequent interviewing of Chamulas confirmed this deductive reasoning. I then went back to my data and to further interviewing in Zinacantan and found that this simple, straightforward principle explains the counterclockwise circuits in Zinacantan as well. I was amazed I had not thought of it before. But my Zinacanteco informants took the principle *so much for granted* that it never occurred to them to state it to me in so many words. They had been previously responding

*This raises the interesting methodological question that will occur elsewhere in the book: isn't the counterclockwise circuit merely a matter of history, something the Catholic friars introduced to the Highlands of Chiapas in the sixteenth century? My response is twofold. First, although history certainly accounts for the introduction of many items of ritual in Chiapas, it does not explain what the ritual means to the Indians today, nor why they are continuing to perform it as they do. Whatever the ultimate origins of a ritual (Maya, Aztec, Spanish, or however syncretistic), the rituals we observe today have a shape, form, and coherence which is distinctively Zinacanteco, and my task is basically to discover the ordering principles which underlie this coherence. Second, in the case of the counterclockwise circuit, there is evidence from the Dresden Codex, from the Chilam Balam (Roys 1933), and from the Uayeb rites described by Landa (Tozzer 1941) that the pattern was a pre-Conquest one. So if sixteenth-century Catholic processions were counterclockwise, they coincided with a pre-existing pattern of counterclockwise circuits.

1. With incense burning and candles lighted, a shaman prays to the ancestral gods

"it's the custom," instead of adding for *my* benefit, "it's the custom to start off to the right." Their response to further interviews were to the effect that "anyone in his right mind knows that!" This Maya pattern is not the only way that right-hand symbolism may be stressed in ceremonial circuits. It is also possible (see Hertz 1960) for ritualists to keep sacred space or a sacred object *on the right hand* in proceeding around it—and this produces a clockwise circuit.

A second example comes to mind. For nearly ten years I puzzled over seating arrangements for Zinacanteco religious and political officials. The Zinacantecos are a very rank-conscious people, their concern with order being made unequivocably clear on ritual occasions by the seating arrangement on benches of various kinds. Seating arrangements are "metaphors of hierarchy" (R. Rosaldo 1968), and no one has ever been known to sit "out of place" even when all of the ritualists are intoxicated beyond reason on cane liquor. Sometimes high-ranking men sit at the right end of benches, sometimes at the left, from the perspective of the seated men. Especially interesting was the seating order of the highest political officials in front of the *cabildo* (town hall) where the Presidente sits at the left end of the bench. The interview data were confused and not very helpful. Finally, in 1969 I had an opportunity to spend a full day on the subject with an excellent Zinacanteco informant who was at Harvard teaching Tzotzil. We recorded all the seating arrangements each of us could reconstruct from religious and political contexts in Zinacantan, and searched together for principles of explanation. What emerged was, again, an economical and elegant interpretation using three simple principles that apply in a fixed order of priority: (1) other things being equal, the highest ranking man sits on the right end of a bench, and his juniors sit to his left. However, (2) if for any reason principle (1) conflicts with having the senior man seated closest to the "rising sun," then the sun takes precedence, and the order is reversed. This explains the seating order of the political officials at the cabildo which was built facing south; it would be unthinkable for the Presidente to sit on the right end of the bench and be closest to the "setting sun"—hence he sits on the left, toward the east. Principle (3), a combination of (1) and (2), applies when two sets of ritual officials (the Alféreces and Mayordomos) sit on each side of the door to the Church of San Lorenzo, the principal church in Zinacantan Center. The Alféreces, being of higher rank, sit to the right of the door (as one faces the church) and, as they face outward, the highest rank sits on the right end of the bench, his juniors to his left. The Mayordomos sit on the left of the door but, contrary to the Alféreces, the highest ranking Mayordomo sits on the left end of the bench, and his juniors on his right. Thus, the highest ranking officials in each group are closest to the door of the church—that is, closest to the principal saints on the main altar inside the church and, correspondingly, to the direction of the "rising sun." If, as the informant explained, you folded the two benches into the church, placing them along the "path of the sun," the highest ranking official in each order would be toward the east. Because the Alféreces are of higher rank, their seating order conforms to both principles: the primacy of "rising sun" over "setting sun," and the primacy of right over left. The lower-ranking Mayordomos, on the other hand, occupy the place which can conform to only one principle. Significantly, proximity to the "rising sun" takes precedence over "right-left" as an ordering principle. Figure 2 expresses this diagrammatically.

Some symbolic solutions, though initially obscure, are often simpler than anticipated. On the other hand, much symbolism evident in Zinacanteco ritual proved subtle and intricate, with unexpected levels of meaning. For example, in Zinacantan plants are crucial exponents of symbolism. They are, to borrow a phrase from Lévi-Strauss (1963), "goods to think with." They

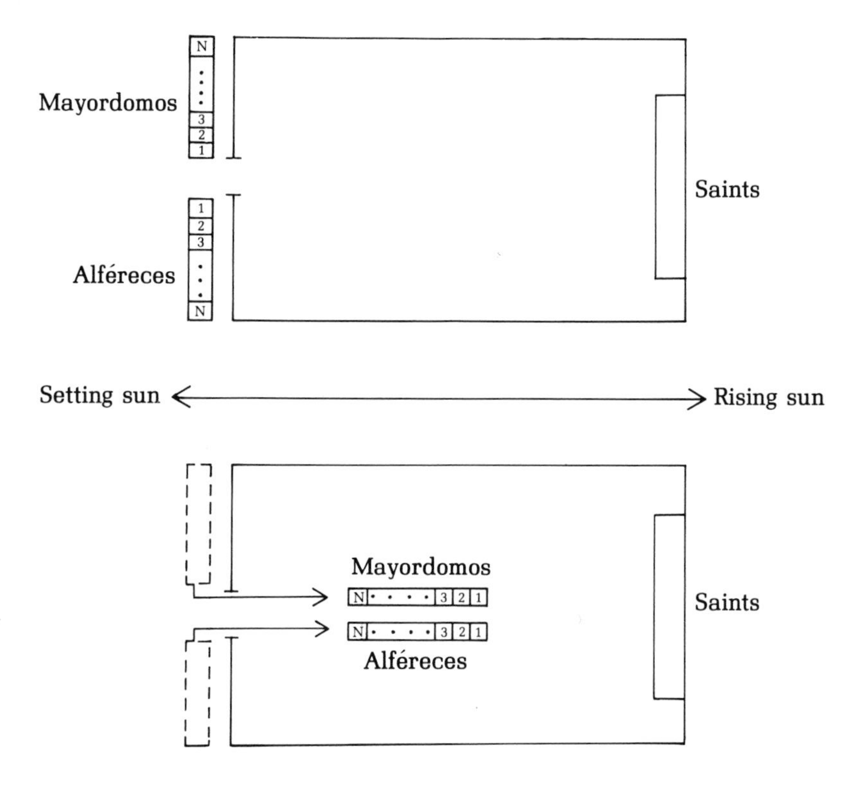

2. The principles of rank order followed by the cargoholders at the Church of San Lorenzo

are used in a logic constructed of observed contrasts in the sensory qualities of concrete objects; they figure prominently in the Zinacanteco's "science of the concrete" (Lévi-Strauss 1966). Thus, plants provide a rich canvas for the portrayal of crucial messages in the symbolic code. As Berlin, Breedlove, and Haven (1974) and Robert Laughlin (1975) have discovered, Tzotzil and Tzeltal identify and classify hundreds of plant species. But from these hundreds of species, Zinacantecos use only about twenty plants for ritual purposes. These ritually salient plants appear in various assemblages, depending on the type of ritual, in virtually all ceremonies. Although I had known about these plants for many years, I could say little about them beyond listing the species used for each ritual. But because I believed our theorists in symbolic anthropology were correct, I was convinced that these plants *must* have meaning, that they *must* be selected in accordance with, make sense in terms of, the Zinacanteco cultural code.

In the summer of 1970 I was stimulated by the field data and theoretical insights of a young colleague, Michelle Rosaldo, who had been working on ritual plants of the Ilongot (M. Rosaldo 1972), to launch a fresh attack on the problem. My procedure was to collect the ritual plants in the mountains with an experienced shaman and take them back to our field headquarters where we could work together without the usual interruptions from the shaman's curious (and sometimes suspicious) Zinacanteco neighbors. There the shaman showed me in precise detail how the plants were tied into bundles and placed on cross shrines. We reconstructed a number of typical full-scale ritual settings which I then used for intensive interviewing. I soon discovered a number of critical plant attributes we had not recognized before. Not only is each plant classified as wild or domesticated and highland or lowland but each also possesses an innate soul, defined as "hot or cold," and "active or quiet." Further, each soul has a color which, not surprisingly, comes from one of the five basic Zinacanteco colors of red, black, white, yellow, and blue-green. Ordinarily, the innate soul color does not correspond to the color of the blossom, leaves, or needles. Like other Mayas, the Zinacantecos do not differentiate "blue" from "green" in the manner that we code colors in the spectrum; this range is YOX (G. Collier 1966). These five colors are generally the most salient in all Maya cultures, and often have directional associations: red with east, black with west, white with north, yellow with south, and blue-green with "the center of the world" (see Thompson 1934; Roys 1933; Marcus 1970).

Arranging the plants in patterned clusters provides a highly effective vehicle for conveying symbolic messages. Consider the use of flowers in Zinacanteco curing ceremonies in light of Mary Douglas' (1966) concept of symbolic boundaries and Lévi-Strauss's emphasis upon the importance of the opposition between Nature and Culture. In Zinacantan this Nature-Culture contrast finds explicit emphasis in the labeled and opposed domains of NAETIK, "the houses," and TE?TIK, "the trees" or "forest" (E. Vogt and C. Vogt 1970).

In Zinacantan wooden crosses stand at the foot and on top of those mountains conceived to house the ancestral gods. These crosses represent more than is implied by the Catholic-Christian symbols: crosses are described as "doorways" to the houses of the ancestral gods. "Doorways" evoke images of corresponding walls, or boundaries of some kind. Thus, these Zinacanteco crosses are both boundary markers for, and gateways to, the sacred houses of the ancestral gods. By extension, all Zinacanteco cross shrines—at the edge of the houses, at the waterholes, and so on—delineate and provide entrance to highly significant social and supernatural spaces in the Zinacanteco world.

For any kind of ceremony involving these cross shrines, the first step—before the arrival of the ritual party—is to fasten three small pine trees to the crosses and cover the base of the crosses and the ground directly in front with pine needles, thereby creating symbolically a "forest," in miniature. Pine trees, growing wild in the Chiapas mountains, are symbols par excellence of the domain of TE?TIK. The three pine tree tops also symbolize the three pines which surround the supernatural corrals located in the mountain homes of the gods where the wild animal companions of the Zinacantecos are kept. It is the pine tree, not the cross per se, that is critical: if a shrine contains only one wooden cross, two pine tree tops are added on the sides to make the triadic symbol of TE?TIK; if no cross exists at a place of ritual, three pines may be erected to form the shrine.

When the ritual party arrives with the shaman, assistants tie a bundle of red geraniums onto the three pine trees. These red geraniums are cultivated in the house compounds of the Zinacantecos and symbolize the domain of "culture," and, indeed, of the essences, "the hearts," of people (Laughlin 1962). The placement of the pine trees is always *outward* toward the world of nature, while the red geraniums always face *inward* toward the world of culture: inward toward the house patio, or, in the case of the mountain shrines, inward toward HTEK-LUM* (Zinacantan Center)—toward the

*The Tzotzil name for the ceremonial center of Zinacantan, as well as all the other ceremonial centers of the Tzotzil-speaking communities in the Highlands of Chiapas, is HTEK-LUM. Literal translation of this term is difficult, but it appears to be derived from the word

churches (where the saints are housed), the cabildo (the seat of community government), and MIXIK' BALAMIL, the "navel of the earth," all located in the ceremonial center.

The messages in the code become more complex with the larger numbers of plants used in the more intricate ceremonies. In the largest curing rite (the Great Seeing ceremony), the patient is placed in a platform bed which symbolizes the corral of his animal companion. Not only do pine boughs surround this bed, but thirteen bundles of plants, each containing four types (see Vogt 1970a; E. Vogt and C. Vogt 1970), surround the patient lying upon it. We had long known the types of plants included and that the thirteen bundles symbolize what the Zinacantecos conceive to be the thirteen parts of a patient's innate soul. Yet I had never studied the arrangement of the plants in the bundles or the placement of these bundles with reference to the patient in the bed. Only when my shaman informant in 1970 showed me precisely how to tie up the bundles and place them around the bed did I discover that, for this shaman, each bundle contained (in order from a position toward nature to a position toward the patient): (1) a bright red flower from a wild bromeliad, VOHTON ʔEC' (with a hot, active, red "inner soul"); (2) leaves from a wild plant (*Synardisia venosa* [Mast.] Lundell) called K'OS in Tzotzil (with a cold, quiet, blue-green "inner soul"); (3) leaves from the wild laurel, called the "fart of the opossum" (with a warm, medium quiet, white "inner soul"); and finally (4) the domesticated red geranium (with a cold, quiet, blue-green "inner soul").* Later in the ceremony, the shaman ties the same types of bundles on the mountain cross shrines, with the same arrangement running from the hot, active, red, wild bromeliad on the outside, toward Nature, to the cold, quiet, blue-green domesticated geranium on the inside toward the "center," toward Culture. Since the curing ceremony can serve, among other things, to resocialize a Zinacanteco who has been wildly impulsive and unruly in his behavior, I believe that I discovered a code in the precise arrangement of these ritual plants which symbolically says with the forceful redundancy characteristic of ritual in human society, "cool it, man!" as the patient is brought back from the wild and dangerous domain of nature to the domesticated and safe domain of culture.

There is much more to this ritual sequence and the symbolic meanings of these ritual plants than I have been able to reveal in this cursory analysis of a ceremony that typically lasts up to forty-eight hours. But it illustrates my point about methodology: the first examples of ritual interpretation involved a sudden insight on the part of an observer, or the sustained cooperative work of ethnographer and informant, but this second set of examples required a method that depended not only on persistent probing for increasingly precise ethnographic data but also on the help of certain analytical concepts to reach the "meta-messages."

Ritual as a Communications System

In trying to interpret Zinacanteco rituals a key concept is that of "symbol," by which I mean (following Langer 1953, 1960, and Geertz 1965) "any object, act, event, quality or relation that serves as a vehicle for conception—the conception is the symbol's 'meaning' " (Geertz 1965: 5). Leach argues that anthropologists are in the main concerned with three types of behavior:

1. Behaviour which is directed towards specific ends and which, *judged by our standards of*

---

meaning "brood," as in "a brood of chickens." In the case of ceremonial centers it means something like "the land of a brood of people," or "the land of a group from one set of ancestors."

*Since each shaman receives knowledge of the plants in dreams, there is variation concerning the attributes of the "inner souls."

verification, produces observable results in a strictly mechanical way . . . we can call this "rational technical" behaviour.
2. Behaviour which forms part of a signalling system and which serves to "communicate information" not because of any mechanical link between means and ends but because of the existence of a culturally defined communication code . . . we can call this "communicative behaviour."
3. Behaviour which is potent in itself in terms of the cultural conventions of the actors but *not* potent in a rational-technical sense, as specified in (1), or alternatively behaviour which is directed towards evoking the potency of occult powers even though it is not presumed to be potent in itself . . . we can call this "magical behaviour" (1966: 403).

I accept Leach's proposal that (2) and (3) be classed together as "ritual" behavior. This is a productive way to conceptualize the data since it emphasizes the important functions of ritual in nonliterate societies: storing and transmitting information. This information is stored in rituals that serve as "communications systems," either "verbal rituals"—what many anthropologists call "myths" or, more generally, "oral narratives"—or "nonverbal rituals," sequences of behavior that fit together into ceremonial dramas. The performance of either type of ritual, or more typically both in conjunction, constitutes the "communicative behavior" that serves to perpetuate knowledge essential to the survival of the culture.

Because Zinacanteco "nonverbal rituals," in contrast to their "myths," are particularly well-developed and systematically patterned, I have chosen to focus mainly upon these rites. I shall use, however, when the data proves illuminating, particular examples of "verbal rituals," in some cases "myths" but more especially types which are situationally part of a nonverbal ritual process (prayers, for example) in order to clarify the attributes and contextual connotations of specific rituals.

The basic units of ritual behavior which actually store the information communicated in rituals are called "symbols." Turner (1969: 8) suggests that we call them the "molecules" of ritual behavior. They are "storehouses" of traditional tribal knowledge, a set of messages about some sector of social or natural life which a society considers worth transmitting down the generations (Turner 1968: 2). The "messages" are of two types. One, which I shall simply call "messages," emerges from the explicit, validating, and social context of the ritual. The second, which I shall call "meta-message," is composed of the connections of symbols, either paradigmatically (in parallel association; a metaphor which relies on the recognition of similarity) or syntagmatically (in the dialectic of a sequence; a metonym which relies on the recognition of contiguity). The "meta-message" is revealed through an understanding of the logical structure of the attributes of symbolic materials and symbolic actions which a particular ritual puts into operation.

The information transmitted in the ritual symbols is not ordinarily practical knowledge about how to grow maize or build thatched roof houses, although the everyday activities of Zinacantecos may provide secular models for the development of particular rituals. The ritual messages, from, and often about, the gods, are charged with mystical efficacy. Thus, as well as "storehouses," the symbols are "powerhouses": the information transmitted consists of authoritative, axiomatic, ultimately valid propositions about society, about nature, about the cosmos (Turner 1968: 2). To provide an example, on Christmas Eve in Zinacantan the birth of the Christ child is re-enacted in an elaborate ceremony attended by all the high-ranking religious and political officials. However, not one, but *two* Christ children are in the manger: "older brother" and "younger brother"! This "storehouse" of symbols reveals not only a basic principle of Zinacanteco culture—age-ranking into "senior" and "junior"—but also a message *about* this principle: it comes from the gods, has mystical authority and sanctity, and is universally valid.

If ritual is viewed as a "communications system," then the peculiarly repetitious quality of the human rituals we observe makes eminent sense. The function of this redundancy factor is twofold: to reduce ambiguity and to certify validity. Leach provides an apt example of the clarifying function:

> If a sender seeks to transmit a message to a distant receiver against a background of noise, ambiguity is reduced if the same message is repeated over and over again by different channels and in different forms. For example, suppose that on a windy day I want to say something to a companion standing on a hill some distance away. If I want to make sure that my message has been understood I will not only repeat it several times over in different forms, but I will add visual signals to my verbal utterances. In so far as human rituals are "information bearing procedures" they are message systems of this redundant, interference loaded, type (1966: 404).

After a Zinacanteco shaman lights candles at the household shrine of a patient who has lost his innate soul, he kneels and prays to the tribal ancestral gods for their aid in returning the wandering soul:

Divine KALVARYO,* holy Father,
Divine KALVARYO, holy Mother,
KALVARYO, holy ancient ones,
KALVARYO, holy yellow ones,
Take this, then, Father
Receive this, then, Lord . . .

Unitedly now,
In unison now,
Will you stand up in holiness,
Will you stand firm in holiness,
Behind the lowly back of,
By the lowly side of,
Your sons,
Your children,
Your flowers,
Your sprouts . . .
Take these my words,
Take these my prayers,
At the circuit,
At the circling [ceremonial circuit to mountain shrines],
Of your divine countenances,
Of your divine faces . . .

Receive, four holy Fathers,*
Receive, four holy Mothers,
Four holy ancient ones,
Four holy yellow ones,
Holy white cave [entrance to great mountain], holy Father,
Holy white cave, holy Mother,

Receive, holy senior great mountain, holy Father,
Holy senior great mountain, holy Mother . . .
(Vogt 1969: 659-664).

He continues addressing over and over again all of the important ancestral gods in their mountain homes. The redundancy of the parallelism in the lines and of the semantic similarities throughout the prayer thus elucidates, in a variety of ways, man's intimate and dependent relation to the gods.

But there is more to this redundancy than reducing the ambiguity of the message. By conveying the message in prayer form and repeating it in ritual action, and again in the arrangement of ritual plants used to restore the lost soul to the patient, the Zinacanteco shaman affirms the ultimate validity of the information. That is, when the essence of a ritual message is an irrevocable principle of reality, it must be transmitted through the praying, singing, dancing, and gesturing of ritualists, and through the

*KALVARYO is the meeting-place of the ancestral gods.

*Refers to the four principal mountain homes of the ancestral gods; they also have symbolic associations with the "Sky Bearers."

symbolic arrangement of candles, plants, incense, and other paraphernalia used. Each time the ritual is performed, it recreates the categories through which Zinacantecos perceive reality, restates the terms in which they must interact if there is to be a coherent social life.

Ritual as a Meaning System

Symbols of ritual also contain a periodic restatement of a "system of meanings." For, as Clifford Geertz (1965) so eloquently argues, the symbols found in culture patterns are both models *for* and models *of* "reality." Symbols not only provide information, like a blueprint, *for* the correct performance of social and cultural behavior in a given society, but they also supply, like a grammar, models *of* the patterned processes of believing, feeling, and behaving in a society.

If we view rituals as "systems of meanings," we find that important ritual symbols always carry a penumbra of meanings. They are always multifaceted or multivocal with a "fan" or "spectrum" of meanings (Turner 1967). As Turner (1967, 1968, 1969) suggests, ritual symbols often display a bipolarity of meanings: on the one hand, ideological, conveying norms and values that guide behavior; on the other hand, sensory, conveying emotional meanings that are "frankly, even flagrantly physiological."

For example, every January in the Zinacanteco fiesta of San Sebastián men costumed as jaguars and black-men carry stuffed female squirrels, painted red on their undersides to emphasize their genitals and adorned with necklaces and ribbons around their necks. The men carry red-painted sticks carved in the form of bull penises, which, to the accompaniment of lewd joking, are inserted into the genitals of the squirrels. The squirrels symbolize the wives of those religious officials who failed to appear for this fiesta and complete their year of ceremonial duty. Here it is clear that, at the "ideological pole" of meaning, the ritual play expresses social and moral norms: the necessity for responsible fulfillment of religious duties. At the "sensory" pole of meaning, the ritual play, as the bull penis trembles with excitement in entering the vagina of a squirrel, provides a vivid public display of sexual intercourse for all to laugh about and enjoy. Both poles of meaning are expressed as the black-man says to the hostess of the house in which the action is taking place: "Look also at Marian Peres from Masan! He does nothing but fuck all the time at the foot of a mango tree. . . . How shameless they are, always fucking each other, even when not in their own home" (Bricker 1973: 58). The squirrels are later thrown to the ground and soundly whipped for placing sexuality above religious responsibility.

The importance of the interaction, or conjunction, of the two types of meaning in ritual symbols cannot be overemphasized when it comes to solving a particular puzzle of ritual behavior: ritual may express and regenerate the social order, while, at the same time, appearing to mimic basic norms and values of a society. The same symbols can explicate the moral code *and* give stereotyped expression in mime to the unruly biological impulses that stem either from the basic organic needs of individuals buffeting against the expected code of behavior, or from lines of tension growing out of paradoxes in the social or conceptual system of a society. Turner (1969: 52-53) suggests, and I agree with him, that ritual at the sensory pole of meaning thus serves to divest of their antisocial quality the powerful drives and emotions associated with human physiology, especially reproduction, and attach them to the normative order, thereby energizing the ideological pole of meaning "with a borrowed vitality."

Ritual symbols display other critical properties: "condensation," "scaling," and "framing." Victor Turner has emphasized condensation. The term implies that a single symbol is saturated with both cognitive and emotional meanings: a national flag may, among other things, represent the political order, inspire the emotions necessary to lead men into battle, and symbolize the history of a nation. A high degree of symbol condensation is provided by the cross in Zinacantan. The cross implies that the Zinacantecos are Catholic; indeed, the presence of so many crosses has led casual observers to assume that Zinacantan is a devotedly Catholic community.* But, as already mentioned, the Zinacanteco cross is also a doorway to the homes of the ancestral gods, marking the boundary between social and supernatural spaces and providing entrance into and exit from these spaces. When decorated with pine and red geraniums, it symbolizes the contrast between nature and culture. In this form it also symbolizes an ancestral god himself, with "clothing" of pine and geraniums. (Some informants associate the red geraniums with the "heart"; others speak of them as representing the red tassles on the neckerchief worn by the god.) In a word, the cross is "saturated" with symbolic meanings for the Zinacantecos.

Scaling refers to small or large-scale models of culturally perceived realities or categories. In Zinacantan the pine trees and needles decorating household shrines reproduce TE?TIK in miniature. During a curing ceremony, a black chicken of the same sex as the patient, sacrificed and left in a small cave for the gods in the mountains, is a small-scale symbol of the patient whose life is to be spared by the offering of the chicken substitute. The seating, drinking, and eating order of a ritual meal symbolizes the pervasive hierarchical relations among men and the division of labor between the sexes.

*There is evidence that the cross was also a pre-Hispanic Maya symbol at, for example, the site of Palenque (see Greene, Rands, and Graham 1972: 28). But whether there was a relation between the so-called "foliated cross" of Palenque and the cross introduced by the Spaniards is unclear.

Conversely, the scaling may run the other way, using a large-scale model for a smaller perceived reality. The massive mountains which house the ancestral gods are large versions of Zinacanteco houses. The largest waterholes, "bathing places" of the gods, are amplified symbols of the waterholes used daily by Zinacantecos.

A Zinacanteco house provides a visual tour in miniature of the Zinacanteco universe with its four corners and its center. Imagine a Zinacanteco climbing to the top of the highest mountain (the Senior Great Mountain, a volcano which lies just east of Zinacantan Center) and looking around. As he turns, he sees his world spread out before him: the ceremonial center, the churches, the houses, the sacred mountains, the forests on all sides. He does not see a square; he sees an irregular, round horizon. Why, then, does he imagine the universe to be square? It is "like a house, like a table," one informant put it. Houses are square-cornered, and so are tables, beds, maize fields, blankets, and altars—in short, all preeminent cultural symbols are square. By making the universe square instead of round, as it is perceived from a mountaintop, Zinacantecos associate it with the sane, systematic, well-ordered world of culture, as opposed to nature. And by scaling, they can run the gamut in their thinking about houses, tables, fields—and the universe (Lennihan 1970).

Another important attribute of ritual symbols is their capacity for "framing," which, Mary Douglas (1966: 63-64) cogently argues, serves to focus attention. Frames delineate things in two ways. The frame may be a slice of time, such as the hours of a curing ceremony, the days in the ceremonial calendar, the times for planting, weeding, or harvesting maize, the time of "rising" and "setting sun," or the arrival and departure of the rainy season. Alternatively, it may be a specified sequence of events in time; for example, the Zinacanteco shaman always bathes the black chicken before it is sacrificed. In addition, frames may ritually define space. A church with its walls lined with saints, a thatched roof house whose corners receive ritual attention in a dedication ceremony, the area enclosed by the ceremonial circuit during a waterhole ceremony, the platform bed in which a patient lies at the end of the "Great Seeing" ceremony—all these frames focus a high degree of attention upon the ritual proceedings performed within them.

On Binary Oppositions

My interpretation of Zinacanteco ritual symbols makes use of some general concepts concerning the structure of human thought that have been advanced by structural anthropologists. The key notion is "binary oppositions" or "binary discriminations." Lévi-Strauss suggests that the whole structure of primitive thought is binary. Leach, on the other hand, recently pointed out that: "there is not the slightest doubt that the human brain does have a tendency to operate with binary counters in all sorts of situations—but it can operate in other ways as well. A fully satisfactory mechanical model of the human mind would certainly contain many analogue features which do *not* occur in digital computers" (1970: 92). In my view, until we have such an "analogue model," close attention to binary oppositions can take us a long way in understanding the structure that underlies much of the ritual observed in tribal societies.

What accounts for the binary oppositions? The cultures of men may be viewed as symbolic codes that program systems of categorization, communication, and exchange. Although the human mind is part of nature, of the orderly physical and biological processes in the universe, it is not a videotape which records the manifold, complex stimuli emanating from the natural and social world in which man lives. Rather, men have evolved ways of reducing complexity, of eliminating ambiguity, of certifying order by classifying almost limitless discrete bits of information into manageable form. Some binary discriminations are universally recognized as a way of constructing meaning and order: Male/Female, Right hand/Left hand, Up/Down, Day/Night, Raw/Cooked, Wet/Dry, Nature/Culture, Men/Animals. Other oppositions are undoubtedly culturally specific: Up river/Down river, Highland/Lowland, Forest/Clearing may occur only under special ecological circumstances. Likewise, Cross cousin/Parallel cousin, Mother's brother/ Father's brother may occur only in societies for whom these distinctions are sociologically important.

In specific cultures binary oppositions may also result from social paradoxes which lead to social tension, and from cognitive contradictions that pose logical incongruities. Victor Turner (1968) shows how the combination of matrilineal descent and virilocal marriage in Ndembu society creates a social paradox that emerges throughout a wide range of the ritual symbolism focused on the opposition between these two principles. In Zinacanteco society the opposition between principles of hierarchy and equality results in a social paradox that emerges in the symbolism of drinking and eating rituals. Utilizing the basic ranking principles of age and sex, the Zinacantecos insist on a rigid hierarchy expressed in the order of serving cane liquor and food, with males taking precedence over females, older members of the society taking precedence over younger members. On the other hand, equality is stressed in that all persons must receive equal portions. Thus, Zinacantecos are locked into a ranking system based upon sex and age, yet, at the same time are equal and equally valued. The contradiction between these two principles, recognized by Zinacantecos, results in delicately patterned relations among participants and the "sacred" quality of the ritual eating and drinking episodes which occur daily in Zinacanteco houses.

2

Zinacanteco Cosmology and Socioreligious Organization

THE RUGGED LIMESTONE and volcanic mountain terrain reaching into the clouds of highland Chiapas is the visible surface of the Zinacanteco world (BALAMIL) which is conceived as a large quincunx. The center of the upper surface of this world is "the navel of the earth," a low, rounded mound located in the ceremonial center of Zinacantan. The world extends outward from this navel; even Mexico City is regarded as a remote place off toward the edge of the universe.

The quincuncial world rests on the shoulders of the VAXAK-MEN, the local version of the "four-corner gods" or "sky-bearers" who played an important role in the cosmology throughout ancient Mesoamerica (Thompson 1934). When one of these gods tires and shifts his burden to his other shoulder, there is an earthquake which lasts until the burden is again secure. Since the population of the earth is increasing, the burden is ever greater and earthquakes are more frequent. But because these quakes kill enough people to keep the burden down, the gods continue to carry on their eternal duties.

K'ATIN-BAK (place warmed by bones) is a deep hole, somewhere inside the earth, which is similar to the Christian Hell. It probably also contains elements of the prehispanic underworld (see, for example, Edmonson 1971: 68-75).

Below the visible world, separated from it by open space, is the Lower World (ˀOLON BALAMIL), also a quincunx. It is not so thick as the upper world. Its surface is inhabited

The cosmology and social and religious organization of Zinacantan have been treated in detail in a number of publications, notably Blaffer 1972; Bricker 1973; Cancian 1965, 1972; Colby 1966; J. Collier 1973; Fabrega and Silver 1973; and Vogt 1966, 1969 and 1970b. The remarks in this chapter will therefore be limited to a brief overview to provide background for the analysis of the ritual symbolism discussed in subsequent chapters. A section on the life cycle in Zinacantan is also included, with cursory descriptions of associated rituals. More detailed information on the life cycle may be found in J. Collier 1968 and Vogt 1969.

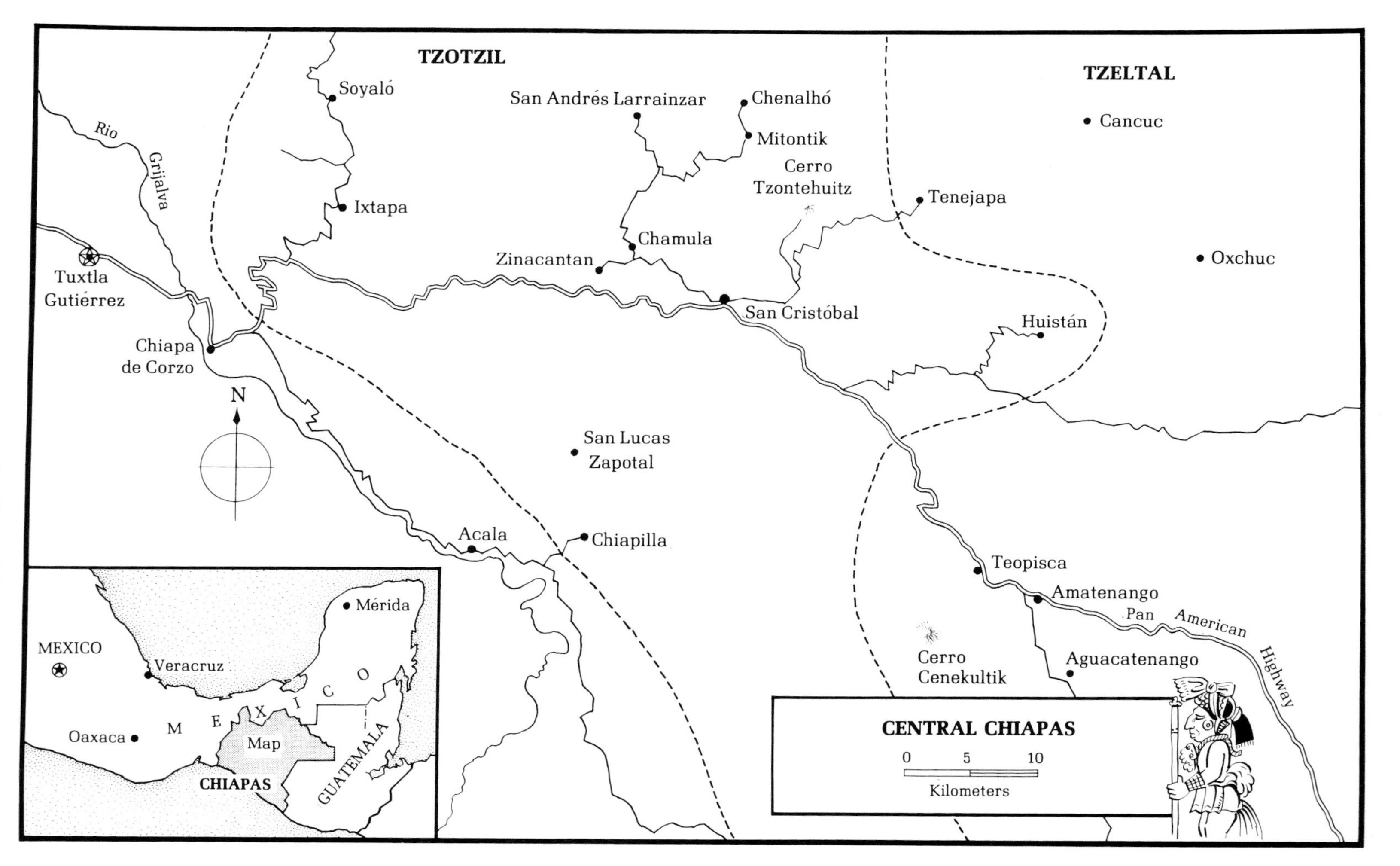

3. Central Chiapas

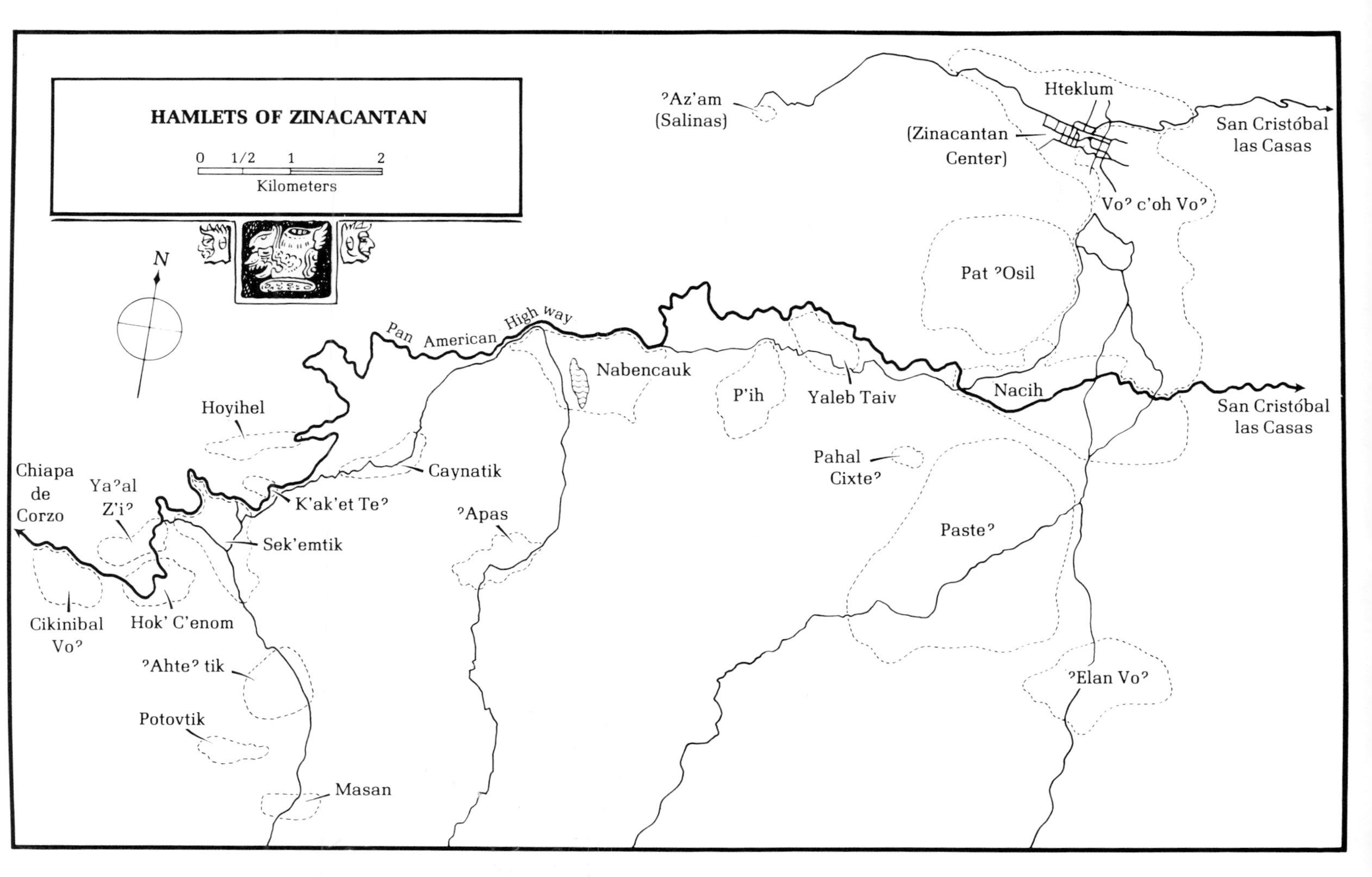

4. Hamlets of Zinacantan

by dwarfs who, with monkeys, were created in the mythological past when the gods first attempted, abortively, to create man.

In the sky or heavens (VINAHEL, "open up there") above the earth is the domain of the sun, the moon and the stars. Some Zinacantecos describe the sky as being supported by the four-corner gods. The sun, HC'UL TOTIK or HTOTIK K'AK'AL ("Our Holy Father" or "Our Father Heat") travels on a path that encircles the earth each day, creating a vertical plane which gives basic expression to the conception of "time" in the universe; it intersects the horizontal plane of the earth, which provides "space" in the Zinacanteco world. "The Sweeper of the Path," Venus (MUK'TA K'ANAL, "Large Star"), precedes the sun along its path daily. The sun appears each morning, pauses at noon to survey the daily affairs of the Zinacantecos, and disappears each evening. The sun at noon is usually conceived as San Salvador. As the sun rises and sets, it passes close to the oceans and makes their waters boil. At night it continues on its path between the earth and the "Lower World," generating such heat that the dwarfs of this world must wear mud hats to protect themselves.

There is no way of saying, abstractly, north, south, east, and west in Tzotzil. The directions are conceived by their relation to the path of the sun. East is therefore approximated by LOK'EB K'AK'AL, the "rising" or "appearing" or "emerging" sun, west by MALEB K'AK'AL, the "setting" or "disappearing" or "waning" sun. These terms express simultaneously time and space; they state both *where* and *when* the sun appears and disappears each day. These points are the intersections of the vertical (time) with the horizontal (space) planes of the universe. North and south are designated as XOKON VINAHEL (the sides of the sky or heavens). The two are differentiated by whether they are on the right hand or the left hand of the path of the sun. The place of the rising sun holds by far the greatest directional significance for Zinacantecos.

The moon, HC'UL ME?TIK (Our Holy Mother), travels a similar path around the world. The stars, K'ANALETIK (The Yellow Ones), exist in a layer of the sky above the clouds but below the paths of the sun and the moon. They provide light at night, "like candles in the window of a house."

Under the influence of Spanish Catholicism, the Zinacantecos have come to associate the sun with God the Father or with Jesus Christ, and the moon with the Virgin Mary. These associations have served to reinforce the traditional Maya conceptions of these bodies as symbols of contrasting maleness and femaleness.

Many mountains and hills located near the Zinacanteco settlements are homes of ancestral deities (TOTIL ME?ILETIK, "fathers and mothers"). The ancestral gods figure most prominently among the deities in Zinacanteco life, judging by the frequency with which they are referred to and prayed to and from the number of rituals performed on their behalf. Remote ancestors of the Zinacantecos, in the mythological past they were ordered by the four-corner gods to take up residence inside the mountains. They are pictured as elderly Zinacantecos, who live eternally in their mountain homes, where they convene and deliberate, monitor the affairs of their descendants, and wait for the ritual offerings of black chickens, candles, incense, and liquor which sustain them. These ancestors are both repositories of social and cultural knowledge and the active and jealous guardians of the Zinacanteco way of life. Deviations by living Zinacantecos from social and cultural mores are noted by the ancestral gods, and punished.

Next to the ancestral gods, the most important deity is the "Earth Lord" (YAHVAL BALAMIL). He has multiple manifestations, each associated with a particular place—an opening into the earth, like a cave, a limestone sink, or a waterhole (C'EN). The god can be pictured as a unitary being, or as many, but he is always described as a large, fat ladino living under the ground, who possesses vast quantities of money, herds of cows, mules, horses, and flocks of chickens. At the same time he has the attributes of thunderbolts and serpents. He owns all the waterholes; he controls the lightning and the clouds that are believed to emerge from his caves, rise into the sky, and produce rain for crops; and he claims all the products of the earth as his own—the trees felled to build houses, the mud used for walls, the limestone from which lime is manufactured. The Earth Lord rides on deer; iguanas serve as blinders for his mounts and a snake as his whip. The shell of the land-snail is his powderflask. The gunpowder is used in making skyrockets and for firing his shotgun, both of which are seen as lightning bolts. Communication with this god is regarded with the deepest ambivalence. There are glorious myths about how men have acquired great wealth in money and livestock by going into caves to visit him. But this god, who needs many workers, may also capture a man and force him to work in the earth for years, until the iron sandals provided him are worn out.

In the centuries since the Conquest, the Zinacantecos have acquired more than fifty-five sacred objects that they call "saints" (SANTOETIK). Most of these are carved wooden or plaster images of Catholic saints, many are pictures of saints, and a few are crosses. The images range in size from less than eight inches to life-size. Forty-two of them are kept in the three churches in the Center; the others are kept in the houses of the cargoholders and in chapels in outlying hamlets. They are usually dressed in flowing robes derived from Colonial styles, but almost all of them also wear some items of Zinacanteco dress—ribbons, necklaces, shawls.

The most important saints have distinctive personalities, and myths explain their arrival in Zinacantan. To mention only a few, the image of San Lorenzo (Saint Lawrence), the major patron of Zinacantan, occupies the place of honor over the main altar of the principal church, which is named for him. Santo Domingo (Saint Dominic), whose image stands just to the right of San Lorenzo, is a secondary patron. He was the major patron up to the end of the eighteenth century, but, for reasons we do not yet understand, was supplanted by San Lorenzo at that time. San Sebastián occupies the place of honor over the center of the altar of his church. The Virgen de Rosario (Virgin of the Rosary) is, like the moon, called HC'UL-ME?TIK (Our Holy Mother). She is the patron of women, often identified with the moon, and considered the mother of Santo Entierro. The latter, also called HMANVANEH ("The Buyer"), is a Christ-in-the-Tomb image kept in an enclosed case in the church of San Lorenzo. According to the Zinacantecos, Santo Entierro used to live on earth. He was chased by demons who, having captured him, put him up on a cross in Zinacantan to kill him. When the demons departed to eat, Santo Entierro came down from the cross, took a blue rock and threw it skyward, creating the blue sky. The demons returned from their meal and placed him back on the cross where, by dying, he paid the price for Zinacanteco sins—thus "The Buyer." Señor Esquipulas is a Christ-on-the-Cross image, found in a sacred cave called NINAB CILO?, and now kept in the third chapel in Zinacantan Center, the Hermitage of Esquipulas, where religious officials take their oaths of office. He is associated with the salt trade, and ritual salt is delivered to high religious officials in his presence in the Hermitage.

These saints are the most sacred objects in Zinacantan, judging by the ritual attention they receive and the Zinacantecos' resistance to attempts by outsiders to see or photograph them. To Zinacantecos, the saints are gods with extraordinary power, each with an "innate soul" located in the image. Their "homes" are the Catholic churches. They must be bathed in water from the sacred waterholes and their clothes must be periodically washed and censed. Like the ancestral gods, they expect prayers and offerings of candles, incense, and music.

The Catholic Mass, according to Zinacantecos, is an elaborate prayer for the saint whose fiesta is being celebrated. Because the saint "is a very human person who likes nice things," at his fiesta he desires a Mass with all the elaborate ornaments and vestments of the Catholic priest; if the Mass is not celebrated, he is enraged. Accordingly, Zinacantecos travel to San Cristóbal before each fiesta to petition the priest for a Mass. If the priest is otherwise occupied and refuses, the Zinacantecos, who have fulfilled their responsibility by asking, are not upset. The saint will undoubtedly be enraged and send punishment; but he will blame the priest, not the Zinacantecos!

Interaction between living Zinacantecos and their gods takes place via the associated concepts of two types of companions, which every human being has: the "innate soul," and the animal companion. In a general way, the Zinacantecos are "animistic" (Tylor 1873), believing that many natural phenomena, all animals, and even some manufactured objects have "innate souls," but only human beings also have animal companions.

The C'ULEL is an innate, personal "soul" located in the heart of each person; it is also found in the bloodstream, recognized as being connected to the heart. This soul is placed in the body of an embryo by the ancestral gods. It has thirteen parts, and the loss of one or more of these parts necessitates the performance of a special curing ceremony to recover them. While the C'ULEL is temporarily divisible into its component parts as a function of the various types of "soul loss," it is considered eternal and indestructible. Only at the point of death does the soul finally leave the body. It is then associated with the grave for as many years as it inhabited the body of the deceased on earth, and eventually enters the pool of innate souls kept by the ancestors. It may then again be implanted in another embryo. While the person lives, the soul can, during sleep, leave the body and visit the innate souls of other Zinacantecos or appear before the ancestral deities. It can travel great distances; it may "drop out" of the body temporarily in periods of intense excitement, as at the point of orgasm. A small child is especially susceptible to "soul loss," as the soul is not yet accustomed to its new receptacle. The mother of a small child will, in unfamiliar surroundings, always sweep with her shawl the ground on which she has been sitting as she departs, thereby gathering up all the parts of her infant's C'ULEL. One of the major purposes of the baptismal rite is to "fix" the soul more firmly in the child's body. However, the baptism cannot prevent "soul loss" from occurring through fright or punishment by the ancestral gods later in life. There are a number of immediate causes for "soul loss," among them falling down suddenly, seeing a "demon" on a dark night, or any unexpected fright. The Zinacantecos still relate how a large number of people experienced "soul loss" when the first airplane swept low over Zinacantan some thirty years ago. The shamans were busy for weeks afterward performing ceremonies to restore the dispersed pieces of "innate souls" to their bodies.

At a more profound level of causation, however, "soul loss" is ordinarily attributed to the wrath of the ancestral gods who punish bad behavior by causing a person to fall or by ordering a lightning bolt to knock out one or more parts of the innate soul; or to an evil person who performs witchcraft to "sell" parts of the victim's soul to the Earth Lord. Without all thirteen parts of the innate soul, a person cannot be healthy; he feels or possesses CAMEL (sickness), and a shaman must be summoned to perform the ritual necessary to recover the lost parts.

Virtually everything important and valuable to Zinacantecos also possesses a C'ULEL: domesticated animals and plants, salt, houses and household fires, crosses, the saints, musical instruments, maize, and all the other deities in the pantheon. The most important interaction in the universe is not between persons, nor between persons and objects, but among the innate souls of persons and material objects.

Rising up 9,200 feet to the east of the ceremonial center of Zinacantan is a majestic volcano called BANKILAL MUK'TA VIZ (Senior Large Mountain). Within this mountain a series of supernatural corrals house the approximately 11,400 wild animal companions of the Zinacantecos, one for each person. The corrals contain jaguars, coyotes, ocelots, and smaller animals such as opposums and squirrels. There is no abstract term in Tzotzil for these animals; CON is the general noun for "animal," and using the adjectival form one refers to "the animal of so-and-so" as "SCANUL———" when talking about one's animal companion. These animals are watered, fed, and cared for by the ancestral gods, under the general supervision of the Grand Alcalde, who is the divine counterpart of the highest ranking member of the religious hierarchy in Zinacantan. His home is located inside the mountain and his household cross is the shrine that Zinacantecos visit in the course of rituals on top of the mountain.

A Zinacanteco and his animal companion are linked by a single innate soul. When the ancestors install a C'ULEL in the embryo of a Zinacanteco, they simultaneously install the same innate soul in the embryo of an animal. The moment the Zinacanteco is born, that animal is also born. Throughout their lives, whatever happens to either human or animal also happens to his alter ego. If, for example, an animal escapes from the corral and is left to wander alone in the forest, he may be injured or shot, in which case the Zinacanteco with whom he shares his innate soul falls ill. It follows that a wandering animal companion, which implies neglect by the ancestral caretakers, signifies grave danger for the corresponding Zinacanteco. A shaman must be summoned quickly to perform the proper ceremony, which asks a pardon of the ancestral deities and petitions them to round up the lost animal companion and to restore it safely to the super natural corral. It is usually during childhood or early adulthood that a person discovers what kind of animal companion he has. He receives this knowledge either in a dream, when his innate soul "sees" its companion, or from a shaman, when an illness is diagnosed as this particular type of trouble.

There is a clear relation between these two concepts and social control. Any type of deviant behavior that stirs the anger of the ancestors against a particular Zinacanteco can lead directly to punishment: the person may suffer "soul loss," or, in more extreme cases, his animal may be expelled from its corral to wander in the woods. Deviant behavior may mean breaking important moral rules or flouting the central values of Zinacanteco society. An individual who fights with or mistreats his kinsmen; a man who fails to accept community service in the religious or civil hierarchies; a man who fails to care for his maize field properly or a woman who mishandles the maize after it is brought into the house; a person who does not wash regularly and wears dirty clothes; a man who fails to make contributions when the officials arrive to collect "taxes" for fiesta expenses—all are prime candidates for sickness.

The Life Cycle

The life cycle in Zinacantan is marked by four major life-crisis rituals: birth, baptism, marriage, and death (Vogt 1969: 180-223). Puberty rites, common in other tribal societies, are lacking.

Birth

Conception results from the mixing of the

man's with the woman's HPWERSA (from the Spanish *fuerza*, "force"), the vital essence in the blood of the mother and father. The father's is the major contribution; the mother's role is to provide nourishment and a receptacle for the fetus as it develops. After delivery, in which both the husband and a midwife participate, the midwife bathes the infant in warm water which has been boiled with aromatic leaves (of ZIS ʔUC and ʔAHA-TEʔES) and prays to the ancestral gods to accept and guide the child. The baby is censed with copal during the prayer, then dressed in clean clothes. The rite that follows establishes the sex identity of the child, initiating the socialization process, and helps fix the innate soul into the new body. The midwife rubs salt twice on the top of the baby's mouth, and presents the child with three red chilis, giving much-needed "heat" to a still "cold" body. The baby's hands are touched with the implements it will use during life: for a boy, a hoe, a billhook, a digging stick, and a splinter of pitch-pine which he will use to light his father's way home after sunset. A girl receives a spindle, a carding comb, and a sword for the loom on which she will weave, a *mano*, a needle and thread, and a tumpline for carrying burdens. The midwife then returns the child to its mother and the two are swathed in blankets to protect them from the potentially harmful view of others. The umbilical cord and the placenta (SNA ʔUNEN, "house of the baby," and SMEʔ ʔUNEN, "mother of the baby") are buried behind the house, and are used in various ways to divine and to influence the number of children of each sex the woman will bear in the future (Anschuetz 1966).

For a period of weeks following the birth the mother is treated as though she were recovering from a dangerous illness (in fact, her condition is called in Tzotzil a "sickness"): she takes a series of three sweat baths with the midwife, she is confined to the house, she does not perform her usual tasks, and she may eat only "hot" foods. This careful treatment seems directed toward restoring her to a normal condition of equilibrium and protecting her from possible injury in her weakened state. In a similar fashion the baby is kept guarded from view so that its soul will not be lost and it can gain the necessary strength and "heat" to survive.

Baptism

To Zinacantecos baptism is the most important of the seven Catholic sacraments. It firmly fixes the innate soul in the infant's body and creates bonds of ritual kinship, *compadrazgo*,* between the child's parents and "godparents." The bond so established is between the parents and the chosen *compadres*, not between the compadres and the child. Involving mutual rights and obligations, it creates a network of interdependence among Zinacantecos which extends beyond the bounds of kinship and constitutes a most important basis to the dynamics of society. Compadres are selected by the infant's parents with four factors in mind: that they be members of another patrilineage; that they will be, or have been, called upon to serve as such for at least three children of the family; that they live nearby, preferably in the same hamlet; and that they be willing and able to provide economic and political services in the future. This last-named im-

*Compadrazgo is the system of ritual kinship universally used in the European-derived cultures of Latin America, and the form observed in Zinacantan is obviously derived from the Spanish Conquerors and their ladino descendants. For members of the Catholic and Episcopal churches in the United States, the important reciprocal relationship established is between godparents and godchildren; but in southern Europe and Latin America it is between the godparents and the parents of the child who address and refer to each other as *compadre* ("co-father") and *comadre* ("co-mother"). In Tzotzil these terms become KUMPARE and KUMALE and are widely extended to additional persons in the rites of baptism and marriage (see Vogt 1969).

plies, ideally, that the godfather should have passed a cargo and be a respected, relatively well-to-do member of the community.

The actual baptismal rite may be performed on the occasion of a fiesta in the Church of San Lorenzo, or, more commonly, it may take place in the Cathedral in San Cristóbal on a Sunday, when a priest is regularly present. The prospective godparents are requested, in a ritual exchange well in advance of the ceremony, to serve as "embracers" of the infant. The godparent of the child's sex holds it during the ceremony. A ritual meal follows the baptism, at the home of the parents. In the months that follow the child is the recipient of gifts of food and clothing from the godparents. In the course of these ritual prestations, more compadres are created by the intermingling of the two families and their relations.

The ceremonies associated with birth and baptism may be seen as a linear sequence characterized by phases of separation, transition, and incorporation (Van Gennep 1909): separation from the mother, handling by the midwife, and the normal acceptance of the baby by the family; a transition period during which the baby is hidden from view, still "impure" and only precariously in possession of its innate soul; and incorporation into society, firmer possession of the soul, and protection by the gods from harm. Note that both mother and child are involved, in the birth ritual, with a *rite de passage*, the woman going from the state of pregnancy to that of motherhood, the child from being a fetus to the state of infancy. The role of the midwife is to emphasize the separation of the infant from the mother; she helps to purify the baby, freeing it from its unclean state. The removal of the umbilical cord and placenta from the house underscores the physical detachment of the baby from its former condition. The first rite of incorporation is the baptism, which ends the most dangerous period of the transition. Membership in Zinacanteco society is conferred with the ritual gift of a complete set of clothes by the godmother, the surrogate parent.

Marriage

It is not until a young man in Zinacantan is married that he can properly serve in an important cargo position or be treated as a full member of his society. At the age of sixteen or seventeen, therefore, he begins to look over the available girls from among those he sees along the trails, at fiestas, or visiting the homes of relatives. Courtship is a lengthy, expensive process which cannot be correctly carried out without the cooperation of the boy's parents, relatives, family friends, and compadres. Once the boy has convinced his parents that his choice of a wife is wise, two "petitioners" are selected who are good talkers and capable of presenting persuasively the boy's petition to the girl's father. Traditionally there is a great reluctance on the part of Zinacanteco fathers to give their daughters away in marriage; as a result much secrecy and cunning are required to catch the girl's family at home and force them to listen to the petition. If the petitioners are successful, the girl's father will accept the liquor offered him; if he refuses, the party must abandon the attempt and will probably go on to the house of the boy's second choice. A trial period follows, in which the boy serves the girl's family and both sides try out the relationship to see if it will work in practice.

The payment of the bride price is gradual; as one informant expressed it, "little by little the boy pays; little by little he removes the girl." It may take up to two years of payment of food and labor before the girl's father permits the "house-entering" ceremony (ˀOCEL TA NA) to take place. This occasion is accompanied by more gifts from the boy's family to that of the girl, and thereafter members of both families call each other KUMPARE and KUMALE, signifying that a permanent compadrazgo relationship has been cemented. The girl's father selects an "embracer" to serve as ritual adviser to the couple, assisted by his wife—or an older woman (SNUP HPETOM, "companion of the embracer") if the wife is too young. After the house-entering, the boy moves into the house of the girl's family and continues to work for her father. Occasionally during this period the young couple is permitted to sleep together (J. Collier 1968).

The wedding itself has three phases: a civil ceremony, a church ceremony, and a house ceremony. The first takes place in the morning, when the families meet in the Center to record the union with the Secretary in the cabildo. In the afternoon the couple visit the Catholic priest and give him the wedding certificate they have received from the Secretary. The priest records their names and collects a fee for the ceremony. By 5 A.M. the next day the bride and groom are dressed and at the ceremonial center. The groom's dress is that of an Alferez who is going through a change-of-office ceremony. The bride wears a new blouse and two new skirts, covered with a long white *huipil*. A large white shawl covers her, partially hiding her face. The church ceremony follows, with the priest saying Mass and all those being married receiving communion.

The party returns to the home of the groom for a ritual meal, served by his family in the patio. The new couple do not eat, but give their food to the embracer and his consort. The embracer and consort then take the bride and groom into the house and remove their wedding clothes, formally introducing the girl into her new home and family unit. The embracer advises the couple on their mutual responsibilities, and the bride's family is invited into the house for the first time. After the ceremony married couples of the two families dance. The mothers of the boy and the girl hold hands as they dance, and the embracer and his consort dance in a counterclockwise circle around the whole group, thereby welding together the two families. All participants keep drinking until they fall into drunken stupors.

The long process of courtship and marriage is sometimes abbreviated when the families cannot afford to make such a great outlay of goods and money as is traditionally considered correct. Various episodes may be eliminated, or the couple may elope. Courtship may be broken off by either party, in which case the boy's family will demand repayment of the money spent. Divorce may be obtained from the cabildo for three hundred pesos. The Secretary erases the names of the couple from his records, the Church is not consulted, and the individuals may remarry.

Because in Zinacantan descent is patrilineal and residence is patrilocal, courtship and marriage ceremonies serve to remove the woman conclusively from all ties to her family. Bride payments cancel whatever claim her family may have over her person or her services as a tortilla-maker or bearer of children. The suitor first becomes a member of the girl's family by giving gifts as well as his labor and thereby earns the right to take her from them. The house-entering ceremony is the *final* point of acceptance of the union by both parties. The girl's father no longer has the option of breaking off the agreement and returning the gifts. He has relinquished control over his daughter, and all that remains is for the parental substitutes to finalize the wedding. In these stages, the ritual relationships supplant the personal, biological ones and the male and female ritual advisers become the girl's "parents."

Marriage unites not only two individuals and two families but also the innate souls of the bride and groom. The embracer cares for the souls, symbolically planting them together as candles at the feet of San Lorenzo and Santo Domingo.

Death

Death, in Zinacantan, does not result from "natural causes." It may result from soul loss; from having one's animal companion released from its corral; from having one's innate soul sold irrevocably to the Earth Lord; or, much less commonly, from physical injury.

At the moment of death, whichever of the thirteen parts of the innate soul remain in the body, depart. The body is washed before it becomes too stiff to handle and is placed with its head toward the "setting sun"; the area is fenced off within the house by household articles. A period of mourning ensues, with the gathering of relatives and the serving of ritual meals. Late that same night the body is placed in a coffin and supplied with small bags of money and charred, ground tortillas to provision the innate soul in the afterworld. Shortly after dawn, the coffin is removed from the house. If the deceased was a married woman, at this time her husband is asked to announce who will be his new wife—making known his choice even if he has not yet spoken to the woman. Once the coffin is outside the house, an adult woman performs a rite to "loosen the soul from the house" and "prevent the soul from returning to see its possessions" and "make it forget its house and not come back to frighten the living." At the cemetery various symbolic actions are taken to discourage the dead from returning and taking more souls away. When the coffin is half-buried, clothes and objects associated with the dead person are placed in the grave, each somehow cut, burned, or broken—like the charred tortillas—to prevent their malevolent use on the living. The filled grave is covered with pine needles, a simple wooden cross is erected and later decorated with pine-tree tops and red geraniums, providing a means of communication, like a cross shrine, with the deceased. After the innate soul leaves the body, it retraces the course of its life in the person's body, gathering up all pieces of flesh, hair, or nail left behind. The journey keeps the potentially dangerous innate soul away from the house during the wake. This first journey is followed by another, more arduous, to K'OTEBAL (the place of arrival); here the soul must cross a large river on the back of a black dog and follow a trail to a junction marked by a cross shrine. It learns there whether it will continue on by the broad road to K'ATIN-BAK or, by a narrow, crooked path, to VINAHEL, somewhere in the sky. Unless a person has seriously deviated from the moral code of Zinacantan, his soul may take the path to VINAHEL, which is much like an earthly Zinacantan with similar social responsibilities. If someone has sinned and is condemned by his kinsmen and neighbors as a witch or a murderer, public denunciation and ritual neglect may characterize the funeral, and the soul of the deceased is banished to K'ATIN-BAK.

The funeral proceedings are undertaken at considerable cost to the kinsmen of the deceased. Because they are the heirs, a degree of social tension is dispelled by this outlay; otherwise, the inheritance might incur the envy of neighbors. Similarly, tensions between the living and the dead can be eased by this public display and sacrifice on behalf of the dead.

A great deal of ritual activity is directed toward creating and maintaining a new relationship with the immortal innate soul of the one who has died. Much of this takes place each All Saints' Day when special rituals are performed on behalf of the dead, who are believed to return at this time to Zinacantan to visit their living relatives (Pope 1969).

Although everything else in the Zinacanteco universe contains a fixed amount of heat, is either "hot" or "cold," human beings possess a variable quantity. Beginning their lives with virtually no heat, Zinacantecos accumulate it throughout their lives, then, at the moment of death, become cold again, like a fetus. Illness is often explained as a temporary disequilibrium in the amount of heat appropriate to a person of a certain age and social accomplishment. Symbols of heat proliferate in the rituals associated with birth, courtship, and marriage as a Zinacanteco grows into an adult. After death, the innate soul must be supplied with sufficient heat, by means of burning candles, liquor, and the censing of the body, to make the journey safely to VINAHEL, although it is now completely "cold." The maximum amount of heat acquired by a Zinacanteco during the course of a lifetime comes from serving his society in an exemplary fashion: the man who is very old, a high-ranking shaman and a veteran of all levels of the cargo system, possesses the greatest heat possible for a human being.

Much attention is given to the protection of the innate soul in the life-crisis rituals. In birth and baptismal rites, every attempt is made to fix the soul solidly within the body of the infant, and therefore assure his survival past childhood. The uniting of two souls in marriage is another crucial juncture; if the souls are not firmly cemented together, the lives of the bride and groom as well as their union may be threatened. The funeral, in turn, protects the soul long enough to enable it to reach VINAHEL, and assures that it will not return to threaten the souls of the living.

In all life-cycle rituals surrogates take the place of parents or close relatives who are too emotionally involved. This is a recognition of the delicacy and importance of these transitional rites. The midwife, the godparents, the "embracer," and those who carry out the funeral proceedings on behalf of the family all play mediatory and conciliatory roles which make these vital transitions much more smooth and broadly based in the social order than if only the immediate family were involved.

Social Organization

The domestic group of the Zinacantecos typically consists of a patrilocally extended family occupying two or more adjacent single-room houses constructed either of wattle and daub with thatched roofs or of adobe with tile roofs. This domestic unit, which retains fathers and sons and imports wives, dwells within a compound ordinarily surrounded by a fence. Small plots of maize separate one compound from another. Each domestic group is symbolized by the KRUS TA TIˀ NA, "cross at the entrance to the house," erected just outside the principal house. The correlation between the domestic group and this house cross is close: a simple count of all of these crosses in Zinacantan provides an approximate total number of domestic groups living in the municipio. The house cross, representing the smallest unit in the patriline within the patrilineage, is the symbolic focus for the domestic group living in its compound. It signifies the unity of the group and provides a means of relating it to other parts of the social structure.

The exact composition of the domestic group varies as the unit moves through a developmental cycle and responds to economic and social pressures.The rules of patrilocal residence and patrilineal inheritance ideally construct domestic units each generation with wives from other lineages. Most Zinacanteco domestic groups have this patrilocally extended structure, although domestic units with different composition can always be found.

Another way of looking at the domestic group is as a small cluster of kinsmen that must contain both men and women, for each sex controls technological skills required for the successful operation of any domestic unit. To simplify the Zinacanteco view: men must grow and bring home the maize supply; women must make the tortillas. Although the most common arrangement is a married couple, other combinations can provide maize-growers and tortilla-makers: for example, widowed mothers with unmarried sons; widowed fathers with single daughters; two elderly sisters, one widowed and one a spinster, with an unmarried son of the widow.

Zinacanteco domestic groups are embedded in a larger social unit: the localized lineage (or SNA). In Tzotzil there is no generic name for either the small domestic group just described, or for the larger groupings of domestic units. Both may be talked about only as specific groupings of relatives in particular contexts. SNA means "the house of." A Zinacanteco who hears of SNA H?AKOVETIK (the house of the Wasp Nests) judges from the context that a collection of domestic groups making up a localized lineage unit is being discussed. A single domestic unit within the Wasp Nests might be called SNA XUN ?AKOV, "the house of John Wasp Nest." I use the word SNA to refer in the abstract to the larger unit, the one composed of various localized patrilineages that are extensions of patrilocally extended domestic groups. Genealogical connections can be traced in localized patrilineages, but they extend back no further than about four generations. The members of such a patrilineage live on adjacent lands inherited from their ancestors. The unit is characterized by some jural authority in that important decisions for its members are made by the most senior men. Some patrilineages also own important ritual paraphernalia which they keep in their houses and regularly send, on request, to the ceremonial center for ritual purposes.

The SNA takes its name from the localized patrilineages. If it contains two or more, its name derives from the lineage which first settled on the lands now controlled by the SNA. SNAs vary in size from those containing one patrilineage, with only four houses and less than fifteen people, to very large ones with at least thirteen patrilineages and over one hundred and fifty people living in more than forty houses.

Each SNA maintains a series of cross shrines. Some are erected on nearby mountains for communication with the ancestral deities; others are built in caves for communicating with the Earth Lord. All of the shamans who live in the SNA assemble to perform the ritual for the K'IN KRUS ceremony. If a small SNA does not have a shaman, it must import one from a neighboring SNA for ceremonies.

The next unit in ascending size in Zinacanteco social structure is what I call the "waterhole group." Again, this group does not have a generic name in Tzotzil, but it can be described with reference to the name of the waterhole around which the group lives. Waterhole groups vary in size from two to thirteen or more SNAs, depending primarily on the amount of water available for household use and for watering livestock. The amount of available water varies seasonally. During the summer rainy season waterholes have a very ample supply; even small ones can support many households. In the winter dry season, however, many of the smaller waterholes dry up completely, so that more households have to depend on fewer sources of water. This seasonal fluctuation leads to a corresponding fluctuation in the size of many of the waterhole groups. In the hamlet of ?Apas eight waterhole groups draw water from eight waterholes in the rainy season; in the dry season the same households regroup into four large groups drawing water from the four waterholes which contain water the year round.

The waterholes are highly sacred. Myths are told about each of them, describing the circumstances which led to the ancestors' discovery of the water and the way in which the waterhole acquired its distinctive name. Each waterhole group maintains a series of cross shrines for its waterhole, again for communicating both with the ancestral deities and with the Earth Lord. All of the shamans of the waterhole group gather to perform the K'IN KRUS ceremony for the waterhole. The waterhole group also holds some jural authority: men who refuse to contribute to the expenses of ceremonies or to the labor needed for cleaning out the waterhole may be fined by the shamans or even denied access to the waterhole.

The next larger unit in the social structure and the largest subdivision of the total municipio is the hamlet. Each hamlet is named; its borders are clearly known to its inhabitants. The fifteen hamlets range in size from 121 people to 1,227 (1960 census). The largest are Nabencauk and Paste?. Some are extremely compact in settlement pattern, like ?Apas and ?Az'am; others very dispersed, like Paste?. Zinacantan's hamlets are recognized officially in two ways: they are units for the Mexican census, taken every decade; and each has at least one, and normally two, *Principales* (KRINSUPALETIK) whose duty it is to represent the municipal government. At least one of the Principales reports to the Presidente every Sunday in the ceremonial center. They carry official messages to their hamlets, help apprehend culprits to be brought to the cabildo for trial, and assist in collecting taxes to pay for major fiesta expenses. They also have extensive ritual responsibilities, especially during Year Renewal ceremonies.

The civil officials who perform their duties at the cabildo in the ceremonial center constitute a crucial element of the municipio's social organization. They are ranked: after the *Presidente*, the *Síndico* and four *Alcaldes Jueces* sit in order on a long bench on the front porch and to the left of the door of the town hall. To the right of the door the *Mayores*, serving as the policemen and errand boys, sit on another long bench. Inside, behind a desk with an imposing-looking typewriter, sits the *Secretario*, the only ladino in the civil government of Zinacantan. In back of his desk is an ancient telephone which connects him with the officials in San Cristóbal, but it is used only in an emergency. Everyday governmental affairs are managed by the Indian officials; the secretary merely keeps the town records.

Civil officials serve three-year terms and, in theory, are elected to office. Actually, they are selected at annual political meetings attended by the important *caciques* (political bosses) of Zinacantan—the men who control the ejido (lands held under the agrarian reform laws), past *presidentes*, important schoolteachers, and so on. Although the civil officials have a variety of duties, which include greeting official ladino visitors, collecting money for and supervising construction of public works (such as roads and bridges), carrying out a few ritual functions, and appointing committees to organize for fiestas, their major concern is the settling of disputes. Day after day the Presidente, Síndico, and at least two of the jueces, who rotate the duty—and more recently some added civil *Regidores*—sit on their bench and wait for law cases. If the Presidente is absent, the Síndico takes the Presidente's silver-headed baton (containing a strong inner soul placed there by the ancestral gods), moves to the Number 1 position on the bench, and hears the cases.

While some Zinacantecos seek out the Presidente in his home during the night or early in the morning so as to obtain an uninterrupted hearing, the more common procedure is for the plaintiffs to approach the Presidente at the cabildo. The plaintiff bows to the officials in rank order, presents a bottle of cane liquor, and describes his complaint, such as "somebody has stolen my chickens." The Presidente and the others listen, and, if persuaded, summon two of the Mayores to bring the accused to the cabildo. The defendant appears, also with a bottle of cane liquor, bows to the officials, and presents his defense. Usually both parties are accompanied by relatives, known to be "good talkers," who serve as "lawyers." Witnesses may be called to provide additional testimony. All talk at once and one wonders how, in the ensuing pandemonium, a judgment is reached.

The case may have one of three outcomes. First, it may be settled in this Zinacanteco "court," with the officials passing judgment by expressing disapproval of an argument or hooting with laughter at a defendant who is telling an obvious lie; in such a case the culprit will be required to return the stolen property and be fined, or jailed (the jail is adjacent to the cabildo), or both. Second, if the case has more serious implications than the Zinacanteco court is willing to deal with (as in a case of murder), it is passed along to ladino officials in San Cristóbal. Third, it may be impossible to reach a clear-cut decision, in which case the Presidente entreats the two parties not to bear grudges against one another, and to live harmoniously in the same hamlet (J. Collier 1973).

Religious Organization

The religious life of Zinacantan is directed by the shamans and the cargoholders. A shaman is called an H?ILOL, literally "seer." Zinacantecos believe that in mythological times all men could "see" into the mountains and observe their ancestral gods directly; today only the shamans possess this ability.

There are at least two hundred and fifty shamans in Zinacantan. Most are adult males, though some are women, and some are as young as fifteen. Usually to become a shaman, a person dreams three times that his innate soul has been called before the ancestral gods in the Senior Large Mountain. In the first dream, which commonly occurs when a person is ten or twelve years of age, the innate soul of a supernatural Mayor (the celestial counterpart of the cabildo errand-runners) appears and directs the innate soul of the novice to accompany him to the house of the Alcalde within the mountain. The novice is conducted inside, where the supernatural Grand Alcalde is seated at the east end of a long table, flanked by all the Zinacantan shamans in order of their rank. After bowing to all present, the novice kneels at the west end of the table. The Alcalde asks if he is prepared to become a shaman. He must answer "yes"; otherwise he will die. The novice then receives all the types of candles, flowers, and other paraphernalia required for a curing ceremony, and is given instructions about the proper performance of the ritual. Dressed in the black ceremonial robe given him by the Alcalde, he kneels again while the senior official makes a sign of the cross on his forehead to indicate his acceptance. A patient is then brought in for the novice, who must diagnose the affliction and execute the proper ceremony in the presence of the Grand Alcalde and the shamans. The second and third dreams, which usually occur about a year apart, differ from the first only in that the patients and the illnesses vary. (If the patient in the first dream was an old man, it may be a woman in the second dream, and a child in the third, each suffering from a different sickness.)

The new shaman does not enter public service immediately, but practices cures on his family and neighbors for some time. Typically, indication of the gods' insistence on his public role comes when the novice himself falls ill. At this time he goes to the highest-ranking shaman in his hamlet, describes the dreams, and asks permission to reveal himself. After praying to the ancestral gods in the sacred mountains, the ranking shaman grants permission. The novice then travels to the lowlands where he cuts a bamboo staff to be carried henceforth in his left hand as a symbol of his office. Returning to his hamlet, he reveals his new ritual status, and begins to perform ceremonies.

The shamans in Zinacantan are all potentially ranked from one to two-hundred fifty. Order depends not upon age but upon time in service, that is, the number of years that have elapsed since the shaman made his public debut. Occasionally a shaman becomes incompetent for various reasons and his order is lowered by the ranking shaman in his hamlet; similarly, a shaman may be promoted by exhibiting special competence. There are reliable operational measures for observing rank order in Zinacantan. The marching order in processions always places the junior man in front and the senior man in the rear. There is also a ranked seating order at ritual tables, regardless of the size of the table or the ceremony.

Besides the shamans, the other important group in the religious organization of the ceremonial center is composed of the members of the official hierarchy, or cargo system. When a Zinacanteco speaks of a cargo, or ?ABTEL TA HTEK-LUM, he is referring to important "work" or "service" provided by men who hold positions in the religious hierarchy. ʔABTEL implies "bearing a burden," as when carrying a heavy load of maize on the back. In the context of the religious cargo system, the concept is probably related to the ancient Maya idea of the "Year Bearer." This is supported by the fact that, like the ancient Maya gods, who carried the year on a tumpline and passed it along to their successors, a contemporary Zinacanteco carries the burden of office for a year, at which time the responsibility is transferred to another (Bricker 1966). In Spanish, this burden-carrying concept translates as the *cargo*. While the positions involve great responsibility, they also provide enormous prestige and hence are much sought by Zinacanteco men who have requested them as many as twenty-two years in advance.

The cargo system consists of sixty-one positions grouped into four levels of ranked prestige and importance (see Figure 5). Zinacantecos must begin at the lowest ranking subdivision, ascending through the system only as a cargo in each level is successfully completed. All cargoholders must reside in the ceremonial center for the duration of their office. They participate in, as well as pay for, ritual activity. It has been estimated that as much as 14,000 pesos (about $1,100 US) is spent for ritual food, liquor, and paraphernalia by some cargoholders. Thus, in addition to the official requirement of consecu-

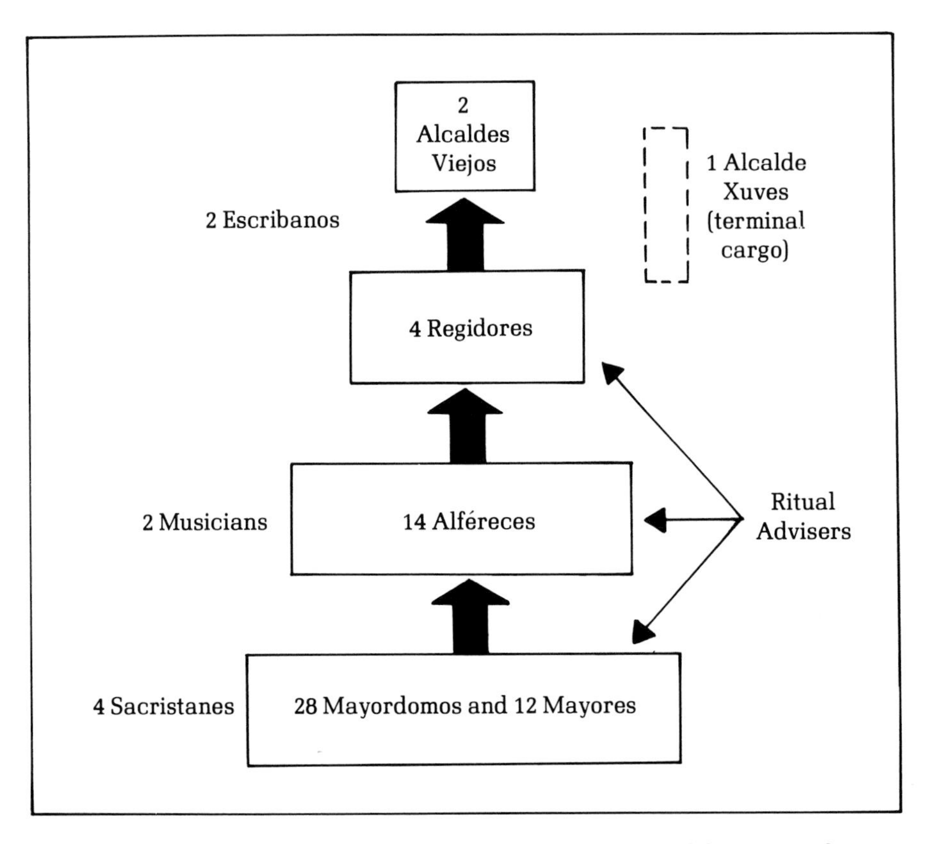

5. The religious hierarchy of Zinacantan, showing 61 cargos on four levels and four types of important auxiliary personnel

tive fulfillment of positions, ascendance through the system depends on the prospective cargoholder's ability to meet the often exorbitant expenses of his office. Generally, a cargoholder must work for several years after the termination of his office to pay off accumulated debts and begin to save for his next position.

In the first level there are Mayores and Mayordomos. The twelve ranked Mayores, in addition to serving as civil policemen and message-bearers, take part in important ritual activities. The twenty-eight Mayordomos are associated with particular saints in either the churches of the ceremonial center or the chapels of outlying hamlets. The Mayordomos are named and ranked according to the saint for which they take responsibility. Thus, the position of Mayordomo of San Sebastián does not have the same degree of prestige as the position of Mayordomo of Sacramento, who cares for the principal patron, San Lorenzo. The twelve Mayordomos serving saints in the churches of San Lorenzo and San Sebastián in the ceremonial center are further subdivided into ranked pairs. (In the Chapel of Esquipulas, ranked pairs of Mayordomo Reyes and Mesoneros take charge of the saints.) Thus, two officials, senior and junior, serve each of the major saints.

The second level in the hierarchy consists of seven ranked pairs of Alféreces associated with,

6. Mayordomos, with flags, in procession

and taking their names from, particular saints. They may at one time have played a significant role in caring for the saints; today their principal activities consist of feeding each other at ritual meals and dancing for the saints. Compared to other cargo levels the economic investment required at this level of service is exorbitant.

Four ranked Regidores and two ranked Alcaldes Viejos, at the third and fourth levels respectively, manage the entire cargo system, serving as overseers and advisers for all municipal ritual activity. The combined levels are collectively referred to as the MOLETIK, or "Elders." There is one position, that of *Alcalde Xuves*, to which an old man can be appointed as a terminal cargo when it is evident that he is not going to achieve a top Alcalde post.

Officials at the first three levels of the hierarchy are assisted in all ritual matters by Ritual Advisers. These advisers, chosen individually by each cargoholder, must have completed at least two years of cargo experience and demonstrated the ability to speak well and command respect. The name of this group of men is the same as that of the ancestral deities: just as the supernatural TOTIL ME?ILETIK, possessing great wisdom and experience, supervise and direct the lives of Zinacantecos, so the Ritual Advisers, experienced in ritual matters, advise cargoholders on the technicalities of ritual procedure.

While each cargo position is of a year's duration, the auxiliary personnel affiliated with a particular level of the ritual hierarchy serve for longer. The four *Sacristanes* daily open and close the church doors, ring the church bells three times each day (sunrise, noon, and sunset), and assist the Mayordomos in caring for their saints. The *Músicos* (musicians), a violinist and a harpist who play for the Alféreces, advise the latter on ritual procedure. Two *Escribanos* (Scribes) keep detailed records of tax collection for fiestas and waiting lists for cargo positions, in addition to assisting the Elders in ritual matters. With the Ritual Advisers serving as "masters of ceremonies" and the auxiliary personnel as dependable attendants and consultants, a cohesive system of ceremonies and ritual behavior in Zinacantan is maintained and perpetuated with an annual turnover of cargo positions.

3

Recurring Episodes in Zinacanteco Ritual

THE RITUAL SYSTEMS of most, if not all, societies contain series of recurring episodes that can be combined to form the longer ceremonial dramas. If, like "molecules," symbols are the basic units, these episodes are like "cells." They have their own inner organization, their own inner consistency. When cells occur alone, their internal ritual symbols carry a small, complete set of messages that codify and communicate information about and certify the validity of key propositions concerning the nature of sociocultural life or the natural universe.

More commonly, these episodes occur in the wider contexts of long ceremonial dramas. The fact that the cells are replicated over and over again (Vogt 1965b) in the mosaic arrangements of ritual life underscores each unit's importance in the cultural code and provides a way of breaking the ceremony into smaller, more manageable units for analysis. As an episode unfolds it reveals a set of symbolic actions which, when compared, disclose the basic elements of the complex ceremonies. These sets of actions are subject to the same basic principles of organization which characterize the long ceremonial dramas.

A Matrix of Binary Discriminations

The social and natural world of the Zinacantecos is categorized by binary discriminations in the cosmological, and correspondingly, the ritual system. Some are expressed at a more general level of contrast; others at a more concrete level, as the Zinacanteco *bricoleurs* (Lévi-Strauss 1966), evolve a cultural code out of their experience.

The critical recurring binary discriminations, general and concrete, are as follows (see next page):

Spatial-Temporal Oppositions

The Zinacantecos live in a world in which there is almost no flat land: mountains surround their

Spatial-Temporal
- Above/Below
  - highlands/lowlands
  - sky/earth
  - mountain/cave
- Day/Night
  - sun/moon
  - red/black
- Year/Day
- Rain/Drought
  - water/frost

Bio-Social
- Male/Female
- Old/Young

Cultural
- Culture/Nature
  - houses/woods
  - innate souls/animal companions
- Indian/Ladino

General Operators
- Rising Sun/Setting Sun
- Right/Left
- BANKILAL/ʔIZ'INAL
- hot/cold

settlements, trails wind up and down gradual to precipitous slopes and highlands tower above lowlands. The Zinacantecos contrast ʔOLON ʔOSIL, the "land below" or Lowlands—especially 5,000 feet down in the Grijalva River basin where they rent fields to grow maize—with ʔAK'OL ʔOSIL, the "land above" or Highlands of central Chiapas in which they live. They contrast VINAHEL with BALAMIL, and discriminate conceptually between the mountains (VIZ), homes of the ancestral gods, and caves and other openings such as waterholes and limestone sinks, which are passageways to the domain of the Earth Lord. This Above/Below opposition finds, to some extent, symbolic expressions in other domains of life: men always sit on chairs, women kneel on the ground. It also contains an apparent contradiction in that the Highlands, closer to the sun, are consistently cooler than the Lowlands, further from the sun (Gossen 1972:143).

Day/Night (K'AK'AL versus ʔAK'UBAL) provides the most basic temporal opposition as the sun appears and disappears each day. Although the moon is often seen in the daytime, its basic symbolic associations are with night. The sun is associated with day, as is indicated by the literal translation of K'AK'AL: "heat." Colors also symbolize this opposition: red is associated with the direction of the rising sun, black with the direction of the setting sun, white with day, black with night.

In longer cycles of time, the year, called HABIL, is contrasted with the day. The year finds expression in the annual calendar round of ceremonies. The intermediate unit, secondary to the Year/Day distinction, is composed of a series of days (twenty in the ancient Tzotzil calendar) designated as ʔUAL, or "month." In recent decades the week (called XEMANA, a loan word from the Spanish *semana*) has become an increasingly important measure of time for the Zinacantecos, especially as they have become accustomed to a holiday on Sunday which is now used as the day for important political meetings and as the date for certain ceremonies.

The Rain/Drought opposition is fundamental in highland Chiapas where a rainy season (May through September) and a dry season (October through April) effect important changes in the lives of the Zinacantecos. The cultivation of crops is determined by this annual fluctuation of the seasons. The seasons are in turn delineated ritually by the K'IN KRUS ceremonies. A more concrete manifestation of this opposition is between "water" and "frost": water falls in the rainy season, frost in the dry season. In the rainy season the Milky Way is called BE VOʔ (road of water), in the winter BE TAIV (road of frost).

Bio-Social Oppositions

Age and sex, expressed in the oppositions between Old and Young, and Male and Female, figure most prominently in symbolic discriminations derived from biological differences and social life. These oppositions occur with monotonous repetition in almost every ritual—from the simplest episode to the most complex ceremonial—indicating their importance to Zinacantecos. Through kinship terms, the patrilineal organization, the division of labor between maize-growers and tortilla-makers, dress, and municipal politics such distinctions order the social world.

Older Zinacantecos are believed to have more "heat," thus more sacred power. They are deferred to by women and younger men, always seated toward the rising sun or on the right, and served food and liquor first. Males are "on top" in this strongly patrilineal society—in rank order, in "heat," in ritual and political power, even in the traditional sexual position. (Our informants were shocked by the suggestion that a women might assume the upper position in a copulating couple.) The primacy of the male is also expressed in religious experience: the sun is male, the moon female. San Lorenzo occupies the central location above the altar on the "rising sun" side of the principal church; next in importance is Santo Domingo to the right. The principal female saint, the Virgen de Rosario, is placed, significantly, to the viewer's left. With the exception of ˀApas, which has installed a Señor Esquipulas image in its chapel as a symbol of independence from Zinacantan Center, all hamlet chapels house subordinate female saints as patrons.

Cultural Oppositions

For the anthropologist the Culture/Nature binary discrimination in Zinacanteco culture creates order out of a vast complex of ritual behavior. Although the opposition is not expressed abstractly, it is eminently apparent in the clearly defined distinctions between the houses and the woods, and the innate soul and the animal companion.

NAETIK symbolizes the essence of social order, civilized behavior—whether out in the hamlets with their clusters of house compounds or in the ceremonial center with the "houses for the saints" and the "navel of the earth." TEˀTIK, an undomesticated domain populated by wild plants, wild animals, and demons (PUKUHETIK), symbolizes essential Nature.

This fundamental opposition is expressed in and mediated on a spiritual plane by the "soul" concepts which *contrast* the well-socialized aspects of Zinacantecos (the C'ULEL, or "innate soul") with the unruly, uncontrollable, "wild," and impulsive side of their behavior (the animal companion living in TEˀTIK), and also *conjoin* Culture and Nature in the belief that the C'ULEL is shared by a Zinacanteco and his animal. These relationships have a "totemic" quality in that Zinacantecos use the same verbal classification to order nature as to order and categorize human society. A series of wild animal companions forms a natural hierarchy that corresponds to the social ranking system: important political leaders and shamans have jaguars as animal companions; minor political leaders, ocelots; less important but still noteworthy Zinacantecos, coyotes; and citizens of no civic or religious distinction, oppossums. In addition, some of the patrilineages have old Tzotzil names derived from the natural order, such as "coyotes," "wasp nests," and "lime head."

The Indian/Ladino opposition reflects the four century old bicultural system that exists in the Highlands of Chiapas. The ladinos, generally called HKAXLANETIK, ("Castilians") are regarded with mixed, often conflicting emotions. They are admired and respected for their economic and political power, yet resented for their use of this power to interfere with Zinacanteco life. In the belief system this contrast is most vividly portrayed in the opposition between the "fathers and mothers," the ancestral deities, and the Earth Lord, pictured as a fat, greedy ladino. Although both the ancestral gods and the Earth Lord must be prayed to and given offerings, they exercise control over quite distinct spheres of life. The gods monitor and control behavior and values, the intangible qualities so diagnostic of cultural identity; the Earth Lord controls commodities, tangible evidence of economic status and well-being, and there are great dangers involved in courting his aid.

General Operators

By "general operators," I refer to four master

binary discriminations, oppositions which appear in virtually all important domains of Zinacanteco life as ordering principles. Rising Sun/Setting Sun establishes the focal directional symbolism in the universe. Intimately associated with the concept of the rising sun are the highest ranking ancestral god (the supernatural equivalent of the Grand Alcalde in the terrestrial religious hierarchy), the supernatural corrals of the animal companions, the placement of the most important saints, "above" (ʔAK'OL), the color red, the oldest Zinacantecos, the male side of the house, and "life." Associated with the setting sun are the lower ranking ancestral gods, the placement of the Virgen de Rosario image in the chapel in ʔAz'am, "below" (ʔOLON), the color black, the youngest Zinacantecos, the female side of the house, and "death." The discrimination also provides the basic unit of time, the "day," in the daily movements of the sun.

Right/Left (BAZ'I K'OB/Z'ET K'OB—with BAZ'I meaning "genuine") is an opposition deriving from body symbolism. It establishes directional symbolism for what we call north and south, north being "the side or edge of VINAHEL on the right hand" (if the speaker is facing west), "the side or edge of VINAHEL on the left hand" (if the speaker is facing east). Unlike what Gossen (1972) reports for Chamula symbolism, in Zinacanteco thought north is not always "on the right hand," and south "on the left hand"; it depends on whether the speaker is facing west or east. The other symbolic associations are roughly equivalent with the east-west opposition: right connotes more importance, higher rank than left. In spatial delineations within a house, and in seating arrangements, right is associated with maleness, left with femaleness.

BANKILAL/ʔIZ'INAL (roughly, "senior/junior"), expressing rank, segments much of the Zinacanteco universe: older and younger brother, senior and junior sacred mountains, senior and junior crosses in shrines, drums, fireworks, caves, saints, cargo officials, shamans, Christ children, necklaces (ʔUALETIK) for the saints. Symbolic associations make it clear that the BANKILAL member is older, more important, more senior—and outranks the ʔIZ'INAL. This crucial principle of rank is based upon age or, more precisely, upon time elapsed since an event occurred in the life of a person or in the transformation of a natural object, such as a mountain, from secular to sacred status. Thus, when Zinacantecos say that people or mountains or crosses are senior as opposed to junior, or that a certain man or shaman is MAS BANKILAL, or MAS ʔIZ'INAL, they are expressing a principle of ranking that is embedded in the flow of time in their universe. The model for this flow of time may be biological aging in persons, historical aging (such as the time elapsed since a shaman made his debut), or "mythological aging" (time elapsed since the ancestral gods performed some act establishing an item of ritual paraphernalia, or a geographical feature within the ritual system).

Finally, the all-important Hot/Cold which derives from temperature differences in nature, and ultimately from the "heat" of the sun, orders persons and objects by degrees of heat in a way that seldom corresponds to measurable temperature. For example, strong cane liquor is labeled hot, weak liquor as cold; old and powerful men are hot, young and powerless girls cold. Sicknesses are classified hot or cold; hot and cold plants are metaphors in curing ceremonies; hot and cold foods are necessary for a healthy diet.

Focal Symbolic Action in Ritual Episodes

The ritual episodes that recur most frequently in Zinacanteco ceremonial life are: drinking, eating, processions, and offerings at cross shrines.

Ritual Drinking

Over his left shoulder every Zinacanteco man

carries a bag, whether a fancy, hand-tooled leather MORAL or a net bag with a leather shoulder strap. The bag is used for carrying any number of objects—money, cigarettes, a pineapple—but most frequently it contains a bottle of cane liquor.

The cane liquor (distilled from the brown sugar derived from sugar cane) is purchased in one of the small stores that abound in Zinacantan Center and the hamlets. The storekeepers purchase it either in San Cristóbal, where it is likely to be legal POX, or from Chamulas, who make a fine grade of bootleg liquor in stills hidden in the mountains. (A few Zinacantecos now distill their own bootleg POX.) Although beer, or even Coca-Cola, may be served in a drinking ritual, POX, referred to as "dew-drops of the gods," is preferred, and *must* accompany any kind of crucial transaction. Medicine is called POXIL, which means "POX-like," signifying that cane liquor and medicine have the same internal effects; they cure illness, repair social relations, and restore health.

The most frequent episode of "communicative behavior," a drinking ritual, occurs whenever cane liquor is presented or offered by one Zinacanteco to another or by one group of Zinacantecos to another. An episode may be triggered by a chance encounter on the trail, in the San Cristóbal market, or elsewhere. If one Zinacanteco is indebted to the other (perhaps he owes him money), he will stop and offer a drink

7. Drinking rituals in progress

(to appease his creditor and explain why he has not repaid the loan). Or one man may be seeking some favor, goods, or services from the other—perhaps he is courting his daughter, or hopes to enlist his aid in building a house or assisting at a curing ceremony—and so offers the liquor. Or the two men may have a special relationship: they may be compadres, in which case they usually exchange drinks, or perhaps brothers-in-law, a delicate relationship since one has removed the other's sister from her lineage.

Words of greeting exchanged as they approach are followed by either a shaking of hands—signifying approximate equality of status—or, more often, a bowing-and-releasing sequence in which the junior man raises his hat and bows to the senior man, who "releases" the bow with the back of his right hand. As he releases the younger man, the senior usually says LAʔ CABOT, which translates approximately as "may you be protected." This bowing-and-releasing signifies that the junior respects the seniority of the older man and that the senior man accepts the gesture of respect and also ritually accepts responsibility for caring for, protecting, the younger man. The man offering the liquor then extracts the bottle from his bag, removes the cork (usually rolled-up maize leaves or husks), and offers "a little bit of cold water." (Zinacantecos are masters of understatement!) When the bottle is accepted, the drinker says KIC'BAN, "I receive," followed by the appropriate term of address, such as TOTIK, "Sir," if the offerer is an older man. At the same time he will again bow politely to his senior, who will in turn release him and say ʔIC'O, "receive it" or "drink it." If, in the opinion of the offerer, the drinker has not consumed enough, even after he has grimaced and commented that the cane liquor is "hot," the offerer may insist that he accept a second round—and the sequence is repeated. Depending on the circumstances, and supply of POX, it may now be time for the original receiver to become the offerer—and the whole sequence is repeated with the second man's bottle. Before they leave each other, the bowing-and-releasing sequence will be repeated again, sometimes several times.

More common than trailside rituals are the instances when cane liquor is carried to another's house and presented with the express purpose of requesting a favor. For example, Palas, who is serving as a Mayordomo, visits Xun, a musician, to persuade him to play the violin for the flower-renewal ceremony of his house altar. He comes to the gate outside Xun's house, with a liter of hot POX in his shoulder bag, and initiates the action by addressing the wife of the household, since it is assumed that the wife will always be at home by the hearth, even when the husband is away.

PALAS: Are you there, Loxa? Is Xun there?

LOXA (Xun's wife): I'm here. Yes, he's here.

PALAS: Are you there Xun?

XUN: I'm here. What's up?

PALAS: May I come in and visit you a minute?

XUN: Sure. Come on in. What's on your mind?

PALAS: I'll visit you for a second, Xun.

(*Palas enters.*)

XUN: Fine. Won't you sit down? There's a chair.

PALAS: Well thanks. How are things going? (Literally, are you still home?)

XUN: Things are OK for now. (Literally, I'm still home for the moment.)

PALAS: Good. Are you going anywhere today?

XUN: Not today. Tomorrow I'm going to San Cristóbal. I'm going to sell two bags of my corn in order to buy four chickens.

PALAS: What do you need the chickens for?

XUN: My wife's going to have a curing ceremony.

PALAS: When (what day?)

XUN: Day after tomorrow.

(*Palas takes out his bottle.*)

PALAS: Well, listen, I've come to talk to you, Xun. Please excuse this little cold water (i.e., weak liquor).

XUN: What's the POX for, Tot (meaning "father," used as a term of respect for an older man.) Palas? What do you want?

PALAS: Oh, nothing. I have a request. Won't you please play my music for me for the flower-change ceremony?
XUN: What day? When do you want?
PALAS: Late tomorrow.
XUN: But I'm not free since my wife has her curing ceremony. Who knows what time you'll begin.
PALAS: I guess we'll start about four o'clock.
XUN: But won't it last a long time?
PALAS: No, not very long.
XUN: Oh, but won't I get drunk? I really can't lose the time.
PALAS: No, no. We only have a little liquor.
XUN: Well, OK. I'll go.
PALAS: Please do. Please excuse this tiny bit of cold water.
XUN: Thanks, Tot Palas. Let's drink it.

(Dialogue from John B. Haviland)

Xun picks up the bottle of POX. He may either serve as the HP'IS-VOʔ (literally, measurer of water—or drink-pourer) himself, or if a younger male is present in the house, will hand the bottle to him and ask him to serve as pourer. Xun then asks his wife to locate a P'IS (usually a one-ounce shot glass, though sometimes larger) for the pourer to use. Bowing and being released, the pourer asks permission to serve, then thanks Tot Palas, again with a bow, for bringing the liquor. The pourer calculates the size of the servings carefully, since the bottle should be finished in exactly three rounds. He first serves Tot Palas, who not only presented the POX but is also the senior male present, bowing and being released as he does so. Tot Palas accepts the glass with his left hand, keeping the right free for releasing bows. He then makes a round of toasts, saying KIC'BAN (followed by the appropriate term of address) and receiving an ʔIC'O response, and receiving and releasing bows, from all in the house except the youngest children. He begins with the senior male present, proceeds down the hierarchy of adult males; then toasts all the females of the household. Shifting the glass back to his right hand, Tot Palas downs the shot of POX in one gulp and returns the glass to the drink-pourer, who serves a shot to the next male in the status hierarchy—that is, Xun, who receives the POX and the toasting is repeated. The drink-pourer continues, pouring a shot for each male in rank order, then serving the females, and finally himself, to complete the round. There is a pause while the bottle is corked and placed beside Xun. Conversation about the maize fields, gossip about people and ceremonies, stories of what is happening at the cabildo follow, until Xun decides it's time for the second round. He hands the bottle back to the drink-pourer and the whole action is repeated. Then there is another pause and more conversation until Xun signals for the third round.

Since POX in its hot form is strong (usually about 70 proof), a "pouring-off" procedure often begins during the second and continues into the third round. At this time, men use small funnels attached to their shoulder bags to pour the shot into their own bottles, *after* they have toasted and gone through the bowing-and-releasing sequence, for it is obligatory to accept the liquor and go through the amenities. Women often pour off the liquor into small bowls near their *metates* (stones for grinding maize). Alternatively, a shot may be handed to someone else in the family group to drink.

At the end of the third round, the drink-pourer hands the bottle to Xun, who returns it to Tot Palas and goes into an appropriate sequence of thanking behavior. Tot Palas puts the empty liter bottle back in his shoulder bag, staggers to his feet, and makes his departure, confident that the bargain has been sealed and that Xun, the musician, will appear on schedule and play for the flower-renewal ceremony.

Analysis. These little episodes of drinking ritual are revealing examples of communicative behavior: small-scale models which structure everyday Zinacanteco social life. The material paraphernalia is very simple: a bottle of cane liquor, a shot glass, and a funnel. The ritual sequences consist of serving liquor in highly patterned order; of appropriate toasts; and of bowing-and-releasing behavior.

Recall that the essential communication in the universe occurs among innate souls. Since the innate souls are conceived to be lodged in the blood and in the heart, there is a rich set of phrases for talking about "hearts." "What does your heart say?" "Rest your heart," "His heart is at ease," "His heart starts up" (meaning "He gets angry"), "His heart ends" (meaning "He calms down") are all metaphors for the varying conditions of the innate soul. POX has a "hot" and "strong" innate soul which serves to open channels of communication and to reduce noise and distortion which might interfere with transactions between men or between men and the gods. The flow of POX in Zinacanteco society, if it could be measured and charted, would provide both a blueprint and a mirror of social relationships.

The sequence expresses two fundamental features of Zinacanteco life: that the society is hierarchically organized with age taking precedence over youth and men taking precedence over women; and that the scarce good (POX) is distributed equally to all, regardless of rank.

The hierarchy of status is expressed in the strict order in which the drink-pourer serves the POX and in the bowing-and-releasing behavior. These two orders are strictly homologous with one exception: although all males are served before females, younger men *bow to* older women. So, although age and sex are conflicting principles, they are given simultaneous expression as ranking principles in the society.

These facts fit nicely into the Zinacanteco view of the life cycle. Babies are born without status, without heat. As the individual moves through life, by acquiring more heat his innate soul becomes more fixed and, therefore, less susceptible to "frights" that may cause soul-loss. Having noted in the drinking ritual the importance of age (with its heat) as a ranking principle, the Zinacantecos are simultaneously reaffirming the patrilineal descent and patrilocal residence patterns of their society.

Unlike many other societies with strict status hierarchies, the drinks are distributed equally. A twelve-year-old girl may have to wait, but when her shot of POX comes the serving will be equal to that of the eldest, most important man present. The same glass is used for everyone. This not only symbolizes equality of distribution but also provides a communal sharing that links all "souls" (and "hearts") into a harmonious social whole.

Ritual Eating

A more complex episode occurs in the "ritual meal," the VEʔEL TA MEXA (literally "meal on a table"). Ordinary meals in Zinacanteco homes are served on the earthen floor. The men sit on small chairs and eat the tortillas and beans from pottery, gourd, or enamel bowls. The women eat later, sitting on the ground near the cooking hearth. For a ritual occasion there is always a "meal on a table" which follows a carefully prescribed format (Vogt 1969: 574-575).

The meal is served on a rectangular wooden table whose axis must be oriented from rising to setting sun, and which is covered with a pink-and-white striped cotton cloth, called a MANTREX. The tables, usually about 30 x 45 cm. to 60 x 90 cm. in size, may be constructed by Zinacantecos, but are more often made by the neighboring Chamulas. The tablecloth is woven by women from cotton thread bought in San Cristóbal. At the center of the rising sun end of the table are placed a bottle of cane liquor, a shot glass, and a bowl of salt. The participants in the ritual meal are seated on small wooden chairs on both sides of the table, generally in the rank order shown in Figure 8. The highest ranking person is seated at the southeast corner, and the next highest ranking opposite him in the northeast corner. The ranking pattern proceeds in symmetrical pairs down the length of the table (A, a, B. b . . .), simultaneously expressing two basic principles: the primacy of the rising sun and the primacy of right over left.

In many Zinacanteco ceremonies, especially the public rites for cargo holders, and for shamans in K'IN KRUS, the participants are all male. The women remain in the cooking area by the hearth. However, in domestic ceremonies, such as curing, baptismal, marriage or house dedication rites, some of the participants are women who take their places in appropriate rank order at the table. The other women remain by the cooking hearth.

The ritual meal always includes cane liquor, maize tortillas, chicken cooked in a broth with chili, salt, and KOKOˀON (Mexican tea, *Chenopodium ambrosioides*), coffee, and small, round wheat-flour rolls made by ladinos. Although pork, beef, or dried fish may be substituted for chicken, this deviation is critically noted. There are seventeen basic steps in the eating of the meal, which may be summarized as follows:

The senior man signals the young man designated as drink-pourer to serve the first round of liquor from the bottle at the head of the table. The senior man prays over the shot of liquor before he drinks it, saying in part:

Well, then, I drink first, Father,
I drink first, then, Mother,
Thank you a little.
In the divine name of God, Jesus Christ, my Lord,
Take this, then, Father,
Take this, then, Lord,
There is still a little left,
There is still a drop left,
Of this dew of your holy mouth,
Of this dew of your holy lips,
I will share with you,
I will stand in your shadows [under your cover] . . .

Appropriate bowing-and-releasing behavior accompanies this episode, and the bottle and glass are replaced at the head of the table. The tablecloth is rolled up—either to the head of the table or from both sides to the middle, and a gourd of warm water is passed to the server from the women at the hearth. The young man places the gourd in the center of the table, and each participant washes his hands in it in rank sequence, initiated by the senior man, who says HAX HK'OBTIK', "let's wash our hands." The gourd is returned to the women by the server. A second gourd is passed by the server to the senior man; again he initiates the sequence, one of rinsing out mouths and spitting on the floor (LAˀ HSUK' KETIK, "come, let's rinse our mouths").

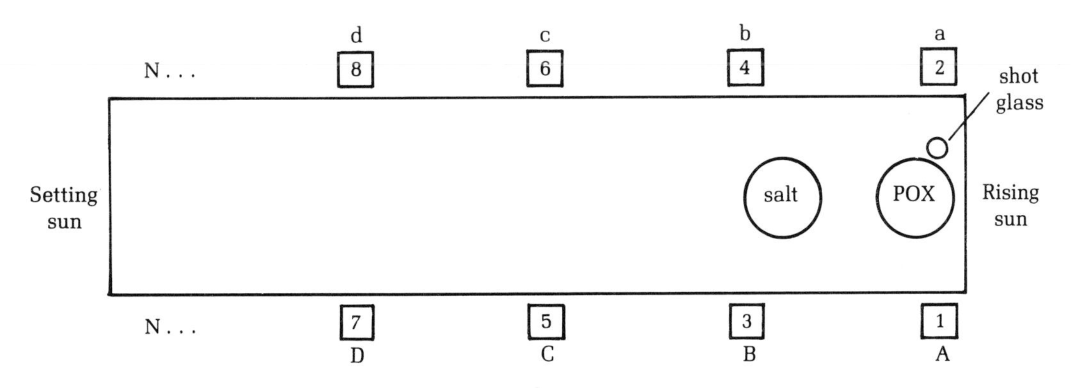

8. The rank order of participants at a ritual meal

The gourd is returned to the women. The tablecloth is unrolled back over the table.

The server places a pottery bowl of chicken parts in broth before each participant, always in rank order. A stack of tortillas is placed in the center of the table. Saying ZAKO ME AVAZ' AMIK (please take your salt), the senior man leads the eating sequence by putting a pinch of salt into his bowl of chicken; the others do the same. Taking a tortilla in his right hand, the senior man says LAˀ YALANIK ME ˀUN (come, fall to!), shifts to his left, tears off a small piece, dips it in the broth, and eats it. The others follow, as when the senior man signals ˀUC'BEIK ME LI YAˀLELE' (drink the broth, please), picks up his bowl in his right hand, and drinks the broth. More broth is offered to those who wish it by the server; most accept, for, with the consumption of many tortillas, the meal is otherwise quite dry.

TAMBEIK ME LI SBATEBE (please take the chicken to make the flavor of the tortillas better) signals the eating of the chicken itself, each person following the lead of the senior man, who takes a piece of chicken in his right hand, places it in the tortilla, and eats it, a small bite at a time. All finish eating at about the same time, and the bowls and gourds are returned to the women by the server. All of the chicken must either be eaten or wrapped in a tortilla to be taken home. A second round of liquor is served by the drink-pourer upon direction by the senior man, followed by a cup of hot coffee for each, sweetened with brown sugar and topped with a wheat-flour roll. The senior man says VOˀ ˀUC'EL ("five drinks," but the meaning is obscure) and begins to eat the roll by tearing off a piece and dipping it into his coffee. After coffee and rolls are eaten, the tablecloth is removed and the hand-rinsing and the mouth-rinsing sequences are repeated. The third round of liquor follows. The bottle, now empty if the drink-pourer has been careful with his measurements, is returned to the host's collection of empty bottles in the corner of the house. This marks the formal end of the meal and the table is removed.

These patterned sequences of behavior apply to ritual meals at all levels in the social system. For small domestic ceremonies, such as curing or house-dedication rituals, a very small table is used and as few as four or five people eat at it. The shaman sits in position 1, followed by other men, then women. In the K'IN KRUS ceremonies of a SNA the table is larger and more people sit at it. The senior members of the lineage are seated in the honored positions, followed by the shamans in rank order and finally the more junior ritual assistants. For K'IN KRUS of a waterhole group the scale increases. As many as eight to ten shamans have to be seated, along with the ritual assistants; often two or more tables are placed together. For the Year Renewal ceremonies of an entire hamlet the scale is even larger, involving as many as fifteen to twenty shamans, plus assistants. The maximum is reached at the Fiesta of San Sebastián, when the entire religious hierarchy of cargoholders, plus the Presidente and his assistants, sit down in shifts at an enormous table and are served a whole chicken per person.

Analysis. The ritual meal is more intricate than the drinking ritual episode contained within it—a nice example of Mary Douglas' view of society as something like a set of Chinese boxes, "each sub-system having little sub-systems of its own" (1966: 138).

Consider the ritual paraphernalia. As well as the bottle and shot glass of the drinking episode, there also appears a wooden table, tablecloth, and seats for the participants. (The chairs themselves are not as important as "seating spaces" along the sides of the table. Houses which lack sufficient chairs often provide seating spaces by improvising a bench from a plank supported on two chairs.) There are also a bowl of salt, gourds of warm water for washing hands and rinsing mouths, and the meal's two courses: tortillas and chickens, and coffee and rolls.

One of a cluster of right-angled symbols, Zinacanteco tables are always rectangular. Congruent with the view of a right-angled universe, they symbolize social order as opposed to the natural world which appears as an encircling, irregular horizon. The shape provides a long axis that can be placed along the "path of the sun" with the head toward rising sun and the foot toward setting sun.

Although Zinacantecos of low status may sit around the foot of the ritual table, no one sits at the head. There the ancestral gods preside and partake of the liquor and food served. Their living descendants are arranged in such a way that the elder ones are seated at the sides of the head of the table, next to the gods; more junior members, of lesser heat, with more time to live, are seated farther away. The hot POX, placed at the very end of the head of the table, is the medium of contact with the gods. The salt, placed just west of the POX, serves as an "insulator" to protect the living Zinacantecos from too much exposure to the gods' supernatural heat. Salt is "cold," contrasting with the "hot" cane liquor and the "heat" of the gods; it serves, in a variety of ritual contexts, to "close circuits" as effectively as POX "opens circuits." As a circuit-closer, salt keeps demons out of food and is, therefore, invariably sprinkled on food before it is eaten. The relationship of POX and salt is homologous with that of rising and setting sun in respect to the dimension of "hot"-"cold," this also being symbolized in the directional orientation.

The POX, rather than the shot glass, is placed closer to the most senior ritualist because, as the "dew-drops of the gods," it connects the most senior participant and the gods; the glass is placed in a more junior position, near a more junior ritualist.

What of the tablecloth? Here another cluster of symbols comes into the setting. The pink or red stripes, always running length-wise on the table, emphasize its long axis and may also symbolize the rays of the sun. The relation of the tablecloth to the candle offerings provides another set of symbolic associations: the candles are carried from San Cristóbal in the cloth; they are placed on it for prayers by the shaman and the participants; they are later carried to the mountain shrines wrapped in the same cloth. In a ritual meal the Zinacantecos eat tortillas and chicken on the tablecloth; it serves, in effect, as "clothing" for the table and for the candles ("tortillas") for the ritual meal for the gods. The cloth also is a reminder to the male eaters that women prepare the food for men.

The ritual action begins with a drinking episode which is repeated in the middle and the end. The three rounds thus are signals that initiate the meal, divide it between two courses, and conclude it. When the senior man accepts the first shot of cane liquor, he turns to the head of the table and offers the POX to the gods.

With the gods invited to join and partake of the meal, liquor is served from the same glass to *all* in the house, an action expressing communality and continuity from the deceased ancestors down to the youngest Zinacanteco capable of drinking a shot of POX.

Next come the two washing sequences: hands that will hold the food, mouths that will consume it. When the food appears there is a contrast between the tortillas, served in a common gourd; and the individual bowls of chicken and individual cups of coffee topped with the wheat-flour rolls.

Ritual drinking and ritual meal episodes serve complementary symbolic functions. The drinking emphasizes social continuity, serving all from same shot glass; but, at the same time, hierarchical discontinuity of age and sex through the order of serving and the bowing-and-releasing. The ritual meal emphasizes communality in gourds for washing and in bowls of salt and tortillas; but individuality through separate bowls of chicken and cups of coffee with rolls.

Tortillas need little explanation. They explicitly signify a man-made meal; humans, unlike animals, eat their meals *with* tortillas. But why chicken, and why coffee and wheat-flour rolls? Chickens, probably replacing turkeys as the staple for ritual meals after the Conquest, are "food for the gods," and the substitute for the life of a patient in the curing ceremonies. The bird thus assumes a symbolic meaning as a mediator with the gods. Chickens, coffee, which probably replaced chocolate in recent decades, and wheat-flour rolls all come from the ladino world. In addition to being expensive, and affordable only for rituals, they come from a domain that stresses individuality, as opposed to tortillas that symbolically unite Zinacantecos, that stress communality in Indian life.

Ritual meals are used partly to mark time, as a symbol of completion. In a curing ceremony, for example, a meal signals the end of the preparations; another marks the beginning of the actual ceremony. They are served at the end of other major stages in the ceremony: following the bathing of the patient and the sacrificial chickens; after the sacrificial chicken is placed in the cave at KALVARYO; after the patient enters the platform bed; and at the end of his postceremonial seclusion in bed.

A number of our field workers in Zinacantan have been so impressed with the frequency of and emphasis upon drinking and eating rituals that they have been tempted to characterize the culture as an "oral culture" (e.g. B. Colby ms. 1959). I am not qualified to pass judgment on this psychological characterization, but I agree that drinking and eating are major concerns. Rather than stress "orality," I perceive the domain of ritual "drinking and eating" as symbolizing in microcosm the quintessential principles of everyday Zinacanteco life. The behavior sequences trigger symbolic actions—the etiquette of the toast, the bowing-and-releasing, the order of serving, the seating order of the participants—that provide models *of* and models *for* the building blocks of the social system.

Ritual Processions

Although there is no generic term in Tzotzil for ritual processions, it is possible to speak of them as XCOLET ʔEC'EL (literally, "they are walking in formation"). A procession essentially consists of a group of ritualists walking single-file, in fixed rank order, from one shrine to another. It may include a handful of ritualists walking from a house shrine to one or more mountain shrines or to visit the saints in the churches; at the other extreme it may consist of the entire hierarchy of cargoholders, accompanied by musicians and helpers, marching to a cross shrine at the edge of Zinacantan Center to meet a saint from another municipio. But whatever the context, ritualists are invariably on foot, single-file, in a fixed rank order, and usually carrying ritual paraphernalia on tumplines.

Rank order requires that the most junior ritualist march first, the most senior ritualist last. If the procession is enclosing sacred space, as occurs in completing a ceremonial circuit, the direction taken is almost always counterclockwise. Music of three types (flute and drums; violin-harp-guitar; brass band) and fireworks of two types (skyrockets and small cannons) are added to certain types of processions.

The smallest, least elaborate ritual procession occurs during a small curing ceremony when ritualists set off from the house of the patient to visit the mountain shrines. The shaman marches in the rear, directly preceded by the patient, then by the candle-carrier. If the patient is married, the spouse marches directly in front of him. If the patient is a woman, some shamans have her husband walk behind her, rather than in front—a position consistent with sex ranking. These three positions are fixed; MAYOLETIK, helpers who carry food and liquor, may, on the other hand, walk ahead, behind, or at times, off to one side.

The more elaborate K'IN KRUS processions include two types of music. The order of march, front to rear, is: flute and drum players, Mayordomos, stringed-instrument players, and shamans, from junior to senior.

An even more elaborate example is provided during a major fiesta when, to meet a visiting saint coming to the Church of San Lorenzo, the cargoholders form, from front to rear and junior to senior, as follows: flute; large drum; small drum; Junior Mayordomos (in rank order); guitar; harp; violin; Senior Mayordomos (in rank order); Junior Alféreces (in rank order); guitar; violin; Senior Alféreces (in rank order); Regidor 4; Regidor 3; Regidor 2; Regidor 1; Second Alcalde; Grand Alcalde; Ritual Advisers. A brass band (usually hired from San Lucas, a more acculturated Indian town) accompanies the procession, marching to one side, apart from the ranked formation. The fireworks shooters likewise accompany the procession, but not in fixed order; rather, they run ahead in order to shoot off fireworks as the procession arrives and departs from cross shrines en route.

Analysis. Any observer of the Zinacanteco scene can recognize one of the quintessential features of the way of life: walking single-file along narrow mountain paths while carrying maize on a tumpline to market, carrying firewood or water, or traveling from hamlets to the ceremonial center. One almost never sees Zinacantecos walking abreast; even along the Pan American highway or on the sidewalks of San Cristóbal, they move in single-file. It is interesting to note that the ancient Maya gods, the Year Bearers who carried the year on a tumpline, are depicted as proceeding along the path of time, single-file. Thus, ritual processions, though special in purpose and function, express this common characteristic. In a word, the processions are modeled on one of the most essential Zinacanteco activities; they are models *of* and models *for* one of the most programmed features of Zinacanteco reality.

I have already discussed why processions move counterclockwise, but why are the ritualists arranged with seniors in the rear? There are a number of interpretations, including the possibility that Zinacantecos simply model their processionals on Catholic custom, with the choir preceding the priests, the priests preceding the bishop, and so on. But I believe there is more to the order than that.

The outstanding feature of processional rank order is that it *reverses* the normal, everyday order of Zinacanteco travel. Although the order of a nonritual group is not as strictly prescribed as in ceremony, the ordinary line of march witnesses the most senior male in front, junior males behind, women and small children in the rear. A reversal of this order for ceremonial occasions serves to shift gears, so to speak, and make a statement about the important differences between ordinary and ritual life.

Gossen further argues that similar ritual processions in Chamula always set out from "conceptual east," and follow the path of the sun: "it follows that the member of the party who has the greatest 'heat,' which is a fundamental attribute of the sun symbol of the east, should remain closest to the source of that 'heat.' It is a simple spatial rule of 'like remains close to like.' And it places the most 'senior' official at the end of the procession" (1972:147). Another aspect to be emphasized is that the ritualists who march in strict formation also sit on benches in comparably rigid formation.

But what might this marching-sitting-marching-sitting sequence represent symbolically? If ritual processions do not merely connect one sacred place with another but, more important, set out from the direction of the rising sun and flow along its path, it follows that they symbolically mark out time in a manner that can be related directly to the ancient concept of KINH (León-Portilla 1968). As the ritualists stop to sit in rank order on benches, perhaps they are symbolically re-enacting the ascent and descent of the sun through the layers or steps of the sky. Recall that the sun rises in the east, preceded by Venus, who "sweeps the path of the sun." The sun then ascends through the layers along a path ornamented with flowers. Ascending a layer every hour, it reaches the zenith at noon and pauses to watch the happenings on earth. As afternoon progresses, the sun descends through the layers to the west.

The inference that the ritualists are enacting the ascent and descent of the sun is buttressed by two points of evidence: first, in the activities of cargoholders there is typically a long pause at high noon, when they sit on a bench and survey a ceremonial scene; similarly, the sun at that hour is said to pause (as San Salvador) and watch happenings on Earth; and second, "sweepers" precede a procession to the mountain shrines to remove the old flowers and add new pine tips in advance of the arrival of the ritualists.

Ritual Offerings at Cross Shrines

In Tzotzil, offerings at cross shrines may be spoken of as YULOˀ KAHVALTIK, "visits to the gods," generally designating the ancestral gods who live in the mountains, although in certain ceremonies, especially K'IN KRUS, communication at selected shrines is with the Earth Lord.

Wooden structures in the form of the Christian cross appear in the following contexts in Zinacantan: on top of the roof of a house (SKRUSAL HOL NA, "rooftop cross"); perpendicular to the main door in the patio outside a house; on top of maize stored in a granary (SKRUSAL ˀIXIM, "cross for maize"); on top of a church (SKRUSAL HOL ˀEKLIXYA, "church-top cross"); in a churchyard (KRUS TA TIˀ ˀEKLIXYA, "cross at the edge of the church"); around the edges of the heart of the ceremonial center, frequently, but not always, at street intersections; beside a waterhole (KRUS TA TIˀ VOˀ, "cross at the edge of the water"); in a cave or limestone sink (SKRUSAL C'EN, "cross for cave or sink"); at the foot and summit of the mountain residences of the ancestral gods (KRUS TA YOK VIZ, "cross at the foot of the mountain," and KRUS TA HOL VIZ, "cross at the head of the mountain"); at the "meeting places of TOTIL MEˀILETIK" that are called KALVARYO; and at the head of a grave in the cemetery (SKRUSAL HOL ˀANIMA, "cross at the head of the dead").

All of these crosses serve symbolically as "doorways" or "entryways"; that is, they are means of communication with deities and boundary-markers between significant units of social space. The crosses on top of houses and churches that are of great importance to Mexican Catholics seem little emphasized; it is believed they "protect" the house or church, but they appear less significant than the other types. On the other hand, the patio crosses, the maize crosses, the boundary crosses, the cross shrines, and the grave crosses are extremely important to Zinacanteco ritual life and receive frequent attention in offerings that relate living Zinacantecos to their deities and to the dead.

To be effective in any kind of ritual activity, a KRUS must consist of three crosses. Many cross shrines contain only one wooden cross; others contain two. These types are symbolically converted into a triple cross by the addition of pine trees next to the standing crosses. If no wooden crosses exist at a place where a ritual must be performed, the sacred triad can be symbolically created by placing three small pine trees in the ground. This has led me to conclude that, for the Zinacantecos, the wooden cross is little more than a handy structure on which to place ritually salient materials and that the pine tips and flowers provide the essential symbols (Vogt 1969: 389).

The crosses are not pushed directly into the ground, but each is tied to a small pole driven into the ground or placed in a cement base. The reasons are twofold: from a practical point of view, the base of the cross, if placed in the ground, would quickly deteriorate in the rainy climate of highland Chiapas; symbolically, crosses must not be YUT BALAMIL, "in the earth," because earth represents and belongs to the domain of the Earth Lord (Priscilla Rachun Linn, Field Notes, 1970). The more elaborate cross shrines have cement or masonry altars constructed in front (see Figure 9). These altars are

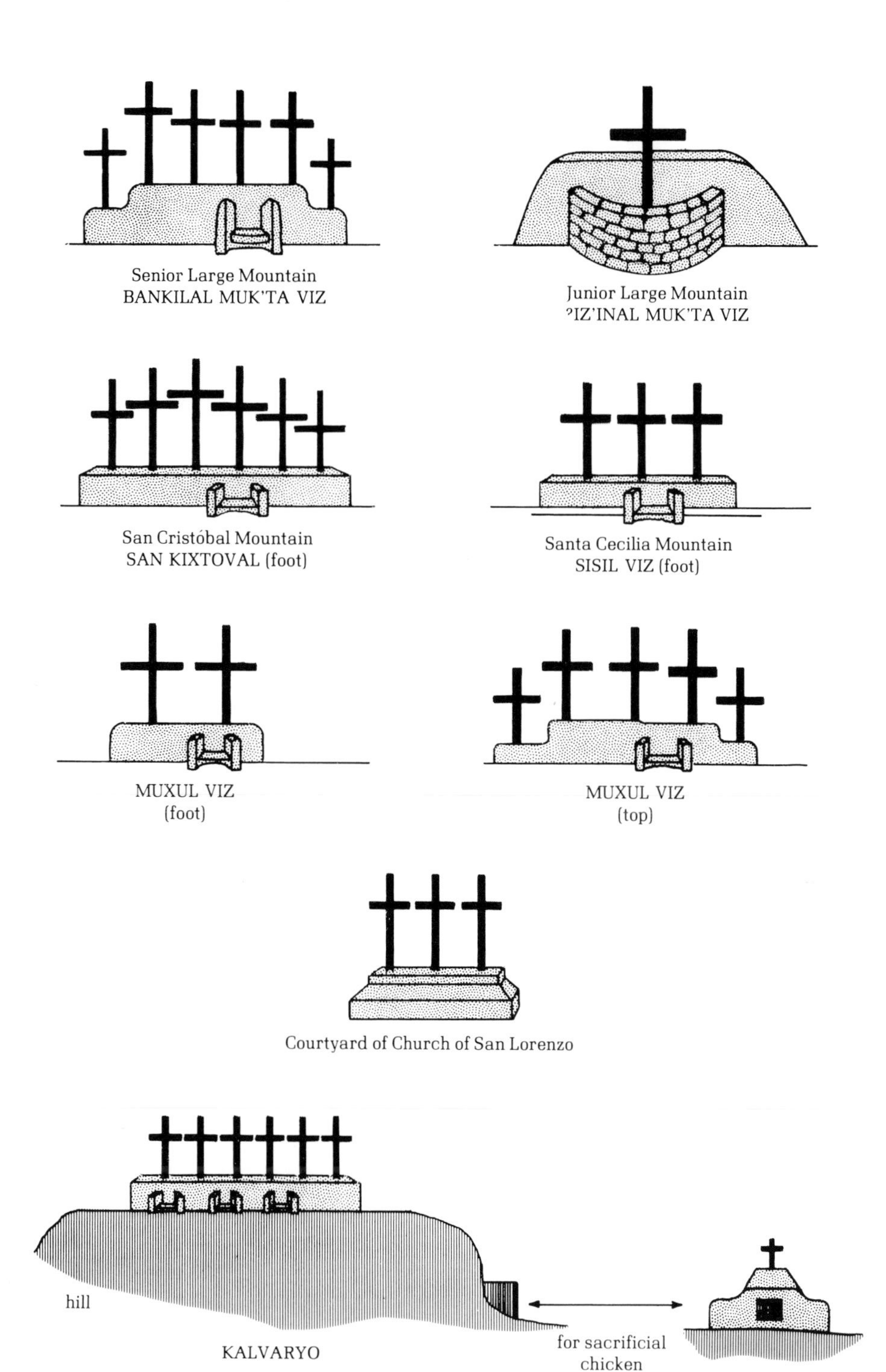

9. Some cross shrines in Zinacantan

called ʔAK'OB KANTELA, "place of the candles," and serve as the receptacle for the offerings to the gods.

Offerings to the cross shrines can be made *only* by a shaman. Whether the ritual occasion is a curing ceremony, a K'IN KRUS or Year Renewal ceremony, or a pilgrimage by an incoming cargoholder to pray to the ancestral gods, a shaman must officiate since he alone can "plant" the candles and serve as the intermediary in communication with the ancestral gods.

The ritual sequence at a shrine is intricately patterned. The pine trees (STEK'EL TOH) are tied on the crosses and the pine needles (XAK TOH) spread in front of the shrine by the sweepers (HMESETIK) before the arrival of the party. The fresh pine needles provide a carpet that insulates the kneeling ritualists from the domain of the Earth Lord; it permits people to come into contact with the gods without losing their souls to the Earth Lord. When the ritual party reaches the shrine, the ritualists kneel to pray briefly, candle-carrier to the left, shaman to the right. Then the candle carrier (HKUC'-KANTELA), who has been carrying the basket of candles and red geraniums on a tumpline and the burning censer in his right hand, places the basket on the left-, the censer on the right-hand side of the base of the crosses. The helpers tie bundles of red geraniums to each of the pine trees (at the level of the arms of the cross) while the shaman prepares the candles. He unwraps

10. A shaman's assistant ties a bundle of red geraniums on a cross decorated with pinetree tops

the cloth from around the candles, removes three of white wax and, using his bamboo staff to poke holes in the earth, "plants" them in the ground in the center of the altar niche. Sometimes the candles are set in the ground separately, but usually the three are tied together with a string. The shaman then places a minimum of three red geraniums in front of the candles—the flowers toward them, the stems toward himself (see Figure 12). The candle-carrier places the basket of remaining candles near the center of the base of the crosses, and the shaman calls for a shot of cane liquor from the drink-pourer. He prays briefly over the liquor then pours it on the ground around the base of the candles, using a counter-clockwise motion. (Some shamans take part of the liquor in their mouths and blow it out three times around the base of the candles, again in a counterclockwise motion, then drink the rest.) The shaman then signals for a round of liquor to be served to all present in rank order. There follows a long prayer to the ancestral gods, led by the shaman, who kneels before the altar, and chanted also in curing ceremonies by the patient (and spouse), or, in other ceremonies, by the cargoholder or more junior shaman, who kneels beside him (see Figure 12). At the end of the prayer, another round of liquor is served to all, who again kneel and pray before departing for the next shrine.

The candles offered by Zinacantecos are manufactured by hand by ladinos in small shops in San Cristóbal. The basic materials used are wax (imported) and tallow (produced locally). Candles are classified by color and price. The seven "colors" are: SERA (from Spanish *cera*, white wax); ZOH (red-coated wax); ʔIK' (black-coated wax); K'ON (yellow-coated wax); YOX (either blue-or green-coated wax; Tzotzil speakers do not differentiate between these colors); ʔORO (wax candles on which flowers made of gold paper were formerly tied, hence the Spanish *oro*, "gold"; now they are coated with alternating bands of yellow, red, and green wax); and XEVU (from Spanish *sebo*, tallow, which is not a color at all but a reference to the material of which the candles are made).

Each of these colors of candles can be purchased in sizes that range in price from 5 pesos each to two for 5 centavos; the in-between prices are: 4, 3, and 2 pesos, 1 peso, 50 centavos, 20 centavos, 10 centavos, and 5 centavos. The Zinacantecos seldom purchase any candle larger than a 2-peso size, the most common used in rituals being SERA of 20-centavos to 1-peso size. The next most frequently used is XEVU, believed to be an offering of "beef" for the Earth Lord; these are usually 1-peso size or smaller.

Zinacanteco ritual infrequently calls for all seven candle colors. When they are used, witchcraft is almost certainly involved; the ritualist is either attempting to perform witchcraft against another Zinacanteco, or is guarding against witchcraft. Most commonly, I have observed the placement of a row of the small two-for-5-centavos candles of seven colors at a house or mountain shrine to provide a kind of "candle curtain" to "close the eyes of witches," to keep them from "seeing" the other offerings at the shrine with their envious eyes.

Analysis. The offerings at cross shrines are charged with symbolic significance. The collection and arrangement of the NICIM—often translated as *flores* (Spanish for flowers) but signifying a domain extending far beyond our concept of them—it includes, among other things, the growing tips of pine trees and pine needles. A better translation might be "a living, growing extremity of a plant," something symbolizing the essence of life and vitality. Note that the small pine trees are tied to the cross shrine and the carpet of fresh pine needles is spread before the arrival of the ritual party. The domesticated red geraniums are added only upon the arrival of the ritualists at the shrine, introducing the symbol of Culture. The placement of the two types of plants is invariably such that the wild pine trees are away from human settlement and toward the

11. A shaman prays for a patient and her husband before a fully decorated cross shrine

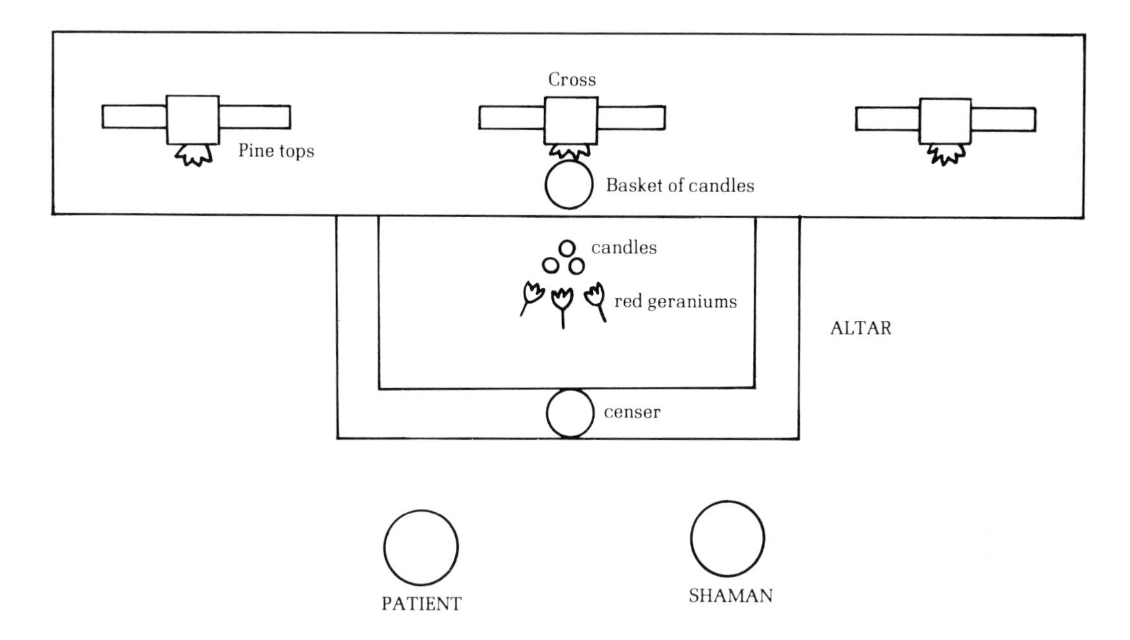

12. The arrangement of ritualists and their paraphernalia at a mountain shrine

woods; the red geraniums face toward NAETIK and away from the woods, from Nature.

Until I understood the principles underlying the arrangement, I was perplexed by the orientation of cross shrines around the valley of Zinacantan Center. I tried repeatedly to connect their placement and orientation with directions, especially with the positions of the rising and setting sun at the times of winter and summer solstice. It is now clear that the best, and at the same time the most parsimonious, interpretation of the orientation of all mountain shrines is simply that *they all face inward*, toward the heart of the ceremonial center and toward MIXIK' BALAMIL, center of the Zinacanteco universe.

But more is evident symbolically in the arrangement of the "flowers" on the shrines. Informants describe them as "clothing" for the crosses, with the red geraniums symbolizing a man's POK', the kerchief with bright red tassels, which are called SNIC POK', "flower of the kerchief." The crosses then resemble three ancestral gods, "dressed and waiting for candles for their food," as one informant put it. (Crosses, especially those inside the churches, are often referred to as SANTOETIK and are classified with the saints' images.)

The burning copal incense that is carried in the procession by the flower-carrier and used by the shaman to wave counterclockwise over the burning candles also carries a penumbra of meanings. It provides a good and rich smell, informants report; it is also "cigarettes for the gods." There are invariably two types of POM burning in the censer: TEˀEL POM, (tree incense), chips of wood cut directly from trees, that is, something wild and undomesticated, and BEK'TAL POM (flesh incense), nodules of resin, which requires that the tree be cut in advance, the sap be allowed to collect in the cut and then be formed by man into balls of resin—in other words, something that requires more human activity, something more "cultural" than the wild "tree incense."

The white wax candles also carry a variety of meanings. They are "tortillas"—some Zinacantecos also say "chicken"—for the gods. The tallow candles are "beef" for the gods. As both types burn, the gods consume them. But because candles are "planted" (unlike the crosses which do not touch the earth), we also perceive an image of the farmer planting his corn. To complete the circular network of interrelated symbols: tortillas are made from maize; maize grows with the heat provided by the sun; candles produce heat energy—hence the symbolic relation of tortilla-maize-candle.

At a deeper level of meaning are the symbolic equivalences between candles and Zinacantecos themselves. The larger, more expensive candles are always placed toward a house altar, toward conceptual east (Gossen 1972: 148). Candles are never placed on the ritual table with tips toward the setting sun, for that is the orientation of death, the placement of a corpse in a grave. The candles, firmly planted and standing up straight before mountain shrines and saints, appear to symbolize an offering of human life. That this is not so farfetched as it first appears is evidenced by the embracer's planting of the candles (representing the innate souls of the bride and groom) at the feet of San Lorenzo in the marriage ceremony. It is further supported by Zinacanteco view that unless people eat maize tortillas, they are never fully socialized, nor can they ever speak BAZ'I K'OP ("the real word," Tzotzil). Our field workers are often urged to eat more maize in order to learn Tzotzil more easily and quickly. Refusal to eat is considered an indication of willful seclusion.

Once the ritual action begins at the cross shrine, the gods receive their cane liquor; the candles burn and the gods receive their tortillas and chicken; incense is waved and the gods smoke their cigarettes. The contented TOTIL MEʔILETIK are now ready to receive messages from the ritualists. These messages cannot be transmitted directly, for such communication requires the mediation of a shaman, who has the power to "see" into the mountains and talk to the gods face-to-face.

The prayer itself, led by the shaman, recited by the petitioner (whether patient, cargoholder about to enter office, or owner of a new house), is accompanied by humbling behavior and loud crying; the tears which frequently pour down the faces of the Zinacantecos as they pray apparently appeal to the gods' parental instincts. The ritualists are always on their knees, periodically placing their foreheads on the pine needles or on the edge of the altar. Indeed, they describe themselves in the prayers as being humble, like children, as they cry and beg forgiveness from the supernatural fathers and mothers for unacceptable behavior that has occurred or may yet occur. The following excerpt is an illustration:

I shall visit your shrines,
I shall entrust my soul to you,
  To your feet,
  To your hands,
    For your sons,
    For your children,
    For your flowers,
    For your sprouts,
      For these I beseech divine pardon,
      For these I beg divine forgiveness.
(Vogt 1969: 649-650)

If the ritual is properly executed, the petitioners are pardoned, restored to the good graces of the gods, and replaced securely into the Zinacanteco social order.

4

House and Field Rituals

FOR EVERYDAY ZINACANTECO life the domains of supreme importance are the house (NA) and the field (COB). The traditional thatch-roofed, wattle-and-daub house (or the more modern tile-roofed, adobe house) provides shelter (Vogt 1969: ch. 4). With a fire constantly burning on the hearth it is also the most important focus of family life. Here tortillas and beans are cooked for the family's meals; babies are conceived and born; children learn Zinacanteco customs; marriages are planned and wedding ceremonies occur; old people die. In short, almost all family interaction takes place here. Zinacanteco women spend most of their lives in and near their houses, working in the patios immediately outside, or fetching wood and water nearby. A house cross erected just outside the door symbolizes the unity of the domestic group occupying one or more houses in a cluster and is the ritual entrance for the group. Collectively, groups of houses constitute the domain symbolizing culture and social order.

Human life in Zinacantan would be impossible without the maize field. Nearly all Zinacantecos utilize some other food sources (wild plants, for example, or commercial products purchased with money earned from the sale of surplus maize or from wage labor), but the overwhelming proportion of calories consumed comes from the fields of cultivated maize, with their supplementary crops of beans and squash. Some of this produce comes from small plots located around the houses, but most is grown in large fields located either on ejido land on the flanks of the Highlands or on rented land in the Lowlands of the Grijalva River valley. Men and their older sons spend much of their lives in the fields—cutting and burning brush in the ancient method of swidden agriculture, planting with digging sticks, weeding with hoes, harvesting the crops (Vogt 1969: ch. 3). Collectively, fields are known as COBTIK, a domain intermediate between the houses and the woods, into which the Zinacantecos venture only to collect wood and wild plants, herd sheep, or hunt.

The domains of houses and fields belong fundamentally to the Earth Lord. To build a new house a family needs not only a plot of land on which to place it but also wood poles, thatch, and mud for its construction. Chopping down and burning the trees and brush to make a field, the Zinacantecos again invade the domain of the Earth Lord. In each case they perform ceremonies in the hope of compensating the Earth Lord for his property and enlisting the aid of the ancestral gods in maintaining stable relations with him.

House Rituals

Preparations for a new house begin in the autumn under a full moon. Then the wood and grasses are cut, and left to dry until spring when construction is usually started.

Two rites accompany the construction of the house. The first, called HOL CUK (literally "binding the head of the roof"), takes place when the walls are completed and the roof rafters are in place. This simple rite does not require a shaman; the workers who are constructing the house direct and perform it. They suspend a long rope from the peak of the house and tie four chickens (one for each CIKIN NA, "corner of the house") to it by their feet. The chicken heads are cut off and buried in the center of the floor; women later cook the chickens. Two men then climb up onto the framework of the roof and "feed" it chicken broth and cane liquor by pouring both liquids on the four corners of the joists at each of the three levels and on the peak of the roof where the rafters come together (see Figure 13). The rite culminates with the workers' eating the chickens and drinking cane liquor.

The second rite, called C'UL KANTELA (holy candle), is performed as soon as possible after the completion of the new house. A shaman performs this ceremony, which serves to compensate the Earth Lord and summon the ancestral gods to provide the house with an innate soul. The participants include the house-owner and his immediate family as well as his father and brothers and their wives and children. This ritual begins with the planting of the house cross (KRUS TA TIˀ NA) in the patio. It is placed parallel with the two doorless sides of the house and is commonly oriented so that prayers to the shrine will be offered in the direction of rising sun. Three stakes are driven into the ground and the shaman lashes the cross to the center one. While musicians (violinist, harpist, guitarist) play, three pine-tree tops are tied on the cross, and bundles of red geraniums are attached to the pine. Pine needles are spread in front, and white wax candles are offered as copal incense burns in a censer and the shaman prays.

The shaman continues the ritual inside the house, which has a fresh pine-needle carpet covering the floor. He prays over the candles at the foot of the ritual table set just to the east of the center of the house. An assistant then hangs a rope from the peak of the house, the end of which marks the center of the floor, where a hole is subsequently dug. A number of roosters and hens corresponding to the number and sex of the family members are hung by their feet from the end of the rope, with their heads concealed inside the center hole. With the exception of one black rooster saved for later burial in the center hole, their heads are cut off with a knife and the blood is allowed to drain into the hole. The bodies of the chickens are scalded with hot water and plucked and prepared for eating; their heads and feathers are buried with the blood as an offering to the Earth Lord. The shaman then censes the remaining black rooster, kills it by pulling its neck, pours a shot of liquor and a handful of earth over him. He then buries the entire bird in the center "grave," head toward rising sun—the position of burial for unbaptized children. The earth is tamped in on top, in the same way used when a body is buried in a cemetery. A small wooden cross about a foot high is planted at the east end of the grave and decorated with pine tips and red geraniums.

Each person then comes forward to "meet" the

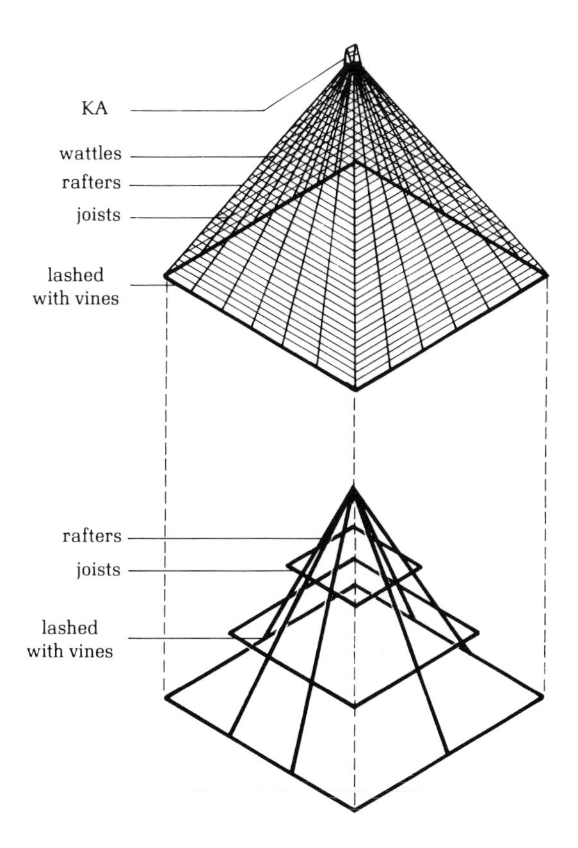

13. Framework for a thatch roof

white wax and tallow candles on the ritual table. The house-owner holding a bundle of pine tips, prays to the gods:

In the sacred name of the holy God,
 Jesus Christ.
Take heed, holy torches,
 Take heed, holy candles,
 Take heed, holy alms,
Take heed, my Father
 Take heed, my Lord!
Thou are ready,
 Thou art set.
Take heed, my Father
 Take heed, my Lord!
They go to stand erect,
 They go to stand firm,
At the thresholds [shrines at foot and summit of
  sacred mountains],
 At the altars,
Of the holy Fathers,
 The holy Mothers.
Is there still holy pardon,
 Is there still divine forgiveness? . . .

So I beg holy pardon,
 So I beg divine forgiveness,
With my spouse,
 With my companion,
With my two gifts,
 With my two travails [children of house-
  owner] . . .

Favor my back,
 Favor my side,
It is only a little I want,
 It is only a bit I wish,
Like some of my fathers,
 Like some of my mothers,
The hot ones,

The warm ones,
Those gathered together,
Those joined together,
With their gifts,
With their travails.
I only wish the same, my Father,
I only wish the same, my Lord . . .
May I not yet reach the mountaintop,
May I not yet reach the hilltop,
May I not yet clothe myself with dirt,
May I not yet clothe myself with mud.* . . .

("The man of the house venerates the candles"; Laughlin, *Of Shoes and Ships and Sealing Wax*)

The shaman then leads a procession, counterclockwise, to each of the four corners, where three pine tips from the bundle held by the house-owner are planted and decorated with red geraniums; he plants and lights candles (usually two white wax and one tallow) and prays at each corner. The shaman also pours chicken broth and cane liquor on the four corner posts and on the center of the four walls. Assistants climb onto the ceiling joists and "feed" the meal to the roof: beginning with the center, they sprinkle chicken broth and POX on the corners and middle joints of the beams and on the lower ends of the six rafters. After lighting white wax and tallow candles in the center of the house, the shaman washes the heads, arms, and hands of all who will live there. After bathing in water which usually contains the aromatic leaves from ZIS ʔUC, ʔAHA-TEʔES, and VIXOBTAKIL, the family puts on freshly washed and censed clothing. The entire group then partakes of a ritual meal of chicken.

After the meal the shaman prepares candles and flowers for a pilgrimage to the mountain shrines. As the procession leaves the house, its owner chants (in part) to those remaining there:

*These four lines refer to burial in a cemetery. Cemeteries are, in general, located on top of hills or mountain ridges.

God,
My Lord,
See here, my Father,
See here, my Lord.
May I pass before Thy glorious face,
May I pass before Thy glorious eyes . . .

For this, my lowly mouth departs,
For this my humble lips depart,
For this, my lowly chunk of incense,
For this, my humble cloud of smoke,
For this, my three lowly torches,
For this, my three humble candles.
I go to beg holy pardon,
I go to beg divine forgiveness, . . .

You shall await my lowly earth,
You shall await my humble mud,
Whatever the hour,
Whatever the day,
I turn back,
I return. . . .

May I pass before Thy glorious faces,
Before Thy glorious eyes,
My Father,
My Lord.

("The man of the house addresses those who remain in the house, as they depart for the shrines"; Laughlin, *Of Shoes and Ships and Sealing Wax*)

After praying at the house cross the members of the procession depart for the mountains in the usual order: miscellaneous assistants, the flower-carrier, the candle-carrier, the wife of the house-owner, the house-owner, and the shaman. Ordinarily four holy mountains are visited—SAN KIXTOVAL, MUXUL VIZ, SISIL VIZ, and KALVARYO—where candles, incense, liquor and prayers are offered to the ancestral gods.

Returning to the patio cross, prayers are again chanted. The procession then enters the house, lights more candles, and prays at the center grave of the rooster. The men don their hats and black ceremonial robes and dance to the music of the violin, harp, and guitar. The formal part of the ceremony ends with a ritual meal.

For the next three days the house must be carefully attended for it now possesses an innate soul and requires special care, "just like a sick person" following a curing ceremony. The cross remains at the grave of the rooster; later it is removed and used for various purposes—for example, as a "cross for the maize." In the days following the ritual the family members remain at home and begin to place their hair combings in the cracks of the walls, signifying their occupancy and symbolizing their belonging (Bardrick 1970).

Field Rituals

Preparation of the lowland maize fields begins in November through February, when the trees and bush covering a new plot of land are cut down. The cut growth is allowed to dry in the hot sun until April when the men return to burn it just before the onset of the rains.

In the Highlands, maize is planted in March on the small plots in or near house compounds. In the Lowlands, where temperatures are higher, it is not planted until the beginning of the rainy season in May. In contrast to the cutting and burning, planting is considered a risky and delicate procedure and is accompanied by extensive ritual activity. The largest and the best ears of seed maize are carefully selected at harvest time for future planting and, stored separately in a burlap bag, hung from the house rafters. After the kernels are planted, the cobs from the seed maize are hung up in trees to rest, for they are believed to be exhausted from having carried the burden of the seeds.

Planting in the ejido lands or the Lowlands is preceded by a ceremony, called SLIMUXNAIL COBTIK (alms for the maize fields) or SKANTELAIL COBTIK (candles for the maize fields). Men who farm on adjacent fields gather to perform this ritual. A shaman directs the ceremony and chants the prayers.

After an ordinary meal at the thatched shelter beside the fields where the men sleep and eat while farming, the procession forms in the usual order: shaman in the rear, preceded by the candle-carrier, then other assistants. If the farming group is large enough to afford them, musicians (violonist, harpist, and guitarist) are recruited to play. The procession moves counterclockwise around a series of cross shrines that mark the corners and center of the field and the waterhole from which the farmers draw water. At each shrine, decorated with pine-tree tops, red geraniums, and pine needles carried from the Highlands, the shaman offers candles and prays to the Earth Lord, while copal incense burns. Cane liquor is served to the Zinacanteco participants and poured on the ground for the Earth Lord.

A skyrocket is set off as the ritual procession leaves the shelter. Three more are fired at each shrine: one upon arrival, a second at the beginning of the prayer, and a third as the procession leaves the shrine. A final skyrocket announces the arrival of the procession at the cross shrine of the farming shelter. Here the last candles are lighted and the shaman chants a prayer, filled with epithets referring to the Earth Lord, which goes in part:

Holy king,
  Holy angel,

Holy snake,
  Holy thunder,

Holy sky,
  Holy glory,

Holy earth,
  Holy world.

The ceremony ends with a formal ritual meal, whose main course, ideally, is iguana, which the Zinacantecos consider the Lowland equivalent of the chicken consumed at Highland ritual meals.

The planting of the maize follows immediately after this ceremony. Because the development of a strong root system is crucial—without it the plant will be blown down by the first strong wind of the summer—ritual precautions are taken. Chicken feet are attached to the bags of seed maize carried by each of the planters to insure that the roots of the plants would grow out like strong supportive feet. Following the same line of reasoning, the planters avoid eating river snails during this time, for the shells resemble maize seed without roots.

The fields must be weeded frequently, for it is believed that if weeds are allowed to prosper, the souls of the maize plants will move to a "clean" field. The number of times a field must be weeded varies. A new field in an area of heavy bush, where large trees were felled and dense weeds have not yet taken root, requires only one weeding; others must be weeded at least twice, usually in June and July. The first weeding is the longest and most difficult; it must be accomplished efficiently early in the season or the weeds quickly take over the field and the seedlings are lost. Another maize ritual, which follows the same pattern as that of the planting ceremony, precedes the weeding.

When the maize tassels appear in mid-July, a third ritual is performed. Green ears are usually ready for gathering and eating by the time of the Fiesta of San Lorenzo in early August.

In the autumn, when the maize is ripe, the Zinacanteco farmers return to the Lowlands to "double" the stalks: they break the shafts a little above the middle and bend the top half almost to the ground. This cuts off the food supply from the roots so that the maize begins to dry and harden on the stalk; it prevents the rain from rotting the ears; and it allows sunlight to reach the crop of beans planted at this time between the rows of maize.

Harvesting, preceded by a fourth maize ritual, begins in the Lowlands in November and continues into December and January. Zinacantecos pick, husk, and shell the maize near the fields so that only the grain needs to be transported back up the escarpment to the granaries located next to Zinacanteco homes. The stored maize is ritually "protected" by a small wooden cross erected on the shelled maize in the bin. This cross is surrounded by still unhusked STOT and SMEˀ ears of maize, symbolic "fathers" and "mothers" which "embrace" the souls of the whole field and of the stored corn. These special ears (see Figure 14) surround the maize cross until the supply of shelled maize dwindles; they are then eaten.

In addition, if ears in the shape of a MAYOL (errand boy) are found, they are also added to the shrine since they helped the "fathers" and "mothers" watch the field. Ears that grow in the form of a HOH (raven) are picked and broken; if left in the field, they will consume all the maize. The symbolism of these various forms of ears is obscure; the STOT, a large ear surrounded by several smaller ears, may represent a father surrounded by children; the SMEˀ a vagina; the MAYOL the billy club carred by a MAYOL who serves at the cabildo; the HOH the beak of a raven.

House and Field Ceremonies as Rituals of Repayment

House and field rituals employ symbols representing reciprocal transactions between Zinacantecos and the Earth Lord: offerings are made in an effort to compensate him for incursions into and utilization of materials from his domain. In the house-dedication ceremony, candle offerings made inside the house always consist of both white-wax and tallow candles, because, as informants put it, the Earth Lord, being like a "fat and greedy ladino," wants meat with his tortillas. (Only white-wax candles are offered at the house cross and mountain shrines to the TOTIL MEˀILETIK during this ceremony; the ancestral gods are Indians who do not eat meat regularly.)

But offerings of candles are not enough. If the Earth Lord does not receive other gifts, he will

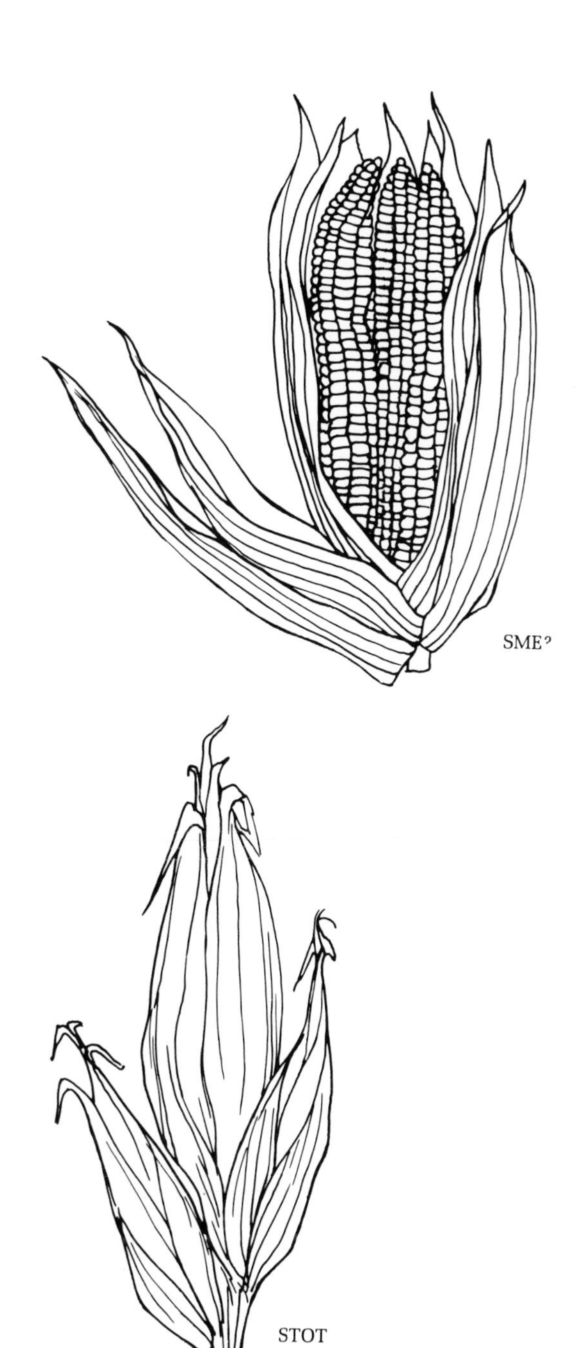

14. The peculiar growths of ears of maize which serve as symbolic "mothers" and "fathers"

some day capture the souls of the inhabitants of the house and put them to work as slaves for many years, until the "iron huaraches he gives all of them wear out"! At the very least, he will make the "earth move" under the house and frighten its inhabitants. Thus, chickens, symbolizing the residents of the new house, are offered as substitutes. In the "Holy Candle" rite the chickens suspended from the peak of the house and beheaded over the central hole are a gift of "souls" as their blood flows directly into the Earth Lord's domain. Although their flesh is consumed in a ritual meal, the heads and feathers are placed in the hole, so in the end, the substitutes are the property of the Earth Lord. The black rooster is a symbolic replacement for the male owner of the house, the person ultimately responsible for this incursion into the Earth Lord's domain. It represents a prestation of both soul and body—an unblemished, undivided whole—as it is ritually interred in the "grave" in the center of the earthen floor of the house.

In the agricultural rituals compensation has concrete meaning: only with appropriate offerings will the Earth Lord permit sufficient rain to fall on the crops and control the destructive winds. Field rituals are characterized by candle offerings, skyrockets, and burning incense; no chickens are involved. Again, the candles are of white-wax and tallow. The skyrockets which signal the progress of the procession symbolize the bolts of lightning which the Earth Lord, or his representatives, the ʔANHELETIK, are believed to "shoot off" in the process of creating the heavy summer rains. Similarly, smoke from the burning incense provides a visual symbol of the rain clouds.

A shaman, performing a field ritual, vividly described this symbolism:

"That," says Telex (hearing the bullfrogs booming raucously in an arroyo), "is the sound of the guitars of YAHVAL BALAMIL." "And that" (as thunder and lightning strike in the West), "is the sound of YAHVAL BALAMIL out hunting . . . "We are having this ceremony for YAHVAL BALAMIL, that he should order the clouds to come out of the earth, clouds to rain on our corn, so our corn should not die . . . Because if it does not rain and our corn dries up and perishes, we would perish too . . . So we are praying to the Lord of the Earth, and we are offering him good peso candles, for we only gave him 50-centavo candles at planting, but now we are giving him peso candles, so he will let our corn grow . . . We have to pray to him in our old language, as we have always done, because he is accustomed to us praying in our old language, and if we did not pray, he would strike us dead with his snake of lightning . . . We do not see the Lord of the Earth, but he is there under the earth . . . And all of us pray to him, for the corn to grow for all the world . . . For there in Zinacantan is the center of all the world, and we must pray for all the world—if we do not, this world will be destroyed, until another one comes . . . And now we are having much rain, because there are many ceremonies tonight, not just here, but all over . . . So we are not sad because we are wet, for we know that the Lord of the Earth has heard our prayers. I believe it is going to rain all night, yes, I believe it is going to rain until tomorrow."

(Field notes by Jack Stauder, 1961; from Vogt 1969: 459-460)

It makes no difference that the wood, thatch, mud, and space were not "given" by the Earth Lord but were "taken" from him; the obligation to repay the transfer of goods remains as strong, if not stronger than if materials had been given. Thus, house and field rituals are a forceful illustration of the Zinacantecos' concern for reciprocity: when a man becomes the new possessor of anything, in any way, someone—man or god—expects and is entitled to recompense.

House and Field as Models of the Universe

Houses and fields are small-scale models of the quincuncial cosmogony. The universe was created by the VAXAK-MEN, gods who support it at its corners and who designated its center, the "navel of the world," in Zinacantan Center. Houses have corresponding corner posts and precisely determined centers; fields emphasize the same critical places, with cross shrines at their corners and centers. These points are of primary ritual importance.

Houses also provide an image of the vertical divisions in the Zinacanteco universe. The lord of the underworld is represented by the earthen floor and the area beneath where the sacrificial chickens are buried. A second vertical division consists of majestic holy mountains, which house the ancestral gods and rise to peaks above, and in opposition to, the domain of the Earth Lord. This mountain part of the universe is mirrored in the structure of the house roof, not only in the obvious visual similarity between mountain and roof shapes but, more significantly, in the use of identical descriptive terms for the two: YOK (its foot) refers to the foot of a mountain and the foundation of a house; SC'UT (its stomach) is the midpoint of a mountainside as well as a wall of a house; SCIKIN (its ear or corner) refers to corners of mountains and houses; and SHOL (its head) can be a mountaintop or a housetop.

Rising above the holy mountains is a quincuncial space with the three layers of VINAHEL: in the lowest the female moon traverses the sky each night; in the middle are the stars which provide light above and below; in the uppermost layer the male sun travels along his path each day. Similarly, a Zinacanteco roof structure has three conceptual "layers," marked by the three sets of joists. These are emphasized during the HOL CUK rite when male ritualists climb to each layer, offering chicken broth and cane liquor to the gods at each of the all-important corners and the center (the peak of the roof).

The critical binary opposition between directional east and directional west is symbolically represented in the allocation of space inside a Zinacanteco house: the men's side is toward "rising sun," with the house altar (if there is one) against the eastern wall; the women's side of the house, with the hearth and cooking area, is toward "setting sun." The men's side symbolizes maleness, hotness, aboveness, oldness, and higher rank; the other, femaleness, coldness, belowness, youngness, and lower rank (cf. Gossen 1972).

House and Field Rituals as Symbols of Social Order

An important ritual transition takes place in house and field ceremonies: materials belonging to the Earth Lord are transferred into the Zinacanteco social order, or from Nature to Culture. Just as fences and gates will later emphasize property rights of the family and protect against outsiders who seek to impose or interfere, so the ritual circuit around the four corners inside the house delineates the area safe from "demons" and the Earth Lord. The close attention paid to the exact center of the house at both the ground and roof levels serves in part to protect against the "demons," which enter especially at these places, because, farthest from the corners, they are least protected (Bardrick 1971). After a successful house circuit, the Earth Lord can never capture the souls of family members who happen to fall down inside the house; nor can the demons enter the house.

Placing the house cross, or soul of the house, in the patio during the ritual symbolizes the transformation of a mere structure into one with a soul, with a place in and significance for society. The cross itself is kept from the territory of the Earth Lord by being tied to a stake pushed into the earth rather than placed directly in the ground. The pine needles laid in front of the cross for ritual occasions further demarcate the domain of the Earth Lord from the domain of the Zinacantecos by creating a dividing carpet. Prayers which refer to the house as "my eyes' awakening" and "my heart's repose" also emphasize the safety and civilized nature of this space.

Such boundary-defining activity—"framing," in Mary Douglas' terms (1966: 63-64)—of houses and fields serves to protect, to keep in and nourish the souls of houses and fields and to shut out demons, the evil, powerful symbols of disorder. The process of socialization apparent in these rituals is similar to the "embracing" process in a baptismal rite, a curing ceremony, and treatment during childhood: in each case objects or persons not fully incorporated into the Zinacanteco social order are looked after, cared for, guided into their proper role in society. Continued "embracing" necessitates an order within, a sustained orderliness on the part of the person or thing embraced: this person or thing must continuously conform to the principles of civilized order sanctioned by the ancestral gods. Thus, house and field ceremonies not only create social order, but perpetuate it in the areas of family shelter and food production which are of crucial importance for Zinacanteco life.

5

Rituals of Affliction: Description

ONE KIND OF Zinacanteco ritual seems designed to cope with tensions that arise in social relations. These "rituals of affliction" are not life-crisis rituals that are performed for all in the course of their life cycles. The situations which trigger them are not predictable, hence not calendrically scheduled. They may occur frequently in the lives of certain individuals, hardly ever in the lives of others.

"Curing ceremonies," broadly conceived, are one type of such ritual; in fact, many ethnographers stretch the concept of curing ceremonies to cover this whole class of rituals. I did so in my 1969 book; but I now believe this complex can more accurately be called "rituals of affliction," following Victor Turner's (1968) definition.

In Zinacantan many of these ceremonies are focused upon an individual "patient" regarded as "ill." But the illness is rarely defined as a physiological malfunctioning per se; rather, the physiological symptoms are viewed as surface manifestations of a deeper etiology; for example, "the ancestral gods have knocked out part of his soul because he was fighting with his relatives." The "ailment" and its "cure" are defined in terms of what we in our society would call a "psychosomatic disorder" and "psychotherapy." The patient's relationship with his social world is reordered and restored to equilibrium by the procedures of the ritual.*

The Great Seeing Ceremony

The longest, most complex ritual of affliction, the MUK'TA ʔILEL, contains the most complete set of ritual episodes performed by a Zinacanteco shaman. Most other rituals of affliction are shorthand versions of this sequence, which typically includes a pilgrimage to at least five

*For more detailed ethnographic data and interpretations of the large corpus of shamanistic rituals in Zinacantan see Fabrega and Silver 1973.

sacred mountains and lasts up to forty-eight hours.

After preliminary attempts to interpret the intricate ritual symbolism in this ceremony (Vogt 1970; E. Vogt and C. Vogt 1970), additional field data and new interpretive discoveries have led me deeper into the symbolic meanings of the MUK'TA ʔILEL. The ethnographic data are based upon field observations of four MUK'TA ʔILEL performances (between 1962 and 1969), as well as repeated interviewing of Zinacanteco shamans since the Harvard Chiapas Project was initiated in 1957.

MUK'TA ʔILEL means literally "Great Seeing," referring to the large number of mountain shrines to be visited and ancestral deities to be "seen." Alternatively, the ceremony is called MUK'TA NICIM, "Great Flower," referring to the large numbers of ritual plants needed for it. The Zinacantecos perform at least twenty episodes for the Great Seeing.

Episode One: Divination by Pulsing

The MUK'TA ʔILEL is performed only after a shaman has diagnosed "illness" in a patient by a technique known as PIK C'IC' (touch blood). This pulsing is a basic technique used by all shamans to determine whether an affliction results from the loss of some of the thirteen parts of the innate soul due to action of the ancestral gods, the Earth Lord, or demons; from the release of the animal companion from its corral; or from witchcraft practiced against the patient by an evil person.

For the pulsing a shaman is usually summoned to the house of the afflicted patient. A member of the family (the father for a child; the spouse for an afflicted husband or wife) takes a bottle of POX to the shaman, presents it, and makes the request. If the bottle is accepted and consumed in a ritual drinking episode, the shaman comes at the appointed time.

Upon arrival at the house of the patient, the shaman sits by the patient and prays:

In the divine name of Jesus Christ my Lord
How much my Father,
How much my Lord,
Holy KALVARYO, holy Father,
Holy KALVARYO, holy Mother,
Take me unto your presence,
Cure the sickness
With one great pulsing
With one small pulsing;

At your feet,
At your hands,
Let your son,
Let your son, then, Lord,
Walk in your holy sight,
Walk in your holy countenance,
My Lord.

The shaman feels the pulse of the patient at the wrist and on the inside of the elbow, first on the right arm, then on the left. It is believed that the blood "talks," and furnishes messages which the shaman can understand and interpret. Shamans are vague as to the exact pulse clues providing the messages; one of the essentials of divination is certainly ambiguity, which permits a great deal of latitude in pronouncing a diagnosis. In an important sense a shaman is "a node of communication" in the social circuits. He has heard all the gossip about the patient and his relationships; he learns more when the request is made that he come to pulse; he talks with the family during the diagnosis. By the time he finishes listening to the blood "talk" he can determine what kind of "soul trouble" the patient has. In the case of the Great Seeing, the trouble is critical: the patient's animal companion has been set loose from its corral by the ancestral gods and is roaming untended in the woods. This ritual he prescribes must be done with some dispatch to round up the lost animal companion and restore it to its corral. The shaman also indicates which sacred mountains should be visited and what quantities of the various ritual materials will be required. He and the patient's family set a time for the ceremony and agree that someone will be sent to fetch him at the proper time.

Episode Two: Preparations

In the interval between the pulsing and the start of the ceremony, the family of the patient works feverishly to make the necessary preparations. Five male assistants called HC'OMILETIK (literally "borrowed ones") are recruited from the patient's domestic group, if they are available; if not, from more distant relatives and neighbors. Four or more female assistants are sought to help prepare food and wash the patient's clothing; these may be the wives of the HC'OMILETIK or other female relatives or neighbors.

On the day of the ceremony the assistants assemble at the patient's house at dawn. The male assistants go immediately to collect a gourdful of water from each of the seven sacred waterholes around Zinacantan Center (see Figure 15). These waterholes are bathing places for the ancestral gods who live in the mountains nearby: (1) PAT TOH (behind the pine) is a male waterhole having water with a white, active, cold soul, where the male ancestral deity living in SAN KIXTOVAL mountain bathes. It is also called YA?AL ?UC, "opossum's water," after XUN ?UC (John Opossum), a man who in mythological times slept in a nearby cave. (2) NINAB CILO?, shortened from NINAB CI?IL VO?, meaning "salty spring" (literally "tip [nose] of salt water lake"), is a brackish, female waterhole having a white, active, hot soul. This water emerges as a spring from a cave in a mountain in which reside the nursemaids (who carry and care for small children) and laundresses of the ancestral gods. The clothes for the patient are laundered here, for the salty water is believed to lock the soul into the body, simultaneously keeping out "demons." (3) VO?-C'OH VO? (five waterholes) is a female waterhole, having water with a white, active, medium soul, where the female deity from SISIL VIZ bathes. (4) POPOL TON means "rock in the form of a reed mat." Since the reed mat was a symbol of authority among the Maya, it is possible that this male waterhole was once considered to be the bathing place for the highest ranking ancestral gods living in BANKILAL MUK'TA VIZ and/or the male gods who meet at KALVARYO. It contains water with a soul that is white, active, and medium, and is significantly located toward the rising sun from the heart of the ceremonial center. (5) TON Z'I?KIN, probably meaning either "wheezing" or "squeaking rock" or "rock with drops of water falling," is another male waterhole, having water with a white, active, hot soul, where the highest ranking gods from BANKILAL MUK'TA VIZ bathe. (6) YA?AHVIL (the water of the flying thing)* is a female waterhole, having water with a white, active, hot soul; it is a bathing place for the female god who lives in YA?AHVIL mountain just above the waterhole. (7) (YOK) NIO?, a term contracted from (YOK) NI? VO? ([foot] of the spring, literally "tip [nose] of water") is another female waterhole, having salty water with a white, active, hot soul, where the female deity from NIO? mountain bathes.

After the male assistants have placed the seven gourds of water under the patient's bed, they go to the mountains with machetes to gather the necessary ritual plants. Enough of each is collected to adorn the household and the mountain shrines to be visited, and to place in the ritual bath and in the bed of the patient. After collecting the ritual plants, the male assistants go out to "sweep" the household and mountain shrines, replacing the dried pine trees and needles from previous ceremonies with fresh pine trees on the crosses and fresh needles in

*From a myth in which soldiers watched a bird dive and bathe in this waterhole before they were swallowed up by a nearby cave.

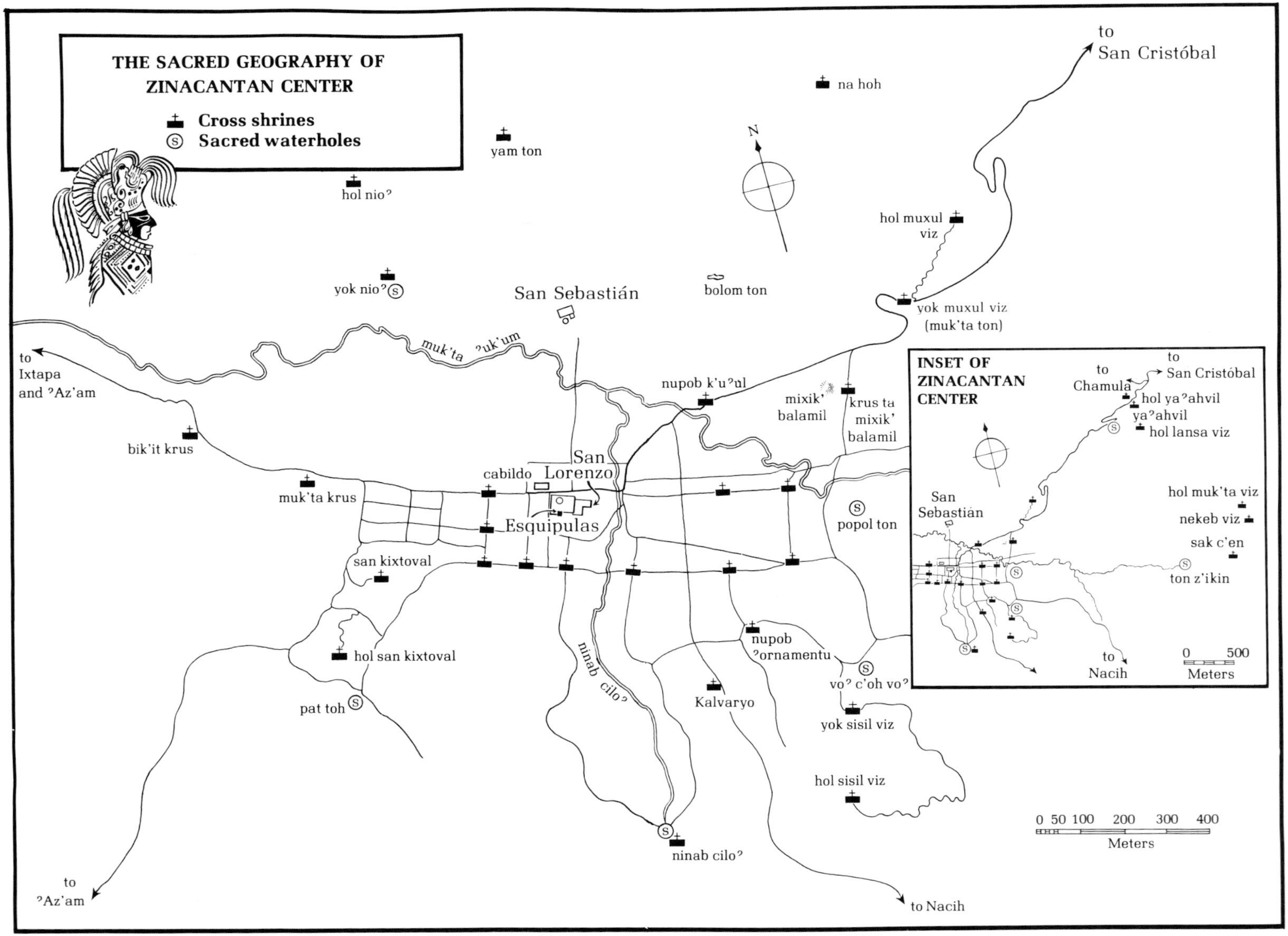

15. The sacred geography of Zinacantan Center

front of each shrine. Each of the sweepers takes care of one of the mountain shrines.

Meanwhile the women remain in the house, grinding maize for tortillas, with the exception of three: one who goes to purchase red geraniums; and two (called H?UK'UMAHELETIK, "washers" or "laundresses"), who go to NINAB CILO? to wash a complete set of the patient's clothing with soaproot (C'UPAK'), the odor of ordinary soap being offensive to the ancestral gods. After the washing is finished, they eat hardboiled eggs and tortillas and drink cane liquor. If they meet laundresses for other ceremonies, they exchange an egg, two tortillas, and shot of liquor with them. These laundresses must be older women without infant children who would be in grave danger of incurring MAHBENAL ("blows" from the ancestral gods).

Two men are sent to San Cristóbal to purchase candles, incense, cane liquor, coffee, and wheat-flour rolls for the ceremony. The family must also purchase two black chickens of the patient's sex, unless available in its own flock. They also must construct an enclosure with poles and planks standing upright around the patient's bed, henceforth referred to as a KORAL (corral).

When all of the assistants have finished their tasks, they return to the patient's house for a meal. If the ceremony is to begin at dark, it is clear why the assistants gather at dawn: it takes hours to complete these preparations.

From the time the gourds of water are in the house the patient is in a delicate ritual state; he may not go outside alone lest he suffer MAHBENAL from the gods.

Why there are precisely seven sacred water-holes is something I still cannot interpret. In the dreams of Anselmo, one of the most knowledge-able shamans I ever interviewed, when he was instructed in the performance of the ritual, the supernatural Grand Alcalde in BANKILAL MUK'TA VIZ had the seven gourds of water from the seven waterholes under the south side of his ritual table. Later they were moved to the center of the table, lined up from rising sun to setting sun, in the order listed above. This order corre-sponds exactly with a counterclockwise circuit of the valley of HTEK-LUM.

There is a Zinacanteco myth about how the Morning Star was a Chamula girl transformed into a "Sweeper of the Path" for the sun. The Morning Star precedes the Holy Sun each day, sweeping the path for him (Vogt 1969: 316-318). If, as I have suggested, ritual processions are conceptually following the path of the sun in making their ceremonial circuits, it follows that the assistants who prepare the path are called "sweepers."

Episode Three: Fetching the Shaman

When all is ready at the patient's house, a male assistant (HTAM-H?ILOL, "shaman's escort") goes to the shaman's house and presents him with a bottle of cane liquor and two wheat-flour rolls. The shaman prays to the ancestral gods, the two men drink the liquor, and the shaman prepares his bamboo staff and black ceremonial robe. Meanwhile, at the patient's house the men orient a table with the long axis running rising sun to setting sun and place on it the package of candles, tips pointing to rising sun. Just before the shaman arrives, the escort runs ahead to give the signal and two incense burners are lighted: one is placed in front of the house cross, the other at the foot of the table.

Episode Four: Arrival of the Shaman

The shaman, dressed in his black robe and carrying his staff under his left arm, stops first at the house cross and crosses himself. He speaks to the people inside the house, enters and kneels to pray at the foot of the table, then exchanges bowing-and-releasing gestures with everyone present.

At the moment the shaman enters the house, the male assistants who were serving as sweepers and assistants become MAYOLETIK, that is, errand boys and messengers like those who serve the Presidente at the cabildo, and like the supernatural MAYOLETIK who run errands for the ancestral gods.

Episode Five: Inspecting the Candles and Plants

The shaman seats himself on a small chair at the foot of the table to inspect the candles and ritual plants. He places the incense burner at the foot of the table, or on the floor near his right foot, while assistants lay down a reed mat (POP) to the south of the table. The ritual plants, water from the sacred waterholes, and other materials are arranged by the shaman, the arrangements differing with each shaman. Figure 16 displays a sample arrangement made by Telex Komis Lotriko, a shaman from the hamlet of Pasteˀ.

Thirteen aromatic ritual plants are most commonly used by shamans for the MUK'TA ˀILEL: ten are the "flowers" of the ritual bath; three additional species serve in other parts of the ceremony. Attributes of the innate souls of the ritual plants vary, since shamans receive information through the three dreams at their debut and continuously throughout their lives. One set of attributes, described by Anselmo Perez of the hamlet of Patosil, follows. Scientific identifications were provided by Dr. Dennis Breedlove, of the Herbarium of the California Academy of Sciences in San Francisco, who inspected each of the plants at our field headquarters.

The bath "flowers" are: (1) Leaves from ZIS ˀUC, a wild laurel tree (*Litsea glaucescens* HBK.) that grows in what Breedlove calls the "mountain rain forest or evergreen cloud forest" of the higher slopes in the Chiapas highlands, including the upper reaches of BANKILAL MUK'TA VIZ. When crushed, the leaves have a very pungent odor. It is also used to decorate the patient's corral-bed and the cross shrines. The same leaves have many other ritual uses, including the ritual bathing of an infant immediately after birth, and the bathing of a mother in a sweat house during the postpartum period. The plant has a warm, medium active, white inner soul. (2) Leaves from ˀAHA-TEˀES (possibly "lordly tree," but the meaning is obscure). This wild myrtle tree (*Gaultheria odorata* Willd.) also grows in the evergreen cloud forest. The leaves are also used to bathe an infant immediately after birth. The plant has a cold, active, white inner soul. (3) NIˀ YIHIL ˀANAL TOH (literally "tip of thick-needled pine," a type of BAZ'I TOH, literally the "genuine pine"). This is a yellow pine (*Pinus montezumae* Lamb.) that is very common in the Highlands of Chiapas. It has a cold, active, blue-green inner soul. An alternative is another type of BAZ'I TOH called HIC'IL ˀANAL TOH (literally "thin-needled pine"), another species of yellow pine (*Pinus pseudostrobus* Lindl.). It too has a cold, active, blue-green inner soul. One of the two types of BAZ'I TOH serves as the pine-tips for the cross shrines, and for the pine needles spread inside and in front of the corral-bed and at cross shrines. (4) VIXOBTAKIL (literally "elder sisters" but meaning "female assistants of the ancestral gods"). This is an odd-looking plant (*Peperomia spp.—Peperomia deppeana* S. & C., *Peperomia galioides* HBK., and many other small, succulent leaved species of this same genus) with a long tail-like growth on top; it grows commonly on the lower branches of oak and other trees in the evergreen cloud forest. It has a cold, quiet, blue-green inner soul. (5) KRUS ˀEC' (literally "cross bromeliad"), also called BAZ'I ˀEC' (genuine bromeliad). This is a highland bromeliad, or air plant (*Tillandsia guatemalensis* L. B. Smith), which grows high in various trees in the evergreen cloud forest. It is an anomolous plant since its roots are attached to, but do not take moisture or nutrients from, a tree. The plant collects water from rainfall and from fog condensation; its nutrients come from a kind of "soup" that forms at the base of its

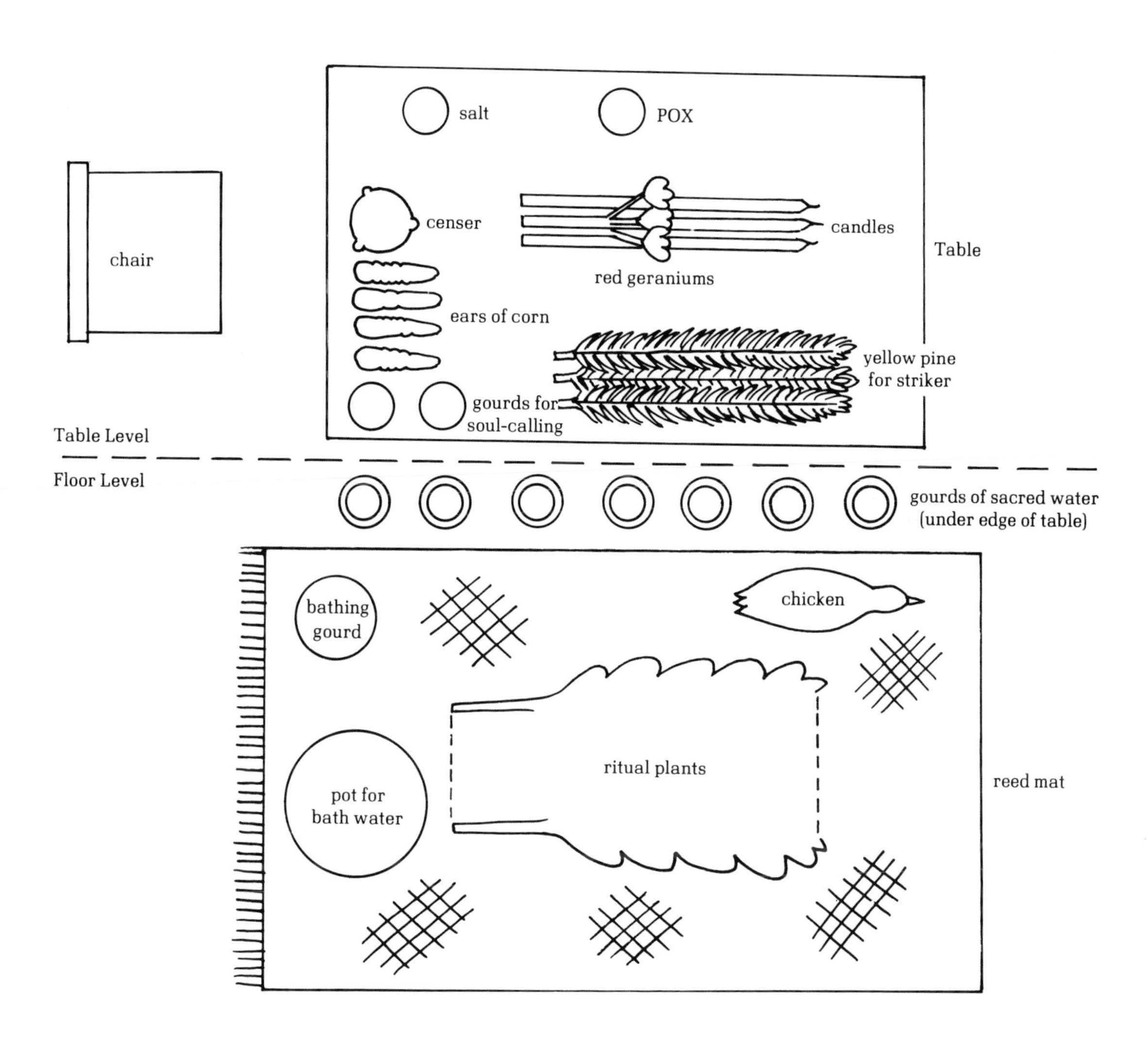

16. The arrangement of ritual paraphernalia used by a shaman

17. Plants used in a ritual of affliction

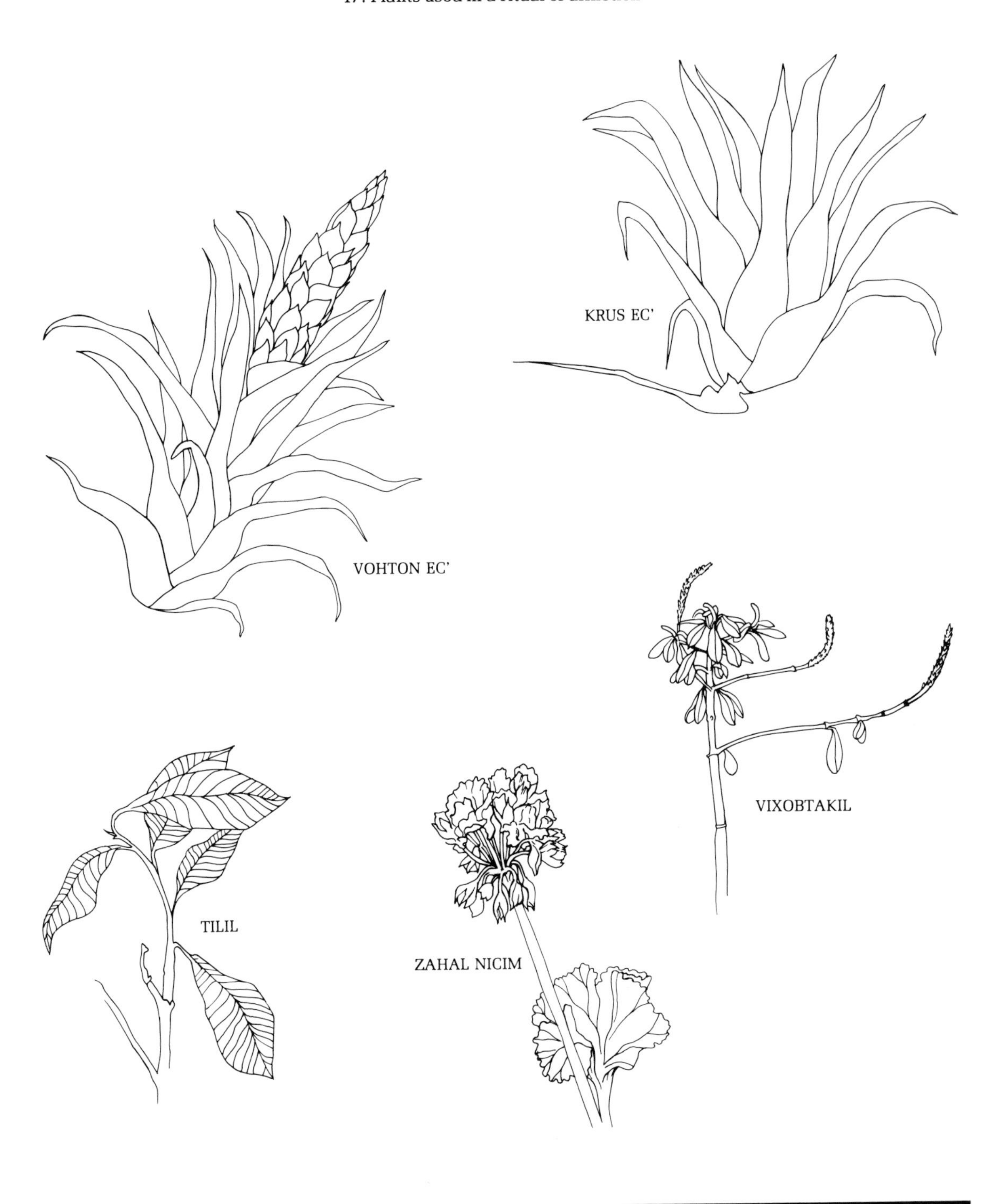

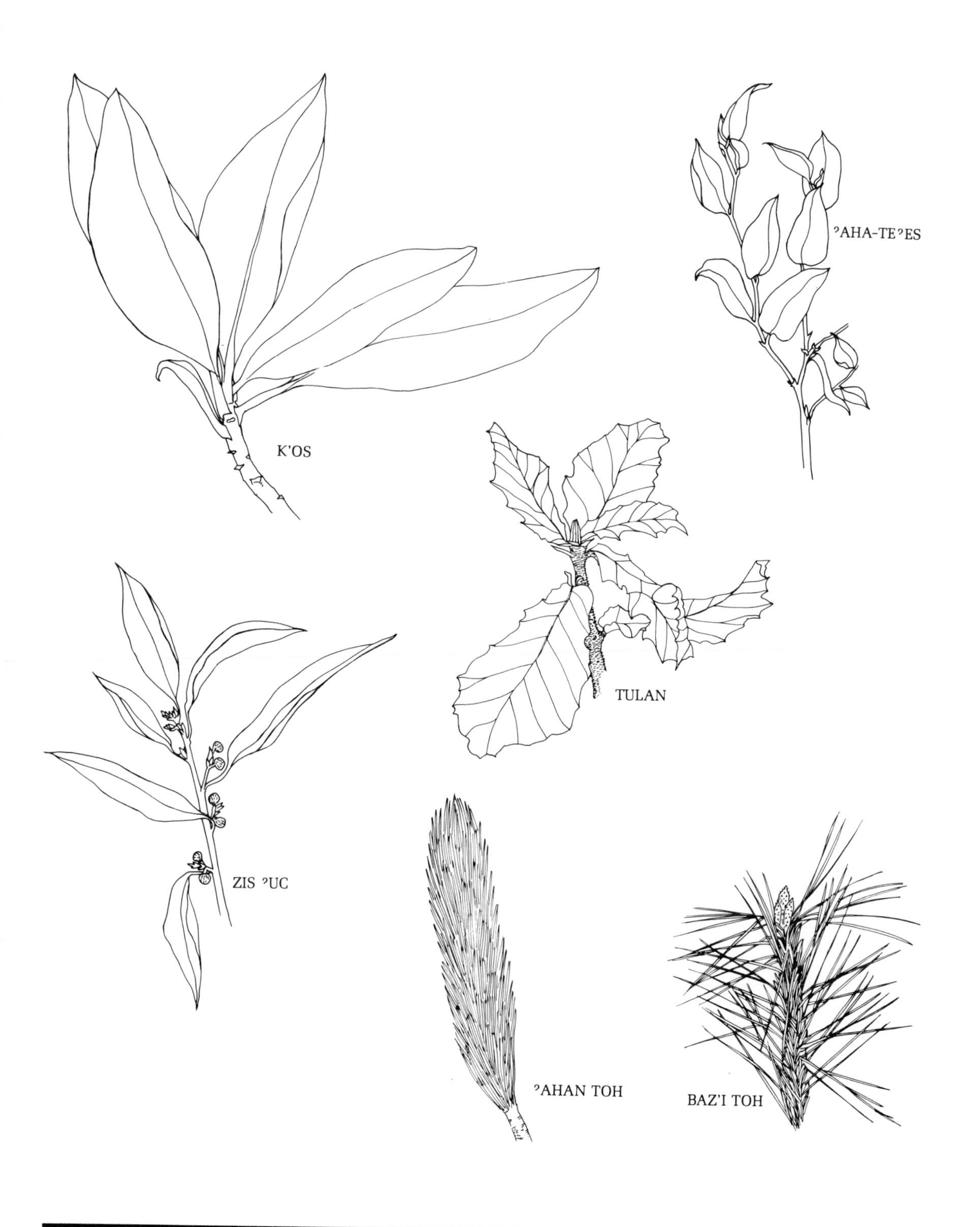

ˀAHA-TEˀES
K'OS
TULAN
ZIS ˀUC
ˀAHAN TOH
BAZ'I TOH

wide leaves as leaves and other debris fall into the bromeliad. The blossoms are used to roof the crèche in the church of San Lorenzo at Christmas-time because in color and form "they look like tile." Only the leaves are used in the MUK'TA ʔILEL. It has a cold, quiet, red inner soul. (6) Leaves from TILIL (literally "flickering"). This wild highland tree (*Rapanea juergensenii* Mez) grows in the evergreen cloud forest. It has a cold, quiet, white inner soul. Some shamans substitute Mexican savory, the "ghost flower" C'ULELAL NICIM (*Satureja mexicana* [Benth.] Briq.), one of the few wild plants sold in markets. (7) Leaves from K'OS (literally "shoots" or "broken-off segments") another tree (*Synardisia venosa* [Mast.] Lundell.) that grows in the evergreen cloud forest. It is also used to decorate the patient's bed and is tied on the cross shrines. Because it has become scarce in the woods, it is now often propagated by cuttings in garden plots near the houses of the Zinacantecos. It has a cold, quiet, blue-green inner soul. (8) ZAHAL NICIM (literally "red flower"). This is the domesticated red geranium (*Pelargonium hortium* L. H. Bailey), which, according to Breedlove, was introduced in the New World from Europe within a few years of the Spanish Conquest. It has a cold, quiet, blue-green inner soul. (9) TEʔEL POM (literally "incense sticks"), cut from the copal tree, called BAZ'I POM (genuine incense)—(*Bursera excelsa* [HBK.] Engl.)—or the bush called ʔAC'EL POM (dripping incense) —(*Bursera bipinnata* [DC.] Engl.). Both grow in the Lowlands and have hot, active, white inner souls. (10) BEK'TAL POM (literally "flesh of the incense"). These are the nodules of resin from the BAZ'I POM.

The additional "flower" used for decorating the corral-bed is VOHTON ʔEC', literally "ear of dried maize bromeliad". This is a very striking bromeliad (*Tillandsia ponderosa* L. B. Smith) that typically grows even higher in trees than the KRUS ʔEC' and has a large, bright red blossom resembling an ear of mature maize. It is used in the bundles of flowers that decorate the patient's bed and also on the cross shrines. It has, according to most shamans interviewed, a hot, active, red inner soul. For calling the parts of the lost soul with a MAHOBIL (striker) shamans use branches of TULAN, which is one of two closely related species of oak, either *Quercus peduncularis* Née or *Quercus rugosa* Née, and/or ʔAHAN TOH, a yellow pine of the species *Pinus oaxacana* Mirov. The TULAN has a warm, active, white inner soul; the ʔAHAN TOH has a hot, active, red inner soul.

After being satisfied that the candles and "flowers" are complete, the shaman censes them with three counterclockwise circuits and chants a prayer known as K'EL KANTELA (looking at the candles):

In the divine name of Jesus Christ my Lord,
So much, my Father,
So much, my Lord,
I beseech your divine pardon,
I beg your divine forgiveness,
At the holy head of the table,
At the holy foot of the table.

Will you stand up,
Will you stand firm,
Behind,
Beside,
Your sons,
Your children,
Your flowers,
Your sprouts,
Who have sickness,
Who have pain,
Who are suffering,
Who are miserable.

At dusk,
At dawn,
They are no longer well,
They are no longer healthy,
For how long will they not receive,
For how long will not possess,
Your beautiful sunbeams,
Your beautiful shade. . . .

Divine KALVARYO, divine Father,
KALVARYO, divine Mother,
Holy KALVARYO holy ancient ones,
Holy KALVARYO holy yellow ones,
Holy seas,
Holy ancient ones,
Holy gathering-place,
Holy meeting-place,
Holy place of recovery,
Holy place of rest. . . .
I shall visit your shrines a little,
I shall entrust my soul to you a little,
To your feet,
To your hands,
For your sons,
For your children,
For your flowers,
For your sprouts,
For these I beseech divine pardon,
For these I beg divine forgiveness . . .

While the rituals performed by cargoholders are theoretically, and indeed actually, almost identical in detail from one year to the next, those performed by the shamans show a bubbling variety. Even an individual shaman may perform the same ritual somewhat differently from year to year.

The variation is not endless, or open-ended, however. All shamans use candles, ritual plants, copal incense, black chickens, and so on. No one dreams, for example, that sheep should be sacrificed in place of chickens or that rattles should accompany the curing chants. But, within the limits of tradition, they hold differing beliefs about details. A common assertion about the plants is that, although living Zinacantecos collect wild plants in the mountains, the ancestral gods cultivate them as *domesticated* plants in gardens; thus, wild specimens are collected from the gardens of the gods.

Episode Six: Preparing the Ritual Plants

With the aid of the MAYOLETIK, the shaman again censes, then assembles the bundles of ritual plants for the KORAL and the shrines. An arch constructed at the entrance to the KORAL is covered with plants, and bundles of plants are placed around the inside of the platform bed. For the arch two small sturdy pine trees, one of the two types of BAZ'I TOH, are fastened to the two posts at each side of the gateway to the corral. A piece of ˀISBON, cut from a limb of one of two species of highland trees (*Cornus excelsa* Kunth, or *Viburnum elatum* Benth.) is used for the arch. (Alternatively, the tops of the pine trees are bent over and tied together.) The shaman assembles bunches of at least four plants—three leaves each of VOHTON ˀEC', K'OS, and ZIS ˀUC, and a cluster of ZAHAL NICIM—and hands them to the MAYOLETIK; one holds the plants together, one on top of the other, while another ties them into bundles with strips of palm. They tie them first to the right-hand pine tree, next to the left-hand one; then tie the balance to the arch, beginning at the top center and working first to the right, then to the left. The placement within the bundle is with VOHTON ˀEC' underneath, next to arch, ZAHAL NICIM on top, toward the people in the house.

Thirteen bundles of the same four plants are assembled in the same order and tied together in bundles for the inside of the KORAL. In this case, *whole* bromeliads are used of the VOHTON ˀEC'. The bundles are placed around the platform as indicated in Figure 18 with the "points" of the "flowers" pointing up, with the VOHTON ˀEC' on the outside, the ZAHAL NICIM next to where the patient will lie. Then the shaman assembles the bundles for the mountain shrines, three of the same four plants for each shrine, and in the same order.

The ˀISBON is also used for the staffs of office of the Regidores, Mayordomo Reyes, and Mesoneros; for the frame of the reed mat bull in the drama of the bull during the Christmas season, and as a stirring rod for maize gruel.

According to native exegesis, the thirteen bundles of plants placed inside the KORAL represent

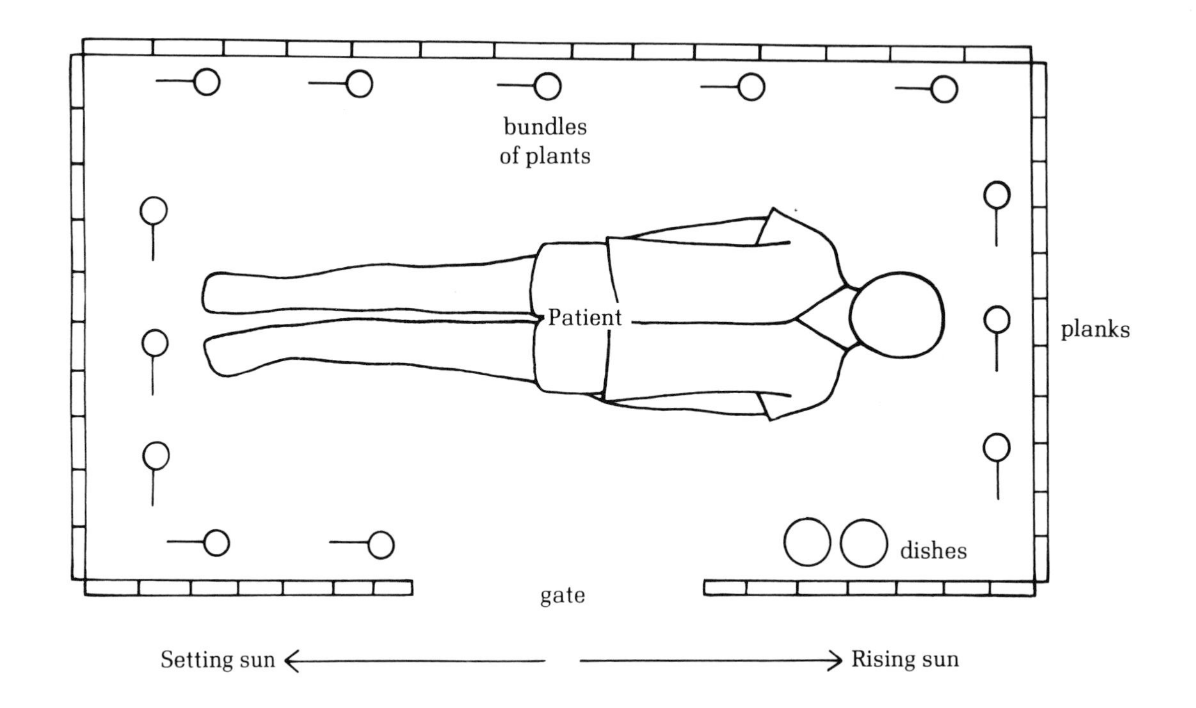

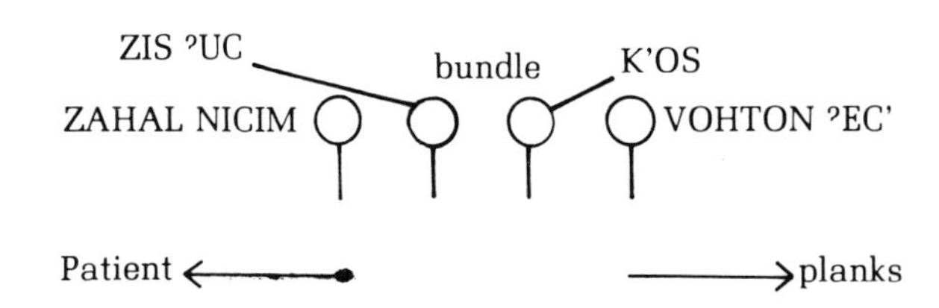

18. The arrangement of patient and bundles of ritual plants used in the corral-bed

the thirteen parts of the patient's C'ULEL. Since there are four kinds of plants in each bundle, the total of fifty-two "flowers" equals the number of grains of maize of the four colors used in the SAT ˀIXIM divination (see Episode Sixteen).

Episode Seven: Preparing the Bath

The shaman calls for a large pot and puts into it three small bunches (or three leaves or pieces) of each of the ten "flowers" for the bath, ordinarily in the order listed in Episode Five. Water from the sacred waterholes is added, usually in the order given in Episode Two.

Episode Eight: Praying over the Candles

The shaman prays over the candles, periodically rotating a smoking censer counterclockwise over the table in an episode called SNUP KANTELA, "meeting the candles." The words he speaks are believed to be received by the gods the moment he utters them. When he finishes, he calls forward each of the adults in the house, in-

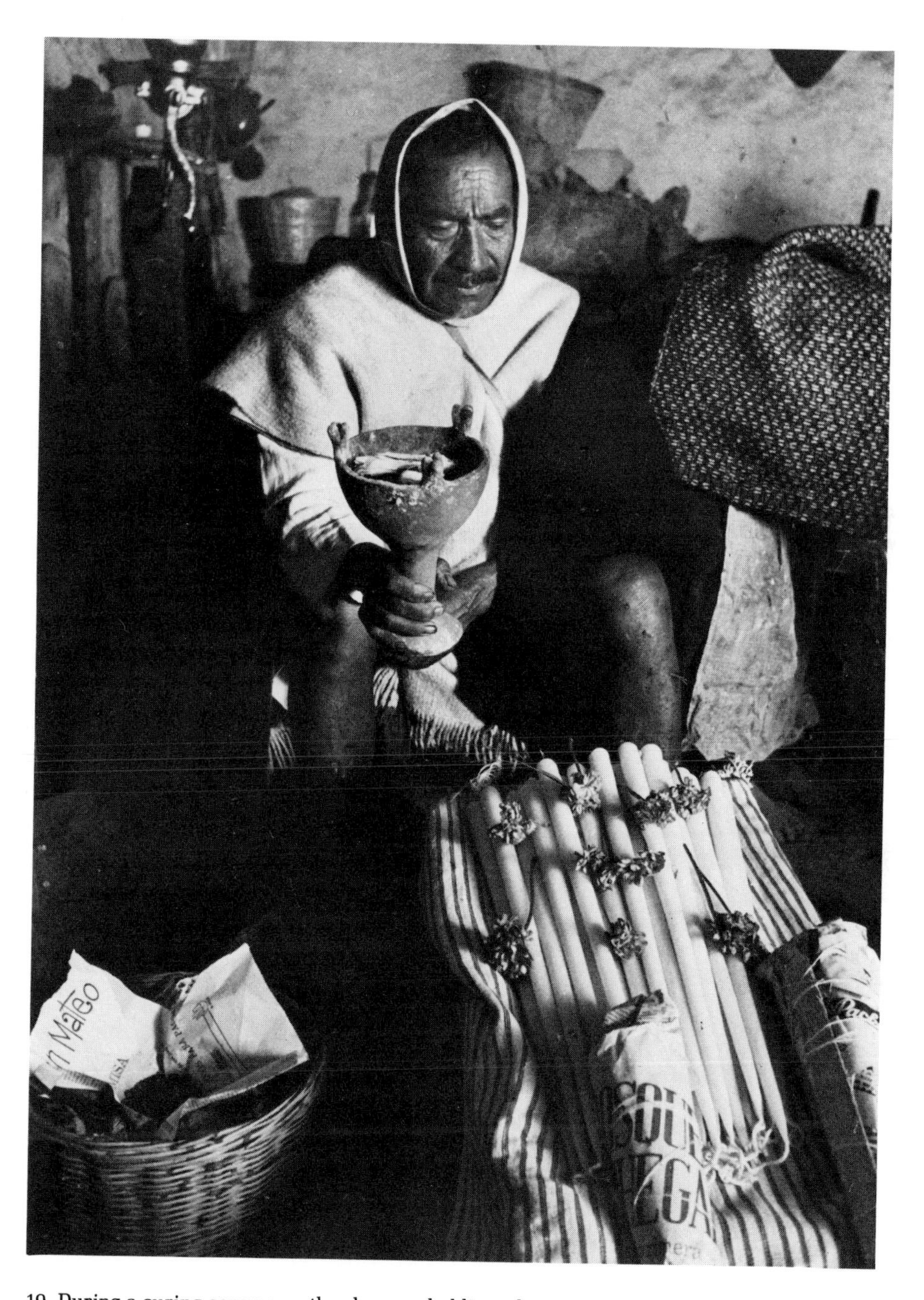

19. During a curing ceremony, the shaman, holding a burning censer, prays over the candles arranged on the ritual table

cluding the patient, in rank order, singly or in pairs, to kneel at the foot of the table and salute the candles. The patient's prayer is as follows (Vogt 1969: 429):

In the divine name of God my Lord,
  Who is thought,
  Who is measurement,
    Will you stand up in holiness,
    Will you stand firmly in holiness,
      Behind me,
      Beside me;

If there is a passing by,
If there is a respite from
  Sickness,
  From death,
  From illness,
  From pain; . . .

See how I suffer,
See how I am weak,
  In one afternoon,
  In one morning,
    No longer is guarded my lowly back,
    No longer is protected my lowly side . . .

Episode Nine: Ritual Bathing

The shaman orders that the large boiling pot of bath water be brought near the table and directs the patient to exchange bowing-and-releasing gestures with each person present, while announcing that he is going to bathe. Everyone tells him to bathe. A half-gourd partly filled with the hot "flower" water, is brought from beneath the KORAL and cooled by adding unsanctified water from a jug. If the patient is a woman, two of the MAYOLETIK hold up a reed mat to shield her from public view. Some shamans bathe the patient; others direct patients to bathe themselves. The head is bathed first; then the arms, stroking toward the hands and fingertips; finally the rest of the body.

While the bathing proceeds, the laundresses (HʔUK̲'UMAHELETIK) cense the previously washed patient's clothing by holding each article over an up-ended basket placed over a censer, allowing the aromatic smoke to permeate the clothes. The patient puts on the clean clothes, blouse or shirt, then skirt or pants. Male patients also put on a black ceremonial robe (XAKITAIL); females a ceremonial poncho with narrow white stripes, called a CILIL. As the patient bathes and changes, he announces each action aloud.

If the patient is married, or an infant, the spouse or parent also bathes and puts on clean, censed clothing. The bathed ones engage in bowing-and-releasing with all present. A MAYOL pours any remaining water under the KORAL so that it spreads across the entire area beneath the platform bed.

The bathing process is accompanied by three rounds of cane liquor for all from a MUK'TA P'IS ("large glass" that holds about three times the volume of the small shot glass).

Episode Ten: Bathing and Bleeding the Chicken

The shaman calls for one of the black chickens. Holding it in his left hand, a shot of POX in his right, he chants a prayer. Then he bathes the chicken in another gourd of the same "flower" water from the large pot, and this water is also poured out under the KORAL.

Using a knife and/or needle, he pulls out a few feathers and makes an incision in the neck vein of the chicken, drains about a cupful of blood into a bowl, and adds three shots of cane liquor. The chicken's neck is either sewn up or swaddled tightly in a cloth to prevent further bleeding. The bird is then placed, still alive, on a layer of pine needles on a plate. Additional pine needles are spread at the sides and on the top; and the plate is wrapped in the ritual tablecloth ready to be taken to the mountain shrines.

The bowl of blood is handed to the patient, who drinks some, then returned to the shaman, who dips a red geranium into the bowl and uses it to daub blood, in the form of crosses, on the patient's forehead and forearms. On the forearms (right, then left) he runs the flower from the inside of the wrist up to the inside of the elbow, then daubs across the inside of the elbow and across the wrist, to make a double-ended cross.

Episode Eleven: Preparing the Ritual Materials for the Pilgrimage

The shaman selects three candles for each mountain shrine to be visited, stating the name of the shrine, and places them upright in the middle of a basket of red geraniums. Candles for the saints in the churches are added, and the basket is placed in a carrying net. The shaman loads the bundles of ritual plants and the sacrificial chicken into nets; the helpers pack liquor and food, firewood, and pitch pine for torches to light the trails at night.

Episode Twelve: Eating a Ritual Meal

A meal of chicken and tortillas is served to the shaman, the patient, the helpers, and the women who washed the clothes.

Episode Thirteen: Departure for the Mountain Shrines

The shaman calls for a bottle of cane liquor, which is left at the head of the table "to ensure that those remaining in the house will not sleep while the others are gone" (Silver 1966a: 176). The bottle, often referred to as a TOTILMEʔIL, apparently is an offering to and a recognition of the presence of the ancestral gods at the ritual table. It is the duty of the women—and perhaps of an old man, if one is present in the household—to remain awake to protect the patient's KORAL from blows from the ancestral gods and from demons who might approach while the curing party is away. The members of the curing party load for the trip; kneel and cross themselves at the table, hearth, and the house cross outside; and line up in rank order.

Episode Fourteen: Visiting the Shrines

The order in which the mountains and churches in HTEK-LUM are visited varies, depending both upon the discretion of the shaman and the direction by which the party enters the ceremonial center. A common order is SAN KIXTOVAL, MUXUL VIZ, SISIL VIZ, and KALVARYO; when BANKILAL MUK'TA VIZ is included, it is commonly last.* The churches of San Lorenzo, Esquipulas, and San Sebastián are ordinarily included on the procession from SAN KIXTOVAL to MUXUL VIZ.

The sequence of behavior, identical at each shrine (except for KALVARYO), has been described in Chapter 3. In the case of the MUK'TA ʔILEL, the "flowers" tied on each of the three crosses by the MAYOLETIK contain, in order from the pine trees toward the praying ritualists, VOHTON ʔEC', K'OS, ZIS ʔUC, and ZAHAL NICIM. Three pine-tips from ʔAHAN TOH forming the MAK KANTELA (shield of the candles) are always placed around the candles in the altar in one of the four positions diagrammed in Figure 21. A common addition to the white wax candle offerings is a cluster or line of two-for-five-centavo candles of all seven colors placed on the ridge in front of the altar, toward the praying ritualists. They provide a shield, a "candle curtain," to keep witches from "seeing" into the offerings. "Policemen," they "close the eyes" of witches who might seek to prevent or pervert the ritual.

As the candles burn, the shaman and patient pray together. An excerpt from what is chanted at the shrine at the foot of SISIL VIZ follows:

*The reasons for this clockwise order probably are practical, and are so described by informants, but a deeper symbolic message may be involved. A reversal of the usual direction may symbolize that time is being reversed, "stopped," in the case of a ceremony whose purpose is to suspend normal time for a patient until he is cured.

20. A shaman praying for the soul of a patient at a mountain shrine; in the background is another sacred mountain, SISIL VIZ—note its resemblance in shape to ancient Maya pyramids

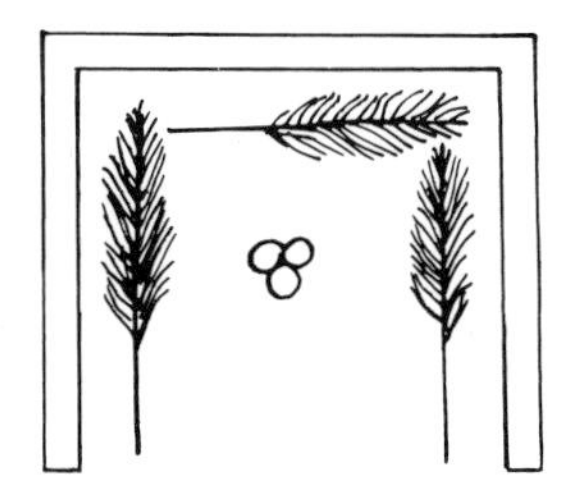

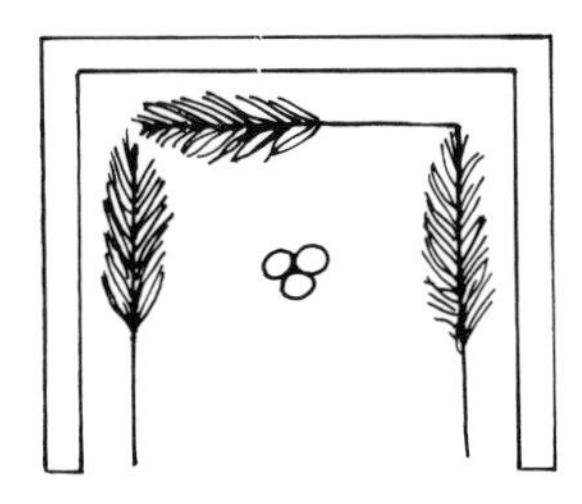

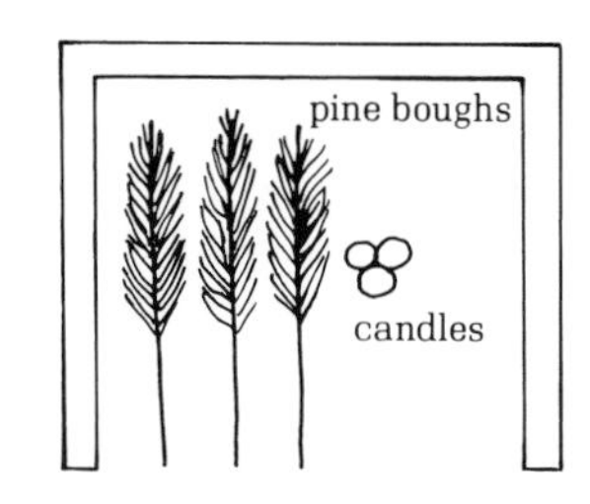

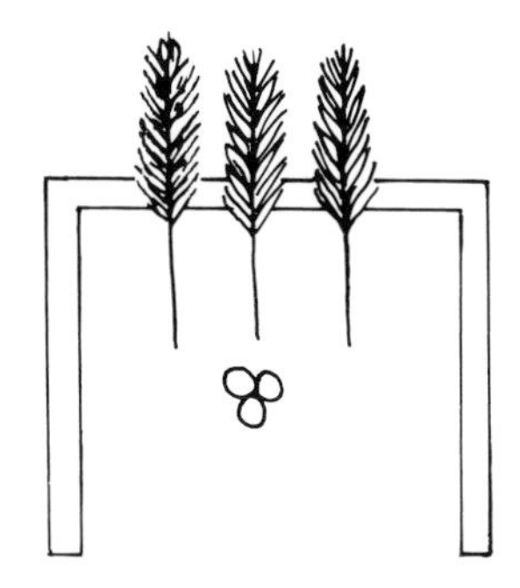

21. Positioning of ʔAHAN TOH to form the MAK KANTELA

In the divine name of Jesus Christ my Lord,
Take this, then, Father,
Receive this, then, Lord,
Divine Maria Cecilia [SISIL VIZ], my Mother,
Divine Maria Cecilia, my Lady,
Who is so much;

I come kneeling, then,
I come bowing low
At your lordly side,
At your lordly front,
Receive this, and let me step,
Let me walk
To the descents of your feet,
To the descents of your hands [the mountain shrines] . . .

If you will accept this graciously,
If you will think well of me,
This lowly little bit,
This humble amount,
These four lowly pine branches,
These four lowly candles,
From your son,
From your child,
This humble bit of incense,
This humble bit of smoke,
From your sons,
From your children,

For this I beseech divine pardon
For this I beg divine forgiveness. . . .

The procedure for paying homage to the saints in the churches is also standardized: the party salutes the cross altar in the patio outside the church, has a round of liquor at the door, enters, and kneels in rank order three times—inside the door, halfway to the altar, and in front of the altar. Here the shaman and patient remain on their knees while the MAYOLETIK rise, set a censer before the altar, and serve a round of liquor. The shaman, accompanied by the patient, lights candles and prays. The assistants light candles and place red geraniums before all the saints in the church. The party makes a circuit of the church, genuflecting before each image. Three genuflections are repeated as the party retreats toward the door. Once outside, another round of liquor is served, and the party moves on (Vogt 1969: 439).

At KALVARYO, or at other mountain shrines where the sacrificial chicken may be left for the gods, the ritual sequence is the same except for the addition of the sacrifice. The patient remains kneeling before the cross shrine at KALVARYO while the shaman and helpers go to the ˀAK'OB K'EXOLIL (place of the substitute) on the west side of the shrine. The chicken is either killed before the crosses at KALVARYO or before the ˀAK'OB K'EXOLIL by the shaman who pulls its head, breaking the neck. It is then replaced on the pine needles on the plate in the enclosure, with head toward rising sun; three pine-tips are placed at the back of the enclosure, and a white wax candle (sometimes two or three) is lighted at the head of the chicken. The enclosure is then walled up with loose stones. (While the K'EXOLIL is most often left at KALVARYO, the great meeting-place of the gods, it is sometimes offered—especially in the MUK'TA ˀILEL ceremony—in an enclosure behind the shrine on the summit of BANKILAL MUK'TA VIZ; it may also be left at the summit of MUXUL VIZ, the foot or summit of SISIL VIZ, or occasionally at NINAB CILOˀ.) When the shaman and helpers rejoin the party, the assemblage eats a meal of cold chicken, or pork, and tortillas, and departs for the patient's home in rank order. Upon arrival, candles are offered at the house cross, and the shaman and patient pray.

Episode Fifteen: Entering the KORAL

Members of the ritual party enter the house, cross themselves at the table and at the hearth, and bow-and-release with all present. The shaman washes the hands and feet of the patient in "flower" water (some the entire body, others the head, arms, and legs). He bathes the second chicken in "flower" water. The water left over from each is thrown under the KORAL. The gourds used for the bathing and the pot with "flower" water are placed under the bed just below the patient's head. The basket and net used to carry the candles are hung above the corral-bed where they remain since "they served the ancestral gods in the mountains."

At this time, the patient climbs through the gate of the KORAL under the arch, and settles down under the blankets on the platform bed. The shaman censes the patient three times and prays to the ancestral gods to come and watch over the patient; then he warns the patient that he is going to kill the second sacrificial chicken. The chicken's neck is pulled and the fowl is tossed onto the patient. If the chicken jumps around a great deal while dying, and its head falls toward rising sun, the patient will improve; if he is to die, it falls toward setting sun. No matter which direction the head falls, the shaman places the dead chicken, head to rising sun, beside the patient's head. Some shamans describe both east and north as "good" directions, west and south as "bad." (Later the chicken is hung for a day, head down, on a hook outside the KORAL, after which it is cooked and eaten by the patient, who carefully saves the feathers and bones.)

Episode Sixteen: Calling the C'ULEL

If the patient has been diagnosed as suffering from XIˀEL ("fright" leading to soul loss), along with the problem of a missing animal companion, the "soul-calling" ritual (LOK'ESEL TA BALAMIL, literally "extracting from the earth") is added to the sequence of events at this point.

First, the shaman performs SAT ˀIXIM (kernel of maize) divination to determine how many parts of the C'ULEL have been lost in different places in the earth. He calls for a gourd bowl about half-filled with water. Salt from Ixtapa is added and stirred vigorously. Then the shaman calls for four ears of highland maize (lowland maize is never used for divining)—white, yellow, red, and black—which have been lying on the table in a large gourd. Using his left thumb, he carefully removes thirteen grains from the white ear, which fall into his right hand. He blows on his right fist and drops the kernels gently into the salt water. The process is repeated with the three other ears. The shaman gently shakes the bowl, and peers into it with the aid of a pine-pitch torch or flashlight to inspect the behavior of the fifty-two grains of corn. The grains whose "mouths" (the part of the kernel originally attached to the ear) point upward indicate soul loss; those "seated" (resting quietly on the bottom of the bowl) indicate parts of the soul that are still safely in the body of the patient. Some shamans report that kernels that are floating indicate soul loss in a waterhole or river. The counting is ambiguous at best because the light is dim, everyone, including the shaman, is in an advanced stage of inebriation, and there are fifty-two grains to transmit signals about thirteen parts of the soul! But the shaman resolves the ambiguity by announcing, for example, that six parts of the soul have been lost at different locations.

Some of the salt water from the divinatory bowl is poured into a small gourd (ZU) at just the proper level to make the gourd into a whistle. The fifty-two grains of maize are placed into a second ZU, and the balance of the salt water is added. These gourds are called ʔIK'OB BAIL ZU (summoner gourds).

The shaman, carrying the gourd with the kernels of maize and accompanied by a MAYOL who carries the whistle, goes out to the house cross in the patio to engage in soul-calling. He prays before the cross, asking the ancestral gods to send their six helpers to call the soul from wherever it has been lost, and asking the Earth Lord to free the soul since it has not "stolen" anything. Then he addresses the lost soul, saying, in the case of a patient named Juan:

Come now, Juan,
Come from where you have stayed in the earth.
  From where you were only seated,
  From where you were only huddled,
    From where you were frightened,
    From where you were affrighted,
      Your feet were frightened,
      Your hands were frightened.

Near you,
In front of you,
  The divine heaven,
  The divine earth;
    The divine Father accompanies you,
    The divine Mother accompanies you,
      The six divine mayores,
      The six divine assistants
        Six divine feet,
        Six divine hands.

Come now, Juan.
  Not only may you be lying there face down,
  Not only may you be lying there on your side,
    The extent to which you were frightened in
      such a place,
    That you were affrighted in such a place.

In whatever place,
In whatever direction,
  Be it a place below,
  Be it a place above,
    Remember your house,
    Remember your dwelling place. . . .

Come now, Juan,
Come.

(Vogt 1969: 442-444)

At the end of the prayer the shaman rises, holds the MAHOBIL in his right hand, and blows water on it from the summoner gourd. Facing a direction in which soul-loss has occurred, he whirls the striker around 360 degrees, and prays again, interspersing the prayer with LAʔ ME, LAʔ ME (Come, please, come, please), and striking the ground at his feet. He faces the directions where the soul has been lost—reminded of them by the patient and the family shouting instructions from within the house—and repeats the process, as the MAYOL stands to his right and blows on the gourd whistle, making an eerie whistling sound "so that the soul will hear and return."

Touching the MAHOBIL again to the ground, the shaman, followed by the whistling MAYOL, leads the lost soul into the house and over to the patient in the KORAL, where, using more salt water in his mouth, from the summoner gourd with the maize, he sucks noisily in four places on the patient's arms, "to call the blood to receive the soul": under the right elbow, inside the right wrist, under the left elbow, and inside the left wrist. Using dry salt from Ixtapa, he makes a cross on the forehead and on the areas where he has sucked, "to keep the soul in."

The striker is placed under the patient's head as part of his pillow; the two summoner gourds, the bowl of salt, and the four ears of maize of four colors are placed to the rising sun side of the patient's head (Figure 22).

Episode Seventeen: Eating the Final Ritual Meal

A final ritual meal is eaten at the table by the shaman, the assistants, and the women who washed the clothes, while the patient eats in his KORAL. They also drink the cane liquor which remained on the table during the trip to the

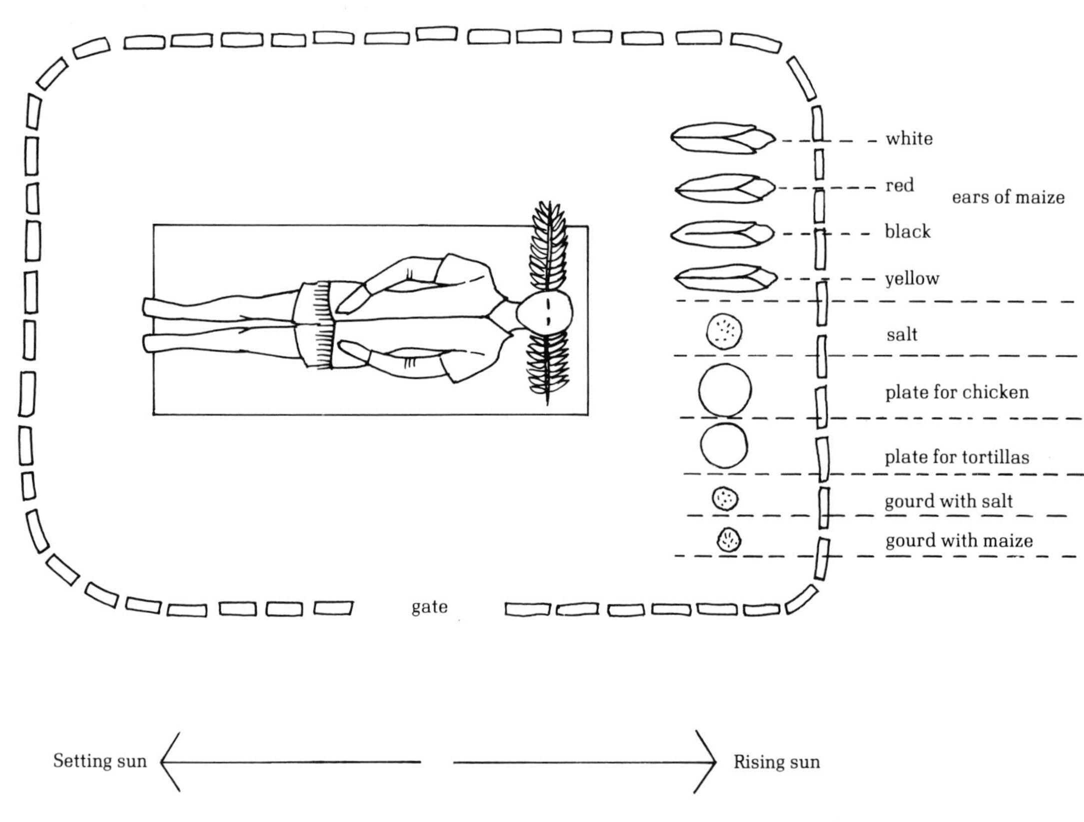

22. The arrangement of patient and various ritual items in the corral-bed

mountains. The shaman is then escorted home by a MAYOL, who carries the shaman's gift of four bottles of liquor, four dead chickens, eighty tortillas, and 2 pesos' worth of wheat-flour rolls.

Episode Eighteen: Postceremonial Seclusion

For a period of two weeks or more there are strong taboos on the patient's behavior and rigid patterns for his care. The patient takes two or three days to finish eating his sacrificial chicken. He must collect the bones and feathers in a pot for the shaman to take away when he returns to remove the flowers; he must eat the maize used for the SAT ˀIXIM divination. (The grains are either parched on a comal, or boiled, then ground and eaten as pozol.) The patient stays in his corral-bed and cannot talk to the guardians; no visitor can enter the house. When the patient goes outside to relieve himself, he must be accompanied by a member of the family, and another person must sit in front of the KORAL to prevent demons from entering.

At least one woman must always be in the house watching the patient; she may not weave or do any other work; her sole duty is to look after the patient. If there are two guardians, one will sleep while the other watches to make cer-

23. Patient in her corral-bed at the end of the ceremony

tain that the patient neither suffers a blow from the ancestral gods or is attacked by demons. If there is only one guardian, she may sleep if a light is kept burning. Neither cabbage nor black beans may be eaten in the house during this period; only white beans, eggs, pork, and chicken are permitted.

During the seclusion the ancestral gods and their assistants come to see how the patient is getting along. The arrival of the latter is signaled by the singing of a sparrow, of the gods by their appearance in the dreams of the patient or a guardian.

Episode Nineteen: Removing the "flowers" from the KORAL

At the end of the period of seclusion, the shaman returns. He prays at the KORAL, censing it three times, then rubs the patient with the thirteen bundles of "flowers" and puts them—along with the plants from the arch, the plants left in the "flower" water, and the pine needles—into a sack. He instructs two assistants to place the sack in the branches of a TULAN tree behind KALVARYO in Zinacantan Center. (Some shamans have the helpers leave the plants in an oak behind the shrine at SAN KIXTOVAL.) The plants, having been originally procured from the gods, must be returned to them, so they are taken to the meeting-place of the gods and placed "united" in a tree behind the shrine. Several of the plants were taken from trees—KRUS ˀEC' and VOHTON ˀEC'—and the rest were leaves or branches. This reciprocating act is a noteworthy example of Zinacantecos' meticulous concern for "micro-adjustment" (Lévi-Strauss 1966: 10).

The shaman removes from under the bed the gourds and the pot of water left from the ritual baths; the "flower" water is saved for the post-ceremonial sweat baths. When the helpers return from KALVARYO, they help the shaman bury the bones and feathers of the sacrificial chicken in a hole about two feet deep behind the house cross. The episode ends with a ritual meal.

Episode Twenty: Post ceremonial Sweat Baths

The symbolism in this episode makes it clear that the patient is believed to have lost too much "heat" either during the course of the ceremony or as a consequence of the illness. He must slowly regain it from the fire at the hearth, from the sun, and from the sweat baths, but for two or three days after removal of the ritual plants, he still cannot leave the KORAL. The patient first begins to leave the bed to warm himself for brief periods by the fire. His bed need no longer be watched, but three ears of maize are left in it to substitute for the patient. The guardians may weave again, but only with black wool, since white wool attracts blows from the ancestral gods. The patient still cannot be left alone in the house.

Accompanied by spouse or mother, the patient takes a series of three sweat baths at three-day intervals. He may enter the sweat house (PUS) only in the morning, because the sun is young and will "give youth" to the patient's body. If he bathes in the afternoon, when the sun is waning, his body will rapidly age.

The PUS is built beside the house or at the edge of the patio. If the former, it usually has two wattle and daub walls and a thatched roof. At the edge of the patio it is tunneled into the bank of earth, either above or below the terrace, which has been dug out of the slope for construction of the house. The sweat house can accommodate two to three persons, either sitting up or lying down. Lava rocks are placed at the back of the structure and heated by a fire of oak. The burning pieces of wood are removed, leaving the coals and hot rocks, and water is sprinkled on the rocks to create steam. Chamarras are placed over the door to keep the heat in. At this time the bathers enter and undress. They sit down and fan the air with palm leaves to make the heat circulate; then lie down with their feet toward the hot rocks for a period of fifteen to thirty minutes. The patient pours over himself the "flower" water left from the ritual baths.

After the first sweat bath the patient can stay alone in the house without his guardians, but still may not go outside by himself. After the second bath he is allowed to go outside in the sun and remain there alone. After the third bath he may leave the house and his bed and need not be watched. He gradually resumes normal activities, at which point the cure is ended.

6

Rituals of Affliction: Interpretations

At the most fundamental etiological level, a sick Zinacanteco usually has "soul trouble." Disruptive social behavior has led the ancestral gods to mete out punishment. They may send a lightning bolt to knock out one or more parts of an individual's inner soul, or, in more extreme cases, let his animal companion out of its supernatural corral.

When the "touching blood" diagnosis of the shaman indicates that the animal companion is wandering loose in the woods, the patient is in maximum jeopardy; Great Seeing is the only ceremony which can successfully retrieve the wandering animal and replace it in its corral.* Fear at knowing of the loss of an animal companion can also cause XIˀEL, since the animal and the man share the same innate soul. Therefore, the "grains of maize" divination and the "extracting from the earth" ritual sequences are added to the ceremony.

In his role of diviner, the shaman serves as an adjudicator of troubles and disputes that have led to a high level of tension and a psychological state producing physical disability. The shaman is typically a sensitive and insightful member of his lineage and waterhole group, always well-informed. In determining the source of the affliction he utilizes all the information he can procure. But since his final diagnosis is based neither upon the sophisticated technology nor the tested principles of modern science, and since he does not possess the legal power of a judge backed by a police force and the threat of fines or a jail sentence, it is crucial that his divinatory procedures have an ambiguity which allows him a measure of latitude in his decision and reenforces his judgment with supernatural sanctions (see Aguirre Beltrán 1963).

Victor Turner (1968: 25) calls the divinatory consultation "a switchpoint between social crisis

*I am indebted to Elizabeth M. Dodd, Victoria R. Bricker, and Francesco Pellizzi for insightful suggestions concerning the symbolism of the Great Seeing ceremony.

and performance of redressive ritual," and shows how the symbolism involved has a pronounced cognitive aspect. The diviner, he says:

> is trying to grasp consciously and bring into the open the secret, even unconscious, motives and aims of human actors in some situation of social disturbance . . . A divinatory symbol . . . helps the diviner to decide what is right and wrong, to establish innocence or guilt in situations of misfortune, and to prescribe well-known remedies. His role falls between that of a judge and that of a ritual expert (1968: 44-45).

When the Zinacanteco shaman "touches blood" he is receiving messages from the soul of the patient. However, the messages are vague: the blood (soul) is described by informants as being hot or cold, strong or weak—scarcely enough information to diagnose an affliction or prescribe a remedy. When the shaman later peers into the gourd of salt water containing fifty-two grains of maize, there is likewise little precision in his divination. Again they are mnemonics, reminders of the parts of the soul still "seated" in the body and the parts "lost." However, both divinatory procedures are crucial, for they do more than function as mnemonics about soul beliefs in Zinacanteco culture: they legitimize the course of action decided upon by the shaman. Using what he has learned through the gossip chains (see Haviland 1971) and the further clues received from intimate contact with the patient and his family, the shaman confidently proclaims that the patient's animal companion has been released from its corral by the angry ancestral gods and that he must undergo a Great Seeing ceremony. On another level, not verbalized but understood by all, he is saying that the patient has been socially disruptive and requires resocialization. But what have corral-bed, plants, black chickens, and maize divination to do with the process of resocializing?

The Corral-Bed

The most distinctive MUK'TA ˀILEL symbol is the corral-bed in which the patient is placed at the ceremony's end and in which he must remain during the period of postceremonial seclusion. The conceptual similarity between the corral inside BANKILAL MUK'TA VIZ, in which the patient's animal is believed to be kept, and the KORAL inside his house, in which the patient is placed, is unmistakable (see Figure 24): both have gates; both are surrounded by mountain plants; inside their corrals, both patient and animal are "embraced" by parental figures and safe from harm (See Vogt 1965b).

The concept of "embracing (-PET in Tzotzil) occurs in many aspects of Zinacanteco life. It is believed that one of the most important duties of the father (TOT) and mother (MEˀ) is to "embrace" a child and care for it well so that it does not lose its innate soul. At the baptismal ceremony a child always has a godfather (C'UL-TOT) and godmother (C'UL-MEˀ)—literally "divine father" and "divine mother"—whose principal duties are to "embrace" the godchild. At a wedding ceremony a HPETOM, or "embracer," introduces the bride into her new home. He is believed to "embrace" the bride and groom, to create a new and lasting relationship.

During the curing ceremonies the shaman is called TOT or MEˀ by the patient, and, as a ritual "father" or "mother," "embraces" the patient in the process of effecting a cure. In the supernatural world, it is the duty of the ancestral gods ("fathers" and "mothers") to look after the animal companions of the Zinacantecos. The job of feeding, watering, and caring for the animals is supervised by the supernatural Grand Alcalde, counterpart of the highest ranking cargoholder in Zinacantan Center. The work is carried out by the HKUCOMETIK, "carriers" of water and food to the animals, and, more significantly, HPETOMETIK who watch the animals carefully. Thus, placing the patient in a corral-bed is a metaphorical way—a piece of "imitative magic" in Frazer's (1911) words—of expressing this symbolic relation between "corraling" the patient

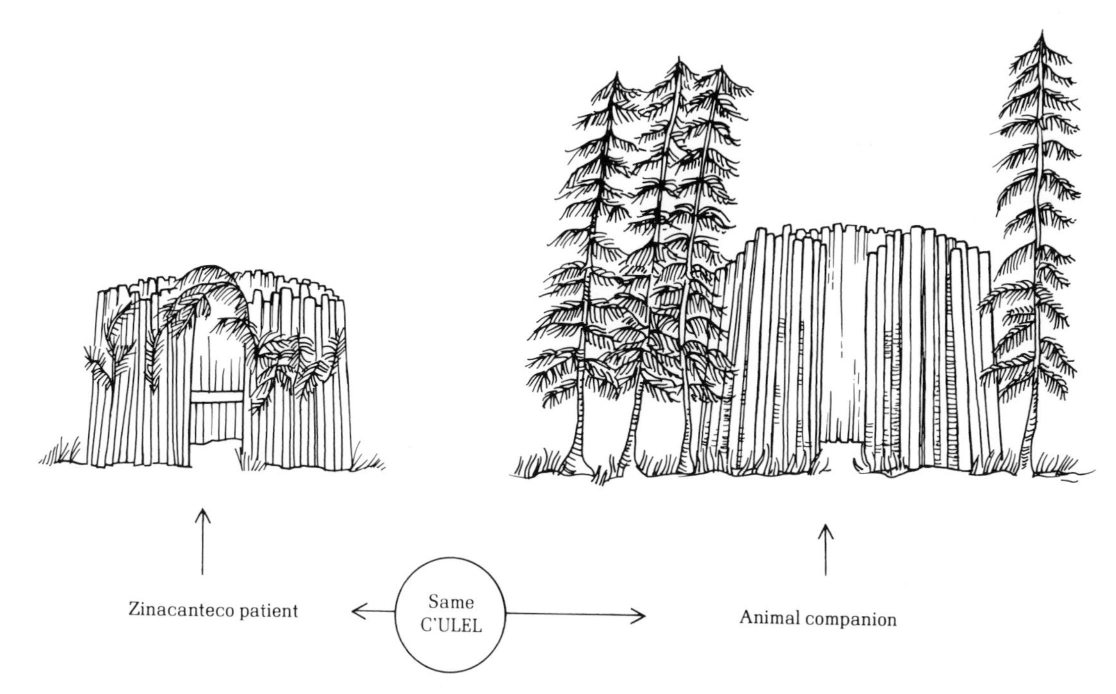

24. The relationship of human and animal "souls" in Zinacantan

and "corraling" his animal companion, properly "embracing" both.

But why should a wild animal companion be kept in a corral at all? Why should the patient be so confined? What does it really mean when this wild animal is out of its corral? Wild animals are not normally corraled, but neither is an animal companion a normal wild animal; for the animal companion, the normal state *is* to be corraled. Zinacantecos are of course not normally corraled in a literal sense, although metaphorically, a well-socialized and well-behaved person is "corraled." The Zinacantecos make a fundamental distinction between NAETIK and TE?TIK—domains which are the equivalent of Culture and Nature.* NAETIK is familiar and safe, TE?TIK unfamiliar and dangerous. In TE?TIK one may encounter PUKUHETIK, demons such as the POSLOM which travels as a ball of fire and hits people, causing a bad swelling, or H?IK'ALETIK, small, black-skinned, curly-haired men with winged feet who soar from caves at dusk, searching for food and sex.*

If TE?TIK is associated with unrestrained or uncivilized behavior, even more so are the wild animals that inhabit it. For example, the illness called CUVAH, which has the symptoms of psychotic disorder, is caused by animals entering the head. The victim acts drunk, howls, and

*A BIX (bamboo staff) is the distinguishing mark of a shaman. He carries it in his left hand whenever he is outside a house (never inside a house). Carrying a BIX, a tree in miniature, symbolizes the shaman's superhuman powers over Nature.

*H?IK'ALETIK are reported to suck the blood of men and rape women with their two-meter-long penises. So potent is their sexuality that their progeny appear three days after conception (Laughlin 1963: 190-191; Blaffer 1972).

wanders around in an animal-like way. The cure is an herbal remedy dropped in the nose, and the illness comes out by vomiting up little red and white animals (Lennihan 1970).

In all men there exist deep-rooted, anti-social impulses which we cannot understand and therefore we fear. Zinacantecos make them intelligible by associating with each person's body two other concepts: the C'ULEL, associated with the heart and the blood, and the wild animal companion. Viewing the animal companion and the corraling episodes of the Great Seeing ceremony in these terms, it is obvious why the animal is set loose when a Zinacanteco engages in anti-social behavior. Most of the time it is penned up, as are the unruly elements of the owner's personality; but when the Zinacanteco seriously breaks a social rule, his animal is no longer tamed and under control, but free and running wild, like the man's disruptive tendencies. Only when the animal and the patient are penned is the situation under control again (Lennihan 1970).

I believe the concepts of the soul and the animal companion provide the Zinacantecos with a cognitively satisfying statement concerning this relation of Nature to Culture. The relations are as follows:

Culture	*Intermediate*	*Nature*
NAETIK	COBTIK	TEʔTIK
Man	C'ULEL	Animal Companion

COBTIK includes the cultivated fields which by the process of swidden agriculture temporarily transforms patches of TEʔTIK into fields of maize, beans, and squash. It is significant that there is an equivalence here between domesticated plants and the concept of the C'ULEL, which is often symbolized by maize.

How is this related to the corrals? I propose that the concept of the Zinacanteco's sharing his inner soul with an animal involves two complementary thought processes: the culturization of Nature and the naturalization of Culture. The resulting symbolic structure balances these opposites.

A Zinacanteco is naturalized (conceived as being part of Nature) by sharing his soul with a wild animal companion. Throughout his life this cultural being is consciously aware that he shares his essential innate soul with an animal within the domain of Nature. Nature, in turn, is culturalized in the corraling of the wild animal. The role of the ancestral gods in the "corraling" and "embracing" of his animal symbolically culturalizes Nature; it is comparable to the controlling of a person by the rules of Zinacanteco society, and to the "embracing" of a child by his parents.

The balance between Nature and Culture is established and maintained so long as a Zinacanteco behaves within the socially approved norms. His good behavior guarantees that his animal will be "embraced" within the corral by the deities—and, by extension, that he will enjoy good health. Imbalance occurs when a Zinacanteco transgresses the social norms. The deities then set loose his animal and endanger his life. The Great Seeing is the means of symbolically re-establishing balance between Nature and Culture: man enacts an animal role in allowing himself to be led into, and cared for in, a corral. This compensatory act for his animal companion demonstrates to the deities that the man is cognizant and repentant of his antisocial behavior. Because the man initiated the trouble by his behavior, causing his animal to be turned out of its corral, he must initiate the resocialization. Just as the animal followed the lead of the man in leaving his corral, so, it is hoped, will he follow the man's lead in re-entering it.

The point at which the patient enters the corral-bed is the crucial moment in the ceremony—from the point of view of curing the patient and from that of restoring a cognitive balance between Nature and Culture. While in the corral, the patient will be gradually reintegrated into the safe, rational world of society. In the meantime, he is in his most vulnerable position: he is out of harmony with the culturalized world; his animal, and quite possibly a large part of his C'ULEL, are lost. Ringed with tight restrictions, he must stay in the corral until he is ready to resume his daily life.

Note that the patient is dressed in freshly washed and censed clothing. Clothing is an important symbol of personal identity in Zinacanteco society; the patient's fresh clothing symbolizes that he is starting afresh, that he is being restored to his proper place in society.

Note also that the patient passes under a flowery arch in entering the corral-bed. These flowery arches apparently represent the path of the sun across the sky (Laughlin 1962b), and therefore the passage of time. As the patient passes under the arch, normal time is suspended for him, as are all normal daily activities. Only at the end of the long period of postceremonial seclusion does the patient re-emerge from the hole punched in normal time and live again by the normal temporal patterns of Zinacanteco society (Lennihan 1970).

Ritual Plants as Metaphors

The large array of ritual plants that are collected, bundled, and manipulated in the Great Seeing ceremony result in the Zinacantecos' alternative term for it: MUK'TA NICIM (Large or Great Flower). Four instances of plant use in the ceremony merit close analysis: (1) the ten "flowers" boiled in the bath water for the patient and his substitutes; (2) the bundles of four "flowers" placed around the KORAL and on the mountain shrines; (3) the pine-tips used for constructing the "shield of the candles" and brushing the patient at the shrines; and (4) the "flowers" used for the MAHOBIL which summons the lost parts of the C'ULEL.

According to Anselmo, the salient features of the souls of the ten "flowers" used for the ritual bath are as displayed in Table 1. The first thing to note is that all are wild, save for the ZAHAL NICIM (red geranium) which serves in almost all Zinacanteco rituals as a symbol of domesticity and social order, and the BEK'TAL POM ("flesh" of the copal incense) which is domesticated in the sense that men must work on the *Bursera* tree to produce these nodules of resin. This suggests

Table 1 Some characteristics of plants used for the ritual bath.

	"flower"	hot/cold	active/quiet	color
1	ZIS ʔUC	medium	medium	white
2	ʔAHA-TEʔES	cold	active	white
3	YIHIL ʔANAL TOH	cold	active	blue-green
4	VIXOBTAKIL	cold	quiet	blue-green
5	KRUS ʔEC'	cold	quiet	red
6	TILIL	cold	quiet	white
7	K'OS	cold	quiet	blue-green
8	ZAHAL NICIM	cold	quiet	blue-green
9	TEʔEL POM	hot	active	white
10	BEK'TAL POM	hot	active	white

that by being washed with wild plants, the patient and the sacrificial chickens are being brought into intimate contact with the domain of Nature. On the other hand, because these plants are domesticated in the gardens of the ancestral gods and used by the gods for their baths, it could be said that the patient is imitating the gods' own actions in an effort to conform to their ideal of behavior.

Only two of the "flowers"—the two types of POM—have hot inner souls; another (ZIS ʔUC) has a warm soul; the remaining seven are cold. Apparently the patient has too much "heat" and the bathing is intended to cool him off.

The plants have predominantly "quiet" inner souls; only the ʔAHA-TEʔES, the YIHIL ʔANAL TOH, and the two types of POM are "active," with the ZIS ʔUC being "medium active." Not only is the patient being cooled down, but it appears he is also being quieted by the "flowers" as he bathes in their water.

Finally, note the color characteristics of the plants' inner souls: red, white, and blue-green. YOX symbolizes the center of the universe in most Maya cultures; for the Zinacantecos the "navel of the earth" is Zinacantan Center, which in turn symbolizes the essence of civilized behavior. Hence, blue-green souls appear in the ZAHAL NICIM, symbolizing social order, and in the VIXOBTAKIL, symbolizing the "elder sister assistants of the ancestral gods," who care for the children of the gods at NINAB CILOʔ.

Red symbolizes life blood, a positive force; but if one dreams of red clothing (perhaps because the association implies spilled blood), murder is believed to be imminent. The directional symbolism inherent in color is quite consistent. As is traditional in most Maya cultures, red implies the rising sun. White is associated with waxing sun, increasing in power as it moves northward and provides the longer days of summer. Thus red and white correspond to positive cardinal directions. Zinacantecos sleep with their heads toward the east, alternatively toward the north, but never toward the west or south. The souls of the flowers therefore provide additional protection from the evil associated with the west and the south by re-enforcing these directions through color symbolism. Similarly, the blue-green elements symbolize the process of bringing the patient's soul back into the "center" of social order; the red and white elements reiterate an association with positive directions (east and north) and symbolize the long-range hope that the cooling and quieting of the patient will lead to life, not death.

The explicit message of the bath plants is that they represent the "flowers" with which the ancestral gods bathe; the meta-message that I detect is that the patient has acquired excessive heat and become overactive as his antisocial impulses have channelled him into a socially disruptive situation. He needs to be infused with the cooling and quieting influence of cool and quiet plants from the gardens of the gods. But because being completely cold and quiet is the state of death, limits are placed on the process by use of the hot, active POM. It is crucial that a balance be achieved: neither excessive heat, nor too little heat is desirable. Illness may be associated with either; the ceremonies seek to re-establish a harmonious balance.

According to Anselmo's interpretation, the salient features of the four "flowers" that are bundled to be placed around the corral-bed and tied to the mountain shrines are shown in Table 2. This collection contains a "bundle" of relationships in the thirteen groups of four "flowers" that symbolize the patient's soul. Note especially the order of placement of the "flowers," in a continuum from Nature (outer) to Culture (inner).

The VOHTON ʔEC', which grows higher in trees than does the KRUS ʔEC', resembles a dried unhusked ear of maize at the end of its growth cycle. It appears to symbolize a Zinacanteco who is hot, active, and perhaps approaching prematurely the end of his life—too close to the sun for

Table 2 Some characteristics of bundles of ritual plants.

Order of placement		flower	hot/cold	active/quiet	color
Nature	A	VOHTON ʔEC'	hot	active	red
↓	a	K'OS	cold	quiet	blue-green
	B	ZIS ʔUC	medium	medium	white
	b	ZAHAL NICIM	cold	quiet	blue-green
Culture (patient)					

his own welfare. The K'OS is cool and quieting. The ZIS ʔUC, "fart of the opossum," implies an additional metaphor. The opossum is an anomalous animal that carries its young in a pouch, and hangs by its tail in trees. The "fart" is incompletely digested food; hence, the ZIS ʔUC appears to symbolize something strongly liminal with an unpleasant odor emanating from an anomalous animal. The final element in the bundle is, not surprisingly, the familiar red geranium symbolizing again the "center" of things Zinacanteco, of civilized social order.

In addition, the sequence of plants follows the characteristic arrangement by ranked pairs. VOHTON ʔEC' and ZIS ʔUC are hotter and more active than the plants which immediately follow them, with the former hotter and more active than the latter. Thus, the transition in the sequence of the plants, from hot and active to cool and quiet, is not linear, but progresses by paired degrees. The sequence of A, a, B, b corresponds to the Senior/Junior (BANKILAL/ʔIZ'INAL) arrangement.

The same series is found on the crosses of the mountain shrines, running from the hot, active, red, wild VOHTON ʔEC' on the outside toward Nature to the cold, quiet, blue-green domesticated geranium on the inside toward Culture (facing HTEK-LUM).

The SNIʔ TOH used for the MAK KANTELA are cut from the pine called ʔAHAN TOH, which has a hot, active, red inner soul, the same distinctive features as the VOHTON ʔEC'. But, whereas the latter symbolizes an ear of corn at the end of its growth cycle, the pine symbolizes a green, still growing, vital ear. It is used to brush the patient at the shrines to make him a vital, still growing person and to sweep away the illness. It is then used to "shield the candles," to frame them, and to show the gods that as they consume their tortillas they should reciprocate by making the patient like a green ear of corn rather than a mature, almost dead one.

The Sacrificial Chickens

The black chickens sacrificed in the Great Seeing ceremony are known as K'EXOLILETIK or HELOLILETIK ("substitutes" or "replacements"). Two chickens are generally used: the Senior Substitute, which is sacrificed and left at KALVARYO for the ancestral gods, and the Junior Substitute, which is killed over the patient. In theory, however, a shaman may decide that a black chicken should also be sacrificed and left at anv or all of what Pellizzi (1973) has called the other "nuclear shrines": SAN KIXTOVAL, MUXUL VIZ, and SISIL VIZ. Further, the shaman may decide that a chicken should also be left at BANKILAL MUK'TA VIZ and at the house cross of the patient's house.

Chickens, like the aboriginal domesticated turkeys and other birds which were probably sacrificed in pre-Conquest times, exemplify an overdomesticated or overculturalized nature figure. They have wings, yet cannot fly; they walk on two legs like people, yet are "corraled" by depending upon people to feed them grain; they stay near houses even when not penned and roost in the trees of the house patio at night. Thus, the chicken is an appropriate symbolic mediator between Culture and Nature. They are also prized for food, being preferred for ritual meals; therefore the ancestral gods appreciate it when they are left as offerings (Vogt 1970a; E. Vogt and C. Vogt 1970).

One reason why the chickens *must* be black is probably historical: they replaced the black turkey as ritual mediators. Another reason is that black chickens are believed to have a stronger inner soul—just as black bulls, black goats, and the HʔIK'ALETIK are all believed to be very powerful. And we know that black and red are critically important ceremonial colors in Zinacantan as evidenced by the black ceremonial robes and the bright red turbans worn by the high-ranking cargoholders during their rituals. In this ceremonial regalia, the cargoholders look very like the chickens, whose black feathers and red combs and wattles combine these colors in a similar way. Furthermore, the Tzotzil word for cargoholders and sacrificial chickens is identical: K'EXOLILETIK. The cargoholders are "substitutes" for the ancestral gods that held these positions in the mythological past (in fact, still hold these cargos in the supernatural world inside their mountain homes). The sacrificial chicken serves as a substitute or replacement for the life of the patient when it is offered to the gods. The cargoholder sacrifices time, energy, and resources for the sake of the gods and the benefit of the community; the chicken sacrifices his life for the sake of the patient.

The identification is even closer in some of the cargoholders' prayers. The Grand Alcalde administers the oath of office to an incoming Alférez with these words:

. . . He came to receive,
He came to take,
The holy, divine oath,
Here under your feet,
Here under your hands,
Your servant,
Your rooster.

(Vogt 1969: 490)

Some symbolic mysteries remain. Why two chickens? Why does the patient drink the blood of the first before it is killed at a mountain shrine? Why is the second chicken killed and placed in the corral-bed? Why does the patient consume all of this chicken, and why are the bones and feathers so carefully buried?

Through the name given the chicken—K'EXOLIL or HELOLIL—and through a number of ritual actions, the senior chicken is identified with the patient. It is bathed in the same "flower water" as the patient, censed with the same POM, prayed over as the patient is, and placed on a plate with pine needles and red geraniums—"a bed of flowers." The blood is drained from the chicken's neck, mixed with POX and given to the patient to drink, then daubed on the patient's face and arms, thus transferring the soul of the chicken to the patient.* The patient takes possession of the chicken's soul by drinking its blood, as indicated by one of the verbs used in the prayer at this moment: TA XʔUʔUNIBE, meaning "he incorporates," "he takes possession"—a verb also used for a man taking a wife. The Zinacantecos also express this by saying that the strength of the chicken is thereby absorbed by the patient, giving him more HPWERSA: only the body of the chicken is symbolically given to the gods.

However, if it is the patient's soul which the gods must return, why give them in exchange the

*Although Fabrega and Silver (1973: 184) report that the soul of the chicken is offered to the gods with the body, other field data indicate that the drinking of the blood does indeed transfer the soul of the chicken to the patient.

body of a chicken whose soul has already been consumed? Pellizzi (1973) suggests that the gods must return the patient's *soul*, which is necessary for his survival, in exchange for his *body*, represented symbolically by the bloodless (and soul-less) but still living body of the chicken:

> The gods are rather materialistic after all, and they definitely like flesh, or meat, just like Ladinos and witches . . . this is at the same time a ritual that follows an exchange model—the body of the chicken for the soul of the patient—and a ritual that follows a sympathetic magic/analogical model—the strong soul of the black chicken is supposed to strengthen or attract back the weakened or missing soul of the patient. It appears that the relationship between men and gods is covertly antagonistic. At the onset of the illness a dangerously close relationship has been established in the form of a shaky equilibrium that cannot last. Because if the soul, in the power of the gods, can lead the body to follow, the body, in the power of man, cannot by itself lead the soul to return. It is in this situation that a mediating element must be introduced—the chicken—that can provide the gods with what they were going to get anyway—a body—and the patient with the needed soul. Through this transaction a new equilibrium is established in which the patient seems to get an edge, since the chicken's body cannot really be thought equivalent to man's. But if one considers the whole story from the beginning, when the gods had no food and no souls, one realizes that everybody has gained at the expense of the poor chicken. And the chicken is, one mustn't forget, a domestic animal, belonging to the cultural realm of man from the beginning, like all sacrificial animals. For clarity, the various steps of this process can be summarized by the following diagram:

The junior, or "lesser," chicken is killed over the patient and eaten by him in a procedure that still puzzles me. This act may be construed as helping to restore a balance between Nature and Culture—an offering left out in Nature is balanced by one left in Culture. If this is the case, then the reason the feathers and bones *must* be saved and deeply buried behind the house cross (so deep that dogs or other animals—Nature—cannot dig them up and eat them) is that they are to remain in the domain of Culture.

Another interpretation is embodied in the chicken's relation to the future condition of the patient. Although Zinacantecos are not as explicit about the junior chicken's representing the patient as they are about the senior bird, an identification is clearly being made by its being bathed in the same bath water. (This is further substantiated by the fact that some shamans bathe the patient a second time after returning from the mountain shrines, just before bathing the junior chicken.) In a ritual action emphasizing the decisive act, the shaman calls attention to the fact that he is about to kill the bird. The way the bird dies predicts the patient's future condition. The identification is strengthened by the fact that the shaman tosses the dying bird onto the body of the patient, as if the knowledge of how to die, in which direction to fall, must be procured from the body whose fate that process foretells. The future condition having been revealed, the focus of ritual returns to the present relationship between man and bird: the chicken is placed beside the patient, its head pointing in the same direction; the meat of the dead bird is consumed by the sick man; the inedible bones

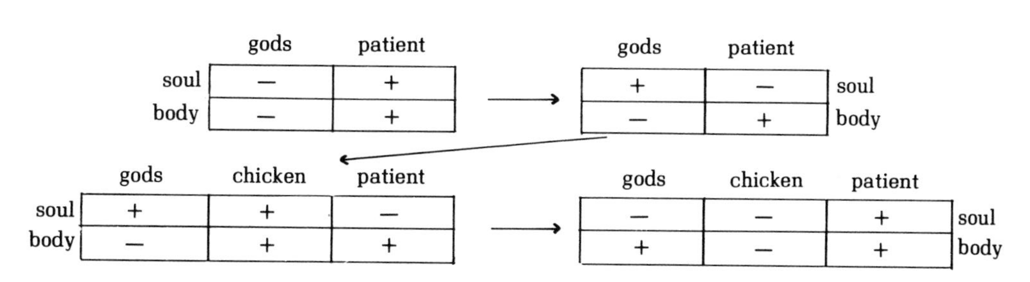

and feathers are interred behind the house cross, the most significant symbol of the dwelling-place of the patient.

Apparently both sacrificial birds are means of establishing communication between men and gods. Symbolically offering himself, the patient sends urgent messages to the gods by way of the senior chicken. He asks that his animal companion be restored to its corral and, as a consequence, that he recover his inner soul and perfect health. He is asking forgiveness for his transgressions, a return to the graces and good favor of the gods. In the case of the "junior" chicken, the flow of communication is in the opposite direction; the message emanates from the gods to the patient. The gods respond to the requests of the patient, making known their answer to his pleas, be it favorable or otherwise, through the behavior of the dying bird. Senior chicken asks the question; junior chicken answers it.

One of the most intriguing aspects of the use of sacrificial chickens in the Great Seeing ceremony is that it represents an exact reversal of details of their use in the house ceremony, C'UL KANTELA. In both ceremonies, communication has been set up between men and gods with the aid of sacrificial chickens. In both cases, mortals seek to please the gods through these sacrifices. In both cases the sacrificial birds are substitutes for the mortal participant (s).

However, in the "Great Seeing," the allocation of the sacrificed chickens is not merely different from, but a neat reversal of, the allocation apparent in the house ceremony. In the former, the blood (inner soul) of the first chicken is consumed by the mortal member (patient) of the interaction between men and gods; in the house ceremony, the blood of the first sacrificial birds is consumed by the gods (the Earth Lord).

The flesh of the first bird is received, in the Great Seeing, by the ancestral gods, and in the house ceremony by the mortals (house-owners). The entire second sacrificial bird (blood and body) is consumed: in the Great Seeing by the mortal participant (patient); in the house ceremony by the deific one (Earth Lord).

Reasons for each specific reversal are elusive, but a clue to their logic can be found in the respective positions of the mortal participants of the two ceremonies vis-à-vis the bounty of the gods. In the Great Seeing the patient's illness results from the gods' disfavor. The patient is not receiving their "gifts" which are necessary for good health—that is, necessary for attaining the equitable, balanced relation between men and gods that is prerequisite to good health. The intent of the Great Seeing, expressed through its prayers, gifts, and other ritual components, is to move the patient from a position of enjoying less than a desired share of the gods' bounty to that of enjoying a "proper" share.

The mortal participants in the house ceremony stand in a significantly different position vis-à-vis the beneficence of the deities. As discussed in Chapter 4, at the time of the ritual the house-owner and his family have already received numerous favors from the gods in the form of mud, thatch, wood, and ground space. Man's concern is to repay, to "give back" favors in an effort to attain a favorable, harmonious relation between men and gods. Thus, the house ceremony seeks to move the house-owner (and, implicitly, all members of his family) from a position of possessing more than a deserved share of the gods' bounty to that of an "ideal" share.

Although the two ceremonies seek to place man in his "ideal" relation to the gods, it is apparent that the direction of one is a reversal of the other.

Maize Divination and Calling the Lost Soul

This ritual complex may be seen as a sequence of episodes which, by a process of creating contiguity, symbolically puts the patient's soul back together again. The shaman blows on the striker, sucks on the patient with the water from the summoner gourd, places the striker under the patient's head and the gourds, salt and ears of maize to the east, all in a process of "micro-adjustment" which culminates with the consumption by the patient of the fifty-two kernels of maize. The kernels are a direct model for the structure of his innate soul. The behavior of the kernels in the bowl of salt water provides a kind of inventory of the current state of the soul, how many parts are "lost." The placing of all fifty-two kernels in one of the summoner gourds provides a symbolic representation of the "complete soul" which the ceremony is supposed to recreate.

The number of kernels is paralleled in the thirteen bundles of four plants each placed around the patient's KORAL and may be a remnant of an earlier belief that relates to some pattern of numeration, calendrical reckoning (in which fifty-two years constituted one cycle), or multiple animal companions. The last is to me a most intriguing possibility: perhaps Zinacantecos once believed that a person's soul was shared with four animal companions located in mountains in the four directions—represented by the white, yellow, red, and black colors of maize—and that each of these shared thirteen parts of the soul. Such a hypothesis would conform to the traditional correspondence between these colors and Maya directional concepts (see Thompson 1934). Another possibility derives from what is known of beliefs in the early colonial period (Calnek 1962): apparently a powerful person in Indian communities could possess a maximum of thirteen associated *nahuals*—wild animals and natural phenomena—while less powerful people possessed proportionately fewer nahuals (see Villa Rojas 1963). The kernels of maize in the divination gourd may therefore somehow represent the greatest possible number of parts of the soul, each associated with all four colors of the maize. Anselmo explained that each color of maize represents three parts of the soul; the thirteenth is represented by the salt. No more than three kernels of each color can be involved in soul loss.

What would happen if the number of kernels pointing upward represented *more* than thirteen parts of the patient's soul? Shamans say this never happens, and, in fact, I have observed that they consistently divine the number of parts lost as being in the range of five to eight. The shamans are, I believe, selecting a "reasonable" number for the missing parts of the soul. If more than eight parts should be lost, the patient would be in serious condition indeed; perhaps he would be beyond the help of a shaman. If fewer than five parts were missing, the family paying for this expensive ceremony might question whether or not it was worthwhile!

The final three episodes focus upon carefully watching and guarding the patient in his very delicate state—delicate because a super dose of heat has been removed in the process of cooling and quieting him down. It is now necessary slowly to build up his heat. In the end, if all goes well, the correct balances between hot and cold, Nature and Culture, and gods and patient are re-established, and the patient, now "healthy," resumes his normal life.

In contrasting games and rituals Lévi-Strauss has written:

> Games thus appear to have a *disjunctive* effect; they end in the establishment of a difference between the individual players or teams where originally there was no indication of inequality. And at the end of the game they are distinguished into winners and losers. Ritual, on the other hand, is the exact reverse; it *conjoins*, for it brings about a union (one might even say communion in this context) or in any case an organic relation between two initially separate groups. In the case of games the symmetry is therefore preordained . . . Asymmetry is engendered . . . The reverse is true of ritual. There is an asymmetry which is postulated in advance between profane and sacred, faithful and officiating, dead and living, initiated and uninitiated, etc. and the "game" consists in making all the participants pass to the winning side by means of

events, the nature and ordering of which is genuinely structural (1966: 32).

In this Zinacanteco Great Seeing ritual there is an asymmetry postulated in advance between Nature and Culture—in the sense that both the patient and his animal companion have become overnaturalized. The ritual moves with a complex but consistent set of metaphors to restore a balance between the two domains as the animal spirit is safely returned to its supernatural corral and the patient is controlled in overt behavior and restored to good grace with his fellow men and the ancestral gods.

In the redundant prayers and behavioral sequences in this rite the Zinacantecos are not only making certain that a message, or lesson, gets transmitted to the patient, but also expressing metaphorically with corrals, "flowers," candles, chickens, maize, food, cane liquor, salt and incense a set of assertions about the paradoxical contradictions in the universe, in their society, and in the soul of man.

7

Waterhole and Lineage Rituals

WATERHOLE AND LINEAGE rites belong to a class of rituals different from those already discussed. Waterhole, lineage, and cargo rituals of various types are called K'IN; this label is seldom applied to house, field, life crisis, or affliction ceremonies.

The difference between K'IN and non-K'IN rituals can be explained in part through analysis of the term. K'IN, which occurs in all Mayan languages, is undoubtedly derived from a Proto-Maya word that means "sun," "day," or "time" (Kaufman 1964: 111). In a book about time and reality in ancient Maya thought, Miguel León-Portilla (1968) provided a brilliant analysis of the concept of *kinh* which is represented as the sun or sun god in the glyphs, the codices, and the post-Conquest texts, such as the Chilam Balam and the Popol Vuh, and symbolizes the basic passage of time. After establishing that the concept of kinh had a divine nature in Maya thought, he discusses more specifically how time was an attribute of the gods. Each period of time was associated with the face of a god, and was "carried" by the god until turned over to his successor at the end of the period. Kinh, therefore, "is a primary reality, divine and limitless . . . In it can be distinguished innumerable moments , each with its own face, carrying a burden which displays its attributes" (León-Portilla 1973: 54). He concluded that space, with its color-directions and layers, was merely a kind of stage for the basic conjunctions of various cycles of time. Kinh was the "cosmic atmosphere" with faces of gods that manifested themselves cyclically, the spatial universe being an immense stage on which the forces of divinity were oriented, entering and leaving the stage in unbroken order. Indeed, according to León-Portilla, the Maya world view might be best characterized as a kind of chronovision, "the conception of a universe in which space, living things, and mankind derive their reality from the ever-changing atmosphere of *kinh*" (1973: 112).

In contemporary Zinacantan the concept of

K'IN designates those ceremonies that are regularly scheduled by the annual solar calendar, now expressed in the succession of saints' days in the Catholic ritual calendar.* Solar symbolism continues to be a crucial aspect of this calendrical reckoning. As Gossen expresses it for Chamula:

In referring to a certain day in relation to the fiesta cycle, one says, for example, "SK'AN TO ˀOSIB K'AK'AL TA K'IN SAN HUAN" ("It is three days until the fiesta of San Juan"). This is usually understood as I have translated it, yet the relationship and similarity of words (K'OK', "fire," and K'AK'AL, "heat" or "day"; K'IN, "fiesta," and K'ISIN, "hot") in the concepts noted above is such that it is possible to understand this as: "three daily cycles of heat before a major (religious) cycle of heat." [This suggests] . . . that the sun and his life-giving heat determine the basic categories of temporal and spatial order (1972: 138).

The basic distinction is thus made between non-K'IN and K'IN ceremonies in Zinacantan. One group of the non-K'IN rituals includes those in which the life cycle of an individual determines when the ceremonies are performed. These rites cannot be locked into solar time. Babies are born approximately nine months after conception, but birth can occur on any day of the year, and the birth ritual must follow immediately. Likewise, the child is baptized, matures and marries, builds a new house, then grows old, dies, and is given a funeral ceremony—all in terms of his or her unique biological cycle. Nor can Zinacantecos predict in terms of the solar calendar the dates and times when illness will occur, or when social and psychological tensions will reach the point at which a ritual of affliction must be performed. All of these rituals are, broadly conceived, "crisis rites" geared to the life cycle.* Other non-K'IN rituals are the maize ceremonies. The maize cycle is more closely related to the solar calendar, since the annual movements of the sun are causally linked to the arrival and departure of the rains and set, within broad limits, the time of planting, weeding, and harvesting of the maize. But since these field ceremonies are not strictly scheduled by certain days in the solar calendar, they are never designated K'IN in the labels applied to them.

The K'IN rituals, strictly calendrical, are repeated each year as the annual ceremonial round unfolds. They are precisely scheduled in terms of solar time, so the designation of K'IN, utilizing the ancient proto-Maya concept, is especially appropriate. These ceremonies have a second defining characteristic: they are public as opposed to domestic. The rites for the life crises of birth, baptism, marriage, death, affliction, or for the new houses or the maize fields, are restricted to the domestic groups for whom they are being performed. The K'IN KRUS and the cargo rites, on the other hand, are being per-

*Because waterhole and lineage ceremonies take place on or around the Day of Santa Cruz, it has been suggested that the word KRUS, of K'IN KRUS, refers to this Catholic saint's day. The explanation is only partial, however, for K'IN KRUS ceremonies are performed not only in May but also in October, at the beginning of the dry season.

*In recent years house-dedication rites, weddings, and funerals that are elaborate enough to include music and fireworks have come to be called SK'INAL, probably indicating that this set of festal characteristics became associated with the "crisis rites" which involved larger groups of people. There was a kind of spill-over from the K'IN ceremonial pattern designated by the term SK'INAL, adding the combined possessive form "s" and "-al" to K'IN, signifying that these rites partake of the more complex "fiesta" pattern. SK'INAL therefore appears to designate a kind of hybrid ceremony, combining certain attributes of the public, calendar-determined K'IN with the basically domestic nature of the non-K'IN ritual (John B. Haviland, personal communication, 15 May 1974). It seems possible that the form has evolved in response to a changing social situation in which increasing numbers of Zinacantecos have both the means and the desire to elaborate a personal and traditional rite with traits that are essentially ladino.

formed for larger groups within the system—lineages, waterhole groups, hamlets, the whole municipio. The domestic rites typically have only one shaman or priest officiating; the public rites involve groups of ritual practitioners.

A third defining characteristic of K'IN ceremonies is the use of percussion (fireworks, drums, rhythmic stamping of dancing feet), something generally absent in non-K'IN rituals.

Waterhole Ceremonies

To survive the long dry season, the Zinacanteco family needs water for cooking, drinking, laundering, and livestock.* Springs, emanating either from caves in the mountains or from fissures at the bottom of limestone sinks, produce abundant waterholes. The lineages living around each form a waterhole group, taking its name from that of the waterhole. Thus, in the hamlet of Paste?, a family might live in BIK'IT VO? (Little Waterhole) or KORAL BURO (Burro Corral). Each waterhole group relates a myth about an ancestral deity who first found the water and established rights to it for his living descendants. These descendants were given access to the waterhole in exchange for proper care of it—that is, cleaning it out and performing the K'IN KRUS ceremony for the waterhole and its associated group twice each year. In May 1960 I attended one of these ceremonies at the Paste? waterhole (Vogt 1969: 447-454, 671-690).

K'IN KRUS TA VO? TA PASTE?

The waterhole called VO? TA PASTE? is located in a limestone sink in the southern part of the hamlet of Paste?, only a few hundred meters from the escarpment that drops off some 6,000 feet to the Rio Grijalva lowlands to the south. The water bubbles out of fissures in the limestone on the side of the sink, where the Zinacantecos have dug and enlarged five openings to provide two for household water, two for laundering, and one for watering livestock.

The waterhole as a whole rarely dries up, severe dry seasons not withstanding, and provides water for some 523 people who live in thirteen SNAs (Figure 25). The waterhole contains two subdivisions. To the west is C'ENTIKAL VO? "water by a cliff," with one opening excavated in the side of the hill and walled in with a cement retaining wall; it is used by SNA CIKU?ETIK and SNA LANTUETIK, lineages living south and west of the waterhole, for drinking water the year around. Another opening to the south is used by the same lineages for washing clothes. To the east three openings around a large sacred tree are called C'IXAL VO? (hawthorn waterhole) and are used by the rest of the SNAs. The three openings provide separate water for household use, for watering animals, and for washing clothes during the rainy season. In the dry season C'IXAL VO? goes dry and all the SNAs use C'ENTIKAL VO?. Because all the households of this waterhole group make use of the water in C'ENTIKAL VO?, they share in the K'IN KRUS ritual for VO? TA PASTE (Vogt 1969: 174-175).

According to the myth related by the inhabitants of VO? TA PASTE?, the original settlers of the hamlet were looking for water when they came across a large live oak tree (CIKIN-IB, *Quercus acatenangensis* Trel.). They decided to dig for water near the tree, working continuously throughout the day. Returning to the site the following morning, the men saw a person standing in place of the oak tree. As they approached, it lost its human form and became the stump of another kind of oak (TULAN). According to my informant, the elusive figure was Marian Perex Xulubte?, an important ancestral deity for the waterhole group, who, through various self-transformations, was indicating to his descendants where water might be found. With new in-

*The hamlet of Paste? and Zinacantan Center have recently built pipelines which carry water from springs on the side of BANKILAL MUK'TA VIZ to hydrant outlets throughout the communities.

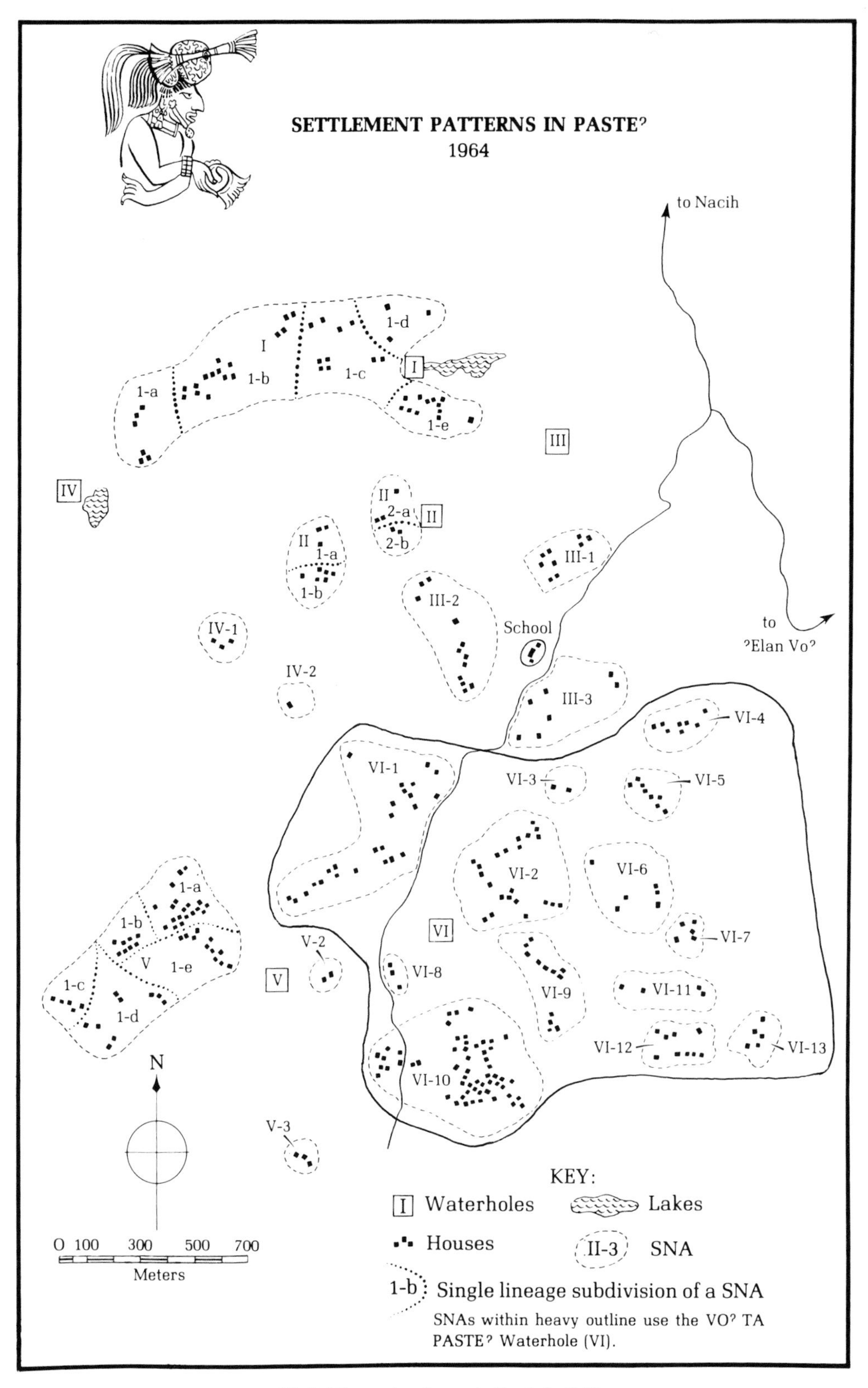

25. Settlement patterns in Pasteˀ, 1964

centive, the men continued to dig and, shortly thereafter, discovered water beneath the tree stump. The site was henceforth called VOˀ TA PASTEˀ, which means "water where he [the ancestor] makes a tree." The TULAN is the sacred MUK'TA TEˀ (Great Tree) which figures prominently in the ritual episodes that follow.

Ceremonial Roles

Shamans. The key figures in the ceremony were the eight male shamans who live in the VOˀ TA PASTEˀ waterhole group. (Female shamans do not participate in public rituals.) They were ranked for seating, walking, drinking, eating, and praying, with the most senior shaman directing the entire ceremony. Each shaman carried a bamboo staff under his left arm while marching from one sacred place to another, and carried or wore his black ceremonial robe. Under his Zinacanteco hat, each wore a kerchief.

Mayordomos. Four Mayordomos were involved: a Senior and Junior Outgoing (or incumbent) Mayordomo, and a Senior and Junior Incoming Mayordomo. Unlike the Mayordomos in Zinacantan Center who are stewards of particular saints, these waterhole group mayordomos had no sacred property to care for, but served, rather, as hosts for the ceremony. All ritual meals and prayers for the candles took place in the house of the Senior Outgoing Mayordomo, which served as headquarters for the ritual. He and the Junior Outgoing Mayordomo shared the cost of the food (maize gruel and tortillas, beef, coffee, and cigarettes). Having held their offices for one year, they were to be replaced by two Incoming Mayordomos; the duty was thus rotated among the heads of all the households in the waterhole group.

TOTILMEˀILETIK. The two eldest and most respected men of the CIKUˀETIK lineage, the largest and dominant SNA of the waterhole group, served as ritual advisers. They sat in honored position at the table for the ritual meals and received food before the others. Their duties consisted primarily of supervising the performance of the ceremony.

Musicians. Two sets of musicians had been recruited by the Outgoing Mayordomos for the ceremony: violin, harp, and guitar players, as well as a flute and two drum players.

Fireworks Men. Two sets of percussion specialists were present: the helpers who carried and set off skyrockets, and other assistants who fired the small hand-held cannon called a KAMARO.

Other Male Helpers. These included men who collected money for the ceremony and made the journey to San Cristóbal for the purchase of candles, liquor, and fireworks; men who gathered the pine-tree tops and pine needles, the palm leaves (C'IB, *chamaedorea* sp.) and the white roses for cross shrines; men who carried the candles and flowers in the ritual processions to the shrines; and, finally, drink-pourers.

Female Helpers. One woman was dispatched to purchase red geraniums from families who grew these flowers in their compound gardens; two were in charge of measuring out the cane liquor from large bottles and pouring it into smaller ones for distribution; another two served as ritual hostesses and supervised the work of twelve other women, who prepared the corn gruel and tortillas for the ritual meals.

A total of some seventy members of the waterhole group participated as ritualists or ritual helpers in the ceremony; not counting small children too young to assist, I estimate that fully one-fifth of the members of the waterhole group were actively involved in designated roles for this one ritual. The K'IN KRUS ritual drama began in the early morning of May 1 and lasted until the early morning of May 3, unfolding in a series of thirteen episodes.

Episode One: Collecting and Counting Money for the Ritual Paraphernalia

Early in the morning of May 1 the men designated money collectors gathered at the house of the Senior Outgoing Mayordomo to discuss with the ranking shaman how much money would be needed to purchase ritual paraphernalia. Having settled on two pesos per household, the men went in pairs to collect. When they returned that afternoon, a table was covered by a cloth, and, under the shaman's supervision, the money was counted. Grains of maize were used: a grain represented 20 centavos; a half-grain 10 centavos. Once the total was calculated, the shaman allocated the quantities to be spent for peso candles, cane liquor, incense, and fireworks. The counting procedure, accompanied by ritual drinking, ended with a ritual meal served on the same table.

Episode Two: Preparing Maize Gruel and Tortillas

In the afternoon of May 1 the women recruited as cooks by the Senior Mayordomo arrived at his house to begin the long process of maize gruel preparation and make the large number of tortillas needed.

Episode Three: Dispatching Assistants for the Ritual Materials

At dawn on May 2 the men who were to purchase or collect ritual materials came to the house of the Senior Mayordomo. They were served a meal and given money and instructions. Those going to San Cristóbal received the money collected from the households and were furnished with tablecloths in which to wrap the candles, kerchiefs to tie around the skyrockets, and jugs in which to carry the cane liquor; they returned at noon with the materials purchased. Other men were sent into the forest to collect wild plants. One man was dispatched to find and bring back white roses from the woods, and a woman was sent to purchase red geraniums from neighboring house compounds. The shamans and musicians, having shared the early morning meal, marched in ritual procession to the waterhole (see Figure 26 for a map of the sacred geography of this ceremony).

The contrast between the tablecloth container for the candles and the kerchief container for the skyrockets should be noted. Both types of ritual materials are "clothed," but the tablecloth (as mentioned in Chapter 3) is similar in design and color not only to women's shawls but also to the material in which they carry babies and wrap tortillas; the association here is with things feminine. The POK' is male attire, worn around the neck or on the head; skyrockets denote the masculine sphere. A second contrast between the sexes is manifested in the collection of the ritual flowers: the white roses are always collected by a man, the red geraniums by a woman.

Episode Four: Cleaning the Waterhole

All available men in the waterhole group gathered at the waterhole shortly after sunrise on May 2, meeting there the already assembled shamans, Mayordomos, and musicians. The string musicians (violin, harp, guitar) formed in rank order on the rising-sun side of the waterhole, the drum and flute players on the setting-sun side. The two groups played alternately while the men, including the shamans and Mayordomos, worked for three hours cleaning out the various openings—removing dead leaves and branches, shoveling out rocks and earth that had fallen into the water caches from their steep banks, and so on. This ritual cleaning brings men into contact with the waterhole openings; during the rest of the year these are part of the domain of the women, who fetch water, launder clothes, and water the sheep. Only when a man waters his horse or mule does he visit the waterhole, and even this is frequently done by women. In contrast, no women were present at the waterhole during the ritual cleaning.

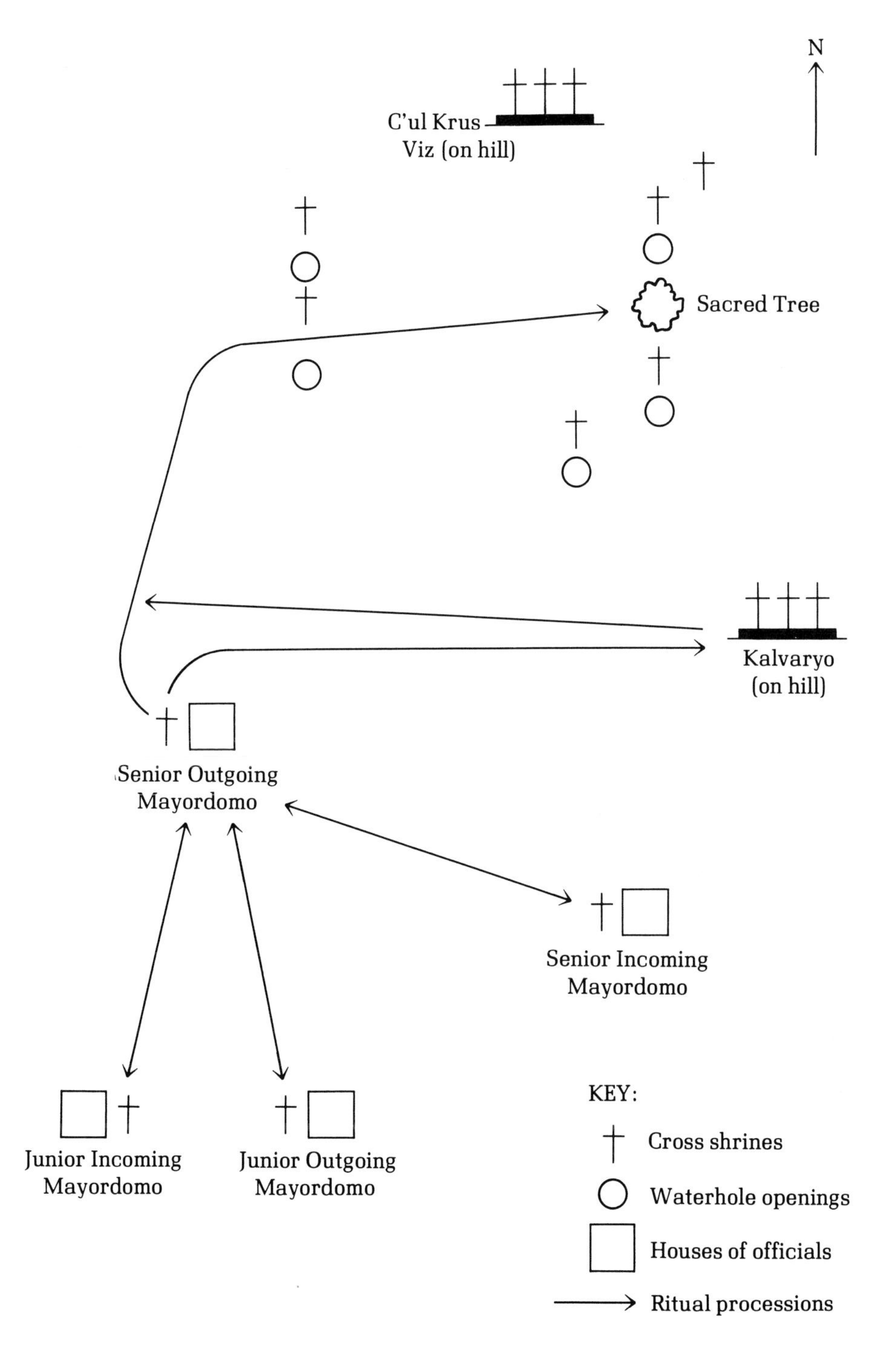

26. The sacred geography of the ceremony

Episode Five: Decorating the Cross Shrines

At 10:30 a.m. the BANKILAL HʔILOL signaled a change in activities. The shamans and Mayordomos formed in rank order, prayed to the waterhole cross by the C'ENTIKAL VOʔ opening, then marched in procession to the sacred tree by the C'IXAL VOʔ openings. Placing their staffs together against the sacred tree, the shamans sat down with the Mayordomos around the trunk in rank order (see Figure 27). Here, under the direction of the Senior Shaman, the shamans divided the pine-tree tops and needles, the palm leaves, and the geraniums and roses among the nine groups of assistants; the latter were then dispatched to decorate the six waterhole cross shrines, the shrine called C'UL KRUS VIZ (Holy Cross Mountain, located on a hill to the north from which the water flows into the waterhole), the KALVARYO for the waterhole group, and the house shrines of the Mayordomos. Each group marched off in rank order, from junior to senior, carrying the materials as follows: the carrier of the pine-tree tops led, followed by the carrier of the palm leaves, the carrier of the geraniums and roses, the carrier of the pine needles, and, finally, the carrier of the skyrockets.

Upon arrival at each of the waterhole and mountain shrines, the assistants tied three pine-tree tops on the cross, then the palm leaves on an arch, then alternated small bunches of red geraniums and white roses on the palm. Finally, the pine needles were sprinkled on the ground to make a carpet in front of the shrine. The house shrines were decorated in a similar manner, but instead of arches, the flowers were tied to the crosses themselves. When the decoration was complete, each group announced the fact by setting off a skyrocket.

Meanwhile, the Senior Shaman held court beside the waterhole, listening to disputes within the waterhole group and trying to settle them equitably. The most serious case that day concerned one family's having refused to pay the two-peso levy for the waterhole ceremony; the family was forced to pay.

Episode Six: Eating the Ritual Meal

Around 2:00 p.m. the entire group marched from the waterhole to the house of the Senior Outgoing Mayordomo. The Mayordomos and shamans knelt and prayed before the house cross—Mayordomos in pairs, Juniors followed by Seniors; shamans in groups of three. The prayer, in part, went as follows:

In the divine name of Jesus Christ, my Lord,
  How much, my Father,
  How much, my Lord,
    My lowly earth has come
    My lowly mud has come [I am in your presence].

How strongly I beseech divine pardon,
How strongly I beg divine forgiveness;
  So shall we make ready,
  So shall we perform it [the ritual].

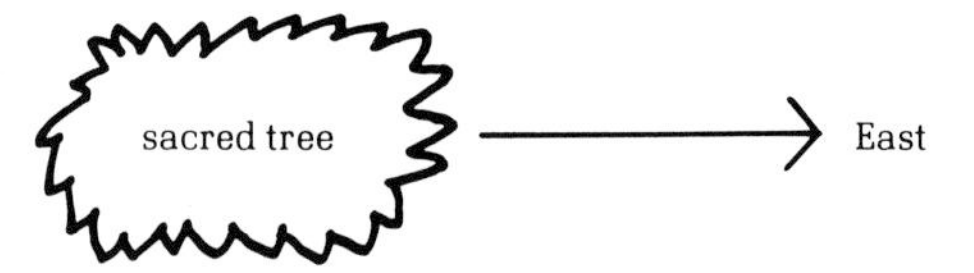

27. The seating order of the ritual specialists

Receive this lowly little bit, then,
This humble amount, then,
If you will accept it with good grace,
If you will await it with good grace,
This lowly little bit, then,
This humble amount, then.
Receive this lowly splinter of our pine,*
Receive this lowly dripping of our candle.
. . .

Receive this, that you let nothing happen to them,
That you let them encounter nothing,
All the little ones,
All the big ones,
All the running ones,
All the perched ones,†
For this I beseech divine pardon,
For this I beg divine forgiveness,
At your holy sides,
At your holy front. . . .

I cannot beseech if there is not pardon,
I cannot beg if there is no forgiveness,
Do not ignore our crying,
Do not ignore our sobbing,
We, your sons,
Your children,
Your flowers,
Your offspring . . .

The ritualists then entered the house and bowed to the two old women hostesses. The shamans placed their staffs against the wall in the northeast corner, then the ritualists seated themselves for the ritual meal in the order shown in Figure 28. The meal followed the patterned sequence described in Chapter 3, except that the first course consisted of maize gruel served in gourd bowls and the second of tortillas and beef in broth flavored with chili and mint. The innate souls of beef, chili, and mint are considered extremely "hot"; these foods denote the intensified heat of the ritualists.

When the ritualists and the violin-harp-guitar players had finished, they left the house in order to make room for other assistants, and the drum and flute players, at the table. The younger male helpers were served later outside the house, the women eating at their place by the fire after the men and boys had finished.

Episode Seven: Viewing the Candles
[K'EL-KANTELA]

Two paper bundles of one-peso white wax candles were placed on the ritual table, previously covered with the tablecloth used to carry the candles from San Cristóbal, tips toward rising sun, bases toward setting sun. A very careful distribution of other materials followed: a jug of cane liquor was poured by the women "measurers" into liter bottles and, from these, redistributed in small bottles provided by each ritualist and helper; cigarettes, too, were distributed among ritualists and helpers. The candles were unwrapped and placed on the table as before, with the paper flowers which came tied to the candles from the San Cristóbal store, and the red geraniums arranged symmetrically around their tips.

Episode Eight: Praying over the Candles

The shamans donned their ceremonial robes, placed their untied kerchiefs over their heads, and began chanting a long prayer. The praying was initiated by Number 1 and Number 2 shamans, holding smoking censers of two kinds of POM in their right hands. As they prayed, they intermittently rotated the censers counterclockwise over the candles. Numbers 3 and 4 shamans then took the censers and led the praying, fol-

*Refers to the "torch," the candle. Such passages suggest that pine torches may have been used in these rites before the Spaniards introduced candles.

†"little ones," "big ones," "running ones," "perched ones" refer to ages, with "running ones" small children and "perched ones" babies carried on their mothers' backs.

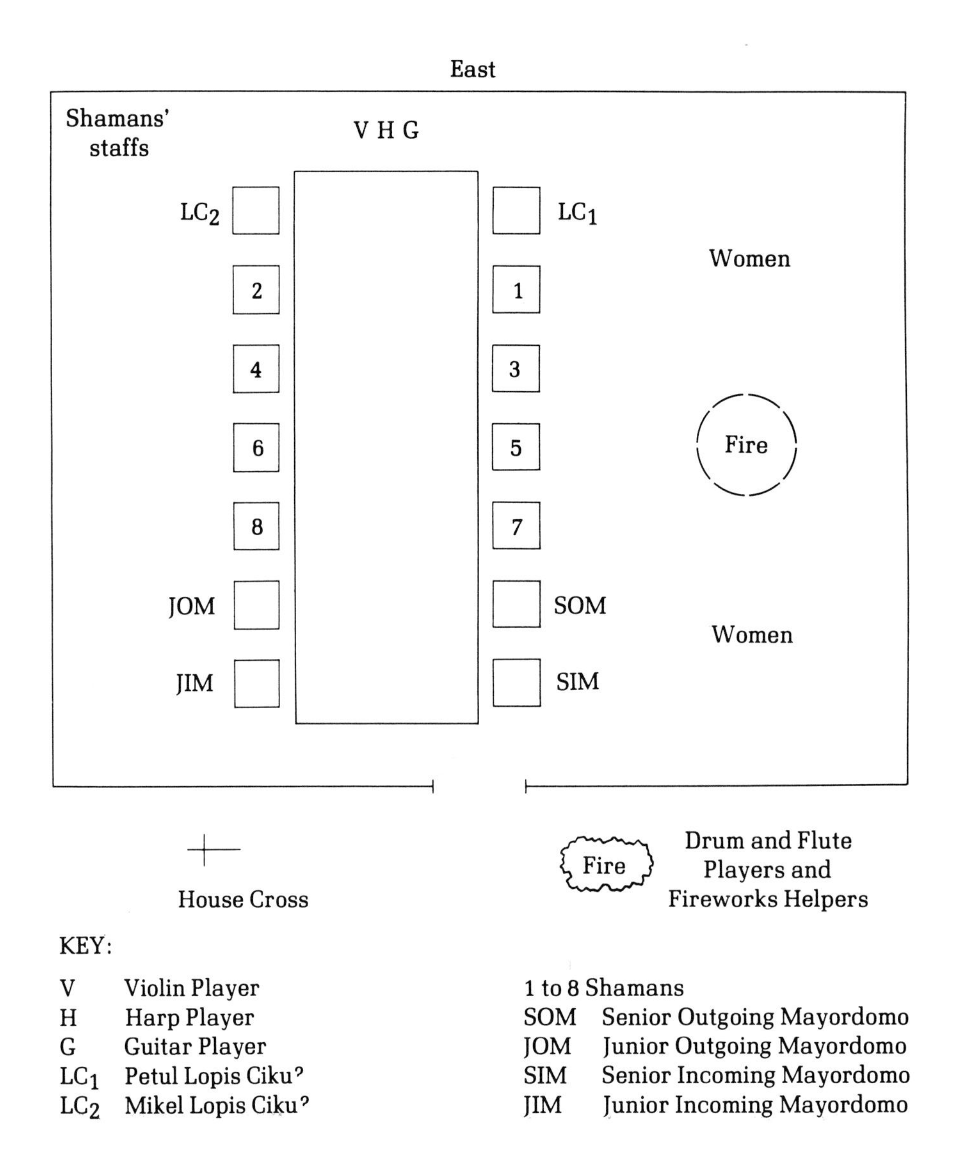

28. Seating order in the Senior Mayordomo's house

lowed in turn by Numbers 5 and 6, 7 and 8, and then 1 and 2 again. This procedure was repeated three times.

Episode Nine: Offering Candles at House Shrines and KALVARYO

The four Mayordomos, each having received three candles wrapped at the bases with a tablecloth, knelt at the foot of the table to pray. They set off then for their respective house crosses, each man accompanied by a junior shaman (Numbers 5, 6, 7, and 8); the Mayordomo, carrying the candles, walked in front, followed by the shaman with his staff. At the house cross both greeted the shrine. The shaman lit the candles in front of the cross and poured cane liquor on the ground around them. Both men knelt, the shaman on the right chanting a prayer that the Mayordomo repeated antiphonally. Three rounds of coffee, laced with cane liquor, followed.

The two senior shamans and the stringed-instrument players remained at the house of the Senior Mayordomo. Numbers 3 and 4 shamans, accompanied by a candle-carrier and the drum and flute players, went to the KALVARYO of the waterhole group. A passage from my field notes described the scene:

> The spectacle was one to excite the interest of even the most jaded anthropologist. Never have I seen a wilder scene! Flickering light from the three candles tied as one in the altar pit and from a small fire the drums and flute players had made to keep warm in the cold night air illuminated the cross with its pine and flower decorations, and the shamans were kneeling and praying before it. From time to time, they bowed low until their foreheads touched the ground, chanting continuously. Incense was thick in the air despite the strong wind; skyrockets were being shot off periodically, and the flute and drum music vied with the wind, the chanting, and the fireworks resounding in one's ear (Vogt 1969: 453).

The prayer went, in part:

In the divine name of God, Jesus Christ, my lord,
Take these, then, my Father,
Take these, then, my Lord,
Holy Fathers,
Holy Mothers, . . .

Holy KALVARYO, holy Father,
Holy KALVARYO, holy Mother,
Holy KALVARYO, holy ancient one,
Holy KALVARYO, holy yellow one [face of very old person],
Holy seas [aged persons],
Holy ancient ones,
Holy meeting-place,
Holy gathering-place,
Holy place of recovery,
Holy place of rest; . . .

Receive, San Cristóbal, holy Father,
San Cristóbal, holy Mother,
Receive, divine salty spring (NINAB CILOʔ) of the holy Fathers,
Divine salty spring of the holy Mothers,
Receive, divine María Cecilia [SISIL VIZ],
Divine Maria Mushul [MUXUL VIZ],
Four holy Fathers,
Four holy Mothers;* . . .

Receive, holy white cave, holy Father [SAK-C'EN],
Holy white cave, holy Mother,
With the great mountain, holy Fathers [BANKILAL MUK'TA VIZ],
With the great mountain, holy Mothers,
Great mountain, holy ancient ones,
Great mountain, holy yellow ones,
Receive, three holy hearthstones, holy Fathers,†
Three holy hearthstones, holy Mothers, ...

*The four important mountain homes of ancestral gods visited most commonly by ritual pilgrimages: KALVARYO, SAN KIXTOVAL VIZ, SISIL VIZ, MUXUL VIZ.

†That is, ʔOX YOKET, the ritual term for BANKILAL MUK'TA VIZ and the other two peaks nearby; the three surround a crater of an extinct volcano, and, from a distance, look like three gigantic hearth-stones —hence the name ʔOX (three) YOKET (hearthstones).

Receive this much, you who are with our holy purchaser,
With our holy payer,
With the Señor Esquipulas, my Father,
Esquipulas, my Lord,
With the divine martyr, my Father,
The divine martyr, my Lord . . .

You are seated then,
You are on bended knees,
In the middle of the holy sky,
In the middle of the holy sky,
In the middle of the holy glory [center of VINAHEL]; . . .

VAXAK-MEN, holy Fathers,
VAXAK-MEN, holy Mothers,
Receive this, then, Father,
Receive this, then, Lord,
This much that you have left,
This much that you have abandoned,
When the holy earth was made,
When the holy world was made. . . .

In unison, then,
In accord, then,
Do the favor,
Take the trouble,
Observe us here ever,
Encircle us here ever,
That we borrow still,
That we share still,
Your holy grace,
Your holy benediction. . . .

Episode Ten: Offering Candles at the Waterhole Shrines

After the shamans (except Numbers 3 and 4) and Mayordomos returned to the host's house, the remaining candles, wrapped in tablecloths, were given to the Incoming Mayordomos, who were to serve as candle-bearers in the ensuing procession. At 11:00 p.m. all the ritualists marched to the sacred tree by the waterhole, joined en route by shamans 3 and 4. There they seated themselves in the pattern described in Episode Five and engaged in ritual drinking until midnight—the beginning of May 3, the Day of Santa Cruz.

At midnight, the four senior shamans rose, lighted three candles, and prayed at the shrine south of the sacred tree; the four junior shamans lighted three candles and prayed at the shrine north of the sacred tree. Subsequently, they lighted candles and prayed at the waterhole shrines, moving from south to north and east to west. When all the shrines had been visited, they returned to the sacred tree for another period of ritual drinking.

Episode Eleven: Offering Candles at C'UL KRUS VIZ

Around 3:00 a.m. the entire procession climbed the hill to the north known as Holy Cross Mountain where the shamans placed candles in front of the shrine and prayed to this C'UL KRUS VIZ, the source of water for the waterhole group. The relation of the houses of the waterhole group (represented by the houses of the four Mayordomos) to its KALVARYO shrine, where the ancestral gods gather to meet and to receive their candle-tortillas, is structurally paralleled by the relation of the waterhole openings, from which the Earth Lord allows the people to draw water, to the Holy Cross Mountain shrine, which is the source of that water and the residence of the local Earth Lord.

Episode Twelve: Dancing by the Waterhole

At dawn the ritual procession descended the mountain and returned to the waterhole; there the junior shamans and Mayordomos danced to the music of the violin, harp, and guitar.

Episode Thirteen: Eating the Final Ritual Meal

Shortly after sunrise the procession returned to the Senior Mayordomo's house. After praying at the house cross, the ritualists entered in rank formation, greeted the hostesses, and seated themselves at the table for the ritual meal which concluded the waterhole ceremony.

Lineage Ceremonies

Each localized patrilineage in Zinacantan lives on inherited lands consisting of house sites and small surrounding fields of maize. One or more of the localized patrilineages who live on adjacent lands form a basic subdivision of a waterhole group. A SNA's structure is most clearly revealed by the K'IN KRUS ceremony, which expresses the rights and obligations of its members to the lands they have inherited. What follows is a description and interpretation of the K'IN KRUS TA SNA CIKUˀETIK that I attended in May 1960 (described also in Vogt 1969: 454-455, 690-695).

K'IN KRUS TA SNA CIKUˀETIK

SNA CIKUˀETIK is large, compact, and cohesive, situated on the very edge of the escarpment at the southern end of Pasteˀ. From its thatched houses distributed over several small hills, one can look down to the Grijalva River, 6,000 feet below, and beyond to the distant mountain ranges.

The CIKUˀETIK draw their water from VOˀ TA PASTEˀ. The SNA is centered around the LOPIS CIKUˀ lineage, whose members were the original settlers on these lands; it also includes members of three other lineages (VASKIS XULHOLETIK, MARTINIS KAPITANETIK, and KOMIS LOTRIKOETIK) who married into the unit and acquired neighboring lands. The SNA is comparatively large—(185 members in 1960)—and possesses special sacred property in the form of a Virgen de Rosario, kept in a small, improvised chapel.*

*In 1971 this Virgen de Rosario became the focus for the construction and formal establishment of a Catholic chapel comparable to those in the hamlets of ˀAz'am, Nabencauk, ˀApas, and Nacih.

Ceremonial Roles

Shamans. Four SNA shamans were key figures in the ceremony. The number of shamans was increasing, I learned from one elderly informant; a few years previous there had been only one. The three who had recently made their debuts were ranked Numbers 2, 3, and 4 under the senior shaman, who directed this ritual. All four carried or wore their black ceremonial robes, had kerchiefs tied about their heads under their traditional palm hats, and carried bamboo staffs when they walked in procession.

Mayordomos. As in the K'IN KRUS TA VOˀ, four Mayordomos hosted this K'IN KRUS TA SNA: a Senior and Junior Outgoing Mayordomo and a Senior and Junior Incoming Mayordomo. The Senior Outgoing Mayordomo's house served as headquarters, and the Outgoing Mayordomos shared the cost of the food, which, in this case, included chicken in place of beef. These Mayordomos were stewards of the Virgin of Rosario, in charge of caring for the statue of that saint. The Senior Incoming Mayordomo was a very young boy, no more than eleven or twelve years of age. Upon questioning, I was told that every older man had served his tour of duty as a Mayordomo; according to the scale of seniority, the boy was the logical choice for the position.

TOTILMEˀILETIK. Petul and Mikel Lopis Cikuˀ, the two old men who had served in the K'IN KRUS TA VOˀ, again were the ritual advisers.

Musicians. The same sets of musicians as had performed at the K'IN KRUS TA VOˀ took part in this ceremony.

Fireworks men. Skyrocket men, but no cannoneers participated.

Other male and female helpers. The roles of these assistants were the same as those observed in the K'IN KRUS TA VOˀ. A total of some forty members of the SNA assumed ritualist or assistant roles of various kinds. Not counting small children, more than one-third of the members of the SNA were actively involved in the ceremony.

The nine-episode ceremony began on May 4 and ended on May 6.

Episode One: Collecting and Counting Money for the Ritual Paraphernalia
Episode Two: Preparing Maize Gruel and Tortillas

These first two episodes occurred on the first day and were similar to the corresponding ones described for the waterhole ceremony, the only difference being that in Episode One the shaman distributed money for the purchase of 50-centavo, rather than one-peso size, candles.

Episode Three: Dispatching Ritual Assistants for Collection of Ritual Materials

This took place the morning of May 5 and followed the format described for the waterhole ceremony.

Episode Four: Decorating the Shrines

The eleven shrines to be visited on the ceremonial circuit were decorated by the sweepers and other ritual assistants early in the afternoon of May 5. Each cross shrine was decorated with pine trees, palm leaves, and red geraniums. An arch of alternating bunches of red geraniums and white roses was added to the shrine for the Virgin of Rosario.

Episode Five: Eating the Ritual Meal

Around 3:00 P.M. the ritualists and helpers assembled at the Senior Outgoing Mayordomo's oak-brush shelter, which had been constructed adjacent to his small house to accommodate the numerous ritualists. They sat down in rank order to a ritual meal of maize gruel followed by chicken and tortillas.

Episode Six: Inspecting the Candles
Episode Seven: Praying Over the Candles

Episodes Six and Seven followed the same patterns as observed in the waterhole ceremony.

Episode Eight: Offering Candles on the Ceremonial Circuit

This began around 7:00 P.M. on May 5 and lasted throughout the night and past sunrise on May 6. The most important episode, it was the one that most differed from the waterhole ceremony. Eleven sacred shrines were visited by the procession, which made a counterclockwise circuit around the homes and lands of the CIKUˀETIK.

After lighting three candles and praying at the house cross of the Senior Outgoing Mayordomo, the procession set out in the following rank order: the two skyrocket men; flute and drum players—flute followed by large then small drum; the Mayordomos—Senior Outgoing, Junior Outgoing, Senior Incoming, Junior Incoming; the stringed instrument players—guitar, harp, then violin; and the shamans—junior to senior.

Upon arrival at the decorated crosses, the shamans lit the candles carried by the Incoming Mayordomos and prayed. Arrivals and departures at shrines were heralded by two skyrocket blasts. The shrines, in order visited, were: the house cross of the Junior Outgoing Mayordomo; C'UT TON (rock on the side of a cliff), located at the base of a small cliff in a limestone sink, below a prominent rock also called C'UT TON; the house cross of the Senior Incoming Mayordomo, where chairs and benches were arranged around the patio for ritual participants observing the candle offerings and prayers of the shamans; a cross under a very large *matasano* tree, known as YOLON ˀAHTEˀ (beneath the matasano tree). The fifth shrine was the SNA HC'UL-MEˀTIK ROSARIO, the small wattle-and-daub chapel of the Virgin. The Virgin was striking: she had a very brown face; long, colored ribbons streamed down her breast; and the tiny face of her infant peeked out from the folds of her shawl. The meter-high platform on which the statue stood was decorated with three pine-tree tops, palm leaves, and an arch of geraniums and roses. The floor was covered with a carpet of pine needles.

Four candleholders had been placed on the floor in front of the image: three everyday ones, and a ritual one shaped like a bull. After the shamans had offered candles and prayed, the two junior shamans and the four Mayordomos danced to the music of the stringed instruments from 1:30 to 2:30 A.M. (The flute and drums remained outside.) Next came ?IZ'INAL KALVARYO, the junior meeting place of the ancestral gods, located on top of a precipitous hill. Many pine torches held by the assistants lit the way. The seventh, BANKILAL C'UT C'EN (senior stomach cave), was located at the side of another deep limestone sink. Here there is a large limestone rock protruding from the cliff which is conceived to be the stomach of the Earth Lord. Because of the shrine's association with the Earth Lord the participants seemed more subdued; an aura of tension and fear came over the procession. Number 2 shaman, a specialist in the ceremony which retrieves lost souls from the Earth Lord, directed the ritual and initiated the praying. At this shrine, the candles were tied in threes and then stuck into a natural hole in the limestone, explicitly the "stomach of the Earth Lord." Dawn broke at 5:30 A.M. while the ritual was still in progress at the shrine. The last shrines visited were: BANKILAL KALVARYO, the senior meeting place of the ancestral gods; ?IZ'INAL C'UT C'EN (junior stomach cave), where the same kind of ceremony was performed as at BANKILAL C'UT C'EN; the house cross of the Junior Incoming Mayordomo; and, finally, the house cross of the Senior Outgoing Mayordomo, where the last candles were offered.

Episode Nine: Eating the Final Ritual Meal

The K'IN KRUS formally ended with a ritual meal of chicken and tortillas at the home of the Senior Outgoing Mayordomo.

Variations in the K'IN KRUS Rituals

I have described the most elaborate form of the K'IN KRUS rituals performed in hamlets with widely dispersed settlement patterns, such as Paste?, Pat?osil, and Vo? C'oh Vo?. The social composition of K'IN KRUS ceremonies varies somewhat among the different waterhole groups within the hamlet of Paste?, and even more noticeably from hamlet to hamlet within the municipio. The basic determinant appears to be the compactness of settlement. For example, two waterhole groups (VOM C'EN and XUL VO?) in the hamlet of Paste? display significantly greater settlement density than the other four. In these two groups, K'IN KRUS lineage rituals are not performed as distinct SNA ceremonies; rather, the two large K'IN KRUS rituals enacted each year combine the necessary ceremonies for both the waterhole and the lineage K'IN KRUS. The cross shrines of the waterhole and those of both lineages are visited in one long ceremonial circuit (Vogt 1969: 176). Similarly, in compact hamlets such as Nabencauk and Nacih, a combined K'IN KRUS is performed by waterhole groups, with ceremonial circuits visiting both the shrines for the waterhole and those of the lineages living around the waterhole. Finally, in the most compact hamlets, such as ?Apas, where over seven hundred people live in a very small area, the K'IN KRUS is performed cooperatively by the entire hamlet, and the ceremonial circuit includes visits to the shrines of all the waterholes and lineages of the hamlet in one coordinated ritual.

Interpretations of K'IN KRUS Rituals

What distinguishes K'IN KRUS rituals from other Zinacanteco rites?

At the most concrete level these rituals focus on *water* and *land*, two of the most critically scarce resources in the Highlands of Chiapas. They explicitly express the exclusive rights and obligations of particular groups of Zinacantecos concerning the use of specified waterholes and particular lands for their houses and fields. The ritual messages say, in effect: "this is our waterhole which our ancestors discovered and which we now use and care for"; and "these are our lands, settled by our ancestors and now used by us." But both waterholes and lands are believed ultimately to belong to the Earth Lord. One cannot take or use anything from his domain without compensation. One aspect of the ritual thus involves offering candles, prayers, liquor, and incense at decorated shrines to please him. On the other hand, the Zinacantecos would not possess rights to their waterholes or lands had these resources not been discovered and bequeathed to them by their ancestral deities. These TOTIL MEʔILETIK are not only the first possessors of these rights to water and land, but also the source of the traditional knowledge and power which can deal with the greedy Earth Lord. They too must therefore be honored with candles, prayers, cane liquor, and copal incense at florally decorated shrines. This, in effect, is a second function of the K'IN KRUS rituals.

Structure and Phasing of the K'IN KRUS Rituals

According to Zinacanteco informants, the cross shrines by the five waterhole openings at VOʔ TA PASTEʔ are called KRUS TA TIʔ VOʔ (literally "cross at the edge of the waterhole") and are means of communication with the Earth Lord. All of the water comes from the hill immediately north of the waterhole; thus the shrine at this hill is also a communication link to the Earth Lord. On the other hand, the ancestral gods (immediate ancestors of the Mayordomos) are reached via house crosses, and via the KALVARYO, the meeting-place of the ancestral gods of this waterhole group. Finally, the ancestor responsible for finding the water in the mythological past is symbolized by the sacred oak tree, around which the ritualists sit while at the waterhole, and whose presence provides a comforting backdrop for the necessary ritual communication with the Earth Lord at the waterhole crosses.

This waterhole ritual reveals a distinctive spatial and temporal shape. The ceremonial drama is phased between two "stages": the waterhole and the houses. It "pulsates," so to speak, between communication with the Earth Lord and with the ancestral gods. There is a kind of mirror symmetry between these two branches of the ritual, both in geography and in the timing of sequences. Geographically, the waterhole and shrines of the Earth Lord are located at lower elevations, the cross shrines of the Mayordomos and at KALVARYO at higher ones. Similarly, in timing, the action moves from house to waterhole (cleaning the waterhole and decorating the shrines) to house again (for a meal and offerings at the ancestral deity shrines), back to the waterhole (offerings and dancing), before finally returning to the Mayordomo's house for the ritual meal.

The ceremony thus has two spatial and temporal frames (cf. Douglas 1966: 63-64); by combining them (Figure 29), the general structure of the ritual evolves, a structure that builds in a binary discrimination between the Earth Lord and the ancestral gods in a manner that differs significantly from that of the lineage ceremony to be discussed later. Within these two large subdivisions, smaller frames reveal their own pulsations. Thus, in the case of the limestone sinks, the sacred oak tree serves as ritual headquarters. From here groups disperse to decorate the cross shrines and return to the waterhole during early episodes; from here they depart again to offer candles and pray and return to dance in the final episodes at the waterhole. In the case of the houses, where the home of the Senior Outgoing Mayordomo is headquarters, groups alternately disperse to offer candles and pray at the shrines and return to the focal meeting-place.

The interaction between the ritualists and the gods in the K'IN KRUS TA SNA follows a markedly different format. Although the ritualists communicate with both the ancestral gods and

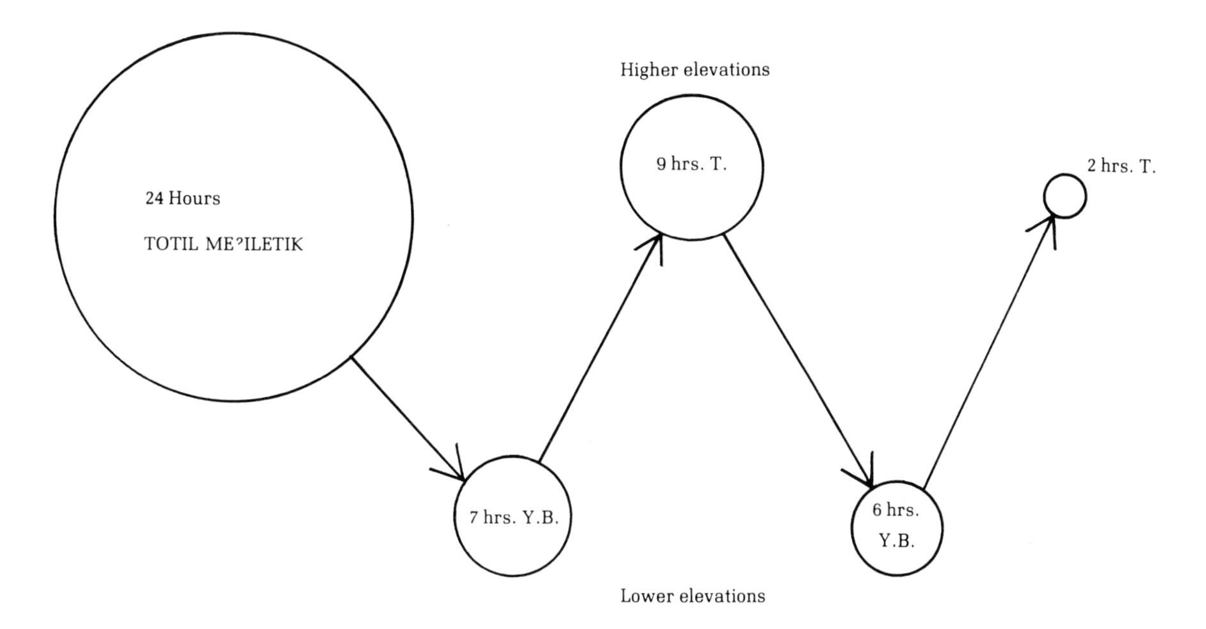

29. Combined spatial and temporal shape

the Earth Lord, as in the waterhole ceremony, the ceremonial circuit reveals a different shape. It commences at the house of the Senior Outgoing Mayordomo, but instead of pulsating between two spatial and temporal frames, it makes one continuous, counterclockwise circuit, communicating as it goes with ancestral gods (at house crosses, KALVARYO shrines, and a sacred matasano tree), the Earth Lord (in three limestone sinks), and with the Virgen de Rosario in her chapel. Thus, its spatial frame connects men, gods, and saints in a continuous and neverending way. Similarly, the temporal frame in this case is outlined in one continuous ritual sequence that progresses unidirectionally from beginning to end, starting and ending at the Senior Mayordomo's home.

The differences in the spatial frames of the two ceremonies seem to reflect different aspects of Zinacanteco life in the hamlets. The pulsation in the K'IN KRUS for the waterhole relates to the daily trips to and from the waterhole; the encircling movement in the lineage K'IN KRUS encloses and protects its lands.

Ritual Delineations

Moving a notch away from the concrete symbolism in the K'IN KRUS—symbolism about which the Zinacantecos themselves are quite articulate—the ethnographic observer perceives metaphoric messages in these rituals that concern the structure and dynamics of the Zinacanteco natural and social universe. One of the important functions of ritual symbols is to reinforce basic cultural categories. This is accomplished in part by the use of "boundary" or delimiting ritual activities. Rituals may delineate temporal, social, or spatial categories.

K'IN KRUS rituals contain many symbols which differentiate crucial categories in the natural and social world and provide means of mediating between oppositions that occur in the categories. The rites differentiate between two fundamental subdivisions of the natural year in the Highlands of Chiapas: the dry and rainy seasons. Recall that the rituals are performed at the time of the onset of the rains, in May, and at the departure of the rains, in October. In one symbolic sense, the May offerings may be interpreted as insuring that all is well in relation to the gods who control the rain; in October, they express appreciation for the rainy season just ended. But in another, perhaps more fundamental sense, the rituals highlight and reconfirm the dry/rainy distinction upon which the Zinacanteco relies. The availability of water and productivity of the land depend on the normal fluctuation of seasons which is the work of the gods. So the smoking copal incense and fireworks are metaphors for the fundamental change of the seasons: cloud and rain symbolism are present in the incense and in the explosive force—like lightning and thunder—of the fireworks.

The K'IN KRUS rites also express differentiation among structural units in Zinacanteco society. The waterhole ritual provides a setting in which a structurally significant unit is confirmed and regenerated twice a year, as male members of the waterhole group congregate to clean the waterhole, compensate the Earth Lord, and make offerings to their ancestral gods. The lineage ritual assembles the SNA for the semi-annual definition of its physical and social boundaries.

These rituals also utilize a series of distinctive metaphors to express the sharp boundaries drawn between male and female domains and to mediate this opposition. The ritualists, as well as the helpers who accompany the processions, are all men; women remain at home to cook. The closest approximation to a female ritual role is found in the woman who collects the red geraniums—the symbol of domesticity—and the two elderly hostesses at the home of the Senior Mayordomo. This male/female opposition is further emphasized in the use of the woman's tablecloth for wrapping the candles, the man's kerchief for wrapping the skyrockets. Even more significant is the mediation between maleness and femaleness achieved in the waterhole ceremony. The waterhole itself, which belongs to the female domain most of the year, falls under the jurisdiction of males during the semi-annual ritual. Its normal usage is suspended, while the men purify it, literally and ritually. This ritual reversal of the normal state of affairs provides for mediation between the two domains as the men interact with and pay homage to the "female" waterhole and the "female" saint.

Certain crucial spatial boundaries in the Zinacanteco universe are drawn in K'IN KRUS rituals. The domains of the Earth Lord and the ancestral gods are differentiated in the two frames I described for the waterhole ceremony: one with the shrines for the waterhole openings and Holy Cross Mountain; the other with the Mayordomos' shrines and the meeting-place of the ancestral gods. The Earth Lord is also definitively separated from the ancestral gods in the two types of shrines visited on the ceremonial circuit of the lineage ceremony. An even more fundamental spatial delineation is achieved in the rituals: NAETIK is separated from TEʔTIK, houses from forest, Culture from Nature. The processions of the waterhole and lineage ceremonies encircle the culturally utilized parts of the local environment; beyond lies the wild forest penetrated by Zinacantecos only for the collection of wild plants or firewood or the pasturing of sheep. This ritual boundary is especially vivid in the counterclockwise circuit of the SNA ritual which encircles the houses and fields of the lineage. Inside the circuit is the safe, familiar, socially ordered part of the universe; outside, the dangerous, unfamiliar, uncivilized. The cross shrines themselves differentiate NAETIK from TEʔTIK. The outsides of all the shrines (facing TEʔTIK) are decorated with pine trees; the insides, (facing NAETIK) with red geraniums (cf. Laughlin 1962b).

The series of ritual episodes performed on the inside, express the fundamentals of Zinacanteco social order in microcosm: ritual meals, ritual drinking, preparation of the candles. Since candles symbolize not only "tortillas" but also the essence of a "standing-up Zinacanteco" (a healthy and respect-worthy Zinacanteco) when offered to the gods at the shrines, the prayers and censing are "civilizing agents," symbolically converting the candles into tortillas, into perfectly socialized persons.

All the "culturalizing" agents in the ceremonies are involved with "heat": the heat of the fire to cook tortillas; the heat of the burning incense over the candles; the heat needed to produce cane liquor; the heat needed to grow flowers for the shrines. The more perfectly socialized a Zinacanteco is, the "hotter" he is—the more he partakes of HC'UL-TOTIK. Therefore, by censing the candles, shamans create acceptable offerings from cold, "uncivilized" ones, reiterating through metaphor the pre-eminence of civilized behavior and the undesirability of antisocial, destructive activity.

Temporal Symbolism

Returning to the point that these ceremonies are designated by the ancient Maya word kinh, it is probable that the ceremonial circuits are also marking the passage of calendrically reckoned solar time.

One of the critical defining characteristics of K'IN-type rituals is percussion. Why should K'IN rituals have percussion, while non-K'IN rituals do not? Rodney Needham (1967: 613) has suggested that "there is a connexion between percussion and transition"—for example, a shaman beating on a drum to make contact with the spiritual world, the setting off of fireworks in a *rite de passage*, as in a Chinese wedding. The rhythmic percussion of Zinacanteco ceremonies appears to conform to this analysis: the drums play when the ritualists are in procession from one sacred place to another; fireworks are set off when the ritualists arrive at or depart from a shrine. The uniquely public character of the K'IN ceremonies is thereby emphasized: episodes and sequences are signalled to the entire social group on whose behalf they are performed. Concomitantly, the progress of time itself is beaten out.

It follows that percussion is absent in non-K'IN ceremonies, for these involve a need to drop out of calendrical and public time and into a time concept determined by an individual life cycle. By avoiding percussive sounds, these rites make "a hole in time" (or avoid time) for a period long enough to create a life (birth), to heal (curing ceremony), to join (wedding), or to put away (funeral). When the quieter "non-K'IN" rite is completed and order re-established, the participating individuals are ready to re-enter calendrical time (Phelps 1969; see also Leach 1961).

Is it any wonder that these waterhole and lineage ceremonies are called K'IN KRUS? K'IN, which means "sun" or "time," and KRUS, the cross shrines which provide the necessary communication points between Zinacantecos and gods, reveal, in combination, the essence of these ceremonial dramas. Above all, K'IN KRUS rituals express and validate the principles governing the spatial and temporal aspects of Zinacanteco society.

8

Some Recurring Cargo Rituals

BY FAR THE most complex rituals of the Zinacantecos are those performed by the cargoholders in Zinacantan Center.* There are few days when some ceremony is not being conducted; often several sequences are being executed simultaneously. Cargo rituals are of the K'IN type. They are calendrical rites, repeated each year in accordance with fixed Catholic saints' days; they are public as opposed to domestic; they are typically accompanied by percussion. In this chapter I provide a description and symbolic analysis of three cargo rites: the flower renewal (BAL-TEˀ), the counting of the saints' medallions (XLOK' ˀUAL), and the change of office (K'EXEL). Not only are these three rites among the most frequent, but they also display many of the key symbols apparent in all Zinacanteco cargo rituals.

The Flower Renewal Ritual

The homes of the MOLETIK, the twelve Mayordomos, and the two Mayordomo Reyes have house altars characterized by arches decorated with "flowers" that must be changed periodically. This ritual, called BAL-TEˀ (which refers literally to the wrapping of the string or vine around the stick of the arch to hold the "flowers" on the arch), is performed in virtually the same manner by all the cargoholders. The schedule varies however: the MOLETIK and the Mayordomos perform BAL-TEˀ before each twenty-three K'IN† and at other stated times (when

*These cargo rituals, including "The Annual Ceremonial Calendar," have been treated in detail by Early (1965), more briefly described in Vogt 1969, and sketched in Vogt 1970b. Cancian (1965) provides a definitive description and analysis of the structure of the cargo system and covers selected aspects of the cargo rituals. Interpretations of selected ritual symbols are found in Laughlin (1962), R. Rosaldo (1968), and Bricker (1973).

†Epiphany (January 6), Esquipulas (January 15), San Sebastián (January 20), Candelaria (February 2), Carnaval, Cuatro Viernes, Semana Santa, Santa Cruz (May 3), Virgen de Leteñia, Corpus, Sagrado Corazon,

there is a long interval between fiestas); the Mayordomo Reyes renew their flowers on alternate Saturdays, or twenty-six times during the year, as well as before fiestas. In addition, the flowers on the arches above the saint statuary and doorways of two of the churches are renewed in rituals performed by the Mayordomos on the first day (called CUK-NICIM, "tying the flowers in bunches") of each of the twenty-three fiestas.

The house altar (ˀALTAL), usually located on the "rising sun" side of the house, rests on a platform of split oak (BAZ'I TEˀ), about 4 feet off the ground, supported by four posts of solid oak (TULAN). Two large reed mats, sewn together to reach from the ground, cover the top of the platform, continuing in back of it and extending over the top, to form a canopy (see Figure 30). On this platform rest the sacred objects: a wooden chest containing clothing and medallions for saints and small saint statues. A branch of ˀISBON (dogwood, *Cornus excelsa* HBK.) tied to the two front supporting posts arches over the sacred objects. Small pine trees of one of the two types of BAZ'I TOH are tied to the two front supports. Three additional "flowers" adorn the tops of the supporting posts and the arch: C'IB, KRUS ˀEC', and ZAHAL NICIM. This collection of "flowers" is renewed in the BAL-TEˀ. The following description is of a rite performed by one pair of Mayordomos.

Episode One: Preparations

Before the ceremony begins it is necessary to procure the "flowers" (pine trees, palm, bromeliad, and red geraniums), food for the ritual meal (beef or pork), cane liquor, and candles, and to request the presence of the retinue of assistants: ritual adviser, musicians, incense-bearer, laundresses, cannoneers, and one or two other helpers. The Mayordomos share a trio of musicians: the Junior Mayordomo recruits the guitarist; the Senior Mayordomo, the violinist and harpist. Each Mayordomo recruits an experienced female Incense-Bearer (never his wife, since the role must be filled by a widow past menopause), who wears a CILIL during the ritual.

Episode Two: Laundering the Clothes of the Saints

At sunrise one laundress arrives at the house of the Junior Mayordomo and is given the washable clothes of the small saint statues. The other laundress goes to the house of the Senior Mayordomo where she is given the bags which contain the sacred medallions, the bags for the Mayordomo's flags, and the bag for ropes, ribbons, and bells which adorn the church saints when they are taken out for processions. Accompanied by the junior cannoneer, the laundresses carry the baskets of clothes and bags to NINAB CILOˀ where they are carefully washed with soaproot. The departure of the women and their arrival at the waterhole are announced by two cannon shots which are answered from the house of the Senior Mayordomo by two shots from the senior cannoneer. This sequence of shots is repeated as they leave the waterhole and return to the houses. The clothing and bags are hung up to dry in the sun, then returned to their chests.

Episode Three: The Ritual Meal

After sunset each retinue of helpers gathers at the house of its Mayordomo to partake of a ritual meal of beef or pork and tortillas.

Episode Four: The Invocation

The Junior Mayordomo, dressed in his black

San Antonio (June 13), San Juan (June 24), San Pedro (June 29), Santo Domingo (August 4), San Lorenzo (August 10), Santa Rosa (August 31), Natividad (September 8), San Mateo (September 21), Virgen de Rosario (October 7), Todos Santos (November 1), Santa Catalina (November 25), Navidad (December 25).

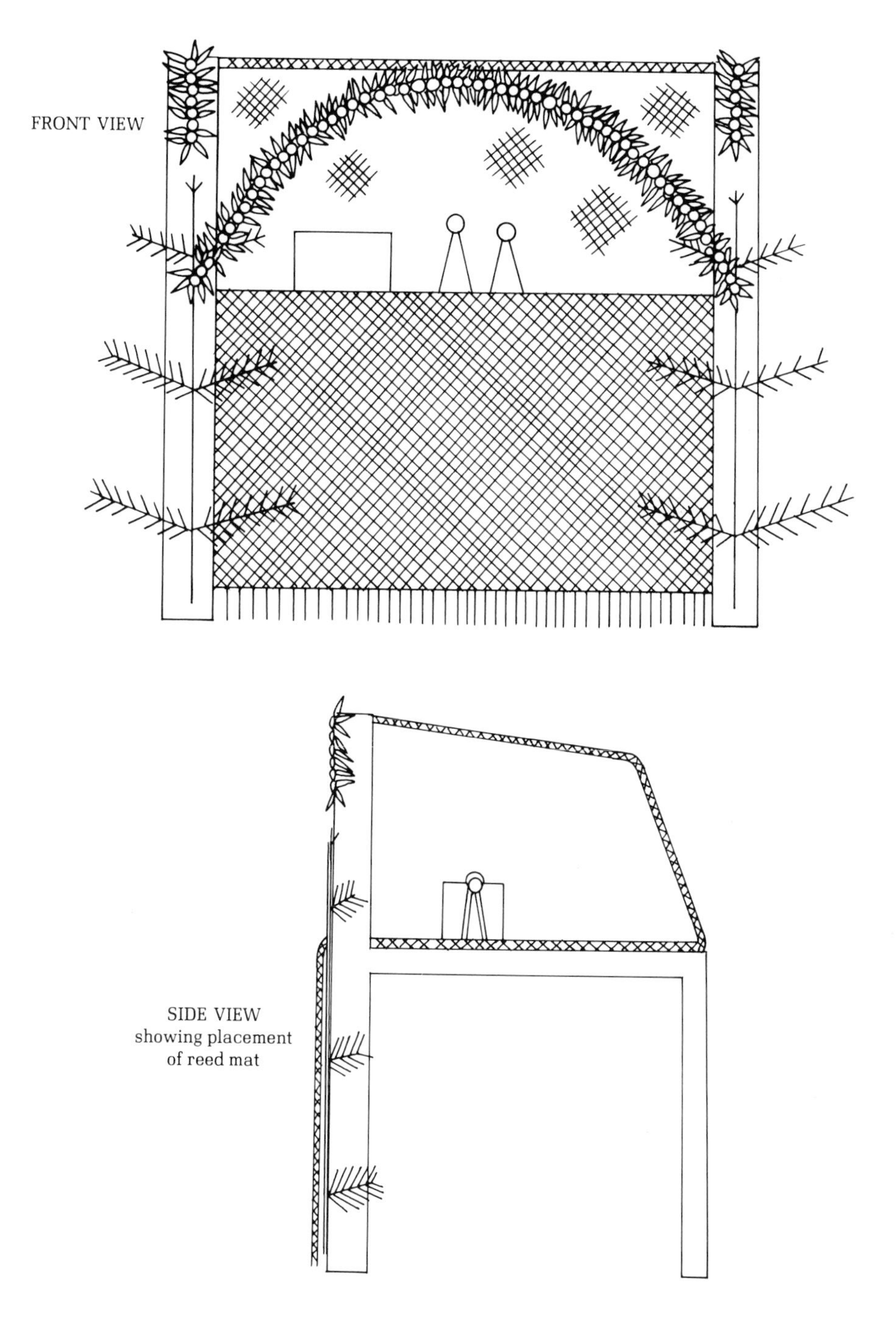

30. A house altar

ceremonial robe and accompanied by his retinue, marches to the house of the Senior Mayordomo; there the group is greeted by the Senior Mayordomo and his retinue. The Senior Mayordomo dons his black ceremonial robe and scarf and he and his junior partner engage in bowing-and-releasing with their three musicians, while reciting the following invocation:

See then, my older brother,
See then, my younger brother [the musicians],
In your presence,
Before your eyes,
We will change the flowers,
We will change the leaves of the tree [the altar decorations],
Of Father San Lorenzo,
Of Father Santo Domingo.*

Now we have arrived at his great feast day,
Now we have arrived at his great festival.
For this we are gathered together,
For this we are united . . .

Lend me the ten toes of your feet,
Lend me the ten fingers of your hands,
I am going to change the flowers,
I am going to change the leaves of the tree . . .

Lend me your instruments,
Lend me your songs,
Older brother,
Younger brother,
For before your eyes,
For before your face
I will change the flowers,
I will change the leaves of the tree,
Oh my older brother,
Oh my younger brother.

Pardon for a moment,
Pardon then for a moment.

(Abridged from Early 1965: 225-226)

The Mayordomos approach the two Incense-Bearers, are released by them with the same type of invocation, and a serving of liquor all around follows.

*The saints' names differ with the Mayordomos.

Episode Five: Removing the Dry Flowers

As the musicians play, a reed mat is placed in front of the house altar. The Incense-Bearers kneel at the "foot" of the mat (the edge with the loose reeds), senior toward the north, junior toward the south. Each places a smoking censer in front of her. The Mayordomos remove their ceremonial robes and loosen their scarves. With Senior Mayordomo working on the north side and Junior Mayordomo on the south, they remove the old flowers from the arch and the front posts, and throw them onto the mat (see Figure 31).

Episode Six: Placing the Fresh Flowers

Two assistants bring in green pine-tree tops and tie them to the front posts of the altar. The two Incense-Bearers tie the palm leaves into bundles, which they hand to the assistants, who in turn hand them to the Mayordomos. The Mayordomos secure them to the arch, beginning at the top and working in both directions, and to the tops of the supporting poles above the arch. The same procedure is followed using the bromeliads, then the geraniums.

Episode Seven: Disposing of the Old Flowers

The Senior Mayordomo places a bottle of cane liquor under the old flowers on the mat and addresses the musicians:

See then, older brother,
See then, younger brother,
Wait for our earth,
Wait for our ground,
Here for a moment,
Here for two moments.

I am going to throw away the rubbish of the feet,
I am going to throw away the rubbish of the hands,
Of the Woman of the Sky,
Of the Lady of Heaven.

(Abridged from Early 1965: 227-228)

The Mayordomos carry the mat outside toward the southeast, discard the old decorations, and

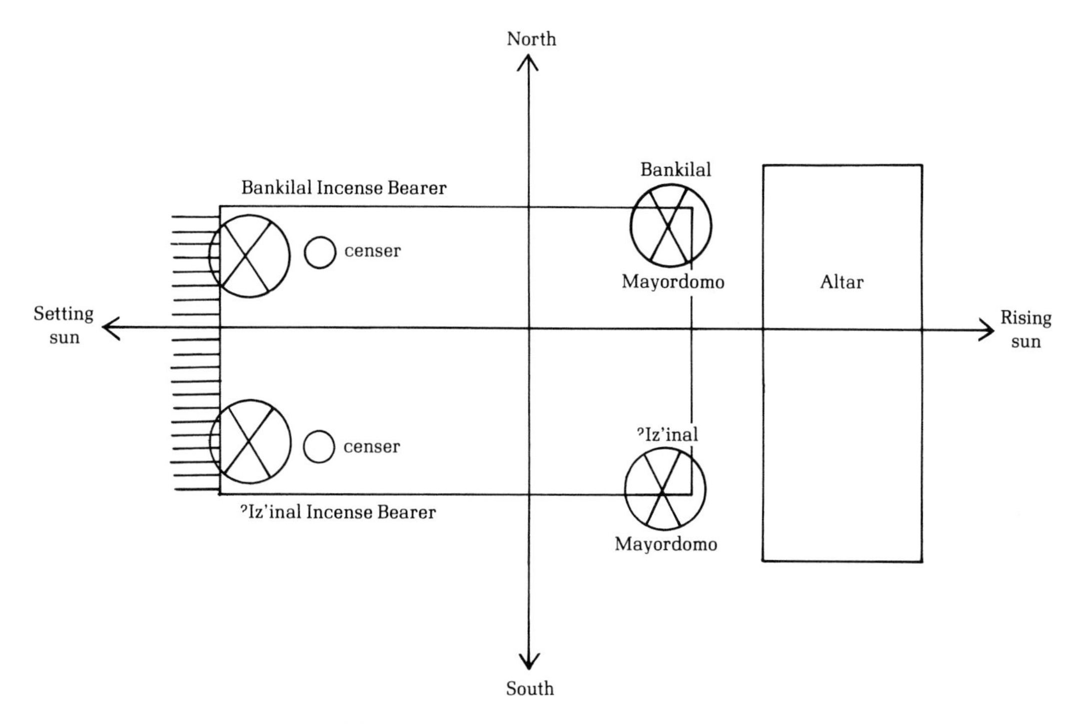

31. Arrangement of the ritual practitioners during a flower renewal ceremony

"discover" the bottle of liquor; they drink some; the rest is saved to be presented to the musicians.

Episode Eight: Offering Candles to the Saints

After the Mayordomos have donned their ceremonial robes again, as offerings of "tortillas," each of the ritualists lights and places white-wax candles in the animal-figure candleholders (some in the form of bulls, others in the form of deer) on the floor in front of the altar. Each Mayordomo offers two candles, one for himself and one for his wife. The candles are arranged according to the hierarchical order of the ritualists, and more generally in the order of relationships—in terms of age and sex—in Zinacanteco society.

The Mayordomos and Incense-Bearers then kneel and pray:

The changing of the flowers is finished,
The changing of the leaves of your tree is done,
Now we have arrived at your great feast day,
Now we have arrived at your great festival. . . .
So receive my candle, my Father,
So receive my candle, my Lord.
Forgive its being so small,
Forgive its being so small, . . .

(Abridged from Early 1965: 230)

Episode Nine: Dancing for the Saints

The Mayordomos put on their hats, face the musicians who are seated beside the altar, and begin to dance. Their Incense-Bearers dance behind them. The contrast between the young Mayordomos and the elderly widows is striking, and the episode displays three characteristic contrasts: older/younger, female/male, and behind/in front. In this paradigm there is a kind of reversal in the sense that "older" is associated with "female" and "younger" with "male", but, as always in Zinacanteco society, women stand behind men.

Episode Ten: Changing the Clothes of the Saints

In procession, the ritualists move from the house of the Senior to the house of the Junior Mayordomo. His altar contains one or more small saints, about 15 cm. high (Vogt 1969: 353). They are heavily clothed in miniature Zinacanteco clothing, which must be changed every fifteen days and, like the flowers, before every major fiesta. The Junior Mayordomo takes the clean clothes from the chest on his altar, while the Senior Mayordomo removes the saints from their cases on the same altar. The Junior Mayordomo hands the fresh clothes to the Incense-Bearers who cense them. The Mayordomos then place the fresh clothes on the saints; this process lasts over an hour, since each statue wears at least five layers of clothing.

Episode Eleven: Offering Candles to the Saints

Again, candles are offered and a prayer is chanted in a sequence that duplicates Episode Eight.

Episode Twelve: Dancing for the Saints

The Senior Mayordomo opens the glass door of the statue case of the small saints, and the musicians begin to play. The Mayordomos put on their hats, and there is more dancing, again with the Incense-Bearers behind the Mayordomos.

Flower Renewal in the Churches

The flower renewal in the churches takes place the day after the rites in the houses of the Mayordomos. The general pattern is similar, the most notable difference being that Incense-Bearers are not involved.

The twelve Mayordomos and their trio of musicians gather at 8 A.M. in front of the church of San Lorenzo. They don their robes, file into the church in rank order, and kneel in a row across the back of the church to recite a prayer to the saints. Then, followed by their assistants, they pass into the side chapel, remove their ceremonial garb, and, supervised by the Sacristans, perform the flower renewal. The old flowers are placed on reed mats and fresh flowers are tied to the arch decorations before each saint. The clothes of the saints, which have been previously laundered are replaced on the statues. The Mayordomos then place lighted candles before the image for which each pair is responsible, kneeling and praying as the candle offerings are consumed. The Mayordomos rise to form a semicircle around their musicians in the front of the church and dance for the saints. The music and songs are the same as those played and sung at the house rituals. The dancing and music, with intermittent rounds of cane liquor, continue until a Sacristan rings the tower bell at noon.

Food, brought by the Mayordomos' assistants, awaits in the churchyard. The Mayordomos present food to the seated Sacristans, who in turn distribute it to the Mayordomos and their assistants before they themselves eat. Rounds of liquor accompany the meal. Afterward, the ritualists move in ranked procession to the church of San Sebastián to renew the flowers there, following the same procedure. In the late afternoon, they return to the church of San Lorenzo, kneel in a row in front of the main door and recite a brief prayer, ending the ritual for the two churches in Zinacantan Center.

Comments on the BAL-TEʔ

This pervasive ritual in Zinacanteco culture provides metaphors for the fundamental social relations between men and women, young and old, in Zinacanteco society, for symbolizing the interrelations between the Ceremonial Center and the hamlets, and for symbolizing the way in which life is renewed with each "rising sun" as it provides light and heat for the Zinacantecos.

During the flower renewal the spatial arrangements, utilizing the principles of rising sun versus setting sun and of right versus left, again underscore the primacy of men over women, old over young. The younger women, who are cooking and tending children around the hearth, sit on the setting sun side of the house; the elderly Incense-Bearers position themselves at the foot of the reed mat as they tend the incense and tie the "flowers" in bundles; the younger male assistants hand the "flowers" to the older Mayordomos, who decorate the altar. Viewed from the altar, the senior ritualists are on the right, the junior ritualists on the left. The same positioning is evident in the arrangement of the candles (one for each ritualist and musician) in their animal-holders, and in the arrangement of the dancers.

A more distinctive aspect of the ritual and a feature which also appears in the necklace counting rite, is the model it provides for the interrelations that exist between the domestic life of the hamlets and the tribal life of the Ceremonial Center. The ritual begins in the houses of the Mayordomos, where flowers and clothes are renewed for the small saint statues. Next it moves to the churches, containing the larger saints that are the property of and sacred symbols for the entire tribe. The final stages take place back in the homes of the Mayordomos. Here we have, I believe, a ritual commentary on and small-scale model of a critical feature of Zinacanteco life: though most Zinacantecos live in the scattered hamlets, spending most of their lives there, they travel periodically to the Ceremonial Center for ritual and political purposes.

The most distinctive aspect of the ceremony is the renewing of a particular collection of "flowers." These plants are, in order from rising to setting sun: pine-tree tops, the palm (which grows at temperate elevations on the edges of the Highlands), the bromeliad, and the red geranium. The familiar contrast between the wild pine and the domesticated geranium is apparent, but what do the additional plants symbolize? The "frame," so to speak, is a symbolic representation of the rising sun as it comes up each day across the flanks of the Highlands (the palm) and strikes the trees on the mountaintops with its spreading rays (the bromeliad). In the model provided by the ritual, the world is symbolized by the reed mat on the altar, and the rising sun by the freshly decorated arch.

The Ritual Counting of the Saints' Necklaces

XLOK' ʔUAL is the uncovering and counting of the necklaces of coins that are placed on the saints' statues. On the eve of each major fiesta, these necklaces are placed on the statues by the Mayordomos and then returned on the afternoon of the saint's day to the sacred house chests of the Mayordomos. The same ritual occurs with even greater frequency for Señor Esquipulas—every Sunday of the year—and I shall use this example for illustrative purposes.

According to the Zinacantecos, Señor Esquipulas, a figure of the Crucified Christ, was found in NINAB CILOʔ and is, along with San Lorenzo, one of the two oldest holy images in Zinacantan. Esquipulas was first placed in the cabildo, where he remained for many years, presiding over the oaths of office for new cargoholders. He was cared for by an elderly Incense-Bearer, who burned incense and lit candles for him, and assumed all the responsibilities later taken on by the Mayordomo Reyes. His first chapel was constructed and the Mayordomo Reyes appointed in

1899 after some soldiers passing through Zinacantan molested the Incense-Bearer in the cabildo. The present large chapel was constructed in 1961.

The two Mayordomo Reyes and two Mesoneros begin their duties as ritual caretakers of the Chapel of Señor Esquipulas on the weekend following their installation on December 30-31. For the three Sundays in January preceding the fiesta of San Sebastián (January 20), all four officials participate in the counting ceremonies for the saint's medallions. On the weekend following the fiesta of San Sebastián, the senior pair takes over the ceremonial performance for three weekends, without the help or presence of the junior pair. On the fourth weekend, the juniors join the seniors to perform the ritual in what may be called a "change-of-duty" weekend. At this time the bags containing the clothing, necklaces, and altar cloths are transferred from the Senior to the Junior Mayordomo Rey, each having a sacred chest for ritual paraphernalia on his house altar. For the next three weekends, the junior officials assume the duty alone. Throughout the year each pair serves six terms of three weekends interspersed with the weekend of joint service. For the remaining one or two weekends of the calendar year in December, they serve jointly.

Every Sunday a Mayordomo and Mesonero must count the coins. (Arbitrarily, I have chosen a weekend when the junior pair has the duty). On Saturday morning the Junior Mayordomo Rey and his drink-pourer purchase supplies in San Cristóbal, while other helpers gather ritual plants. At sundown the Junior Mayordomo Rey goes to the houses of the three string musicians with liquor and requests the presence of each at the ritual. Before they arrive, the house cross is decorated with pine trees and red geraniums, and burning incense is placed in front of it. An assistant goes to the chapel to light candles and burn incense for the saint.

The flower renewal then takes place, following the sequence just described. The Mayordomo Rey removes from the chest the three large bags, passes each over incense, and places them on the mat in the following order from north to south: the SPIXOL KAHVALTIK (hat of our lord), containing the saint's crown and mirrors; the ʔUAL KAHVALTIK, containing the necklaces, and the MANTREX KAHVALTIK, containing the altar cloths and the large tablecloth for the table in the chapel. He and the Mesonero cense them once more and return them to the chest. Having prayed and lit two candles in front of the altar, the Mayordomo Rey and the Mesonero bow and release the ritual participants. The group proceeds to the chapel to renew the flowers on the arch and dance for Señor Esquipulas. Back at the house of the Junior Mayordomo Rey, the counting of the medallions unfolds in the following nine episodes.

Episode One: Eating Bread with Coffee

The ritualists are served coffee and wheat-flour rolls upon their return from the church.

Episode Two: Removing the Necklaces

The three large bags are removed from the chest of the Junior Mayordomo Rey and placed on the altar. The two ritualists kneel on opposite sides of the mat—Mayordomo Rey toward the south, Mesonero toward the north—and loosen the scarves around their heads as a sign of reverence. The Mesonero holds the necklace bag, while the Mayordomo Rey unties the drawstrings of the inner bags containing three necklaces. Each necklace is stored in nine bags, one inside the other. The outer six are made of the pink-and-white striped cloth used for tablecloths in ritual meals; called CUʔIL POK'ETIK (breast bags), they are replaced yearly by the Mayordomo Reyes. The three inner bags—ʔAMARA ʔUALETIK (tying-up necklaces) are of red silk and are never changed. The Mayordomo

Rey censes each of the three innermost bags three times and continues to hold it while all others present bow. Then he returns the bags to the mat, removes the necklaces, and places them carefully in parallel half-ellipses a few centimeters apart, with the loose ends toward the altar (see Figure 32) and the crosses in the center of the necklaces pointing up.

The necklaces are: ʔUAL BANKILAL, comprised of 137 one-peso coins, 24 five-peso coins, and one thirty-peso coin, equal to a total value of 287 pesos; ʔUAL ʔIZ'INAL, comprised of 104 one-peso coins, 12 five-peso coins, 1 ten-peso coin, and 1 fifteen-peso coin, totaling 189 pesos; and ʔUAL SANTORENSO, comprised of 19 one-peso coins, or 19 pesos. The grand total is 495. Most coins are of modern Mexican vintage, readily identified and counted; a few date from the colonial period and are believed to have a value of 15 or 30 pesos each. Each has a hole drilled through it, through which a red silk string passes. These strings are tied to a gold-colored band, which serves as the connecting "chain" of the necklace. Many red and pink ribbons are also attached to the band and to the strings holding the silver coins. The overall effect is a color riot of gold, silver, and red.

Episode Three: Counting the Coins

The Mesonero takes a small sack from the necklace bag and empties its kernels of white

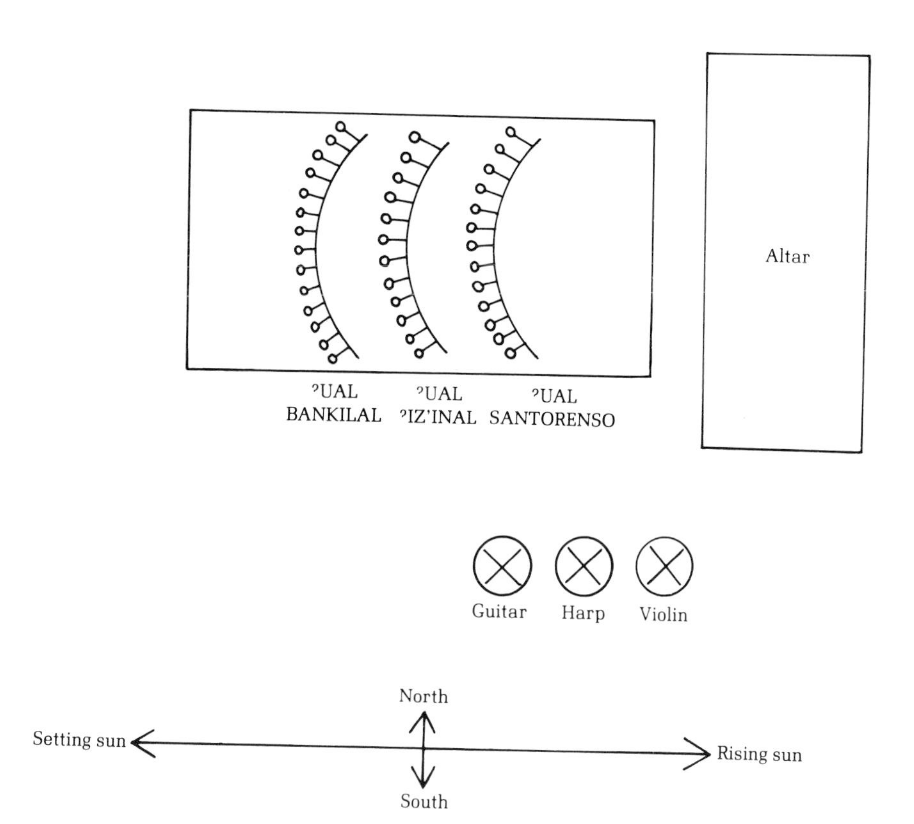

32. Arrangement of necklaces and musicians for the medallion-counting ceremony

maize onto the mat. The number of kernels is supposed to equal the peso-value of the coins on the three necklaces. Starting with the ʔUAL SANTORENSO, the Mayordomo Rey holds one end of the necklace band in his left hand, while the Mesonero holds the other end in his left hand. Using his right hand to draw each coin, dangling on its string, toward him, the Mayordomo Rey calls out its value, and the Mesonero moves a comparable number of kernels from one pile to another with his right hand. The process is repeated with the other two necklaces. The count never exceeds twenty: if a thirty-peso coin is to be calculated, the Mayordomo Rey calls out "twenty," then an additional "ten," and the maize is moved accordingly.

If the final total exceeds 495 kernels of maize the coins have gained in value since the last count, signifying that Señor Esquipulas is pleased with his Zinacanteco attendants. However, if kernels of maize remain in the original pile after the count is completed, the saint has been displeased with the performance of the rituals since the last counting and has "removed" coins in the interim. Consternation and much discussion as to the causes of his displeasure follow a low count. After repeated observation of this counting ritual, we are still not certain why the count varies. There are two possibilities: that the ritualists are intoxicated to the point where errors are bound to occur; that unconscious errors reflect the cargoholders' perceptions of their own performance since the previous count.

After the count the necklaces and the bag of maize are replaced in their coverings. All present bow to the bulging bag, which is censed once again and replaced on the altar, as are the two bags containing the hat and mirrors, and the altar cloths used at the chapel.

Episode Four: Dancing with the Necklaces

As the musicians play, the cargo officials approach the altar, from which the Mayordomo Rey takes the large necklace bag, placing it in his black ceremonial robe which he holds open in front of him. In a similar way the Mesonero places the other two bags in his robe. Thus prepared, the two cargoholders dance—Mayordomo Rey in front, toward the altar, Mesonero behind. As dawn begins to lighten the sky, which can be glimpsed through the smoke hole at the peak of the house, the music and dancing end and the cargoholders rest as a ritual meal is prepared for them and the musicians.

Episode Five: Ritual Meal

A ritual meal of beef and tortillas is served: the seating arrangement is shown in Figure 33.

Episode Six: Placing the Necklaces on the Saints

Just before the full dawn the ritualists leave the house of the Junior Mayordomo for the Chapel of Esquipulas. The procession—led by a helper carrying a smoking censer, followed by another helper carrying by tumpline liquor bottles in a net bag, then the musicians, and last the Mesonero and Mayordomo Rey with the ceremonial bags held before them in their robes—must reach the chapel just after sunrise. The ritualists enter the churchyard, stopping to bow and pray to San Lorenzo in his church, and greet the churchyard crosses before entering the western door of the chapel, whose bells are being rung by another assistant. After kneeling three times at the back, middle, and front of the chapel, the officials place their bags on the altar, while the musicians take seats along the southern wall near the altar.

The Mayordomo Rey removes his ceremonial robe and sandals in order to climb on the narrow ledges in front of the glass case sheltering Señor Esquipulas to reach and open its doors. The Mesonero hands him the adornments after turning each article counterclockwise over smoking

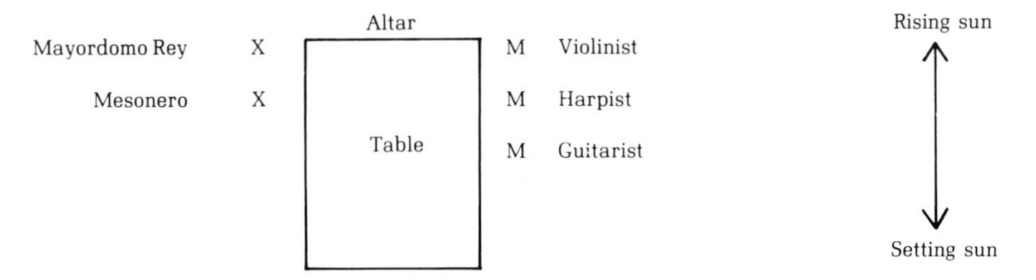

33. Seating arrangement at the ritual meal

censers. During the week Señor Esquipulas wears two mirrors over his heart, two on each index finger, and one on each elbow—a total of eight. Having removed the saint's cap, the Mayordomo Rey adds a crown and seven more mirrors in the following order: right index finger, right elbow, left index finger, left elbow, and three over the heart. Five ribbons (two pink, two purple, one green) are placed around the neck. Then the junior medallion necklace followed by the senior necklace are added. The ʔUAL SANTORENSO is placed on the small statue of San Lorenzo located to the right of Esquipulas.

The Mesonero takes the two altar cloths from the third bag and spreads them on the altar. He also spreads a large tablecloth on the green central table where the Elders, with staffs of office in front of them and red turbans on their heads, will sit to carry on their Sunday business.

Episode Seven: Dancing for Señor Esquipulas

Facing the musicians, the Mayordomo Rey and the Mesonero stand side by side, the former toward rising sun. They dance, with intermittent rest stops, for some seven hours, until approximately 2 P.M.

Episode Eight: Eating Eggs, Coffee, and Bread

The third meal is eaten outside the chapel. Here the Mayordomo Rey, the Mesonero, and the musicians are served on the ground a meal of eggs, coffee, and bread.

Episode Nine: Returning the Necklaces to the House Chest

The Mayordomo Rey removes the necklaces, the ribbons, the mirrors, and the crown from Esquipulas and replaces the saint's cap, eight mirrors, and white and red loincloth. After the sacred bags have been held up for veneration, the ritualists march in procession back to the house of the Junior Mayordomo Rey, carrying the bags in their ceremonial robes and singing. At the house the Mayordomo Rey again dances, holding the necklace bag in his outstretched robe as before. He then replaces the three bags (necklaces in center, clothing on left, and altar cloth on right) in the chest on his altar.

Comments on the Medallion Counting Ritual

The term ʔUAL is derived from the Tzotzil word for month, ʔU.* Its use, coupled with the fact that the counting does not exceed twenty, suggests that the procedure is related to and perhaps derived from the ancient Tzotzil calendar of twenty-day months. Although this calendar is no longer in use in Zinacantan, elderly informants

*There are probably two homonymous roots in contemporary Tzotzil, one meaning "necklace," and the other meaning "month," or "moon." ʔU is also general Maya for "necklace." Bricker (personal communication 29 October 1974) suggests that there may be a semantic relation between the two meanings, based on the possibility that "the ʔUAL of Zinacantan was once used in divining, perhaps for predicting the luck associated with months."

can still name its eighteen months; in nearby Chamula (see Whelan 1967; Gossen 1974b) and in other more conservative Tzotzil municipios, the ancient calendar is still used by the older generation.

The reasons why the necklaces are composed of silver coins continues to be something of a puzzle. In their round and shiny appearance, they may be symbols of "little suns," representing days as they are counted. But it is also important that in a contemporary world where the Indians believe the ladinos have most of the money and they (the Indians) are impoverished and need to increase their supply of money that the necklaces are composed of money which is counted each Sunday in a kind of "increase" rite. Further, the fact that coins are counted against kernels of maize is a sort of bridging ritual in which the symbol of exogenous wealth—money—is equated with the symbol of indigenous wealth—maize—and serves to bring money under control by integrating it into Zinacanteco culture and to affirm the stability of Zinacanteco wealth—maize—in the monetary terms of the ladino world.

This ritual, which follows the flower renewal, perpetuates and intensifies the BAL-TE? symbolism, just as the second line reiterates the first in a couplet of a Zinacanteco prayer. As each necklace is held up for counting beneath the flowered arch above the altar, it evokes an image (in both color and shape) of the full face of the sun rising above the eastern horizon (Hamilton 1970; see Figure 34). The nine bags, from which the necklaces are extracted, may symbolize the nine layers of the traditional Maya underworld (Vogt 1969: 601) through which the sun must pass during the night.

After the counting and dancing, the necklaces of coins, which symbolize sun, heat, money, and the passage of time, are carried *just after sunrise* to the chapel and placed around the neck of Señor Esquipulas, himself a symbol of the sun god who looks out over the world from his position on the rising sun side of the chapel. At the

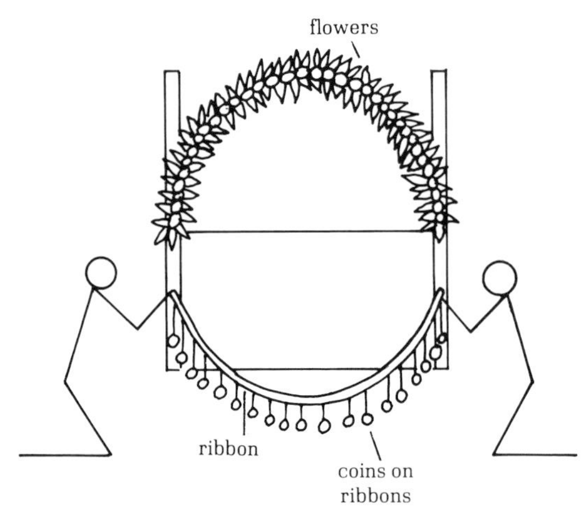

34. The image of the face of the rising sun

end of the day, as the sun wanes, they are removed. The necklaces are then returned to the house of the Mayordomo Rey until the following week when they will again be counted and placed on the saints. This rite again symbolizes the periodicity in the flow of life between the ceremonial center—where ritual is focused upon tribal artifacts and paraphernalia—and the hamlets—where ritual is focused upon domestic artifacts and paraphernalia in the houses of Zinacanteco families.

Change-of-Office Rituals

A third recurring cargo ritual of great symbolic significance is the change-of-office ceremony (K'EXEL) for the cargoholders. All cargoholders serve for one year in office, but change according to different schedules—the MOLETIK (Grand and Second Alcalde and four Regidores) and the Mayordomo Reyes and Mesoneros change on the night of December 30-31; the Alféreces and Mayordomos are installed at specific fiestas during the calendar year (see Vogt 1969: 504, 510). A relatively large proportion of the annual ritual activity performed by cargoholders concerns this installation of new officeholders and the removal of the old. As Bricker (1966) has pointed out, there is a striking similarity between these contemporary cargos and the ancient Maya concept of the Year Bearer: just as the ancient Maya god was thought to carry the year on a tumpline, passing it along to the next bearer at the end of the year, so a contemporary Zinacanteco cargoholder carries his burden of official responsibilities for a year, at which time he passes it along to his successor.

The period during which a cargo is transferred from the outgoing official to the new incumbent is an ambivalent time in the lives of the two men and their families. Consequently, the event is given great attention and is highly ceremonialized. For purposes of illustration, I shall focus on the change-of-office ritual for an Alférez which occurs in thirteen episodes over a period of six days.

Episode One: Announcement of the K'IN

For three consecutive nights in advance of a major fiesta, each Alférez who is approaching the end of his cargo sends out his drum and flute players to announce the forthcoming K'IN. Accompanied by a drink-pourer, the musicians march counterclockwise around the heart of the ceremonial center, passing by the ten streetcorner crosses just after dark and again just before dawn. The two drummers and the flutist play special music to announce the fiesta, stopping for rounds of liquor at each streetcorner cross and at the doorways of the church of San Lorenzo and the chapel of Esquipulas. After the evening announcement they return to the house of the outgoing Alférez for more POX, resting before the dawn announcement, after which they again return to his house.

Episode Two: Preparations

An Alférez passing through a change-of-office ceremony must recruit a large retinue of helpers. In addition to the drum and flute players, he needs a ritual adviser to counsel him on details of the ceremony, one who will visit the sacred mountains to pray to the ancestral gods that the cargo be served well and the cargoholder be pardoned for inadequacies in its performance, who will speak to the other cargoholders when the man he is representing leaves office, again asking pardon and expressing the hope that they are satisfied with the manner in which the duties were performed, and who will stand inside the door of his house and "greet" the other Alféreces when they arrive for a ceremonial visit. The importance of the ritual adviser as a speechmaker and representative is expressed in his alternative Tzotzil name, HTAK'AVEL, "he who answers." Each of his duties expresses the crucial link believed to exist between former members of the community who served cargos long ago in Zinacantan Center and are now ancestral gods officiating in the supernatural world and the present cargoholders who have assumed these traditional responsibilities. An Alférez also needs an old woman to measure out the liquor, liquor carriers and pourers, and a young man to carry his hat and rattle. His wife needs helpers to make the hundreds of tortillas and huge quantities of maize gruel required to serve his fellow Alféreces.

An Alférez must have large quantities of liquor, food, and ritual paraphernalia such as candles and fireworks on hand before the ceremony begins. Each of the two Senior Alféreces (Santo Domingo and San Lorenzo) must purchase and slaughter a bull to be hung in the southeast corner of his house. The meat provides ritual meals for the Alférez's entourage and official visitors throughout the fiesta period. Following the ritual slaughter, everyone present in the house blows three mouthfuls of salt mixed with cane liquor over the carcass, "so the meat won't spoil," and that evening the first ritual meal is served to the entourage.

The symbolism in the slaughtering of the bull is especially interesting. Beef is a very "hot" meat, brought from the Lowlands specifically for this change-of-office ritual. The cargo initiate is like a waxing sun: thus, the meat he eats, the sacrifice he makes to open the channels to the gods, is placed in the "hot"—southeast—quadrant of his house (Wasserstrom 1970: 118).

Episode Three: Praying to the Sacred Mountains

After a ritual meal the Alférez and his wife, the ritual adviser, and a shaman, whose duties are to light the candles and recite prayers, visit the four important sacred mountains and the chapels of Esquipulas, San Lorenzo, and San Sebastián. In preparation, the candles are prayed over, and the Alférez and his wife, like patients in a curing ceremony, after bathing, dress in freshly washed and censed clothes. The ritual sequence at the shrines is similar to that of a curing ceremony. The Alférez asks the gods' help and guidance, and begs them not to afflict him with disease if he should happen accidentally to displease them during his year in office.

Episode Four: Alférez Dresses

In preparation for taking the oath of office, the incoming Alférez, standing on a bullhide mat, is carefully and elaborately dressed. Although the ritual costume of the active Alféreces consists of a black ceremonial robe, red turban (ZAHAL POK'), high-backed sandals (CAK XONOBIL), and a large black hat with green ribbons, the Alférez approaching his term dresses in a long cape with a white collar; blue or green velvet knee pants; long, red knitted stockings; and adds three peacock feathers tied together to his black hat worn over the turban. Outgoing Alféreces dress in the same elegant manner, which is similar to the wedding costume of a groom and defines the men as initiates going through a rite of passage.

Episode Five: Oath of the Incoming Alféreces

During each of the seven major fiestas, two of the fourteen Alféreces are replaced. The oath ceremony for new incumbents takes place in the chapel of Esquipulas. As it begins, the top-ranking members of the religious and civil hierarchies seat themselves at the large, green rectangular table—over whose head and foot hangs Spanish moss (ZONTEʔ)—in the chapel in the order shown in Figure 35. The batons of office of the Alcaldes are placed with the silver knobs toward the foot of the table, ready to "receive" the new Alférez. The four Regidores, accompanied by flute, drum, and firework specialists, lead him in procession from his house to the chapel. The Regidor, who has carried the Alférez's feathered hat, hands it through the doorway to an assistant, who delivers it to the Grand Alcalde seated at the head of the table. The incoming Alférez enters the chapel, genuflects, and positions himself near the foot of the table. Then, in order of seniority, each of the seated officials rises, turns toward him, and delivers an exhortation, part of which follows:

My venerable father,
  Now your person has arrived,
  Now your person has arrived,
    Here before the feet,
    Here before the hands,
      Of the Lord Esquipulas
      Oh my venerable father. . . .

You must be a good servant,
You must be faithful to your trust,
  During the twelve months,
  During the twelve days.
Therefore you must leave your sins,
Therefore you must leave your wickedness,
  Under the feet,
  Under the hands,
    Of the Lord San Lorenzo,
      Oh my venerable father. . . .

(Abridged from Early 1965: 238-239)

The incoming Alférez makes three genuflections, each time moving closer to the foot of the table. Once there, he places the tips of the fin-

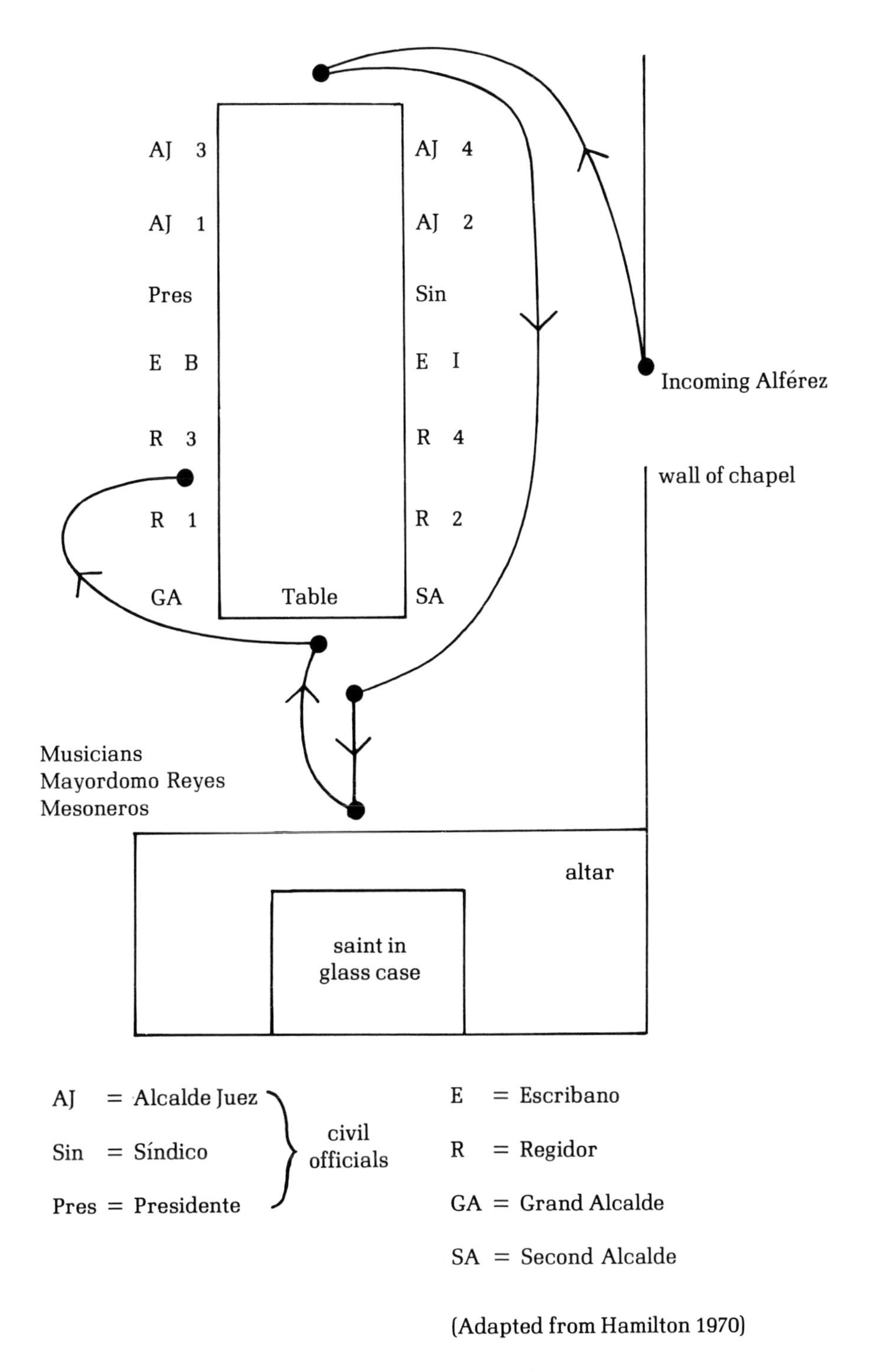

35. Seating arrangements and movements of the Alféreces for the oath ceremony

gers of both hands on the table's edge and bows his head between his hands, touching his forehead to the table top. The Grand Alcalde rises, walks to the side of the kneeling figure, and intones the oath:

Let no one talk against him,
Let no one murmur against him.

May he keep in sight,
May he keep before his eyes,
  His cargo,
  His service . . .
May he see it,
May he watch over it,
  As they saw it,
  As they watched over it,
    His two predecessors,
    His two antecedents. . . .

(Abridged from Early 1965: 239-240)

As the Grand Alcalde pronounces the last three lines, he makes the sign of the cross on the bowed head of the Alférez. The new Alférez walks to the altar of Señor Esquipulas (resplendently dressed in crown, ribbons, extra mirrors, and medallions) to light a candle, as the Grand Alcalde reverses the directions of two batons of office so that the silver heads now face the oath-taker.

After praying to Señor Esquipulas, the Alférez faces the officials for another exchange. The first takes place with the Grand Alcalde, who hands him the peacock-feather hat to hold. The Alférez's ritual adviser comes forward to retie his head scarf in the way signifying a cargoholder. The hat is then placed on the table with the hats of the Alcaldes. The new Alférez serves liquor, coffee, and rolls, and takes his place with the seated officials, between the First and Third Regidor, to await the swearing-in ceremony of the second Alférez. After the second ceremony, the Junior Alférez takes his place across the table from the Senior Alférez, between the Second and Fourth Regidor. Throughout this swearing-in ceremony hand-held cannons are being fired outside the chapel.

The large, rectangular table in the chapel of Esquipulas is called MEXA ʔISKIPULA SKWENTA MOLETIK, "the table of Esquipulas for the Elders." It is painted blue-green, the color associated with the "center of the world," suggesting that a small-scale model of the universe is being set up. The Spanish moss grows on mountaintops and, as it is struck by the rays of the early morning and late afternoon sun, is associated with sunrise and sunset.

The silver-headed batons have red ribbons attached to a half-ring about a third of the way down each staff. The ribbons may suggest red rays of light or heat emanating from the batons, which are believed to have a strong, hot innate soul given them by the ancestral gods. By pointing the silver heads toward the incoming Alférez, the Grand Alcalde confers heat or ritual power on the new cargoholder.

In the second prayer, the incoming Alférez is referred to as "Your [Esquipulas'] servant, Your rooster". In this typical couplet format, the second line restates and intensifies the first. A rooster is a "servant" in more than one sense. Because it serves as time-keeper during the night, certain hours of which are called "the first rooster crow," "the second rooster crow," and so on, and because priests were time-keepers in earlier days, the rooster, by extension, symbolizes the services of the priest in relation to the gods and society. As discussed earlier, it is used as a sacrificial victim for the welfare of mortal Zinacantecos. Thus, the prayer impresses upon the incoming cargoholders the multiplicity and importance of the responsibilities of their new positions.

A longer version of the prayer contains references to the sun god—"May he [cargoholder] walk in thy [sun god's] sight, / May he walk before thy flower-like face." Flowers, because of their brilliance, structure, and vitality, are associated with the sun: each is in effect a miniature sun (Laughlin 1962; Hamilton 1970). This symbolism is further apparent in the figure of Señor Esquipulas, who is positioned not only on the rising sun side of the chapel but also amidst a great array of flowers, wearing red ribbons, shiny mirrors, and a necklace of coins. A Zinacanteco myth illustrates the importance of the relationship between Esquipulas, in his traditional role as Christ, and the sun, believed to have fathered the saint. According to the story, Christ's blood is sucked out by the H?IK'ALETIK (Black-men), and, as a result, the sun loses its heat. The life force of Esquipulas—that is, "blood"—is thereby closely associated with the life force of the sun—that is, "heat."

After offering a candle and praying, the new cargoholder steps to the "rising sun" head of the table. Standing there, the sun god's new priest or servant in effect looks out over the ritual world from the position of the rising sun. After the exhortation by each official at the table, and the receiving of his hat and red turban, the new Alférez gives a bottle of liquor to the Grand and Second Alcaldes, emphasizing the important relation of this ritual liquor to heat and the sun: it is a strong drink which burns the mouth; metaphorically, as described below in the "Dance of the Drunks", the liquor is the "god's flower." Obviously, the symbolic value of POX, as opposed to its physiological effect, makes it a desirable and important ritual element—by drinking liquor, a Zinacanteco symbolically imbibes the essence of the sun and strengthens his innate soul. At this moment the new Alférez passes from secular into sacred time and completes his first step toward divine office.

Episode Six: Coffee and Rolls at the Houses of the Outgoing Alféreces

In the late afternoon the outgoing Alféreces make a farewell ritual gesture to the Mayordomos, Regidores, Grand and Second Alcalde, Sacristans, and two Civil Alcaldes representing the cabildo. They offer liquor, coffee, and rolls to the "guests" who first gather in front of the church of San Lorenzo in rank order. All the Elders wear necklaces of beads ("rosaries," or VENTEXIL) with multi-colored ribbons outside their ceremonial robes. When in position, the Senior Mayordomo of Sacramento (highest ranking Mayordomo) stands directly opposite the Grand Alcalde (highest ranking cargoholder), the Junior Mayordomo of San Sebastián (lowest ranking Mayordomo) faces the lowest ranking Civil Alcalde.

The Mayordomo line, led by the lowest ranking Mayordomo, files by the line opposite it, greeting first the lowest ranking Civil Alcalde, the other Civil Alcalde, the Sacristans, the Regidores, and finally the Second and Grand Alcalde. A greeting, followed by bowing-and-releasing, takes place between each individual of the Mayordomo line and each official in the Elders line (see Figure 36). The Elders are greeted with added ceremomy: each cargoholder lifts the Elder's necklace with his right hand, touches it to his forehead, kisses then releases it before moving on. As the last of the Mayordomos pass by, the lowest ranking members of the line of Elders fall into procession behind them in order to greet those of higher rank within their own line. The greetings end when the Second Alcalde kisses the necklace of the Grand Alcalde—the only person left in his original position.

Each cargoholder, after greeting the Grand Alcalde, has followed the man ahead of him to form a line in the center of the terrace. When the Grand Alcalde joins the line, in the last and senior position, the lowest ranking Junior Mayordomo of San Sebastián leads the long procession, accompanied by the music of the Mayordomos' musicians, to the house of the retiring Senior Alférez.

At the house doorway stand the two retiring Alféreces and their Ritual Advisers, who watch the procession approach and greet the house shrine. After being received by the ritual advi-

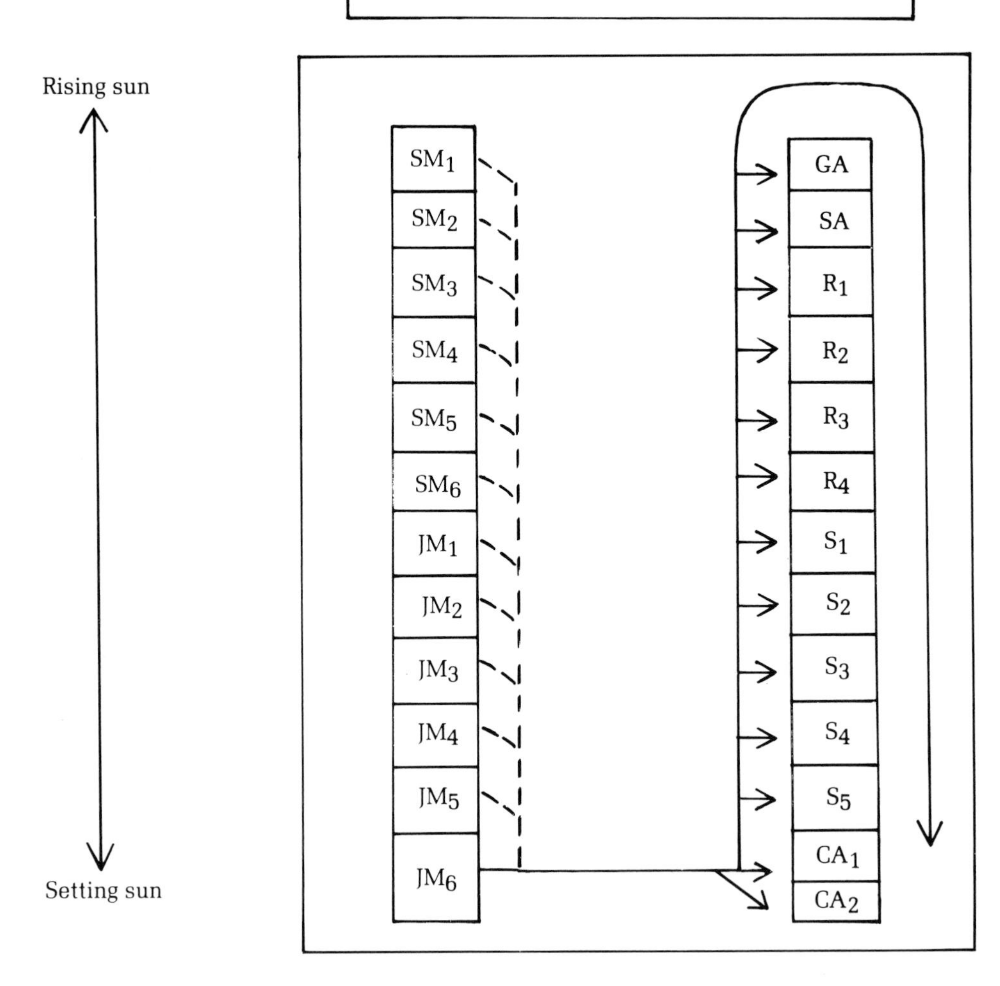

36. Arrangement of cargoholders for a greeting ritual in front of Church of San Lorenzo

sers, the processional group exchanges a series of greetings with the Alféreces similar to that given in front of the church. The Elders and the outgoing Alféreces then turn in the direction of the church of San Lorenzo to recite in unison a prayer to the patron saint, after which they kiss each other's necklaces and exchange more formal greetings.

The procession divides into two groups which seat themselves in rank order on two long benches facing each other, oriented east-west. After a round of liquor, a gourd of warm water used for mouth-rinsing is passed down each line. Next each man receives a small gourd of coffee and two wheat-flour rolls covered with a pink-and-white napkin. When the food has been blessed by the ritual advisers, the coffee is drunk and the empty gourds returned to the servers; the rolls are put into shoulder bags to be eaten later. After another round of liquor has been served and cigarettes passed and smoked, the procession moves to the house of the retiring Junior Alférez where the ritual sequence is repeated.

The ceremonial strategy of passing by in rank, a line of cargoholders bowing-and-releasing and kissing necklaces, is used repeatedly in cargo rituals as an effective and orderly way to convert a standing rank order—when the highest rank must stand closest to a church or cross shrine or rising sun—into marching rank order—when the lowest must move first, the highest last.

Episode Seven: Circuits of the Alféreces

LOK'ESEH-VOB, "extracting the musical instruments," is performed as the Alféreces march from the house of one to another, picking up each Alférez in specified order. The circuit is made on the first evening of each major fiesta and repeated on the second and third evenings. When all are in procession, the Alféreces march to the house of their No. 2 musician (guitar player) where they are served a meal, then to the house of the first musician (violin player) for another.* The group continues to the house of the Alférez of San Lorenzo, where, after a round of liquor, all dance with their rattles in front of the small image of San Lorenzo on the house altar. The assistants then set up a table for a ritual meal of beef and atole (maize gruel).

In the house of the Alférez of Natividad, the Alféreces sit in a circle for rounds of liquor, after which they dance and are served coffee and rolls. Next is the house of the highest ranking Alférez of Santo Domingo where the most elaborate activity of the evening takes place. Liquor, dancing, and singing to the music of flute and drums and violin and guitar precede more liquor and a ritual consumption of one small loaf of wheat-flour bread and a large gourd of coffee, both shared by all the Alféreces in rank order. A full ritual meal of tortillas and beef follows.

The Alféreces visit the houses of the two retiring Alféreces and are served atole. Throughout the night the group continues on to the houses of other Alféreces, in descending rank order. The Alféreces who receive visits vary from fiesta to fiesta, since the holders of lower-ranking, less-expensive Alférez cargos are not expected to entertain their fellows during each major fiesta. At the last house the Alféreces lie down to rest for the remaining hours before daylight.

Episode Eight: "Dance of the Drunks"

At about 7:30 the next morning the Alféreces march to the Church of San Lorenzo. There they sit in rank order on their customary benches on the terrace in front of the church, with the two musicians in the middle, separating the Senior Alféreces from the Junior Alféreces. Each Alférez, upon receiving a bottle of liquor from his assistant, presents it to the violinist, who posi-

*The Alféreces do not have a harp player since their music is considered too difficult for a harp (Haviland 1966).

tions the bottles on the terrace in two rows of eight bottles each—the first row (to the east) for the Senior, the second for the Junior Alféreces. (There are sixteen bottles because, with the addition of two incoming ones, there are now sixteen Alféreces rather than the usual fourteen.)

Accompanied by their ritual advisers, the incoming Alféreces arrive separately from their houses. They, joined by the two outgoing Alféreces, perform the first dance of the morning: the so-called "Dance of the Drunks," a stylized and farcical act that is repeated at intervals in front of the seated Alféreces. The Senior Alféreces (incoming and outgoing) face the Junior pair several yards apart, and as they dance, both pairs periodically shout and leap forward to change positions with the Alféreces facing them. As the dance progresses, they act increasingly intoxicated, their movements become more and more erratic. They end the dance by collapsing in "drunken stupors" beside the lined-up liquor bottles and taking great gulps of POX. They then enter the church to pray:

. . . forgive me, my father,
Forgive me, my lord,
  Thy flower [POX] has knocked me down,
  The leaf of thy tree [POX] has taken me off my feet,
    I have lost my reason,
    I have lost my way.
Do not completely abandon me,
Do not cease to protect, . . .

(Abridged from Early 1965: 256)

Rejoining the other Alféreces outside the church, the four continue their dramatic roles by complaining loudly and incoherently that they have been robbed of their money and their hats. The rest of the Alféreces enter into the resulting drama, as the four sob and protest their misfortune.

After a break for liquor and cigarettes, dancing begins again. The four Alféreces who are changing cargos line up in front of the musicians; the remaining Alféreces form a semicircle behind. The tempo of the music is punctuated by the sound of the rattles, which the officials hold in their right hands, and the slapping of high-backed sandals on the stone terrace. Since rattles and dancing are forms of percussion, this episode is especially symbolic of the change-of-office transition taking place. Dancing continues with short rests for liquor and cigarettes, until about 11 A.M. During one of the intervals, the outgoing Alféreces pass down the line with bottles of liquor in their hands, offering drinks and apologizing for any defects in their performances during the year. Frequently they break into ritualized crying to express repentance for irresponsible behavior.

In the late morning their ritual advisers lead the men changing cargos to the crosses in the churchyard, where the group prays together. It moves to the bandstand and presents liquor to the flutist and drummers seated there. To their music, the "Dance of the Drunks" is performed for the next two hours. It differs from the early morning performance only in that the participants remain on their feet throughout.

Episode Nine: Maize Gruel at the Outgoing Alféreces' Houses

About 2 P.M. this same afternoon (the "vespers" of the saint's day) the Civil Alcaldes and all religious officials except the Mayordomo Reyes and Mesoneros gather in the churchyard in response to invitations given by the ritual advisers of the Alféreces who are leaving cargos. The ceremonial lines are formed for the same greeting ritual as the day before, but are extended by the participation of the outgoing Alféreces and their two sets of flute and drum players.

These musicians lead the cargoholders in rank order from the church to the house of the outgoing Senior Alférez where the ritual advisers are greeted. The same bench formation used the day before has been set up for the "guests" who take their seats as the musicians play. The ceremony is similar to that of the previous day, but on a grander scale. Two shots of liquor are served by the drink-pourers prior to the first of two servings of maize gruel. The generous servings of gruel are barely sipped by the cargoholders, but are handed to small boys standing behind them who pour the liquid from the gourd bowls into buckets which are taken home for family consumption. A round of liquor is followed by cigarettes, one offered to each cargoholder, by the outgoing Alféreces. The second serving of gruel is followed by more liquor and cigarettes.

The procession moves to the house of the outgoing Junior Alférez to participate in another maize gruel offering identical to the first. Inside both houses the musicians are served a meal in appreciation of the music they provide throughout the year-long term of office.

The offerings of food at the houses of the outgoing Alféreces are again reminiscent of the parallel couplet structure of a Zinacanteco prayer (in which the second line of the couplet restates and intensifies the first line). The first day of the offerings, the food consists of coffee and *two* wheat-flour rolls; the second day, of *two* generous servings of maize gruel, more highly prized as a food than the Spanish-introduced wheat-flour rolls. (In both cases the food is not eaten, but taken home to be eaten later.)

Episode Ten: Circuits of the Alféreces

The sequence of events in this episode is identical to that of Episode Seven.

Episode Eleven: Alféreces Dance on the Church Terrace

On the day of the saint, according to the Catholic calendar, the priest arrives from San Cristóbal to say mass. The Alféreces are seated on their benches on the terrace outside the church of San Lorenzo. After the priest has left, they commence dancing and drinking, omitting the "Dance of the Drunks" performance of the preceding day; the Alféreces who are changing office dance in the center. The omission of the "Dance of the Drunks" may indicate that the incoming and outgoing cargoholders, having expressed their ambivalences the day before, are now ready to move with more commitment toward their new roles.

Episode Twelve: Flag Exchange

This episode takes place just before sunset on the last day of a major fiesta. Weather permitting, it is held in the plaza outside the chapel of Esquipulas; if it is raining, it is inside the Church of San Lorenzo.

The Senior Mayordomos, carrying the folded flags of their saints in their shoulder bags, enter the Church of San Lorenzo to pick up the flagpoles from a corner of the sanctuary. Attaching the flags to the poles, they return to the church terrace, where the Junior Mayordomos are waiting. One of the Sacristans hands a folded red-and-white checkered blanket to the Mayordomos, and the entire group files in procession to a position parallel with the front of the Church of San Lorenzo. The Alféreces, accompanied by their musicians, form a line in front of the chapel; the civil officials come from the cabildo and fall in position next to them. The Elders emerge from the chapel and stand beside the civil officials; the ritual advisers of the four changing Alféreces complete the line (see Figure 37).

The Mayordomo with the blanket spreads it on the ground in the middle of the plaza. The Regidores kneel on the setting sun side of the blanket. The two outgoing Alféreces come forward to take the red flags from two of the Senior Mayordomos, being careful to grasp the poles with an end of their red turbans. They kneel with their flags on the rising sun side of the blanket. At this point, the two Regidores and the two Alféreces crawl on their knees toward each

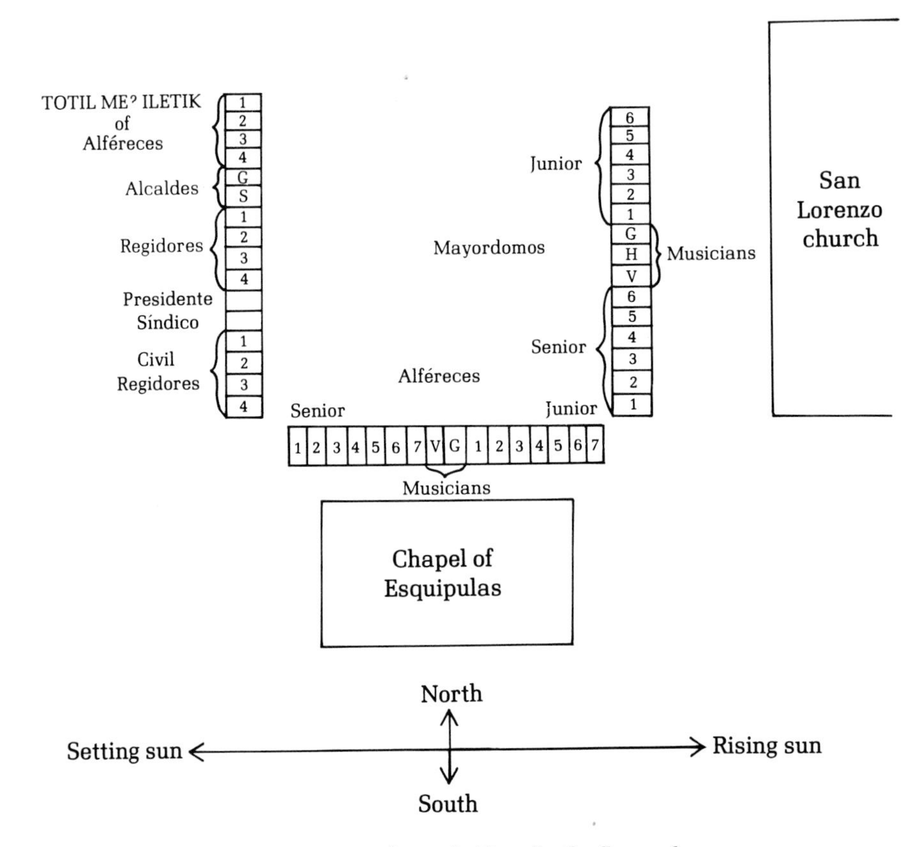

37. Arrangement of cargoholders for the flag exchange

other until they meet in the middle of the blanket where they kiss each others' necklaces, then back up to the blanket's edge. The sequence is repeated a second and third time. On the third approach, the two outgoing Alféreces hand the flags to the two Regidores, saying:

My venerable Father,
Before your sight,
Before your eyes,
The holy divine banner,
Is going to leave my feet,
Is going to leave my hands,
Oh my venerable Father. . . .

I took care of,
I looked after
My cargo,
My cargo, . . .

In the same way they must watch,
In the same way they must have before their eyes,
During a year in the divine world,
During a year on the divine earth,
The two who follow me,
My two successors, . . .

(Abridged from Early 1965: 270-271)

The Regidores respond with the same words, but using the third person to refer to the Alféreces. The Alféreces rise and position themselves on the north side of the grouping of cargoholders.

The Regidores rise and walk around to the rising sun side of the blanket vacated by the outgoing Alféreces; the two incoming Alféreces come forward and kneel on its setting sun side. As before, the four kneeling men crawl toward each other and kiss necklaces. This is repeated a second and third time. On the third approach, the Regidores hand the flags back now to the incoming Alféreces, signifying the official commencement of their new cargos. Throughout this sequence, cannon shots are fired about every five seconds. The four rise, and the flutist and two drummers come forward. The new Alféreces fall in behind them, the two Regidores in the rear, and the group circles the blanket counterclockwise three times while the drums beat and the flute pipes out and the new Alféreces shout with joy. They then march over to the Grand Alcalde at the corner of the square where they are joined by the outgoing Alféreces. The whole group—the old Alféreces with their ritual advisers, the new Alféreces with their ritual advisers, and the two Regidores—passes around the entire square of cargoholders, bowing, releasing, and kissing necklaces with all. When the Junior Mayordomo of San Sebastián, the lowest ranking cargoholder, has been released, all form a ranked procession to march to the house of the Senior Incoming Alférez. The episode finishes at sunset.

The symbolism of the flag exchange episode is very rich. The red flags probably represent ritual power, their color being associated with the sun and with heat. The red-and-white blanket indicates the place where ritual power (red) changes to secular status (white) and vice-versa, as the new Alféreces are invested with their cargos. The significance of the transfer of flags is the transfer of the position of rising sun, as the outgoing Alféreces leave the position, entrusting it momentarily to the Regidores, who in turn yield it to the incoming Alféreces.

Episode Thirteen: Atole at the Houses of the New Alféreces

The final episode of this ritual takes the ranked procession of cargoholders to the house of the new Senior Alférez, where they sit in rank order on benches and are again served maize gruel. The procession moves on to the house of the New Junior Alférez, and the sequence is repeated. The outgoing Alféreces have now finished their ritual duties and have been formally and officially replaced by their successors.*

Structural and Temporal Symbols in the Cargo Rituals

Among the fundamental symbolic features of the cargo rituals, as illustrated by the three recurring rites just described, are the metaphors of hierarchy they provide for Zinacanteco society. The programmed seating and processional orders of the ritualists are condensed, highly charged expressions of hierarchy; the bowing-and-releasing behavior between persons of greater and lesser rank in everyday life is intensified.

Other metaphors to express hierarchy are used in the positioning of the ritualists during the ceremonies. In the Flower Renewal and Necklace Counting rituals the positions of the performers are prescribed with reference to the house and chapel altars and ceremonial tables, whether the ritualists be changing the flowers, counting the coin necklaces, eating, praying, dancing, or marching in procession. All of these programmed sequences position the ritualists in such a way as to constantly remind Zinacantecos of the rank order in their society while also asserting this ranking as imperative for sound social organization. A distinctive metaphor of hierarchy in the change-of-office ceremonies occurs in the sequences of necklace-kissing performed by the Alféreces and Elders and followed by their "peeling off" to convert a standing ranked formation into a marching formation.

*The exception is the four highest ranking Alféreces, who have additional ritual duties in the Fiesta of San Sebastián.

Through adherence to the principles of primacy in Zinacantan, the positioning of ritualists and the programming of ritual sequences underscore the key determinant of Zinacanteco ranking: the contrast between BANKILAL (senior) and ?IZ'INAL (junior). As R. Rosaldo (1968: 525) so aptly expresses the essence of cargo rituals: "they appear to be elaborate, redundant communiques about hierarchy and rank; over and over they emphasize and maximize order among men."

But cargo rituals do more than express hierarchical order. They are symbols of and for structural tensions found in Zinacanteco society, tensions that usually result in the development of ritual in human society.

Four types of structural tensions find expression. One is the strained relations existing between ritual specialists (such as the musicians, chosen because of their ability to play their instruments) and cargoholders (who acquire their cargos in part by virtue of their means to pay the expenses of the ritual). Musicians and cargoholders cooperate, but their relationship is ambiguous. Musicians instruct the new cargoholders in their duties and are paid for their services in food and drink. Cancian states that they "are respected for their knowledge and their services to the saints and the community, but in the last analysis it is the people who supply the money, the cargoholders, who receive the lion's share of the prestige" (1964: 341). The musicians are food-drink receivers; the cargoholders, food-drink givers. They depend on each other. But the structural relation has conjunctive and disjunctive components that lead to joking between the two groups between ritual episodes and provide for a delicate and ambiguous situation that is expressed in the rituals (R. Rosaldo 1968: 533-535).

Another type of structural tension lies in the conflict between ascribed and achieved status. Although age per se is respected in Zinacanteco society and the old are bowed to in daily life, status and prestige accrue to a younger, wealthy Zinacanteco, able to work his way up the ladder of the cargo hierarchy faster than older fellow Zinacantecos. The rank order among cargoholders corresponds to a hierarchy based on relative wealth. A Zinacanteco does not ordinarily have an opportunity to display his wealth because witchcraft threatens those who are ostentatious. To quote Rosaldo:

> In cargo ritual the bowing and releasing behavior—in daily life, a metaphor expressing respect for age—is, in effect, a recognition of economic superiority. A metaphor for ascribed status (age) is translated into one for acquired status (wealth). Not only does the cargo system reflect and confer prestige within the community, but also, in its ritual, its gives men a culturally appropriate way to act out a social order based on acquired status, an order forbidden in hamlet life . . . Adult males live in both worlds, they must acknowledge the existence of both hierarchies. To the extent that this dilemma is felt by the participants, the contradictions between these two systems must give the relation among the cargo-holders its problematic, and its "sacred" quality (1968: 534-535).

A third type of tension is particularly apparent in the change-of-office ceremonies. Cargoholding brings great prestige; it also brings great expenses and subsequent debts. For the incumbent, the prospect of leaving his cargo means abandoning the exciting life of the ceremonial center and returning to rather monotonous maize-farming activities in his hamlet. Yet he is relieved that the year-long drain on his economic resources and energies has ended. For the incoming cargoholder there is the prospect of a stimulating year as he wears special costumes and gains prestige; but he also faces a year-long struggle of expenditure, of keeping his retinue happy and well-fed, of keeping alert enough to perform the necessary ritual. Such tension is expressed in the change-of-office ceremonies.

Despite their extensive use of Catholic symbols and paraphernalia, the rituals described manifest the high symbolic significance of the sun god and the marking off of the days, weeks, months, and year in the annual calendar round.

I suggest that the Flower Renewal rite symbolically represents the rising of the sun on the eastern horizon; that the Counting of Necklaces presents an image of the full face of the sun just above the horizon; that new cargoholders replace the incumbent in the important rising sun position. In the change-of-office ceremonies the incumbent Year Bearer is replaced with a new Year Bearer as time flows by. It is of ultimate significance that cargoholders' ceremonies are called K'IN, that proto-Maya word which variously translates as Sun, Day, Time.

9

End-of-the-Year/ New-Year Cargo Ceremonies I

THE PERIOD FROM December 16 through January 25 is the richest segment of Zinacantan's ceremonial calendar. It is characterized by rituals which dramatize the end of one ceremonial year and the start of a new one. During this time the terms of most cargoholders expire and the positions are transferred to a new hierarchy. Not surprisingly, this crucial transition is characterized by rituals of inversion, parody, farce: men become women, Indians become ladinos, people become animals, the most solemn ceremonies become the subject of mime and ridicule. Normal life is played back to front (Leach 1961: 135), as the social structure is unwired, then rewired, in six weeks of ritual activity.

MIXATIK (Masses)

Each morning from December 16 through December 24, the Mayordomos gather in front of San Lorenzo Church to perform MIXATIK. This ceremony is related to the novena performed by Mexican Catholics just before Christmas, although in contemporary Zinacantan the ritual congruences are few. The nine days of the ceremony, corresponding to the nine months of the Virgin's pregnancy, feature the eating of squash (itself a potent sexual symbol) by ritualists and spectators. The Mayordomos take turns preparing the squash, which must be cooked two nights before it is served. The ceremony of the first night, called SVOK' SMAIL SAKRAMENTU (breaking of the [Mayordomo] Sacramento's squash), takes place at the house of the Senior Mayordomo of Sacramento and, unlike subsequent nights, is characterized by formal ritual. The Sacristans and the Mayordomos' Incense-Bearers supervise assistants who remove rinds from both highland and lowland species with machetes and knives, cut the vegetables into pieces, and place them in cooking vessels containing water and brown sugar. When the pot is placed over the fire, three shots of liquor are added to ensure the quality of the cooked squash; it is also believed that the "soul" of the liquor is transferred to the pot, protecting it against breakage in the hot coals. More squash is prepared the second night. Early on the morning of December 16 all the cooked squash is taken to the churchyard where it is served by a Sacristan to the assembled Mayordomos, other Sacristans, musicians, all helpers, and any others present. Each receives two tortillas filled with squash, and drinks from a large bowl of maize gruel, which is passed and shared (Vogt 1969: 520-521). In this squash-eating ritual the symbols of sex and fertility—one of the two most important categories utilized in the End-of-the-Year ceremonies—become prominent for the first time.

The Posada (Inn) Ceremony

Performed during the same nine-day period, this ceremony, which takes place every afternoon in the side chapel of San Lorenzo, derives from the biblical narrative of Joseph and Mary's search for lodging just before the birth of the Christ Child. The Zinacantecos consider the Virgin Mary a "loose woman, who slept with many different men but did not have a husband." Because of this, no one would provide shelter for the delivery of her child. Only an older brother, Joseph, consented to take her into his stable.

The chapel altar contains two turtle-shell drums (called PAT ʔOK, "turtle-back," and played with corncobs in order to produce more maize), a plain drum, and a rattle—instruments played by four musicians in the procession. Three more musicians (violin, harp, guitar) take positions to the left of the altar, and the statues of the Virgen de Navidad and San José stand before it on flower-bedecked platforms.

The Mayordomos enter the chapel, remove their shoes, and don their ceremonial robes. A procession forms led by musicians playing the instruments from the altar: the turtle-shell drums, then the small drum and rattle. They are followed by four Mayordomos carrying the Virgin, four Mayordomos, carrying San José, then the guitarist, harpist, and violinist. A small bell is suspended from each carrier handle, and as the procession moves around the chapel, greeting the other saints, each Mayordomo strikes the bell on the handle in front of him. The remaining Mayordomos walk behind, followed by two Sacristans, one reading hymns in Spanish from a Catholic hymnal, the other carrying a lighted candle.

Moving counterclockwise, the procession halts at the altar of the Virgen Purísima. The Mayordomos carrying the two statues incline them toward one another until the heads touch, signifying a bowing-and-releasing exchange between Joseph and Mary. Mary's bowing expresses gratitude for her brother's generosity and sympathy. To the continuing accompaniment of drums, rattle, bells, and hymns, the procession circles back to its starting place, where the saints are returned to their platforms and drums and rattles replaced on the altar. Turtle-shell drums are used because when Christ was born and the night "lighted up," all the creatures burst into song, even the turtles in the rivers. The Mayordomos pray to the statues before returning to the church terrace for rounds of POX.

Building the Creche

On December 23 the Mayordomos, Sacristans, ritual advisers of the Mayordomos of Rosario, the Mayordomos' musicians, and other helpers spend the day building an enormous crèche (LECOPAT, literally "brush shelter"), in a niche of the side chapel of San Lorenzo Church where the altar of San Mateo stands. In shape and size the LECOPAT resembles a traditional Zinacanteco house (of wattle-and-daub walls and thatched roof). Its walls are constructed of vertical pine poles, across which strands of reeds are woven horizontally (lower right of Figure 38). Cypress branches are then woven into the walls so thickly that the pine and reed underpinnings are no longer visible (lower left of Figure 38). The roof is also made of poles of pine thickly covered with alternating strips of KRUS ˀEC' and C'IB. The end strips are both of palm. In the middle of the roof beam a small wooden cross is erected, wrapped with alternating pieces of another red bromeliad (VOHTON ˀEC') and dry, whitish corn husks (HOHOC').

Four tiles are removed from the floor to permit the insertion of four white pines which stand at the corners of the crèche. The use of white pine (K'UK' TOH, *Pinus ayacahuite*) is unique to this ritual context. According to Zinacantecos, this is the only species of pine which "talked" in mythological times, repeating over and over again, "K'UK', K'UK'." The word, literally translated, means "feather" or "crest," and may refer to the feathery appearance of the tree. The upper halves of the white pines are hung with lowland fruits brought by the Mayordomos; each Mayordomo must bring twelve pieces of fruit, including oranges, grenadines, and limes. The Mayordomos also bring SCUˀ MEˀTIK (breast of Our Holy Mother), a nipple nightshade (*Solanum mammosum* L.) which closely resembles in shape a female breast, to hang in the pines. In addition, those Mayordomos who have C'UM, a cushaw

by Mary Scott

38. The Crèche

(*Cucurbita Moschata* Duch.), in their lowland fields bring it for the trees.

Banana leaves, sugar cane, and bundles of XAN (the palm used in weaving Zinacanteco hats) are tied on either side of the doorway of the crèche. Two strands of hawthorn apples (K'AT'IX) are strung on maguey fibers, alternating red and yellow apples, and hung over the doorway in scallops. Hawthorn apples and nipple nightshade are also hung inside the crèche.

The two Christ children, San José, and the Virgin Mary are placed within on a table covered with lichens (ZONTE? AL BALAMIL, "Spanish moss of the earth"). As one faces the group, San José is on the left, then the younger brother Christ child, the older brother Christ child, and Mary. From Christmas Eve to New Year's Eve the Christ children lie in small wooden cradles; on New Year's Day they sit up in little wooden chairs. On either side are ears of seed maize and bags of seed beans placed by people who visit the crèche; it is believed that the seed gains strength and fertility through association with the birthplace of the Christ children.

The crèche is completed by late afternoon, and the Mayordomos retire to the terrace to spend the interval before the posada ceremony drinking liquor. Meanwhile, the civil officials from the cabildo are constructing another crèche—much smaller but of the same materials—on the altar in the church of San Sebastián.

The Drama of Ritual Aggression*

A familiar Zinacantan myth explains that a bull was present at the birth of the Christ child. Although the baby was dying from the cold, the animals refused to remain in the stable to warm it with their breath and body heat. Only the bull, at the request of Joseph and Mary, agreed to stay; it, therefore, plays an important part in this fiesta of the Christmas season. On December 24, at the house of the Senior Mayordomo of Rosario, bull-painting specialists (HPINTOLETIK, "painters") from VOM C'EN in the hamlet of Paste? construct a bull (VAKAX, from the Spanish *vaca*). The framework is approximately 2 meters long, 1 meter wide at the lower end of the structure, 1½ meters in height. It is constructed of saplings joined together with string, and a 3 x 9 cm. top runner board. Reed mats cover the entire structure with the exception of the front and bottom sides, which are left open so the performers can enter. The rectangles resulting from the construction of the framework are painted in red, white, and black. Toward the rear of the bull, in the upper left rectangle, and again near the head, in the upper right, a large design—which is the cattle brand of Zinacantan (see Figure 39)—is painted. Near the bull's head brightly painted letters announce in Spanish a "bill of sale," for example:

Zinacantan 1° de	Zinacantan 1st of
Enero 1960	January 1960
Compraron un Toro	Bought a Bull
Valor de 700 Pesos	Worth 700 pesos
de finca	from the
de Santo Tomás.	Santo Tomás ranch.

(Initially the date of the "bill of sale" is December 24, but when the bull is repainted on December 31—CKUX VAKAX, or "revival of the

*Heretofore, this has been referred to as the "Ritual Bullfight" (see Vogt 1969; Vogt 1970b; and more detailed descriptions in Bricker 1973; and Fletcher 1970). Further research, however, has revealed that, although the first act may be modeled in part on the Spanish bullfight, the overall performance bears little resemblance to it. I have decided, therefore, at the suggestion of Elizabeth M. Dodd, to call this rite the "Drama of Ritual Aggression" and to refer to the MAMALETIK and ME?CUNETIK as "fools of aggression," or for stylistic variation as "grandfather" and "grandmother." MAMAL and ME?CUN are Tzeltal terms of address referring to, respectively, an old man, and a father's sister; they are untranslatable in contemporary Tzotzil.

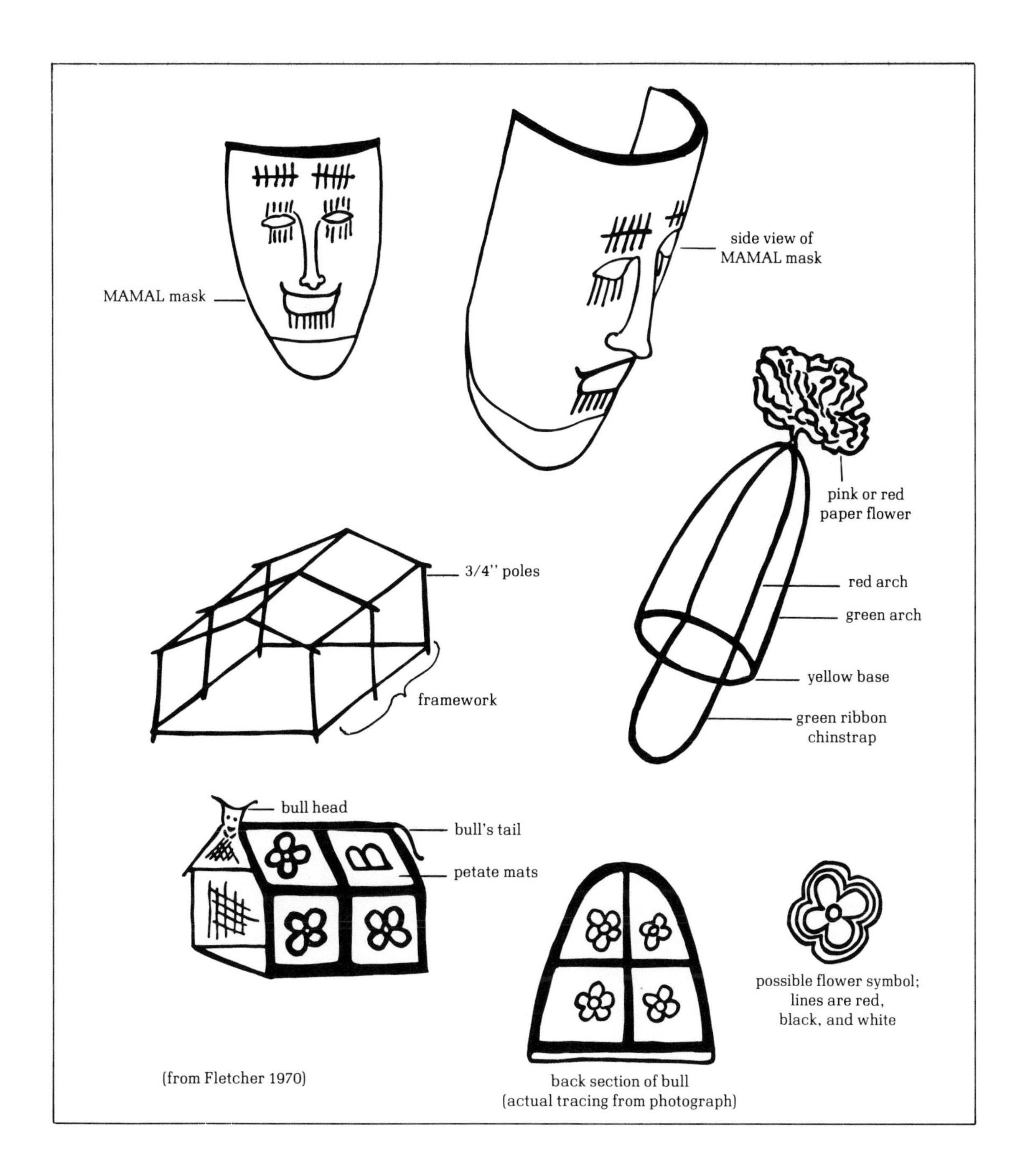

39. The ritual props used in the bull drama

bull"—it is changed to January 1, and the recorded price raised considerably.) On the bull's small triangular head are two tiny horns, painted green, red, and white; the tail is that of a real bull. Between performances the bull is hung in two slings from the roof-overhang of the house of the Senior Mayordomo; it is censed three times each day—possibly to keep "evil spirits" from entering (Bricker 1973: 45).

The bull and its owners—two "husbands" (called MAMALETIK), played by Senior Mayordomos, and two "wives" (called ME?CUNETIK), played by the junior partners of these Mayordomos, and their two children" (called ?ANHELETIK "angels"), played by boys dressed as angels—perform in public places and private homes on December 24-25, December 31-January 1, and January 6. Through humorous misbehavior in events concerning the bull's ownership, taming and killing, acceptable and unacceptable behavior for Zinacanteco men and women are dramatized. Unlike that of the "parents," the role of the "angels" is not humorous: their seriousness and relative passivity depict—in a different manner and for a younger age group—another model of proper Zinacanteco behavior.

40. A close-up of the two stick horses of the MAMALETIK

The Performers

MAMALETIK. The Senior Mayordomos alternately assume the roles of "husbands." When the paint on the bull is nearly dry, two of them enter the house of the Senior Mayordomo of Rosario to dress for a performance. Each wears a scarf tied in ceremonial style around his head; an old Zinacanteco hat hanging around his neck; a face mask painted red with a black beard; a necklace of small red and yellow hawthorn fruit strung on wire; a collarless woolen shirt, brown with black stripes, with three-quarter-length sleeves; brown knee-length chamois breeches; and a pair of high-back, open-toe ceremonial sandals. Each carries a two-meter-long brown wooden stick-horse, with short red leather reins and a hand-carved head with silvered eyes and forehead decor. In his right hand, each "husband" holds the deerbone handle of a rattle made from a gourd and covered with bright pink chicken feathers.

ME?CUNETIK. The partners of the MAMALETIK dress next in the house of the Senior Mayordomo. They wear outfits similar to those of Zinacanteco women: long, dark-blue skirts, pleated at the center front; red sashes; white cotton blouses (though hanging loose over the skirts rather than tucked inside); large white cotton scarves with bright pink pom-poms at the corners (the bride's large white head-scarf). Red and yellow hawthorn apple necklaces and high-back sandals provide a comic contrast to their otherwise feminine appearance. The incongruity is made further apparent through the gestures and behavior of these female impersonators. They do not attempt to imitate a woman's smaller steps or more quiet, modest manner; their performance is characterized by loud shouts, leaping, and masculine postures. They create a ludicrous and unbecoming picture of masculine behavior in women and by implication denounce the efforts of women to exercise male prerogatives. As godparents of the "angels," the two couples are compadres.

ˀANHELETIK. The roles of the senior and junior "angel-children" are played by boys between the ages of ten and twelve. They are selected, on the recommendation of the school principal, because of their reading and writing abilities, industriousness, and interest in becoming Sacristans. The "angels" are present, though not costumed, at the construction of the bull and the performance which follows the dressing of the "fools of aggression." After this, the boys invite the bull-constructors to their homes to witness another performance of the adult actors and the bull while the angels dress. Inside his home, the senior angel puts on high-backed sandals; bright pink or red knee-socks; blue or green knee-length velvet breeches, with tiny bells at the knee fastenings; a red shirt with white bands that cross on the chest and tie around the waist; and a red turban similar to those worn by Alféreces. Many aspects of the costume closely resemble the ceremonial dress of Alféreces who are changing office and of bridegrooms—symbolizing the transitional status of the ˀANHELETIK. The turban is topped by a kind of crown, approximately 30 cm. high, constructed from two bent saplings whose arches cross each other at the top and whose ends are secured on a sapling circlet (see Figure 41). The arches and circlet are painted red, yellow, or green, and paper flowers of red, green, or orange are attached at the crown where the arches cross. The crown rests on the forehead of the boy over the turban, and is held in place with a chin strap. Fully dressed, the senior angel joins the group waiting in his father's patio, and atole is served. The assemblage then moves to the home of the junior angel, where, as the boy dresses in identical costume, it watches another performance and is served another round of atole. The "angels" follow the "fools of aggression" and the musicians to each performance. They are invariably accompanied by members of their family who tidy their costumes and instruct or reprimand as needed. Essentially they are onlookers—learning adult behavior through observing—and errand boys—passing out cigarettes to cargo officials. They take an active role only infrequently: they recite prayers for the bull group in the church; on Epiphany, they dance together and/or with their ritual "parents"; that evening they remove their costumes and join in the capture of the bull.

Musicians. Two well-known and talented musicians, a violinist and guitarist, play throughout the Christmas ceremonies. (The same musicians perform with the T'ENT'EN drum during San Sebastián and for the Pasioneros during Carnaval.) They are second only to the Mayordomos in command of the ritual performances, directing many of the sequences and counseling the actors.

Bull-Masters. Throughout its dances, charges, and other activities, the bull is manipulated by a "bull-master," a young, sturdy Zinacanteco; an "understudy" replaces him when he tires.

The Performance

Full performances take place inside and in the courtyards of the churches of San Lorenzo and San Sebastián, at the houses of cargo officials, and in front of the cabildo. They form a developmental sequence from the first performance, given in the patio of the Mayordomo of Rosario on December 24, to the last, held the same place on January 6, each being related to those preceding and succeeding it. Variations are caused by the

41. The two "angels" who participate in the bull ritual

physical and temporal limitations of the "stages" used, and special episodes may be added.

Each bull performance has three acts of five episodes. Episode 1 is a "fight" between the bull and the stick-horse riders. In Act I, the "grandfathers" take the latter role, while the "grandmothers" stand between them, forming a line of performers which faces the bull some twenty feet away. (If the performance takes place in a house patio, the performers stand near the house cross, backs to it.) The MAMALETIK prepare to meet the bull, with stick-horses in their outside hands, the rattles in their inside hands, while the bull prances and shakes, impatient to charge. Just before the opponents race toward each other, the MEˀCUNETIK lift their skirts, exposing their genitals in an attempt to distract the bull and lessen the chance of his "goring" their ritual husbands. After two charges, in which the opponents meet in the middle, turn, and withdraw to their original positions, the bull succeeds in wounding the riders with his horns.

Episode 2 portrays the agony of the gored riders and the assistance given by their wives. As the victims writhe on the ground, moaning with pain, their wives hover, wailing in fright and sympathy. As the bull retires to one side and stands quietly watching, the wives attempt to assist the husbands to their feet using the stick-horses as lifting devices; they succeed only in pushing the sticks into the men's genitals. A verbal exchange follows, with intensely sexual double meaning, as they discuss where and how severely the men have been hurt. Finally, assisted by their wives, the MAMALETIK crawl along the ground to the highest ranking official seated among the spectators.

Episode 3 involves a request to the official to "cure" the ailing men. The double meanings continue:

MEˀCUN: Please, father,
  Please, my patron,
Mend the bones of my husband,
  My companion.

OFFICIAL: Why, what happened to him?
MEˀCUN: A bull gored him.
OFFICIAL: Well, why did you buy the bull then?
MEˀCUN: He thought it was a good bull, and, besides, I wanted it. I thought it would be good.
OFFICIAL: You shouldn't have bought it, for its goring is causing much suffering. Is anything broken?
MAMAL: Yes, something is broken. Please mend my bones.
OFFICIAL: I'll try to mend them.
MEˀCUN: Please mend them if possible.
OFFICIAL: I'll recite the [curing] formula:
TONTIKIL PUZUL
  ˀI TONTIKIL C'ABEN
Find your place, bones!
  Find your place, muscles!
Don't leave your hole, muscle!
  Don't leave your hole, bone!
Good.
Try it and see if they are well;
  Try it and see if they are healed.
MAMAL: [jumps into the air three times and repeats the following formula:]
MAMAL: Stretch out, bone!
  Stretch out, muscle!
Remember your place, bone!
  Remember your place, muscle!
Don't go to another hole, muscle!
  Don't leave your hole empty, bone!

(Bricker 1973: 22-23)

The "curer" may differ with the performance: the Presidente or some civil official when at the cabildo; a cargo official or the ritual adviser at cargoholders' houses; a musician when official cargoholders are absent.

Episode 4 concludes the "cure." While chanting the curing prayer, the official passes the gourd rattle of the ailing husband over each wound three times, being especially careful to "treat" the genitals of the men. During the cure, the official may reach over to touch the genitals of the wives with the rattle, or push it under their skirts. He brings laughter from the observers by asking the MAMALETIK if their wives are truly female. At this time, one may put his hand on the buttocks of the other's wife, as if to ascertain the answer to the official's question. He is usually struck by the jealous husband, to the further amusement of the crowd. When asked what payment he would like for his services, the official demands to sleep with the MEʔCUNETIK.

Episode 5 dramatizes the recovery of the husbands. With sweeping dramatic gestures, the men rise from their prone positions, leap into the air three times, and gallop furiously about on their stick-horses, indicating eagerness to fight the bull again.

In a full performance, the first act invariably involves the conflict between the bull and the "husbands." In the second act, the bull plays no part; rather, the two MAMALETIK charge each other on their horses, striking the poles together in passing, and accompanied as before by their wives. The third act sees the grandmothers charging each other "on horseback," with the "husbands" running alongside. In each act, however, the component parts remain essentially the same: (1) a "fight," involving the bull and/or horses; (2) dramatization of the agony of the wounded and the assistance of their mates; (3) the petitioning of an official (or musician) to "cure" the wounded; (4) the curing procedure; (5) the recovery of the riders.

When the wives have been thrown from the horses, the husbands tell the official that their "sides (wombs) are damaged." They ask that their mates be restored to health so that they might bear more children. The official adjures the wounded vaginas (as he did the wounded penises in Acts I and II) to remain with their mates after the "cure," implicitly advising marital fidelity. But he tests the couples by asking as payment for his services a "prickly squash," referring to the wife's genitalia and his desire to copulate with her. He scolds the husbands for having purchased a bull and horses too difficult to manage, and reprimands the women for having attempted to ride the horses, for which females are not intended. Throughout the joking runs a sober thread: the injurious effects of unacceptable behavior are being emphatically portrayed before the eyes of Zinacantecos who cannot help but absorb the lessons.

The Birth of the Christ Children

At about 10:30 P.M. on December 24 the ceremonies celebrating the birth of the Christ child(ren) begin at San Lorenzo. The two images of the Christ child, NINYO BANKILAL (Senior Infant) and NINYO ʔIZ'INAL (Junior Infant)—considered to be "brothers" by the Zinacantecos—are carried in procession to the Church of San Sebastián. The march is led by the "fools of aggression" and the musicians, followed by the ʔANHELETIK, Mayordomos, and Sacristans. The civil officials from the cabildo—four Civil Alcaldes, the Síndico, and the Presidente—take turns carrying the statues of Joseph and Mary and serve as "godfathers" for the Christ children. They are followed by the Elders of the cargoholders, who are last in the line of ritualists.

As the procession moves to the music of violin and guitar, the shooting of skyrockets, and the sound of flute and drums, the MAMALETIK, MEʔCUNETIK, and bull dance ahead, periodically returning to bow to the Christ children. At San Sebastián, the two children are placed in the crèche in the middle of the altar by the Presidente, after which the drama of ritual aggression is performed.

The posada ritual that follows has an important variation: the Mayordomos carry the images outside the church, and its doors are shut. With songs the Mayordomos petition to re-enter. They are answered by a group of singers inside, who first refuse, then grant entry. The symbolic moment of birth occurs when the Christ children are replaced on the altar, immediately following the repositioning of Joseph and Mary. In celebration of the event sparklers are handed out to young children, who run and play with them inside the church.

At approximately 1 A.M. the procession

returns to San Lorenzo, where the images of the two Christ children and Joseph and Mary, held by kneeling Mayordomos, are greeted by all present who approach and bow before this Zinacanteco "holy family." The images are then carried to the crèche where the two Christ children are placed in position by the Presidente.

The ceremony of the Birth of the Christ Child(ren) emphasizes annually several essential principles of Zinacanteco life. The ranking of the two Christs reiterates the importance of the Senior-Junior relationship among Zinacanteco men. Both Christs are male, as are the godparents. Further, since one of the more important associations with Christ is the Sun god, the sun is being "reborn" during these ceremonies: the winter solstice has just occurred and the sun is rising earlier again and producing longer days.

Christmas Day and the Spinning Lesson

After a 9 A.M. mass said by the priest from San Cristóbal, the "fools of aggression" execute a full performance inside the Church of San Lorenzo. The usual three acts are followed by a special routine, the "spinning lesson," one repeated in San Lorenzo church on New Year's Day and Epiphany (Bricker 1973: 18-20). The ME?CUNETIK, using gourds and cotton yarn on spindles, demonstrate their skills of spinning and weaving.* These ritual "wives" address the large crowd of female spectators: "Can you spin as well? See how beautiful my work is! If you cannot match this, we pity your poor husband!" The "grandfathers" join in this teasing admonishment, singling out individuals as examples of incompetent spinners and weavers. Such women draw back in genuine embarrassment and shame, covering their mouths with their hands or their entire faces with shawls.

*It may be significant that cotton, which is of pre-Columbian origin and hence preceded the use of wool in Zinacanteco culture, is selected for this ritual spinning lesson.

Although the incident is a humorous one for the majority of spectators, it provides an important lesson for all about the necessary skills of the model wife.

New Year's Day

On the evening of December 31, the Mayordomos and Sacristans sleep in the sacristy of the Church of San Lorenzo until midnight. At that time the Mayordomos, in pairs, light candles and pray to their saints for the protection of Zinacantan in the approaching year, and the Sacristans toll the church bells and fire rockets from the patio. The Mayordomos retire to the house of the Junior Mayordomo of Rosario to sleep until 4:30 A.M. when the performers of the drama of aggression must be readied. A full performance is given for the Christ children in San Lorenzo Church from 5 to 6 in the morning, after which the performers return to the Junior Mayordomo's house for breakfast.

The second performance at the church, following breakfast, is usually interrupted by the arrival of the priest from San Cristóbal to recite an 8 A.M. mass. From a spectator's point of view, the interruption is both interesting and disturbing: the priest halts the performance and demands that the crowd be silent; nuns accompanying him use long sticks to poke and push Zinacantecos into benches near the altar; the Sacristans are ordered to lock the church doors to prevent anyone from sneaking away. The mass is then said for a congregation which must be told when to kneel and stand, for few if any, of those present are familiar with the proceedings. At the priest's departure, the performance resumes. Dancing takes place at the back of the church and near the creche. Eventually the ritualists, followed by a large crowd of spectators happy to share the free liquor and atole, depart to visit the homes of the new cargoholders.

At 4 P.M. the entourage approaches the cabildo in front of which the Presidente and other civil officials are seated, waiting. The presidente asks the MAMALETIK to produce the bull's ownership papers. A ludicrous attempt to explain how the papers were lost follows. Against the background of their exaggerated alarm and shouted protests, the Presidente accuses the "grandfathers" of having stolen the bull and orders them thrown into jail. A lively chase ensues, as the accused flee from the cabildo pursued by the Mayores and a crowd of laughing young boys. The "bull thieves" are captured, only to escape and be captured again and again. They are finally escorted into the jailhouse and placed behind bars, wailing in comic distress. The "grandmothers" plead with the Presidente for their release, and after fifteen minutes of harassment, he gives in. Free, the MAMALETIK join the other performers in enacting the bull drama before the Presidente and other civil authorities.

Late in the afternoon, after a full day of performing, the ritualists return to the house of the Senior Mayordomo of Rosario for the evening meal. Here, the bull is replaced in its slings and costumes are carefully put away to await the performances on January 6.

Epiphany

January 6 marks the end of the three-day fiesta of Epiphany during which two Alféreces (Divina Cruz and Virgen de Soledad) terminate their cargos. The day's many and diverse activities comprise the most strenuous work of the fiesta period for the performers.

In the early morning the Mayordomos place necklaces on the saints in the church and retire to the home of the Senior Mayordomo of Rosario for a meal. When the Mayordomos of Santa Cruz and San Antonio have dressed in their MAMALETIK and ME?CUNETIK costumes, and the ?ANHELETIK have arrived fully dressed, the ritualists dance to special Carnaval music. The Senior "husband," "wife," and "angel" stand in a line, facing their junior partners. In time to the music, the senior performers slowly raise their right legs to touch toes with their junior counterparts. This is repeated with their left legs; then again with the right. At this time the partners exchange positions, crossing to the opposite line, and repeat the steps. When this sequence has been completed three times, the full bull performance is given three times lasting altogether about an hour, the "angels" watching from the sidelines and passing out cigarettes.

The performers and spectators depart for a performance at the Church of San Lorenzo, where, by interrupting the ritual again, the priest is able to swell the attendance at the Catholic mass. As before, his departure signals the resumption of the drama, performed before the crèche and in the west end of the church. During the remainder of the morning, the full performance is given twice in San Lorenzo, twice in the Church of San Sebastián, and once before the Alféreces seated in front of the entrance to San Lorenzo.

At noon, the *nombramiento* (naming), a special board with lighted candles attached at the top and the names of the Incoming Mayordomos of Santa Cruz and San Antonio written at the bottom, is delivered to the chapel of Señor Esquipulas by the "fools of aggression." Leaping, shouting, and dancing, as if in a performance, the ritual husbands and wives place the wooden tablet on the saint's altar, having greeted the Elders attending the presentation. The Grand Alcalde and First Regidor serve POX to the gathering, as the MAMALETIK and ME?CUNETIK, with the help of assistants, distribute coffee and rolls.

The "fools of aggression" rejoin the remaining Mayordomos at the Church of San Lorenzo, where the necklaces are taken from the saint statues, and the roles of the "husbands" and "wives" are reassigned to other Mayordomos. The group members disperse to their own homes where the necklaces of the saints are replaced on the house altars and a meal is consumed. At 2 P.M., all the Mayordomos and the bull and his entourage reconvene at San Lorenzo.

To collect money for the approaching fiesta of San Sebastián a large procession of Zinacanteco officials and their ritual assistants marches through the ceremonial center. It is led by the bull and the "grandfathers" and "grandmothers," followed by the Junior Mayordomos, the Sacristans, "angels," musicians, the Senior Mayordomos carrying flags, Escribanos, and, last, the Elders. The men stop at seven street crosses, where the drama of ritual aggression is performed as the Regidores circulate among the nearby houses asking for donations. At this time spectators feel free to grab the hawthorn apple necklaces of the dancing performers, and assistants are kept busy replacing them. The march terminates at the chapel, where the Alféreces, who have danced most of the afternoon at San Lorenzo, and the Presidente and civil officials also gather.

The assembled cargoholders then commence the flag-changing ceremony signifying the cargo changes of the Alféreces of Divina Cruz and Soledad. As the Alféreces and Regidores solemnly execute this part of the change-of-office ceremony, the "fools of aggression," kneeling next to them, mimic them: as the Alféreces and Regidores bow and kiss necklaces, the MAMALETIK and ME?CUNETIK bow and kiss their necklaces of hawthorn apples; when the officials cross themselves and pray, the "grandfathers" and "grandmothers" cross themselves with the gourd rattles, and pray long, loud, and incoherently; as the cargoholders exchange flags, the "grandfathers" exchange stick-horses. Both ceremonies, earnest and comic, end with a procession of the group's important members.

The bull ritualists retire to the house of the Senior Mayordomo of Rosario to rest up for the evening sorties to the center of HTEK-LUM which precede the midnight killing of the bull. These short excursions are characterized by frantic movements of the bull amidst a crowd of highly excited spectators; the animal charges madly about the main churchyard and streets, as if sensing the approaching fate, while the gathered group chases him, throwing lassos at every opportunity. When the frightened animal is finally roped and pulled to the ground, the bullmaster is offered a drink of liquor by the captor. The liquor soon revives the bull, who jumps up and runs off to a nearby canteen, where he demands that the owner open the bar and serve free drinks to his entire entourage. Afterward the bull group returns to the house of the Senior Mayordomo of Rosario to dance and rest before the next excursion to the center.

Following this first trip, the bright horns of the bull are cut off by the bull-painters and replaced by oak branches. At the end of the fifth excursion into the center, the bull is caught in the patio of the house of the Senior Mayordomo of Rosario and secured with a rope to a thick post; the bull performer climbs out. At midnight the "fools of aggression" climb on the bull and plunge "knives" (made of wood covered with silver foil) into its neck. The "blood" (POX mixed with mint, onions, and chili to produce a red color) which flows from the wounds into a clay pot, is served to all present by the MAMALETIK. Men climb inside the framework and thrash about so as to tear the reed mats from the sapling body; the mangled remains are put aside to be fully dismantled the next day. In celebration of the bull's death, a ceremonial meal, accompanied by more "blood," is served. This is strongly evocative of the curing ritual, during which the patient drinks the blood of the chicken "substitute," gaining strength from its soul.

What can all this ritual activity—which begins with the creation of the bull on December 24 and ends with its "death" thirteen days later on January 6—possibly symbolize?

At a level of analysis about which Zinacanteco

informants are quite articulate it is a commentary on what they regard as acceptable and unacceptable behavior. (This line of analysis is expanded by Bricker [1973] in her study of ritual humor.) The ritual provides a statement not only about the cultural code but, more significantly, about the gap between the abstract principles and their application to everyday behavior.

Some examples will illustrate: the remarks of the officials who "cure" the "gored" "grandfathers" or "grandmothers," adjuring the wounded "bone" (penis) or "hole" (vagina) to stay with its mate; the punning when an official requests as payment a "prickly squash," thereby testing the fidelity of the husband-wife pair; the reprimanding of the grandfathers for having purchased a bull they cannot manage and horses they cannot tame, and of the grandmothers for having attempted to ride horses.

Consider the meek, quiet, and obedient behavior of the boys who play the senior and junior ʔANHELETIK. These angels provide a symbolic human extension of the Senior and Junior Christ children. They sit or stand quietly, arms crossed, respectfully observing and absorbing the rituals performed by the adults; they perform favors and errands without complaint or hesitation; they interact harmoniously and with consideration—unlike real brothers who quarrel. They pass from one mode of proper behavior into another as they ritually become "older" during the course of the Christmas season festivities: during the first days, as symbolic extensions of the Christ children, they behave as meek and obedient early teenagers in the latency period; at the end of the Christmas season, in taking off their costumes and using lariats to help chase and "kill" the bull, the angels behave like assertive and courageous teenagers.

The "jailing of the husbands" comments on events common in Zinacantan: husbands engage in disruptive behavior and are jailed; their wives appear before the Presidente to beg that their husbands be released. The "spinning lesson" is an obvious commentary on the industriousness and skill required of the ideal Zinacanteco wife, and the failure of some to display appropriate willingness and talent.

At a deeper, meta-language, level many more symbolic meanings pervade this drama of ritual aggression. Its sexual "horseplay" would delight a Freudian psychoanalyst. At almost every turn artifacts symbolizing sexual organs are used and double-entendre references to penis, vagina, and sex act are being made. I believe this symbolism is an important extension of the sex and fertility symbols found in the squash-eating "masses," the ritual plants that form the crèche, and the symbolic re-enactment of the birth.

At this level the ritual comments on three of the most important points of stress in Zinacanteco social interaction: relations between the sexes, relations among persons of varying ages, and relations between compadres. Years of observation of behavior and study of myths have provided considerable evidence of the tensions that exist between husbands and wives, between younger and older people, and between ritual kinsmen. It is highly significant that the major roles in the drama are "husbands and wives," that they are played by Senior and Junior Mayordomos, and that the two pairs are "compadres." Using ritual roles that encompass these contradictory and ambiguous relations, the "ritual of aggression" dramatizes both the existing tensions, and the possible reconciliation which can be achieved through a third party: a "shaman," or one who "sees" better than other mortals the ways and wishes of the gods, a high-ranking civil or religious cargoholder, or a musician, all representatives of social order.

What does the "bull" symbolize as he attacks and gores the "fools of aggression" and in the end is slain, dismantled, and destroyed? I have already noted that bulls are considered very "hot." Although heat is traditionally associated with sacred power, an excess spells danger and destruction: an overly powerful sun can wither the maize; an overly powerful shaman can perform witchcraft and bring sickness and death.

Bulls figure prominently in dreams as witches' animal companions (Robert M. Laughlin, personal communication, 18 September 1972). From native exegesis it is clear that the "hot" bull represents an evil power. During the bull performances, the musicians play what is recognized as "bad" music; at the moment of the bull's "death," they begin to play "good" music. The "grandfathers" express the anticipated happiness of Zinacantecos at the prospect of the bull's death when they instruct the women: "when you get home, make a lot of tortillas. People from all the hamlets are going to eat together once we have killed the bull."

Above all, the bull appears to symbolize disorder in the form of uncontrolled power and unruly social behavior: he repeatedly "gores" the "grandfathers" and "grandmothers," who are members of the religious hierarchy. The victims must be "cured" by symbolic representatives of social order. Lasting order is restored only when the bull is "killed" and his "blood" drunk.

10

End-of-the-Year/New-Year Cargo Ceremonies II

THE FIESTA OF San Sebastián requires more preparation, involves more participants, and attracts as large, if not a larger, crowd than any other fiesta in Zinacantan. Although the larger Church of San Lorenzo is used more and its saint is the patron of Zinacantan, the fiesta of San Lorenzo in August does not compare in elaborateness with that of San Sebastián.

The mythological explanations of this extraordinary fiesta lie in the various versions of a myth told in Zinacantan and obviously related to a sixteenth-century Catholic account. Sebastián, born of a noble family and commander of a large company of Praetorian guards, was a favorite of the Roman Emperor Diocletian. Unknown to Diocletian, however, he was a devout Christian—a criminal in the eyes of the Empire. Sebastián's faith was revealed when he exhorted two Christian soldiers being tortured for their beliefs to give up their lives rather than renounce the True Faith. The Emperor, after attempting to dissuade his favorite from "heretical" convictions, ordered him tied to a stake and lanced with arrows. Irene, a widow of one of the Christian soldiers, nursed the gravely wounded Sebastián back to health. Refusing to flee, the young Christian boldly positioned himself in front of Diocletian while pleading for the lives of several Christians. The Emperor took no chances the second time: Sebastián was killed, brutally and certainly, with clubs.

The myths of San Sebastián told in Zinacantan are products of over four-hundred years of cultural syncretism, as is apparent in this version elicited from Cep Nuh, a fifty-five-year-old informant from Nacih:

In olden times San Sebastián was a Captain under the command of a General who had two daughters. The General wanted San Sebastián to marry one of the daughters, but San Sebastián refused and the General announced he was going to kill him. The General took San Sebastián to a rocky place in the woods at the edge of the sea in Oaxaca, and secured him to the trunk of a tree by tying his two hands behind him. Many animals and savages that lived in the woods came by—two BOLOMETIK [jaguars], two K'UK'UL CONETIK [large toucan birds], two ZONTEˀETIK [savages], one male and one female [now, the myth-teller added, we call them BANKILAL and ˀIZ'INAL, instead of male and female], and a number of HˀIK'ALETIK [Blackmen]. Two KAˀBENALETIK [Lacandon Indians], who also lived in the woods, arrived. All the animals tried to kill San Sebastián by eating him; the Lacandons, who saw that San Sebastián was a ladino, tried to kill him with arrows because they hated ladinos and wanted to kill them all. These efforts to kill him were unsuccessful.

Then San Sebastián's younger brother, San Fabián, and younger sister, Santa Catalina, came to be with him and to help him.

Later the two SAK HOLETIK ["White Heads," defined as Aztec Indians] came to see San Sebastián, and observed that he was still alive. They went back to call on the General and to tell him that San Sebastián was not dying and to request that the General send soldiers to kill him.

The soldiers came and tried to shoot San Sebastián with guns. They shot at him, but the bullets would not penetrate, for in front of the tree trunk that held San Sebastián was the K'OLTIXYO [testing target] which protected him. Fabián told them that if you wish to kill San Sebastián, you must first knock down the target. The soldiers grabbed a lance that was nearby and took turns trying to strike the target; but none could hit it. The soldiers then returned to the General to report that they could not kill San Sebastián, and that he had two companions with him—San Fabián and Santa Catalina. The General was furious for he thought that Santa Catalina must be San Sebastián's fiancée. He said: "Tomorrow, I shall go kill him myself."

The next day the General returned to the site with his soldiers. As they approached they heard the T'ENT'EN drum being played by Fabián. Upon arrival, the General asked Sebastián again to marry one of his daughters, but Sebastián did not answer. Instead, Fabián spoke to the General, explaining that he [Fabián] was Sebastián's younger brother, and that Catalina was the younger sister, and that they had come to help Sebastian. The General announced that Sebastián must be killed. But Fabián replied that he must first knock down the target. The General asked what it was, and Fabián said it was Sebastián's heart, already out of his body and hanging in front of his body. The General then grabbed one of the lances and tried to charge the target. He tried several times with both the point and the side of the lance, with no success. The General said the lance was no good, "too light," so he tried the other, made of gold and silver, and weighing 8 arrobas [about 200 pounds]. This lance was so heavy that it fell to the ground as the horse ran fast, and the General suffered a heavy blow on the head by the target. Then many of the soldiers and also the animals tried to strike the target. But all failed; no one could kill San Sebastián; he was left alive.

The next day an ox cart was passing nearby, and the owner of the cart heard the sound of the T'ENT'EN playing. He left his cart and went into the woods to see what it was. There he found three saints' statues—San Sebastián, San Fabián, and Santa Catalina—all lighted with candles. The drum was at the feet of San Sebastián with the drumstick on top of it. Off to the right in front of the drum were the target, the two lances, and on top of the lances the rope for hanging up the target. Nearby there was a book which the owner of the cart opened and read and discovered that San Sebastián would like to leave this rocky place by the edge of the sea in Oaxaca, but that Fabián and Catalina wished to remain there. The owner of the cart went back to tell his companions, but when they returned to the site, they found only San Sebastián, the T'ENT'EN, the K'OLTIXYO, the lances, and the book—Fabián and Catalina having disappeared into the woods. They loaded up the objects they had found and set out eastward, eventually arriving in Zinacantan Center where they camped in a pasture that had good grass for the oxen. When they awoke the following morning, they were startled to discover that San Sebastián (and the other objects) were missing from the cart. But in the early dawn, they saw candles burning in a nearby manchineel patch and thought the saint must be there. They went to the manchineel patch and found San Sebastián tied to one of the trees, with his left hand behind him, his right hand above his head, "as he appears in the

Church of San Sebastián today." The owner of the cart consulted the book again and learned that San Sebastián wished to stay here with the T'ENT'EN, the K'OLTIXYO, and the lances. So they hitched up their oxen and traveled on, leaving San Sebastian in the manchineel patch.

The next day the Zinacantecos discovered San Sebastián and the objects with him. They consulted the book and learned that, although he was a younger brother of their San Lorenzo, he did not wish to live in the same house, but preferred one of his own. The Zinacantecos discussed this and thought of building a house for San Sebastián. But the VAXAK-MEN, who were very elderly Zinacantecos, said they would build the house. They built the house [church] in three days, during which time there was a K'INUBAL [a winter storm from the north] with much wind and rain. In three days the storm passed, and the church was completed, and San Sebastián placed in it. He is called MARTIR KAPITAN, because as a living person he was a Captain.

Later on, when the small T'ENT'EN, the target and the lances were all kept on the altar in the church, a larger T'ENT'EN drum appeared and was kept with these objects. Then there came a time [during the time of anticlericalism in the late 1920s and early 1930s] when the governor of Chiapas told the Zinacantecos that the government did not want saints, and that they should pull the churches down and destroy the saints. The shamans recommended that the large drum [the Senior T'ENT'EN] be taken to LAC CIKIN and hidden in a cave there; and that the small drum [Junior T'ENT'EN], the target, and the lances all be hidden in the hamlet of ʔElan Voʔ After the revolution passed, the image of San Sebastián was returned to the church, but the other objects were kept in ʔElan Voʔ in the houses of the Lopis Cikuʔetik. The people of the neighboring hamlet of Pasteʔ were resentful and wanted these objects kept in their hamlet. A meeting was held to settle the dispute. It was decided that the target and lances would be kept in Pasteʔ, while the T'ENT'EN remained in ʔElan Voʔ.

The original K'OLTIXYO was made of gold and silver; also one of the lances was of gold and silver and very heavy. Some Zinacantecos say the shamans also recommended that the target, which was so heavy it took two men to lift it, and the gold and silver lance, also be kept at LAC CIKIN. Now the K'OLTIXYO and both of the lances are made of wood.

The saint images of San Sebastián's younger brother and younger sister, Fabián, and Catalina, were purchased later and placed in the church.

One time years ago when the two Lopis Cikuʔ brothers, Xun and Martil, were fighting with each other, the T'ENT'EN fled and they were left without a drum. They came to the Elders to report that they had lost the drum. The shamans began to pray and make ceremonies so the T'ENT'EN would return. They looked for it in all the caves. For almost a year it was gone. Then Xun Cikuʔ dreamed that the drum was in POK'EB, a cave below Pasteʔ. He went alone and found the drum, and came to tell the Elders and the shamans at the cabildo. The shamans took candles and skyrockets and brought the drum to ʔElan Voʔ. Many Zinacantecos wanted to bring it back to the church of San Sebastián, but Xun Cikuʔ insisted upon keeping it and built a chapel for the drum. We are not certain today whether it really was the same old drum, or whether Xun Cikuʔ made another one himself.

So the fiesta of San Sebastián goes on today to show the people of Zinacantan what happened in this myth.

(Vogt, Field Notes, 23 January 1972)

Ritual Impersonators*

The fiesta of San Sebastián gives the new cargoholders an opportunity to celebrate their first major fiesta; thus, they are appropriately dressed in official regalia. The outgoing officials, on the other hand, serve as impersonators of mythological figures (HTOY-K'INETIK, literally

*These ritual actors have previously been referred to as "entertainers" (see, for example, Vogt 1969). Since they are ritually acting out the myth of San Sebastián, I have decided to call them "impersonators" or "actors," to emphasize that their function is less to "entertain" than to re-enact the myth.

"lifters" or "elevators of the fiesta," but figuratively "rising heats or suns") and dress for their roles in distinctive costumes.

Six officials of the top three levels of the cargo hierarchy comprise the group of Senior Impersonators (MUK'TIK HTOY-K'INETIK). They are divided into three "couples": MUK'TA and BIK'IT HKAXLAN (Castilians), played by the Grand and Second Alcaldes; MUK'TA and BIK'IT HXINULAN (female Castilians), played by the Alféreces of Santo Domingo and San Lorenzo; MUK'TA and BIK'IT SAK HOL (White Heads), roles assumed by the First and Second Regidores.

The HKAXLANETIK dress as colonial "Spanish Gentlemen," wearing gold-embroidered red coats and knickers, red kneesocks, and high-backed sandals; mirrors dangle from strings around their wrists and necks. The MUK'TA HKAXLAN carries the sacred painting of San Sebastián in a net bag which hangs from his right shoulder by a leather strap. The HXINU LANETIK, "Spanish Ladies," dress in embroidered white blouses, red skirts, knee-length red stockings, and high-backed sandals; rosaries and mirrors hang around their necks. Large veils of shiny purple or red are surmounted by broad-brimmed Alférez hats of black felt with gold bands that hold upright two sets of peacock feathers, one on each side. They carry tiny combs in small white, blue, or red enamel bowls. The SAK HOLETIK, "White Heads," dress in felt hats covered with white *ixtle* (fiber derived from the maguey plant), long-sleeved white shirts, white capes that reach below the hips, and white breeches. A contrast is created by the addition of a red turban below the hat, and bright red knee-socks. A large block "E" of tinsel, turned so that the prongs hang down, dangles on their foreheads, and each wears mirrors and rosaries around his neck, and carries a small bow and arrow in his left hand and a rattle in his right. These impersonators are sometimes called "Moctezumas," or "Aztecs."

The group of Junior Impersonators (BIK'ITAL HTOY-K'INETIK, literally "small lifters of the fiesta," figuratively "small" or "little rising heats" or "suns") is comprised of five subgroups, whose roles are filled by lower-ranking members of last year's hierarchy: the Third and Fourth Regidores become the BANKILAL and ʔIZ'INAL KAʔBENAL; the Alféreces of Trinidad and San Antonio play the BANKILAL and ʔIZ'INAL BOLOM; the two Mayordomo Reyes take the part of the BANKILAL and ʔIZ'INAL K'UK'ULCON; the two Mesoneros play the BANKILAL and ʔIZ'INAL ZONTEʔ; and six Mayores become the six HʔIK'ALETIK. The KAʔBENAL wear dark blue dress coats and breeches, and black hats, covered with dark *ixtle* from which a long red or purple braid hangs to the waist. They carry rattles in their right hands and bows and arrows tied together in the left. Zinacantecos often refer to them as "Lacandons." The BOLOMTIK (Jaguars) are dressed in one-piece, jaguarlike costumes of orange-brown material painted with black circles and dots. Their hats are of jaguar fur. They carry stuffed animals in addition to whips and sharply pointed sticks. The BOLOMETIK make a "huh, huh, huh" sound. The K'UK'UL CONETIK are, literally translated, "plumed serpents," although the costumes suggest, and many Zinacantecos believe, that they represent either the "raven," which brought maize to man after the flood, or a "toucan," which stole and ate Zinacanteco maize and killed people with a peck on the back of their heads. It is also possible that these are some kind of manifestation of KUKULKAN, the Maya version of the plumed serpent deity, Quetzalcoatl. Each K'UK'UL CON wears knee-length trousers, and a white shirt and beaked headdress, each with green and red dots. The beak is held open with an ear of maize (large for the senior, small for the junior); the butts of the ears are to the impersonator's right. Small wooden wings, also painted white, red, and green, protrude from their backs. The K'UK'UL

CONETIK make the sound "hurr, hurr." The ZONTEˀETIK (Wearers of Spanish Moss)—also referred to by informants as PUK'UH HNATIKIL HOL (long-haired demons)—are dressed in green velvet pants, black ceremonial robes, and black felt hats from which long bunches of Spanish moss cascade down their backs to the ground. The six to eight HˀIK'ALETIK wear leather pants and black cotton jackets. Their faces and arms are blackened with ashes; like the "Jaguars," they carry stuffed animals and pointed sticks. Their characteristic sound is "ves, ves, ves."

Props

The performances of the ritual actors require special paraphernalia, with the most significant the K'OLTIXYO lance target, the T'ENT'EN drum, the BOLOM TEˀ or "jaguar tree," and stuffed animals, called C'UC'.

The K'OLTIXYO is the "testing target" for the mounted Senior Impersonators and accompanies them on visits to the homes of new cargoholders. During the year it is kept by a lineage in the Pasteˀ waterhole group of VOM C'EN. The Senior Impersonators formally petition the target from the lineage and are responsible for its care throughout the fiesta period. The target (carried in the left hand of the Big Spanish Gentleman) is a wooden cylinder about 3-4 inches in diameter and a foot long. A hole drilled near the top holds

42. Left to right: ZONTEˀETIK, K'UK'ULCONETIK, and KAˀBENALETIK

a rope by which the target is suspended for action; multi-colored ribbons flow from the bottom. The cylinder is painted red and decorated with a silver cross outlined in black near the top, and five broad silver rings with narrow black and yellow bands (see Figure 43).

The T'ENT'EN, not unique to Zinacantan, is a type of drum called *teponaztle* that is common to many Indian cultures of Middle America (Saville 1925; Phelps 1970). It must be requested from its "owners" in the hamlet of ˀElan Voˀ by the Junior Impersonators, who sponsor and accompany it throughout the fiesta. It is two feet long and six inches in diameter (see Figure 44). It is constructed from two types of wood glued together: C'UT TEˀ (Spanish cedar, *Cedrela odorata* L.), which faces the spectators while the drum is being played, and C'IX TEˀ (black cherry, *Prunus capuli* Cav.), which faces the drum-carrier. (The drum is carried on a tumpline and played from behind with a stick, on alternating tongues.) The Tzotzil dictionary (Laughlin 1975) lists two definitions for T'ENT'EN: "teponaztle," and "short" or "runty" with specific references to a person or animal. These words suggest a small, short, or stunted drum, a description that fits some mythological accounts of the drum as the junior of a pair of teponaztles used by San Sebastián.

Throughout most of the year, the T'ENT'EN rests in a small chapel in ˀElan Voˀ where it has been kept by a Lopis Cikuˀ lineage for at least the four generations remembered by Zinacantecos. The chapel also houses all the paraphernalia used in connection with the drum: the red POK' with which it is covered for special events; the ribbons attached to it; the tumpline used to carry it; the drumstick, made of the heart of an oak and renewed every four years; two sets of small bows and arrows carried by the drum-carrier and by KAˀBENALETIK; and a box in which the drum is kept. Two days before its January 18th trip to Zinacantan Center, the drum is ritually washed in water containing leaves of sacred plants (ZIS

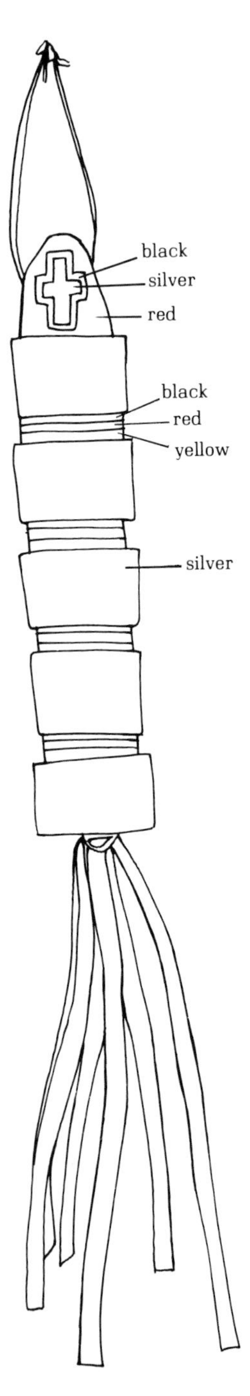

43. K'OLTIXYO, testing target

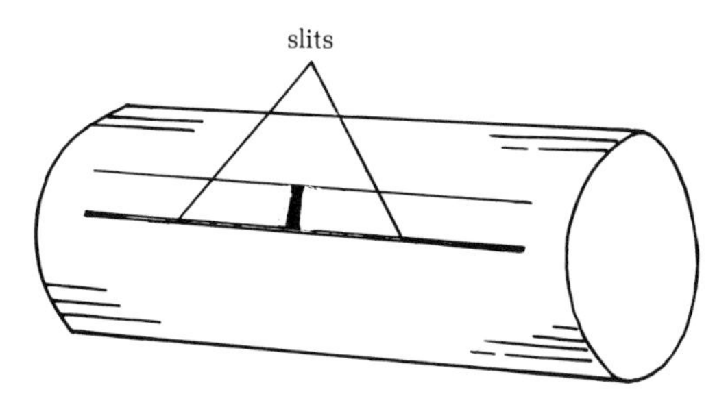

44. The sacred T'ENT'EN

ˀUC and TILIL), reglued, and decorated with bright new ribbons. The similarity between its treatment and that of saint images is striking. Like a saint it is referred to as "Our Holy Father T'ENT'EN," and receives a flower renewal ritual every two weeks and daily offerings of candles and incense; before its major ceremonial appearance, it is washed and "clothed."

The drum is involved in only two rituals each year: the fiesta of San Sebastián and the rain-making ritual, for which shamans must make a long pilgrimage to the top of Junior Great Mountain south of Teopisca. Its appearance at any other fiesta is forbidden. A story tells that some twenty years ago a man in ˀElan Voˀ dreamt the drum wished to go to the fiesta of San Lorenzo. The owner was authorized by the Presidente to take it to the Center for the fiesta in August. Eight days later the man who dreamed died, along with all his family, proving that the T'ENT'EN has a strong and powerful innate soul and that it wishes to appear in the Center only for the fiesta of San Sebastián.

Another special artifact is the BOLOM TEˀ (Jaguar Tree) made of an alder tree (NOK) that grows along the river in the Center. The bark is stripped off its trunk and limbs and on January 17 it is erected by the Jaguars and Blackmen.

Stuffed animals, principally squirrels, but sometimes iguanas, coatis or spider monkeys, are carried by the Jaguars and Blackmen. These symbolize the wives of delinquent cargoholders who have failed to appear and carry out their ceremonial duties, and other personages the actors wish to mock and punish.

The early preparations for the January fiesta begin the preceding summer. Starting in July, the Senior Impersonators must visit the custodians of the K'OLTIXYO and the Junior Impersonators the custodians of the T'ENT'EN three times with gifts of liquor and bread to request that these sacred objects be brought to the Ceremonial Center for the fiesta. The last visit occurs on January 15. While last year's hierarchy prepare for the dramatic aspects of the fiesta, the new cargoholders buy supplies and make arrangements for the ritual details of the change-of-office for the two Mayordomos and the two Alféreces of San Sebastián. Other preparations include visits made to ˀAz'am, Sak Lum, and Nabencauk before January 15 to insure the presence of the visiting saints from those hamlets for the Fiesta of Señor Esquipulas in the chapel.

Schedule of Events

(Vogt 1969: 544-546)

January 16-18. Last year's cargoholders visit church of San Sebastián to ask forgiveness for negligence in their cargos.

January 17 (BAL-TEˀ TA NA, "house flower renewal"). Mayordomos renew flowers on their house altars. Assistants prepare San Sebastián churchyard for fiesta.

January 18 (CUK NICIM, "tying the flowers"). Mayordomos renew church flowers.

Early morning: T'ENT'EN arrives and is met and accompanied by Junior Impersonators to the house of relatives of the owner of the drum. K'OLTIXYO is met and escorted by the Senior Impersonators.

Evening: Junior Impersonators visit new cargoholders' houses with the T'ENT'EN, Senior Impersonators with the K'OLTIXYO (rounds continue every evening until all new officials are visited). Senior Impersonators attend ritual washing of San Sebastián picture at the home of the Grand Alcalde.

January 19 (CAN-K'OBEL, "the learning of the hands").

Forenoon: New MOLETIK meet San Sebastián picture coming from Rancho San Nicolás and escort it to Church of San Sebastián. Alféreces dance outside San Sebastián.

Noon to sunset: Performances in San Sebastián churchyard by both MUK'TA and BIK'IT HTOY-K'INETIK, not fully costumed; "Running of the Horses," followed by Junior Actors dancing to the T'ENT'EN; the Senior Actors "testing" with the K'OLTIXYO; "Running of the Horses" at sundown.

After sunset: Coffee served at houses of Alféreces.

Evening: "Spanish Gentlemen" fetch "Spanish Ladies" from their houses.

Night: Alféreces' oath of office in Chapel of Esquipulas. Both groups of ritual actors continue visits to houses of new cargoholders.

January 20 (BA VEˀEL, the "first" or "waxing banquet").

Early morning: Mayordomos place necklaces on saints' statues. 8 A.M. Mass by Catholic priest.

Forenoon: "Dance of Drunks" in San Sebastián churchyard performed by the four Alféreces of San Sebastián changing cargos.

Noon: Gifts of fruit given by Mayordomos to Sacristans, and by Alféreces to their musicians. "Running of the Horses," followed by arrival of Junior Actors.

Afternoon: Junior Actors divide into two groups; one performs ritual sequence at Jaguar Rock, the other at NIOˀ. Arrival of Senior Actors; "Testing of the Impersonators" with the K'OLTIXYO. Banquet with special food served to new cargo and civil officials at two sittings: new MOLETIK and Civil Officials, followed by Alféreces. Junior Actors perform. Senior Actors serve atole to new Mayordomos near San Sebastián church door. Formal performances by Senior and Junior Actors.

Sundown: "Running of the Horses." After ceremonial leave-taking from saints, crosses, and church, all groups are served atole at houses of new Alféreces.

Night: Circuits of Alféreces. Continuing visits of Ritual Actors to the cargoholders' houses.

January 21 (MUˀYUK VEˀEL, "no banquet"). Activity identical to that of previous day, without banquet or ritual at Jaguar Rock and NIOˀ.

Late afternoon: Alféreces' flag-changing ceremony in the courtyard of San Lorenzo Church, followed by serving of atole at houses of new Alféreces.

January 22 (SLAHEB K'AK'AL VEˀEL, "[day Of] last banquet.") Activity similar to that of January 20. Exceptions:

Forenoon: Mayordomos remove necklaces from statues of saints; return necklaces to house altars.

Late afternoon: Junior Actors light candles at Chapel of Esquipulas and pray for forgiveness for negligence in past cargos, dance, and return to household of T'ENT'EN drum, which they guard through the night; burn stuffed animals.

January 23. Visiting saints escorted to edge of Zinacantan by new MOLETIK. K'OLTIXYO escorted similarly by new Senior Actors; T'ENT'EN by the Junior Actors.

January 24. New Grand Alcalde erects his house altar.

January 25. Retiring Grand Alcalde gives symbols of office to new official in special house ceremony.

Unique Features of the Fiesta

Preparation of the Churchyard of San Sebastián. On January 17 assistants of the ritual actors remove the pasture fence around the churchyard and place small pine trees around the performance area in front of the church door. Two upright posts, which will later hold the K'OLTIXYO, are set in the ground, and an open-ended brush chute is constructed by the Spanish Gentlemen and White Heads. The Jaguar Tree, approximately twenty feet tall, stripped of its bark, is set up in the churchyard.

The cross shrines facing each other—SKRUS BIK'TAL HTOY-K'INETIK at the western edge of the fiesta grounds and SKRUS MUK'TIK HTOY-K'INETIK to the east of the "testing target"—are decorated with pine trees and red geraniums. The arrangement is such that Junior Impersonators face the "setting sun" as they pray and dance before their shrine and Senior Impersonators face the "rising sun" as they strike the K'OLTIXYO and pray and dance before theirs. The shrines appear to delineate the inner core of the sacred area in which most of the ceremonial action takes place.

At the side of the church two shelters are constructed from supporting posts and TULAN branches. One serves as a ceremonial cabildo, where civil officials and new cargoholders partake of the special banquets and from which they view the performances of the ritual actors; the other is headquarters for the Mayordomo Reyes and Mesoneros, whose families and assistants have the duty of preparing and serving the food for the two ritual banquets (see Figure 45).

Visits to Cargoholders' Houses. During the nights of January 18 through January 21 the Senior and Junior Impersonators pay visits to the houses of all incoming cargoholders. These descriptions are based on Bricker's observations of the entertainment on January 20, 1966, in the home of the Second Regidor. About 3:45 A.M., the Junior Actors approach the house, recite the usual greeting prayers at the door, and, once inside,

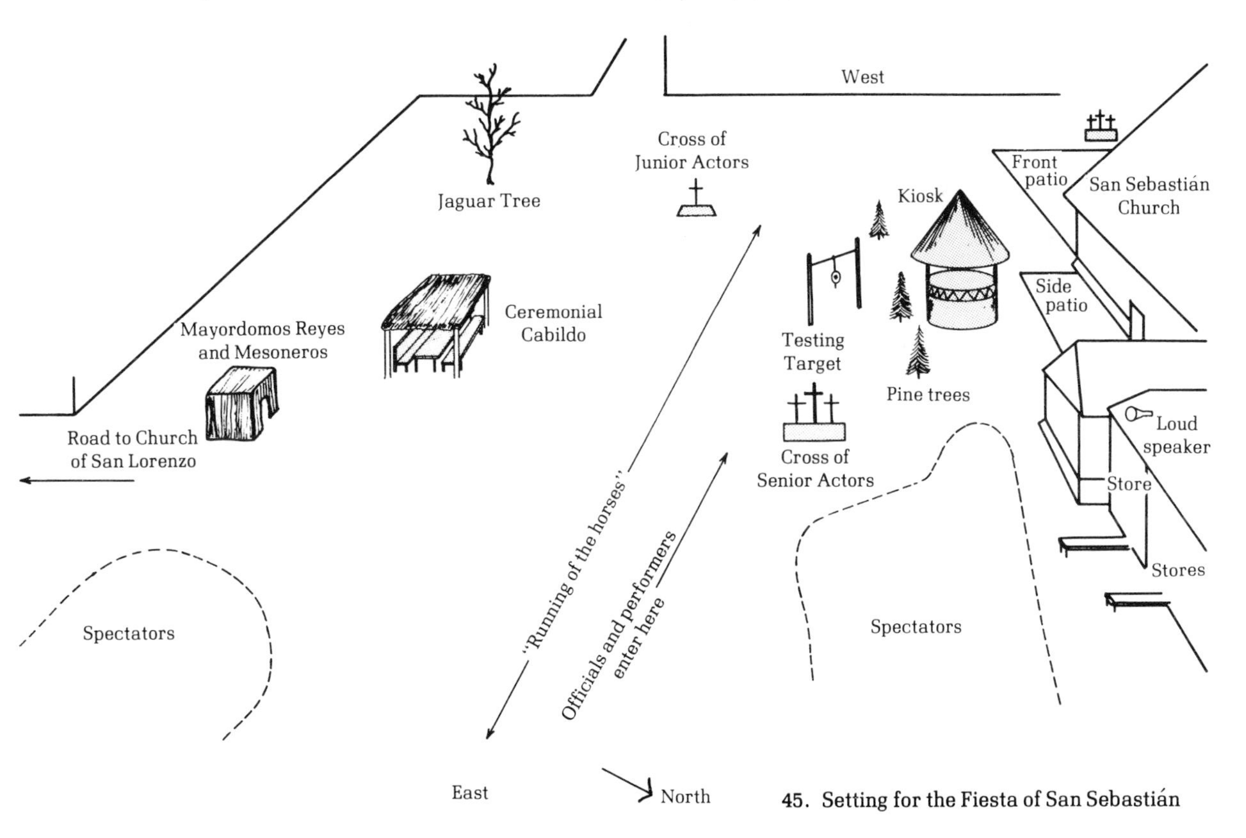

45. Setting for the Fiesta of San Sebastián

begin their performances. Following an episode of simulated copulation between a negligent cargoholder and his wife, using the stuffed animals, a mock curing ceremony is enacted for the child of the deviant couple:

JAGUAR: My mother, my lady, lend me your [ceremonial] robe for a little while, because I am going to extract the soul of Lol ʔUc's little son from the ground. The child took magical fright when his father became drunk while serving as policeman. [Puts on robe and a shawl and kneels near the fire with his stuffed squirrel.] *Hurr-ves-ves-ves.* Come, you know our house. Maruc, join your little child, who took fright when your husband beat you when he was drunk as a policeman. [Audience laughs] *Hu-hu-hu* [blows on a bottle to call missing parts of child's soul which fled when the child took fright].

BLACKMAN: Look! You succeeded in extracting the missing parts of his soul from the ground. Now that he's better, Maruc is kissing him.

(Bricker 1973: 59-60)

From a descriptive point of view, the "curing ceremony" parodies a traditionally serious and formal rite: a man's POK' is placed around the neck of the stuffed animal representing the sick child; the Jaguar wears a ceremonial robe for curing, but it is that of a woman; a bottle partially filled with POX rather than the usual gourd of salt-water is used for "soul calling"; a small sprig of pine is held by the "curer" behind the stuffed animal to represent a cross shrine.

From a prescriptive point of view, the rite is a commentary on the behavior of a cargo official, or, by implication, any responsible male Zinacanteco. Through further ridicule and chastisement of Lol ʔUc, the drinker and wife-beater, a lesson in appropriate behavior is presented.

Other short episodes are enacted before the Junior Ritual Actors leave, to be replaced within the hour by the Senior Ritual Actors. These performers enter the house after formal greetings at the door and are served liquor by the Second Regidor's family.

Next the two Spanish Ladies approach one of the women in the household, saying "We will comb out your lice." She replies, "Please do." The Spanish Lady begins to comb and exclaims, "Oh, how many lice you have! It must be because you worry too much. You are worried by your husband and your child. As for me, my husband does not give me cause for concern. Look at our lovely clothes—mine and those of my husband!" The woman responds, "Yes, I am worried because my child cries all the time and my husband keeps beating me up." If the woman whose hair is being combed happens to be the cargoholder's wife, the Spanish Lady adds, "Your lice have multiplied like crazy. You must be worried about your cargo." The cargoholder's wife replies, "Well, yes, it is because we don't have enough money." The Spanish Lady then walks up to a young girl and begins to comb her hair, saying, "Oh, you have so many lice. It is because your mother scolds you so much. You are very distraught."

(Bricker 1973: 61-62)

As the Spanish Ladies perform the combing skit, the musicians sing a derisive song about them:

María is dancing;
  Luchita is dancing;
María is swaying;
  Luchita is swaying . . . .
I am a woman, I am a woman, I am a woman for sure! . . .
  Pinch away, pinch away, women [the lice]! . . .
    Comb away, comb away girls!
I am a woman, I am a woman, I am a woman for sure!
  I am a girl, I am a girl, I am a girl for sure! . . .
I am a bought woman;
  I am a bought girl;
I am a whoring woman;
  I am a whoring girl.

(excerpted from Bricker 1973: 62-63)

The above interchanges are thematically characteristic of Indian-ladino relations, involving the ladino's perception of the Indian and the Indian's perception of the ladino. The Spanish Lady's preoccupation with finding lice in the hair of Indian women satirizes the commonly held ladino belief that Indians are slovenly, dirty, and inattentive to matters of personal health; the "fastidious" Spanish Ladies are portrayed not only as vain and self-important but also—another common Zinacantecan conception—as promiscuous.

Following several other short dramatic episodes the Senior Actors depart for their performance at the home of another cargoholder.

Fetching the Spanish Ladies. On the evening of January 19 the costumed Spanish Gentlemen visit the houses of their "female" counterparts to court the Ladies as they dress. The father of each Lady engages in a dialogue with the suitor, attempting to discourage the match:

FATHER: When will you marry?

SPANIARD: Not until tomorrow. But it's all right if we sleep together now. We have the right to do so now because it won't be long before we marry.

FATHER: But don't beat your wife.

SPANIARD: But she doesn't mind the blows. I beat her until I was spent but she didn't leave. "Go!" I told her yesterday, but there she was huddled. She didn't want to go.

EVERYONE: Hi, hi, hi. . . .

FATHER: Are you a rich man?

SPANIARD: That's not important. I know how to work well at night—at least that's what some women say. Wealth isn't everything. Fruit and bread aren't everything. All that is important is that there be a man [to sleep with], for that is something that [women] can't get along without.

EVERYONE: Hi, hi, hi. . . .

FATHER: Spaniard, how many children do you have already?

SPANIARD: Only one.

FATHER: Will you kiss her?

SPANIARD: Well, what's it to you if I kiss her?

FATHER: But you are an old man. My daughter is still a girl. See how pretty she is. You are old and pock-marked.

SPANIARD: So, she's still a girl. What good would she be to me if she were already an old lady! . . .
Now look, my father, my Lord, drink up a little. Thank you for giving me your daughter. My foot has received, my hand has received your daughter [ritual terms spoken by the suitor when the marriage is agreed upon].

FATHER: You won't suit my daughter because you are already an old man.

SPANIARD: Please don't interfere. But don't criticize your daughter. You keep saying, "You are already an old man," but your daughter wants me so much that she doesn't see me as an old man. You will just offend her if you keep telling her, "He's too old." Your daughter doesn't view me as an old man, because she wants someone who is a little more mature, someone who has already worked for some time. Younger men have worked less. So, father, what you ought to tell your daughter is, "Sleep with your husband!" Teach your daughter well.

EVERYONE: Hi, hi, hi. . . .

(Bricker 1973: 51-52)

This preliminary performance portrays the pomposity, indolence, and preoccupation with sexual activity of the HKAXLAN; the Spanish Lady's obsession with carnal pleasures can be readily inferred. Thus, an important theme of the ritual action in San Sebastián is established: the condemnation of open sexuality through comic dramatics.

Afternoon Churchyard Ritual. On January 19 a rehearsal is held for the approaching performances of January 20, 21, and 22. Shortly before midday, the civil officials and Elders enter the churchyard of San Sebastián in ranked procession, pray inside the church, then take their places on the benches of the oak-bough cabildo. Eight horsemen, sponsored by the Senior Actors, and two Junior Actors (the K'UK'UL CONETIK) line up their mounts at the east end of the fiesta grounds. At noon, *bombas* are shot off. At this signal the riders run their horses to the western edge, whirl, charge back to the east, then again to the west.

Following the "Running of the Horses" along the path of the sun, the Junior Impersonators dance into the fiesta grounds in a formation unique to San Sebastián. The six Blackmen, carrying their stuffed animals, are followed by the two Jaguars (side by side), then by the Plumed Serpents and Spanish Moss Wearers (side by side in a row of four). All dance *backward*, shouting their animal cries. They are followed by the guitarist, the violinist, and the T'ENT'EN, which is carried by one man on a tumpline and played by another walking behind, and the two Lacandons (side by side), all of whom dance *forward*. The Junior Impersonators stop at the cross shrine of the Senior Impersonators to greet the shrine, then continue to the cross shrine at the setting sun end of the grounds, near the Jaguar Tree, where the T'ENT'EN is kept at the base of the crosses when not in use.

Following the same path of the sun the Senior Impersonators arrive on horseback, accompanied by their musicians and by the HC'AM-TEˀ MOL ("The old man who receives the stick"), who carries the two wooden lances for "testing the target." The order of march is: Little and Big White Heads, followed by the Little Spanish Lady and Spanish Gentleman, and finally the Big Spanish Lady and Spanish Gentleman. (For this rehearsal the actors wear their regular cargoholder regalia; for the formal performances the next three days they wear their fiesta costumes.) The procession greets the cross shrine of the Senior Impersonators, then dismounts at the kiosk. The Big Spanish Gentleman remounts and is handed the K'OLTIXYO. As the band plays, he rides to the "testing target" poles, climbs up on his saddle, and ties the target between the poles. He receives a lance from the lance-bearer, and, having prayed to the sun, to San Lorenzo, Santo Domingo, and San Sebastián, his horse is led through the open chute while he strikes the target. Afterward he enters the church to pray with the rest of the Senior Impersonators. Returning to the churchyard, the group approaches their cross shrine, where the MUK'TA HKAXLAN takes from his net bag the sacred painting of San Sebastián and places it at the base of the three crosses. To the music of their musicians, the Senior Impersonators dance in descending rank order, north to south, facing the cross, for most of the remaining afternoon.

Meanwhile, at their cross shrine and the Jaguar Tree, the Junior Impersonators perform dancing and dramatic skits using the stuffed animals and pointed sticks. They denounce those cargoholders of the past year who have failed to meet their final official responsibility: attendance at the Fiesta of San Sebastián. The negligent cargoholder and his spouse are the subject of lewd jokes and dramatizations. An actor may hold up a stuffed squirrel (representing the wife) and ferociously poke its genitals with the pointed stick saying, "Look at Marian Peres from Masan. He's just a fucker who keeps doing it at the foot of a mango tree!" Or, addressing a woman in the crowd of spectators, "Look, my mother; look, my lady, at what Lol ˀUc is doing with Xunka (his wife). How shameless they are, always fucking each other, even when not in their own home!" (Bricker 1973: 58). The defaulting cargoholders are accused of having placed pleasure above responsibility, for having intercourse in public places and in unnatural positions, for buying ribbons and necklaces for their wives instead of meeting the cost of their cargo.

Later in the afternoon a complete round of "test-jousting" takes place. Beginning with the Big Spanish Gentleman and ending with the lowest-ranking Blackmen, each actor mounts a horse, is given a lance, and attempts to strike the K'OLTIXYO as his mount is led through the open chute. If he fails, his horse is led around (in a counterclockwise direction) and through the chute again, giving the rider a second, and sometimes a third, chance to strike the target. Between each attempt, the remaining Jaguars and Blackmen dance through the chute, also in a counterclockwise direction, calling out their animal cries, and leaping up to strike the target with their stuffed animals.

The performances end about sundown, with a reversal of the "Running of the Horses": the eight horses are run along the path of the sun from the west to the east, back to the west, and then returned to the east. Both groups of actors depart. The Junior Actors dance into the front (western) door of the church of San Sebastián in the same backward-forward formation used in arriving at the fiesta. However, in leaving the church, the order is reversed: the Lacandons and the drum and string musicians dance *backward*, while the Plumed Serpents, Wearers of Spanish Moss, Jaguars, and Blackmen dance *forward* until the group reaches its cross shrine again. Here the Actors revert to the usual order, exiting from the grounds in the same backward-forward formation by which they arrived. The Senior Actors follow. The Big Spanish Gentleman, having had his sandals removed by assistants, climbs on his horse. Standing on the saddle under the target, he removes the target and the rope from which it hangs. Seated again, he is led back to his group, where, having dismounted and replaced his sandals, he is given the painting of San Sebastián. With his sacred objects in hand, he remounts to lead the ranked procession of mounted Senior Impersonators from the fiesta grounds.

Performance at the Jaguar Rock. During the afternoons of January 20 and 22, before the civil officials and Elders partake of their banquets, one of the two sub-groups of Junior Actors performs at the Jaguar Rock, located behind a row of trees in a nearby pasture east of San Sebastián church. At the foot of the large limestone boulder (conceived to be the "home" of the Jaguars) is a shrine of three wooden crosses, at the base of which the Senior Lacandon, flanked by the two Jaguars, places five lighted white candles. These ritualists are then joined by the remaining members of their sub-group—three Blackmen and the Senior Plumed Serpent and Spanish Moss Wearer—all of whom dance and pray before the candles.

The Blackmen, Jaguars, and their ritual adviser climb on top of the boulder in order to light three candles at the foot of the cross located there. On the instruction of their adviser (who, at the 1972 fiesta, was the owner of the T'ENT'EN) they light a small fire of corn fodder and dry grass southwest of the cross, setting the Jaguars' "house" aflame. As the group huddles near the edge, "stranded" atop the rock, they shout for assistance to the crowd of spectators below. As the fire becomes smoky and diminishes, the stuffed animals are tossed down from the rock and back up again, between one group of ritualists and the other. The "squirrels" frequently fly over the heads of those on the rock, and often hit those on the ground, to the amusement of the watching crowd. At length, the Jaguars, Blackmen, and the ritual adviser descend from the rock. At its base, to the left and behind the crosses, the Jaguars crawl into an indentation where they are "killed" by the Lacandon, who repeatedly pokes his arrow, still attached to the small bow, into their bodies. After several minutes lying "dead," the Jaguars rise and enter the crowd of spectators. They seize several young Chamula boys—people being the favorite food of Jaguars—drag them back to the shrine, and have them "killed" by the Senior Lacandon. When the boys have been released, and rounds of liquor drunk among the ritualists, the sub-group, dancing and shouting, returns to the churchyard (see Bricker 1973: 55).

Ritual at NIO?. Meanwhile, the second sub-group, consisting of four Blackmen, the Junior Spanish Moss Wearer, Junior Plumed Serpent, and Junior Lacandon, marches in that order to the shrine of NIO? located on the southern slope of a small mountain northwest of the Church of San Sebastián. In front of the three-cross shrine, the KA?BENAL lights seven white-wax candles, tied into groups of three and four. The ritualists pray, then dance before the burning candles. A grass fire is lighted to the right of the crosses, representing the burning of the house of the Spanish Moss Wearers and Blackmen. These figures are believed to reside in caves, one of which is located near the cross shrine. The fire parallels symbolically the burning of the house of the Jaguars at BOLOM TON. Compared to the activity at the Jaguar Rock, the ritual at NIO? is restrained and formal: no loud jesting or tossing of stuffed animals occurs. After a short interval, the sub-group marches back to the churchyard.

Banquet for New Officials and the Jaguar Tree. On January 20 and 22 banquets are served in the ceremonial cabildo, in two sittings, to the new civil and religious hierarchies. Each receives a half-chicken served with hard-cooked eggs and potatoes in a thick chili sauce. During the first part of the meal the Senior Impersonators amuse the new officials by offering them tastes of quince jam from small wooden containers and by joking and punning. The Junior Impersonators arrive during the second half of the banquet, Jaguars and Blackmen carrying young Chamula boys whom they wish to exchange for food from the ritual table. After hearing threats of castration and consumption of the boys, the members of the new official hierarchies take pity on the frightened captives and deliver part of their meal to the hovering captors. The Jaguars and Blackmen rush to their cross shrine with the collected tortillas and eggs, and divide the food among all Junior Actors.

The Jaguars and Blackmen, stuffed animals and food in hand, circle the Jaguar Tree three times. Leaving the squirrels on the ground, the two Jaguars, followed by the Blackmen, climb to the tree's uppermost branches. Laughing and shouting, they spit and throw pieces of food at the crowd, supposedly "feeding" the stuffed animals left below in the care of the Blackmen. The animals are then tossed back and forth from ground to tree in a sequence similar to that performed at the Jaguar Rock. At length the climbers slowly descend. As they get within reach of the ritualists on the ground, their genital areas are playfully poked with the heads of the stuffed animals. Since jaguars are the strongest animal companions, and squirrels the weakest, it is possible that some social metaphor is implied in this sequence, but its full meaning still escapes me. This ritual is probably the local expression of the tree raising and climbing ceremonies that are widespread in Middle America and the Southwest (Redfield 1936).

Transfer of Sacred Objects of Office

On the morning of January 25, the incumbent and incoming Regidores and Alcaldes gather at the home of the incoming Grand Alcalde. Seated in rank order inside the house, the incoming Elders await the arrival of their outgoing counterparts. Skyrocket specialists set off rockets and cannons in quick succession, and, as the outgoing Elders approach the house, the sound is increased by the explosions of the procession's rockets. The blasts, once alternating, merge into a continuous chaotic sound as the procession enters the house patio. The Regidores, preceded in the usual rank order by their musicians and skyrocket men, carry various sacred objects in their hands: the Fourth Regidor, two clay candleholders; the Third Regidor, two vases containing flowers and four candles; the Second Regidor, a small wooden box with stamp pad and seal inside; the First Regidor, candles and the municipio's branding iron. The Second Alcalde, next in

46. Jaguars and Blackmen climb the Jaguar Tree

procession, carries nothing. Across one shoulder, the Grand Alcalde wears a net bag in which the cloth sack with a red border which protects the sacred painting of San Sebastián can be seen.

After extensive greetings across the threshold between the groups of Elders, both hierarchies turn in the direction of San Lorenzo Church to pray together. During this time the musicians play simultaneously, one guitar-harp-violin combination seated inside the house, the other in the house patio. As the prayer ends, the outgoing Elders begin to shout and dance, shaking feather-decorated gourd rattles and stamping in time to the music. The incoming group returns to seated rank order inside the house.

After several minutes of dancing, the outgoing Grand Alcalde grasps the ribbon attached to the back of the painting of San Sebastián—being careful not to touch the actual frame—and lifts the picture halfway out of the sack. He kneels on the threshold, facing the incoming Grand Alcalde who kneels opposite him looking out into the patio. The incoming Alcalde prays to the picture held before him for over ten minutes, then kisses it reverently in the center and steps aside. The incoming Second Alcalde approaches and greets the sacred object in a similar fashion, though he prays for a shorter length of time. In descending rank order, all of the incoming Elders pass in front of the painting. They are followed by their musicians, other male helpers inside the house, women, and last, all children, who are made to touch the glass covering the painting with their foreheads.

When all inside the house have greeted the saint, the outgoing First Escribano is called to remove the painting from the net of the outgoing Grand Alcalde and place it in a similar net held by the new Grand Alcalde. At the moment of the transfer the musicians play louder than before; the firing of the skyrockets intensifies, percussively marking this key transition (Needham 1967). The new Grand Alcalde, grasping the picture by the ribbon, returns to his kneeling position at the threshold. The greeting process is repeated: starting with the outgoing Grand Alcalde, all in the house patio pass by the saint, saluting it as did the group within the house. The incoming Grand Alcalde takes the picture to his house altar, freshly decorated with a flower arch, and places it in an open coffer. He receives the rest of the sacred objects in similar procedures from the outgoing Grand Alcalde: candleholders, flowers and candles, box with stamp pad and seal, branding iron. All are placed on the altar beside the coffer.

The incoming group forms a semicircle around the altar, in descending rank order from right to left. Kneeling, they pray in unison for approximately thirty minutes, periodically touching their foreheads to the ground. At the close of the prayer, the outgoing Elders enter the house for the first time and replace the incoming group around the altar. Their praying sequence differs only in that the outgoing officials interrupt their sober words to bemoan termination of their cargos.

When all present have knelt before the altar and greeted its objects in shortened versions of the Elders' salutation, the outgoing group dances inside the house, observed by the seated incoming officials. In the middle of the afternoon, the outgoing Elders leave the house, at which time a meal is served to the new officials by the new Grand Alcalde's family. The incoming officials and their entourage disperse to their homes in the late afternoon.

Comments on the Fiesta of San Sebastián

The complex of symbols displayed in the fiesta of San Sebastián is richer in meaning and more complicated than any found in saint's day fiestas throughout Zinacantan's ceremonial year. After repeated observations and extensive interviewing I do not pretend to understand all of the symbolism. However, a number of important strands are beginning to emerge from this rich corpus of data. One interesting line of interpretation is that the fiesta's ritual dramas reenact aspects of Zinacantan's cultural history. Before the Conquest, Zinacantan was in contact with Aztec traders who sought quetzal feathers and amber from Chiapas highland tribes. These merchants gave a Nahuatl name to the place, Tzinacantlán, and may have introduced such concepts as the K'UK'UL CON, Quetzalcoatl or the "plumed serpent," still impersonated at the fiesta. The SAK HOL performers in the fiesta accompany the Spanish Gentlemen and Ladies, recalling their role as guides to the conquerors.

It is highly significant that San Sebastián and the myths related to him, unlike all other saints in Zinacantan, were introduced by the Spaniards. The performances include other Conquest-related events. The Spanish Gentlemen and Ladies ride on horseback, accompanied by retinues, and the Spanish Gentleman initiates the "testing" performance. Some Zinacantecos were conscripted by the Spanish to help fight the "Lacandons." The present term may refer to the antecedents of the present-day Lacandons, who live in eastern Chiapas; more likely, as Thompson (1970: 32) suggests, it refers to various Maya tribes in the lowlands to the north and east who were fighting against the Spanish. KAʔBENALETIK possibly derives from Cabnál, leader of the hostile Lacandons in the seventeenth century (Villagutierre y Soto-Mayor 1933: 223, 241-242), and is frequently translated by the Zinacantecos as "Lacandons."

But even if the ritual dramas do present a Zinacanteco version of the tribe's cultural history, a stronger argument for their central place in the ritual system is that they are symbolic models of the social and natural structures of modern Chiapas. For the members of this municipio the world is divided into Indian and ladino sectors. The ladinos, being superior in political and economic power, are played by the Senior Impersonators, while Indian cultural elements are played by the Junior Impersonators, who are officials of lesser rank in the cargo system. The White Heads occupy the lower ranks of the Senior Impersonators. At the same time, the world is more fundamentally divided into various types of men and animals which appear as both props and characters in the performances of the Junior Impersonators. The dramas restate these divisions in the universe with ritual force each year and pass Zinacantecan "judgments" upon them. For example, while the Spanish-speaking ladinos are "honored" by having their roles filled by high-ranking senior actors, their behavior and attitudes are mercilessly ridiculed. A commentary on the overlap of human and animal realms, and the reprehensible but inescapable "animalism" in all Zinacantecos, is made through the behavior of the junior actors using animals props.

Why is the T'ENT'EN carried on a tumpline, continuously played, and carefully tended throughout the fiesta period? What characteristics make it essential in all performances in the cargoholders' houses and the San Sebastián churchyard, at the Jaguar Rock and the house of the T'ENT'EN in the Center when the stuffed animals are burned?

The *teponaztle* drum was called *tunkul* in Yucatan and *tun* in highland Guatemala (Saville 1925); *tun* was also the Yucatec Maya word for the 360-day year (Thompson 1954). Since the calendrical deities of the ancient Maya are often depicted carrying the burden of the year on a tumpline on their backs, and since the T'ENT'EN appears in the Ceremonial Center only at this fiesta—the time of the ending of an Old Year and the beginning of the New, the time of "rising heat"—it seems to embody, above all, the symbol of the arrival of the New Year (Phelps 1970).

But more may be involved. The rain-making pilgrimages to the top of the Junior Large Mountain begin and end with prayers to the T'ENT'EN. For the Aztecs, Quetzalcoatl was intimately associated with rain: he determined the course of vegetal growth, for it was he who speared the rain clouds, causing drought. He was the deity of new vegetation, prayed to by the Aztecs when they used trees from the forests (Saville 1925). And it is the K'UK'UL CON who lifts the T'ENT'EN out of its box and places it on the tumpline of the drum carrier. If K'UK'UL CON is related to Quetzalcoatl, the small drum's strong symbolic associations with rain and with drought appear justified.

The mimicking, mocking, obscene, and licentious behavior of the outgoing cargoholders contrasts sharply with the solemn, proper, "correct" ritual behavior of the incoming officials. The outgoing cargoholders appear to symbolize "disorder," the incoming cargoholders "order." The number of role reversals and behavioral inversions should be noted: men impersonate women, Indians impersonate ladinos, people impersonate animals, ritualists dance and march backward—all aspects of "playing normal time back to front."

Interpretations of End-of-Year/New-Year Ceremonies

Now, to take an overview look at the distinctive ritual symbols being utilized in this extraordinary series of events that extend from December 16 to January 25, what kind of symbolic sense can be seen in this ceremonialism that occupies so much time and absorbs so much energy and so many resources?

Why does the richest ritual segment of the annual ceremonial calendar occur in December and January? The period corresponds to the end of the maize cycle; for the first time in months Zinacantecos have their granaries full and money in their pockets. This economic factor explains how they can afford to pause and put their energy and material resources into intensive ritual activity, but not why they choose to do so.

Maya cultures appear preoccupied with the passage of time. An important aspect of this is the marking of the solar year, and an emphasis upon the end of one year and the beginning of the next. The period of Christmas to San Sebastián—from the point of view of either the Catholic saints' calendar or the movements of the sun—is the time of transition from the old to the new year. The events begin just before the winter solstice, when the sun reaches its lowest point of waning, and continue through what is appropriately considered "the rising heat fiesta" as the sun is moving higher into the sky, the danger of frost is passing, and the new maize-growing season is about to begin.

The ceremonial schedule is divided into two phases: Christmas-New Year's-Epiphany; then, after a lull of twelve days, there is a period of intense activity in the fiesta of San Sebastián. The phases are like a couplet in a Zinacanteco prayer: the second restates and intensifies the ritual symbols and themes of the first. In the first phase the low-ranking Mayordomos introduce certain symbolic themes as they eat sweetened squash, perform posadas, build the crèche, direct the birth of the Christ children, and perform the mimes and parodies as "grandfathers" and "grandmothers" in the Drama of Ritual Aggression. In the second phase, many of the same themes are stated in a different form, and their meanings intensified with the use of many additional, as well as higher ranking, cargoholders in the ritual dramas of the fiesta of San Sebastián.

To a greater degree than any other time of the annual ceremonial round, this Year-End/New-Year period utilizes ritual symbolism characterized by two crucial bi-polarities. First, in Victor Turner's (1968) terms, there is a marked contrast between the sensory pole—the stress on sexual, fertility, aggressive, antisocial symbolism, much of it flagrantly physiological—and the ideological pole—the stress upon the norms and values of Zinacanteco society. There is another marked contrast between formal and solemn ritual behavior and masquerading and revelry—inversions and reversals for almost all the cargoholders, beginning with the Mayordomos at the

Christmas celebrations and adding most of the rest of the hierarchy in San Sebastián.

It is my thesis that the Zinacantecos are first unwiring, or unstructuring, the system of order and then rewiring, or restructuring, it, as the cargoholders who have spent a year in "sacred time" in office are definitively removed from their cargos and returned to normal time and everyday life. This process serves to make them reflect, as representatives of all Zinacantecos, upon the essence of their way of life: the contrasts or paired opposites and contradictions between husbands and wives, between Senior and Junior in their system of rank order, between men and women as apparent in the patrilineal system, between Indians and ladinos (in their bicultural world), between men and animals. The ceremonies are essentially a "liminal period" between the old and the new year, between being in office and out of office.

Through these terms we can understand the astonishing number of inversions in behavior, of role-reversals: boys become angels, men become women, other men impersonate a bull, cargo officials and musicians serve as shamans, other men become animals, Indians play ladinos, men impersonating jaguars become shamans who "cure" stuffed squirrels of "soul-loss." Men dance and march backward—the only time this occurs during the entire year. Normal life is played "back to front" as the ritualists move into a veritable orgy of inversions and reversals.

Edmund Leach (1961) suggests that "formality" and "masquerade" are paired opposites and, as such, modes for moving in and out of "sacred time." He suggests that, "a rite which starts with formality (e.g. a wedding) is likely to end in masquerade; a rite which starts with masquerade (e.g. New Year's Eve; Carnival) is likely to end in formality."

With respect to Zinacanteco rituals, Leach is correct in two senses. First, taking each of the two phases as a unit, one sees the Mayordomos behaving with rigorous formality in the building of the crèche, the posada rites, and the birth of the Christ children, then ending this ritual phase masquerading as "fools of aggression." With the outgoing cargoholders in San Sebastián the sequence appears to be reversed: they begin with masquerading (as women, ladinos, animals, and so on) and end with intense formality on January 25, after the stuffed animals have been burned, as the sacred articles of office are turned over to the new Grand Alcalde. Second, taking the ceremonial year as a unit, the new cargoholders behave with great formality from the fiesta of San Sebastián throughout an entire year; they end their cargo service at the following San Sebastián celebration in ludicrous masquerade and farce.

An additional and interesting process is occurring *within* each phase of this Year-End/New-Year ceremony: the two modes of formality and masquerade seem to form a kind of dialogue, with the "fools of aggression" and outgoing cargoholders representing the masquerade and the incumbent and new cargoholders representing formality. It is as if two programs are being played simultaneously on the ritual tape that emits messages about the cultural code, its gaps and contradictions, and the attempted resolutions in this complex interaction of formal "proper" behavior and reveling, ridiculous, farcical behavior.

Finally, it is evident that the skillful mimicking of social conflicts through various inversions, role-reversals, and parodies of solemn ritual are ways of divesting of their antisocial quality the powerful drives and emotions associated with human physiology, especially reproduction, and attaching them to the normative order, thereby energizing it with a "borrowed vitality" (Turner 1969: 52-53). The copulating behavior of the stuffed squirrels contains proto-typical condensed symbolism: Lol ˀArias' fucking his wife at the foot of a mango tree symbolically represents the sexuality, the animality in *all* Zinacantecos; all are being punished as the squirrel is whipped.

By January 25 the bull has been killed, the grandfathers and grandmothers have relinquished their stick-horses, the stuffed animals have been burned, the Jaguars, Plumed Serpents, and Spanish Moss Wearers have put away their costumes, the Spanish Gentlemen and Ladies have become Elders once again. By the time of the formal transfer of sacred articles of office to the new highest-ranking cargoholder the system of order has been rewired for the year which is being born.

II

Year Renewal Rituals

FOR THE MUNICIPIO as a whole the most important rituals performed by the shamans are ʔAC' HABIL (New Year), ʔOʔLOL HABIL (Midyear), and SLAHEB HABIL (End of Year). Zinacantecos say they are performed so the year may pass in happiness and contentment, without sickness or death. I call them Year Renewal Rites. They are conducted twice a year. All of the hamlets have the ʔAC' HABIL; some perform the second Year Renewal at Midyear, others at the End of the Year. Only in Zinacantan Center are all three performed annually for the benefit of the entire municipio.

The distinctive feature of the Year Renewal in the hamlet is a pilgrimage by all its shamans to the tribal sacred mountains and to the saints in the churches of Zinacantan Center. The two Principales serve as mayordomos and host the ritual meals which begin and end the pilgrimage. The Senior Principal is ordinarily the New Year host; the Junior Principal for the second ritual, whether it be the Midyear or End of the Year ceremony. In some hamlets, such as ʔApas, the ceremonial circuit includes, during at least one of the Year Renewal rituals, visits to shrines within the hamlet as well as the pilgrimage to the Center; in others—Pasteʔ, for example—the circuit does not include sacred places within the hamlet, only those in the ceremonial center. For ʔApas the pilgrimage to Zinacantan Center takes place at the New Year ritual. The hamlet's Senior Shaman divides his colleagues into five groups: one offers candles and prayers at the shrines within the hamlet; two visit the mountain shrines around the Center; one visits the three churches in Zinacantan; and the fifth group makes its offerings at the mountain shrines located west of the ceremonial center, in the vicinity of ʔAz'am.

These Year Renewal rituals express the unity of the hamlet and symbolize its relation to the ceremonial center. Just as the Principales report to the Presidente, so the shamans must report to and make offerings to the tribal gods.

The Ritual in the Center

Year Renewal ceremonies in Zinacantan Center are more frequent and more elaborate than those conducted in the hamlets. The stage is large geographically, including the entire municipio as well as a number of shrines beyond its borders. The ritual action takes place in the Chapel of Esquipulas, in the houses of the highest ranking shaman and the highest ranking cargoholder, in the churches of San Lorenzo and San Sebastián, and at KALVARYO. The mountain shrines visited include all those located immediately around Zinacantan Center, as well as the collection of shrines around the hamlet of ˀAz'am. The only known tribal shrine not included is Junior Great Mountain, located much farther away, and visited only for special rainmaking ceremonies (Vogt 1969: 473).

Drawn from all the important religious and political hierarchies, the ritualists include:
Shamans. These key figures in the Year Renewal rites include all shamans who live in the Center, plus two shamans from most of the hamlets. (Small hamlets may send only one.) By tradition the highest ranking shaman resides in the ceremonial center; his colleagues in the Center are included regardless of rank. Those from the hamlets, selected by the highest ranking shaman in each hamlet, are usually very junior in rank and younger and stronger since they are sent to the most distant mountain shrines. The total number of shamans participating ranges from about twenty-six to forty-two.
MOLETIK. The Grand Alcalde, highest ranking cargoholder, is host for the ritual meals and praying over the candles. The wives of the Elders, with additional women helpers, gather at his house to prepare the food. The MOLETIK furnish maize for the tortillas.
Mayordomos Reyes and Mesoneros. These cargoholders, whose duty it is to care for the Chapel and the saints therein, attend the meals at the home of the Grand Alcalde and participate in later visits to the churches of San Lorenzo and San Sebastián. The Mayordomo Reyes bring their stringed musicians to play for the ritual; the Mesoneros purchase the candles and other ritual materials in San Cristóbal.
Civil Officials. The Presidente, Síndico, and Alcaldes Jueces from the cabildo, as well as the Principales from each hamlet, who supervise the collection of money for ritual materials, collect incense from the Mayordomos and geraniums from households who volunteer them and serve as candle-bearers during the ceremonial circuits.
Musicians. The violin-harp-guitar trio plays; no flute and drum musicians are included.
Other Male Helpers. Twelve to sixteen men serve as "sweepers."

The Year Renewal ceremony (observed in 1963) has ten basic episodes.

Episode One: Setting the Date

Year Renewal ceremonies are not geared specifically into the Catholic calendar. Their dates are set by the most senior shaman in consultation with the Presidente and Elders. Journeys to the shrines must be scheduled for Tuesday, a day on which the gods are certain to be at home. Hence the all-night prayer over the candles is scheduled for a Monday night; the day for counting the money is the preceding Sunday. The New Year ceremony is set for a Sunday-Monday-Tuesday in late January or early February, following San Sebastián, which symbolizes the end of one year and the beginning of the next. The Midyear rite is scheduled for a Sunday-Monday-Tuesday after June 24, the Day of San Juan. And the End of Year ceremony is assigned a Sunday-Monday-Tuesday following All Saints' Day, usually late in November but occasionally in early December. Since it is important that the Year Renewal ceremonies not conflict with any other important ceremonial dates and that at least three weeks be allowed for preparations, the meetings to establish dates occur early in

January, near the end of October, and in early June. Once a date has been set, the Presidente sends his Mayores to inform all the shamans in the ceremonial center and asks the Principales to convey the information to the senior shaman of each hamlet.

Episode Two: Collecting the Money

Under the supervision of the Principales, money for the ritual materials to be purchased in San Cristóbal is collected by one or two HZOB TAK'IN (money collectors), who request an equal amount from each household to reach the total expected from the hamlet. When the money has been collected the Principales deliver it to the Presidente, who directs them to take it to the Grand Alcalde. The Senior Escribano keeps a list of what is expected from each hamlet and checks off each name as the funds are received.

Episode Three: Counting the Money

The counting takes place in the Chapel of Esquipulas on Sunday, in the presence of the Elders and the shamans. The shamans first gather on the north side of the churchyard of San Lorenzo at about 10:30 A.M and eat tortillas which they have brought with them. At noon, having formed in rank order and knelt in front of the Church of San Lorenzo and at the churchyard shrine, they march into the chapel to pray in unison to Señor Esquipulas.

The highest ranking shamans sit at the central table with the Grand and Second Alcalde; the other shamans stand; the Regidores and Escribanos sit on benches along the wall. The Senior Shaman then requests that the money be produced. The Senior Escribano, who stands at the head of the table, reads off the amounts that each hamlet has delivered and the total. After the Grand Alcalde places the money on the table, the Senior Shaman allocates the funds to be spent for various items: white wax candles, incense, liquor, skyrockets. (The resin incense is purchased at candle-shops; wood incense is furnished by the twelve Mayordomos in the ceremonial center.)

Episode Four: Dispatching the Ritual Assistants

At sunrise on Monday morning, the Mesoneros, accompanied by the Number 3 and Number 4 Regidores and by the Junior Escribano, travel to San Cristóbal to purchase the ritual materials. The "sweepers," who have been recruited by the Principales, go out to renew the pine trees on all the shrines and spread pine needles in front of the crosses.

Episode Five: Gathering of Shamans at the House of the Senior Shaman

On Monday morning the shamans gather again, this time at the house of the Senior Shaman, each with a *media* (pint) of cane liquor to exchange drinks in his honor. They also eat tortillas brought from home, for it will be a long time until the next meal. When a messenger from the Grand Alcalde announces that the candles and other materials have arrived and that the cross shrines have been decorated, the shamans march in formation (most senior in the rear) to the cargoholder's house.

Episode Six: Praying over the Candles

Arriving about sundown, the shamans kneel and pray at the house cross, then enter and pray before the altar-shrine of San Sebastián. They engage in bowing-and-releasing with the Elders, and seat themselves in rank order at the table. The Mayordomo Reyes with their musicians and the Mesoneros are present as are the civil representatives from the cabildo. The placement of the ritualists is shown in Figure 47. The two highest ranking shamans rise and pray to the altar of San Sebastián in the house, to the Church of San

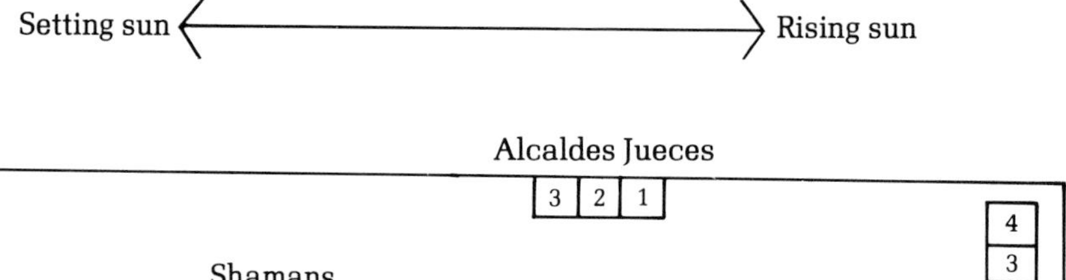

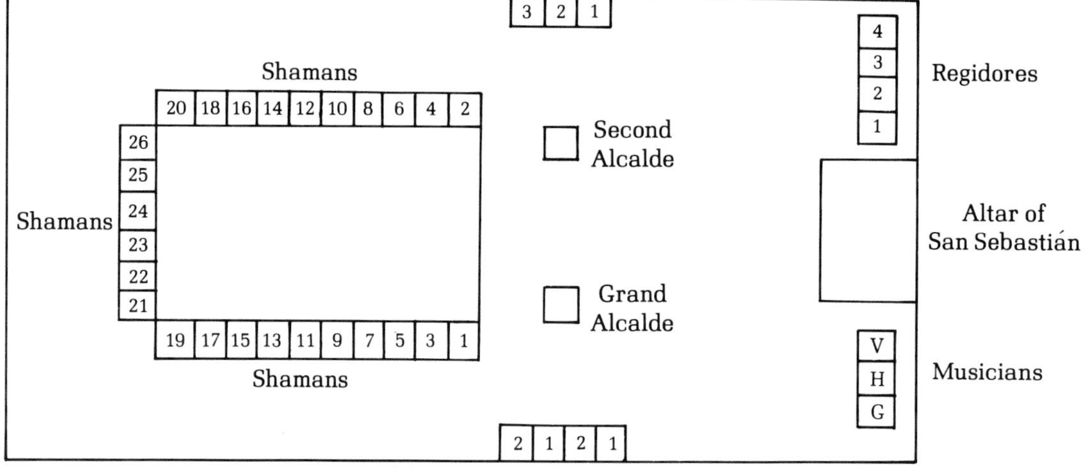

47. Placement of shamans and cargoholders for the all-night praying over the candles

Lorenzo, and to the candles on the table, after which the two Alcaldes stand and release the two shamans.

At about 7:00 P.M. the long prayer over the candles begins; it lasts until 4:00 A.M. the following morning without interruption. The first four shamans stand with smoking censers in their hands, leading the prayer which is recited by all shamans and periodically rotating the censers over the candles in a counterclockwise direction. Periodically they bow and place their heads on the table, continuing to pray, for several minutes at a time. When the first four finish, the censers are passed to the next four shamans in rank order; this rotation pattern continues until all have led the prayer. In 1963 five groups of four, followed by a group of six, led the prayer. When all pray in unison, the chant can be heard several blocks away; the walls of the Grand Alcalde's house reverberate.

The prayer, in part, went as follows during a Year End ritual (from Vogt 1969: 467-471):

In the divine name of Jesus Christ my Lord,
Receive, then, my Father,
Receive, then, my Lord,
Since I come kneeling,
Since I come bowing low.

We shall beseech divine pardon,
We shall beg divine forgiveness . . .

To take this unto the place where the feet descend,
To take this unto the place where the hands descend,
With the divine Señor San Cristóbal holy Father,
With the divine Señor San Cristóbal holy Mother,
With the holy KALVARYO holy Father,
With the holy KALVARYO holy Mother.

To send your holy words,
To send your holy prayer,
  To stand in holiness,
  To stand firmly in holiness
    Behind us,
    Beside us . . .
Receive this, that nothing happen to them,
That they encounter nothing,
  That all be well for a while,
  That everyone feel healthy for a while, . . .

Grant us divine pardon,
Grant us divine forgiveness,
  With this lowly little bit,
  With this humble amount,
    That to all the little ones,
    That to all the great ones,
    That to all the running ones,
    That to all the perched ones,
    That to all your holy sons,
    That to all your holy children,
      Nothing happen;
      That they encounter nothing, . . .

Receive this, then, my Father,
Receive this, then, my Lord. . . .

These offerings are not piled high,
They are not heaped high,
  It is only a small bit,
  It is only a humble amount,
    But grant us thy divine pardon,
    Grant us thy divine forgiveness,
      Receive this humble spray of flowers,
      Receive this humble splinter of pine,
      Receive this humble bit of incense,
      Receive this humble cloud of smoke. . . .

Receive, then: your holy sun has gone over the hill,
Your holy year has passed,
  Take this for the holy end of the year,
  Take this for the holy end of the day, . . .

All the holy Fathers,
All the holy Mothers,
All the holy gods,
All the holy saints,
  To you I speak,
  To you I pray,
    At the circuit of the holy shrines,
    At the circling
    Of your divine visage,
    Of your divine countenance; . . .
Receive, then, my Father,
Receive, then, my Lord,
  So that I may walk in your sight,
  So that I may walk in your countenance,
    My Fathers,
    My Mothers,
      My Lord.

Episode Seven: Eating the Ritual Meal

Following the long prayer a meal is served all the ritualists. It consists of tortillas and chicken —or pork can be substituted for chicken.

Episode Eight: Offerings to the Shrines

At sunrise the groups designated to visit the mountain shrines and the churches form under the supervision of the Senior Shaman. Shamans visit the shrines in groups of two, the more junior ones being dispatched on the more arduous journeys to distant shrines. Assistants carry the candles and other ritual materials, food, and liquor. They may be either the men who served as "sweepers" or the Principales, but once they accept the role, they become MAYOLETIK.

The senior shamans divide into six pairs, each of which is joined by one of the six Elders. The two highest ranking shamans are joined by the Grand Alcalde, the Mayordomo Reyes with their musicians, the Mesoneros, and the various assistants. Their circuit includes the Chapel of Esquipulas, the Church of San Lorenzo, and the Church of San Sebastián; here candles are placed before each saint and prayers recited by the shamans. The important saints—San Lorenzo, Santo Domingo, Virgen de Rosario, San Sebastián, Señor Esquipulas, and others—receive peso-size white wax candles; lesser saints receive 50-centavo and minor saints 20-centavo candles.

At the mountain shrines the helpers place bundles of red geraniums on the crosses; the shamans light three peso-size candles and pray. The distant shrines located in the rugged ravines west of Zinacantan Center include: (1) LAC CIKIN (pricked-up ears), the mountain home of a male ancestral god; it contains a cornet and large drum left there by San Sebastián on his mythical travels before reaching Zinacantan (it is said that the instruments can sometimes be heard playing inside the mountain); (2) NAKLEB ʔOK (Snapping Turtle House), the home of another male ancestral god which serves as a reception room, or office, as one informant put it, for the god inside LAC CIKIN; (3) ROSARIO (Virgen de Rosaric), the principal saint in the chapel of ʔAz'am which contains the sacred salt well; (4) ʔISAK'TIK (Potato Patch), the home of another male ancestral god which is visited in cases of extreme illness, when offerings at Senior Great Mountain fail to cure the patient; (5) C'UL TON (Holy Rock), a "doorway" to ʔISAK'TIK.

The shrines visited around the valley of Zinacantan include the familiar ones already described: SAN KIXTOVAL, MUXUL VIZ, SISIL VIZ, SAK C'EN, NEKEB VIZ, BANKILAL MUK'TA VIZ (ʔOX YOKET), NINAB CILOʔ, NIOʔ, NA HOH, YAʔAHVIL, and KALVARYO. In addition, journeys are made to LANSA VIZ (Spear Mountain), the home of a male ancestral god; YAʔAM TON ("[untranslatable] rock"), home of another male ancestral god; and MIXIK' BALAMIL (Navel of the World). Every sacred shrine is included in this ceremony.

Episode Nine: Praying to the Ancestral Gods at KALVARYO

After all the shrines have received offerings, the entire assemblage of ritualists meets in the late morning at KALVARYO, the central meeting-place of the ancestral gods. The highest ranking shamans and the Elders arrive first, following journeys to nearby churches and mountain shrines; the junior shamans arrive later from their more distant excursions. (Some, who cannot return in time, rejoin the group at the house of the Grand Alcalde.) At KALVARYO the shamans light candles before the shrine of six crosses; then shamans and Elders pray in unison to *all* tribal ancestral gods, turning counterclockwise in kneeling position to face and address each mountain and church in turn.

The prayer having ended at noon, all stand. The most junior shaman starts down the formation, bowing to and being released by other shamans and Elders, then retiring to the open space behind the shrine. He is followed by the next junior shaman, and the process continues until only the Grand Alcalde is left before the crosses. After bowing to KALVARYO, he joins the others for a meal on the ground of tortillas and chicken or pork. The assemblage then returns to the home of the Grand Alcalde in formation, front to rear: musicians, Mesoneros, Mayordomo Reyes, shamans, and Elders.

Episode Ten: Final Ritual Meal

The Year Renewal ritual ends with a ritual meal at the home of the Grand Alcalde. Seated in the order described in Episode Six, the ritualists consume tortillas and chicken or pork, engage in final rounds of ritual drinking and bowing-and-releasing, and disperse.

Variations and Interpretations

The ten episodes described are regular parts of Year Renewal rituals in Zinacantan Center, whether the ceremony be New Year, Midyear, or End of Year. Special renewal rituals may be performed at other times to ward off impending crises: an epidemic threatening to sweep through the municipio, or an incursion into Zinacanteco territory by foreigners. In the case of the former, the ceremony reaffirms the tribal gods and arrests the illness (MAKOB CAMEL, "method of closing sickness"). In the case of interference by outsiders, the ceremony is intended to strengthen

48. Shamans and Elders praying at KALVARYO during a Year Renewal ceremony

the tribal gods and "shut off the power of seeing" (SMAKOBIL SAT) from the foreigners. An example of the latter is the experience of an archaeologist who attempted in 1961 to secure permission to survey and excavate sites in the municipio. Not only was permission denied by the Presidente, but a special renewal ceremony was performed by the shamans to prevent him from "seeing into the sacred mountains."

Special renewal ceremonies are similar to the regularly scheduled ones, except that money is not collected for food and the Elders need not provide ritual meals (ritualists are expected to bring their own food for pilgrimages); also the prayer over the candles is held in the Chapel of Esquipulas rather than the house of the Grand Alcalde.

What *distinctive* meanings do these Year Renewal rituals have for the lives of the Zinacantecos? The very names of the rituals, New Year, Midyear, and End of Year, and the times of their performance indicate a fundamental relation to the cycling of the year. The fiesta of San Sebastian marks the end of the ritual year. What more appropriate time for the "New Year" to restore order and initiate a new annual cycle than immediately following? "Midyear" appropriately follows the fiesta of San Juan, close to the summer solstice. Finally, at All Saints' Day the living pay respect to their ancestors who return to receive food and drink in the houses and cemeteries; shortly thereafter the "End of the Year" is celebrated, before the long cycle of Christmas-New Year-San Sebastián begins. Whether or not the shamans' End of the Year ceremony might have originally fallen closer to the winter solstice, as seems more appropriate to the natural time cycle, is not known. Gossen has found that in Chamula the surviving ancient solar calendar suggests that December 26, 27, or 28 is 1 Z'UN, thus putting the beginning of the year closer to the winter solstice in the Chamula conceptual system. He also argues that the Tzotzil calendar was a winter solstice to winter solstice cycle: "contemporary Chamula interpretation of month names is resonant with the idea that the sequence deals with aspects of the slow waxing and waning of solar intensity. It is also interesting that most symbolic domains of Chamula life (e.g., fiestas and the lifecycle) which are isomorphic with the solar cycle begin with cold, rise to heat, and return to cold" (1974b: 247). This cycle fits well with my interpretation in Chapters 9 and 10 that the Christmas-New Year-San Sebastián period in Zinacantan ceremonializes the end of the old year and beginning of the new year.

Year Renewal ceremonies are unique in the ritual system of Zinacantan in that they are the only rites that renew the municipio's tribal shrines (with the exception of Junior Great Mountain) and articulate all crucial parts of the official structure of Zinacantan—shamans, cargoholders (with the exception of the Alféreces), and civil officers. Indeed, they focus attention upon the two peaks of sacred power—the Senior Shaman and the Grand Alcalde—and the peak of civil power—the Presidente.

Structure and Phasing: Implements of Unification

The ritual sequence has two major parts, separate but related. The first is the interaction between the ceremonial center and the hamlets. The date for the ceremony is set in the Center; information disseminates to the hamlets. Money collected flows in toward the Center; shamans travel there to count the money, then return to the hamlets. The following day, they again travel from the hamlets to the Center. The resulting interchange integrates the numerous dwelling places of Zinacantecos into their central meeting ground; the component parts are united into a whole (the group of ritualists) in the place (HTEK-LUM) that symbolizes that unification.

The second facet deals with integration and unification of the gods. The united whole of "human" Zinacantan, as represented by the group of ritualists, separates to travel to sacred shrines. Having honored the gods, the ritualists do not return to the Center, as might be expected, but unite first at KALVARYO. Here they again "journey" to each shrine; by kneeling and praying from KALVARYO, they revisit them, before their attention again focuses on KALVARYO. An interchange is achieved between the homes and the meeting-place of the ancestral gods. The ritualists create the connection, as they created it between the Center and the hamlets.

Thus, the two parts of the ritual outlined by structure and phasing also express two separate, but related, functional aspects of Year Renewal ceremonies. Structural duplication has produced a functional duplication, merely transposed into another sphere: unification (function) that is the result of the integration of parts into a whole (structure and phasing) is accomplished in Year Renewal ceremonies for both mortal and deific Zinacanteco realities. A similar structural pattern is found in the exchange of saints between the churches in HTEK-LUM and the chapels in the outlying hamlets as well as with churches in neighboring muncipios like Ixtapa and San Lucas Zapotal that probably once were a part of Zinacantan. These saint exchanges also unify in a social, political and economic way the component parts of the Zinacanteco world (Wasserstrom 1970).

Boundary Symbolism

A crucial aspect of the Year Renewal rituals is the drawing of a boundary around the municipio. By making offerings at all the tribal shrines and praying at KALVARYO, the ritualists are symbolically defining Zinacantan, establishing ritual purity within, and setting the municipio apart from the disorder outside. By exaggerating the difference within and without, the rituals symbolically recreate order each year for all of Zinacantan.

The Year Renewal rituals not only separate what is Zinacanteco from what is not but also symbolically underscore the differences between the cargoholders and the shamans and mediate between them. They attempt to deal with "internal lines in the system" and touch upon a critical internal contradiction between the principles of organization of the cargoholders and those of the shamans.

I have noted that the cargoholders are the contemporary equivalents of the ancient Maya Year Bearers. Each carries the burden of office for a year before passing it along to his successor. These are heavy burdens. They require that a man request the office many years in advance and, while on the waiting list, be diligent and enterprising in managing his economic affairs so that he will be able to assume the crushing costs of his cargo. He must also manage his social affairs skillfully so that he will be able to recruit the large numbers of helpers needed for his retinue. Only by expertise and hard work can he work his way through the four levels of the cargo hierarchy and become an honored *pasado*, "passed one" or "one who has passed through" (Cancian 1965).

A shaman, on the other hand, dreams that he has been called upon by the ancestral gods to assume his role. Once he makes his debut, he is a shaman for life. Although he must respond to requests for his services and spends much of his time performing ceremonies, he has neither the economic obligation to furnish food or liquor (they are provided by the family or larger social unit receiving his services) nor the social obligation to recruit assistants (always recruited by others). Hence, the shaman, as shaman, is never expected to be an economic or social entrepreneur;* he holds a position of power and prestige by virtue of his ability to dream about, to "see," and to communicate with the gods.

So, the styles of the two major kinds of ritualists in Zinacantan—what might in this context be called the "Year Bearers" and the "Year Renewers"—are markedly different, indeed contradictory. The former is a man of his own making, the latter a man of the gods' making. Further, the very act of bearing is a quintessentially human act, but the act of renewing a year is a divine act.

The sequence of events in the Year Renewal rites symbolically underscores the differences between the cargoholders, who host the meals and attend to the details of receiving money for and purchasing the paraphernalia and of recruiting the helpers, and the shamans, who take no part in arranging details but only appear at the appropriate time to allocate funds for different types of paraphernalia, eat the food, light the candles, and pray to the gods.

In the early episodes the lines between cargoholders and shamans are carefully drawn. The Elders, the Mayordomo Reyes, and Mesoneros are busy with details of the ritual, but after these are accomplished, they arrive at the house of the Grand Alcalde and patiently await the arrival of the shamans. The shamans gather in the churchyard of San Lorenzo, then march in formation to the Chapel of Esquipulas to check the money and allocate it, after which they return home. They next appear at the home of the Senior Shaman to

*Many shamans also hold cargos; when they do, they are able to call upon individuals for whom they have provided curing or other ceremonies to serve as helpers.

drink together and honor this most senior among them while awaiting word that all is in order for the night-long prayer. Then they march to the house of the Grand Alcalde, where, in the presence of the Elders, they sit around the table and pray over the candles. The mediatory part of the ritual begins to unfold when the shamans arrive at the home of the Grand Alcalde; they honor his cross shrine and his altar; they bow to the Grand and Second Alcaldes. The mediation tempo increases following the ritual meal, as the Elders and the other cargoholders accompany the high-ranking shamans to the churches and nearby mountain shrines. The mediation reaches its peak at KALVARYO where all pray in unison to all tribal shrines and eat together. Here the potential conflict of rank is resolved: the Grand Alcalde, not the highest-ranking shaman, is left at the end of the bowing-and-releasing sequence. The procession back to his house further underlines this rank order, as the shamans precede the Elders in the line of march.

The dreaming and "seeing" power of the Year Renewers is critical for the Zinacanteco ritual system, for it is the shamans who pray to and deal with the ancestral gods living in the sacred mountains that rim the valley of Zinacantan and lie beyond the Center. As one high-ranking cargoholder expressed it to Haviland (personal communication, August 11, 1973), "Without the shamans, none of us would be alive." On the other hand, the economic, social, and ritual expertise of the Year Bearers is utilized to manage the sacred affairs of the ceremonial center. Only shamans make pilgrimages to the more distant sacred mountains; shamans accompanied by cargoholders visit the nearby mountain shrines, and the churches, saints, and house altars in the ceremonial center are cared for by cargoholders. On the continuum from Nature to Culture, it is the shamans who deal with the gods living in, or on the borders of, TEʔTIK and the cargoholders who manage the calendrical rites in NAETIK.

Thus, the Year Renewal rites give both pinnacles of religious power separate and essential functions to fulfill, assign them positions of prestige and power, and place high value on both the Year Renewers and Year Bearers.

One prominent aspect in the Year Renewal ceremonies is what I call the "symbolism of six." A common Zinacanteco myth about the origins of the tribal gods relates how six Elders from Zinacantan were summoned to Mexico City by an Indian king to help the Presidente overcome enemies who were about to conquer Mexico. Whether this war of conquest was related to any actual war in Mexico history is unknown. These ancient Zinacantecos were called XOHOBETIK (sun rays), and, "just as engineers look into the distance," they were able to see into the mountains and perceive the Earth Lord. (Here again "vision" is equated with "knowing".) Each of these mythological culture heroes had specialized powers: one could make fog, a second lightning, a third a whirlwind, a fourth fly like a hawk, a fifth like a butterfly, and a sixth like a fly. They successfully overcame the hidden enemies by laying down a heavy fog and under its cover erecting a series of crosses, like a corral, around them. After consulting the sun god, they proceeded to destroy their enemies by setting the crosses on fire with lightning and having the whirlwind fill the corral with sea water. The water boiled and the bodies of the enemy floated to the surface. It was the duty of the hawk to make certain that none reached the edge of the boiling water, cooled off, and came to life again; the butterfly made certain that no enemy reenforcements arrived; the fly inspected each floating body to confirm its death. The Presidente and the Indian king then came to verify that all the enemies were dead and gave a great fiesta, lasting six days and six nights, for the Elders. The MOLETIK returned to Zinacantan but, fearing reprisals by the enemy forces, rather than returning to their old homes, asked permission from the Earth Lord to take up residence inside the mountains. The Earth Lord agreed and the MOLETIK took up residence in six mountains. The "most senior" went to ?OX YOKET (BANKILAL MUK'TA VIZ), while the other five went to KALVARYO, SAN KIXTOVAL, LAC CIKIN, NAKLEB ?OK, and ?ISAK'TIK. At the same time their wives took up residence in six "female" mountains: MUXUL VIZ, SISIL VIZ, NINAB CILO?, NIO?, YA?AHVIL, and LANSA VIZ. (Other mountains substituted by some informants include SAK C'EN, NA HOH, C'UL TON, and YA?AM TON.) They live today inside these mountains from where they monitor the affairs of their living Zinacanteco descendants.

These six supernatural Elders are believed to meet at KALVARYO, which has six crosses; they are symbolically reincarnated each year in the six Elders (Alcaldes and Regidores) at the top of the cargo system. Further, the concept would appear to be replicated in the six C'UL MOLETIK (Holy Elders), who, along with the Grand and Second Alcaldes, wash the large entombed Christ image (HMANVANEH, "The Buyer") with after-shave lotion on Wednesday of Holy Week, march in procession with the image on Thursday, and place the image on the Large Cross on Good Friday. It was also (until two Alféreces were added some thirty years ago) replicated in two orders (Senior and Junior) of six Alféreces, and two orders of six Mayordomos, and, until the civil Regidores were added after 1962, in the six civil officials who preside at the cabildo: Presidente, Síndico, and four Alcaldes Jueces. I am told by informants that there also used to be six Mayores on duty at the cabildo. Finally, it is worth noting that the number of Senior Impersonators performing at the fiesta of San Sebastián is six.

Through the emphasis on the six Elders and the six pairs of senior shamans who go with them to visit the churches and nearby mountain shrines, this symbolism is strongly reiterated in the Year Renewal ceremonies. Why *six* remains a mystery. Were there six prominent ancestors sometime in the past? Perhaps there were six leading lineages in Zinacantan. Or could this pervasive symbolism result from two times three, three being stressed throughout the ritual life, with the multiplier being either Senior and Junior, Male and Female, or some other binary opposition?

12

Some Dynamics of Change in Zinacanteco Ritual

THE FACT THAT Zinacantecos continue to enlist for cargo positions that will not become available for more than two decades demonstrates their belief in the continuity and stability of their ritual system. Although, like all Mayas, they are acutely concerned with the passage of time, its unfolding does not, in their view, entail corresponding changes in their ritual life. Zinacantecos are not immune to the encroachment of Western society now felt throughout the Highlands. When possible, they do not hesitate to purchase watches, transistor radios, maize-grinding mills, plastic raincoats, and trucks. Yet this acceptance of selected aspects of economic modernization does not lead them to question the essential constancy of the metaphysical universe. History—expressed in oral narrative—and experience with ritual life confirm the Zinacanteco's view that such life is constant.

At least four salient factors help explain change in Zinacanteco ritual patterns. First, as a premise, it can be stated that no culture, no matter how ancient or isolated, is static. Although its rate may be slow or fluctuating, change is an observable constant in all cultural systems. It may be stimulated by such phenomena as ecological variation, economic development, or demographic fluctuation, but appears to occur even in the absence of such factors. Some combination of tensions within the system (Geertz 1957; Vogt 1960) and the propensity of men to "play" creatively with their cultural patterns probably best explains the "drift" characteristic of all cultures. Although it is difficult to factor out the changes that are occurring in this "cultural drift" in Zinacantan, certain ritual details appear to be differentiating from a common historical base in much the same manner that dialect variations occur between the hamlets.

Another source of change is the historical and contemporary influence of the Catholic Church. Since the Spanish Conquest and subsequent "conversion" of the Indian populations of New Spain, Zinacantecos have had to reconcile inherent discrepancies between the imposed and the native conceptual systems. The present-day ladino ritual system is regarded with ambivalent feelings of admiration and respect, bewilderment and confusion, bitterness and resentment.

A third source of change is the impingement of the ladino world on nonritual aspects of life. Zinacanteco population has increased dramatically* as modern medicine introduced by ladino agencies (government doctors and nurses, private physicians, availability of drugs in San Cristóbal pharmacies, and so on) has effectively brought epidemics of smallpox, typhus, and influenza under control and reduced the incidence of lowland diseases such as malaria. There has also been an upsurge in the per capita income as Zinacantecos become more deeply involved in the nonsubsistence, money world of modern Chiapas.

The fourth source of change—the vast increase in numbers of channels of communication between Zinacantan and the outside world—is even more complex. Roads, automobiles, radios, schools, and clinics have brought Zinacantan within range of outside influences in the past two decades at a level not experienced before. Mexican government agents, visiting missionaries, students, and tourists come into daily contact with Zinacantecos in the ceremonial center, the most accessible hamlets, and the San Cristóbal marketplace. Such contact with outsiders has, understandably, led to uneasiness, often outright hostility, on the part of the Zinacantecos.

*This increase (4,509 in 1940, 6,312 in 1950, 7,650 in 1960, 11,428 in 1970), according to the Mexican censuses of 1960 and 1970, should be considered with some reservations. According to George Collier (personal communication, October 25, 1973), there is field evidence that either the 1960 or the 1970 figures for Zinacantan as a whole are in gross error, for the population aged ten and over in 1970 is much greater than the population total of 1960, even though the former population consists of the same individuals as the latter.

Trends, 1942-1972

The Zinacanteco ritual system has been under continuous observation by members of the Harvard Chiapas Project since 1957, providing firsthand data on the continuities and changes in the system over the fifteen-year period from 1957 to 1972. We also have access to relevant data from 1942-43 when Professor Sol Tax and a group of Mexican students spent some six weeks doing field research in Zinacantan Center. The most striking fact about this thirty-year period is the surprising lack of change in the crucial elements of the ritual system. This is all the more startling given the statement in the summary article on the 1942-43 expedition to the effect that "in the Municipio of Zinacantan we find an indigenous culture in the process of change due to Ladinoization, progressive and constant, of its members" (Cámara Barbachano 1943). One might have predicted that thirty years later traditional ceremonial life would show the kind of cultural erosion, with old patterns breaking down or being extinguished altogether, characteristic of many Indian communities under acculturation pressure in Oaxaca, Morelos, and Michoacán (see, for example, Leslie 1960; Lewis 1951; Foster 1948). Instead, the key elements of the 1942 Zinacanteco ritual system are still prominent in 1972. Moreover, there has been a marked increase in the incidence of these ceremonies and an intensification of traditional ritual patterns.

While ladinoization has proceeded apace in the domain of household and community material culture—for example, house types, men's clothing styles, modes of transportation, and bilingualism—it has had far less effect on traditional ceremonial life. There is little evidence that Zinacantecos are any more Catholic now, in the orthodox sense, than they were in 1942; of the seven Catholic sacraments, baptism and marriage were the only ones mentioned as being of importance to them in 1942; in 1972 they are still the only vital ones.

Only four noteworthy changes in ritual behavior can be traced, at least in part, to the direct influence of ladinoization. First, the number of house altars has increased substantially. Although in the Center such altars have long been used by cargoholders, now many houses in the hamlets have interior altars. This shift is of symbolic importance since the traditional Zinacanteco pattern has emphasized the KRUS TA TI? NA in the patio outside, a pattern not followed by ladinos who typically have altars inside their houses. This change *may* be attributable, however, not so much to ladino influence as to emulation of the cargoholders. If so, the trend is one of reassertion and reaffirmation of Zinacanteco religious separateness and cultural identity.

Second, although there has been an increase in the use of modern medicine to cure diseases, the availability of modern services has not eliminated the practice of curing ceremonies by shamans. These apparently contradictory trends can be explained by the Zinacantecos' conceptions of the purpose of each. Modern medicines serve to eliminate the physical manifestations of disease while shamanistic rites deal with the underlying causes of the affliction and accomplish, in our terms, necessary psychotherapy. Good health, dependent on harmony with the moral and religious powers of the universe, thus demands traditional curing ceremonies at a rate equal to the increased administration of ladino medical help. Indeed, it can be argued that increased recognition and treatment of physical ailments by ladino physicians has made the Zinacantecos more aware of "sickness"—an awareness interpreted as an increased occurrence of deviation from behavior sanctioned by the gods. In other words, it may be considered an indication of social illness requiring an aggressive campaign of shamanistic rites to defend society against the corrupting encroachment of ladinoization.

The ladinoization of men's clothing—from short cotton pants to long trousers, from high-backed sandals to huaraches and even ladino shoes—is reflected to some extent in the ceremonial life. While men generally still dress in short pants for ritual affairs, an increasing number of cargoholders and shamans wear huaraches on these occasions. Traditionally, men's clothing styles have been a respected mark of cultural identity.

Finally, there is a trend in ritual paraphernalia away from the traditional gourd and ceramic containers toward a variety of metal, enamel, glass, and plastic containers. This shift appears to have little significance for Zinacantecos, however, who do not find it strange or awkward to substitute in maize divination a fancy enamel bowl for a gourd. A good example was provided by the use to which a purified water container was put, after being presented as a gift by a 1971 Project member to the Alférez of Santo Domingo. Noting its ample capacity and convenient pouring mechanism, the Alférez filled the container with ceremonial liquor, giving up the use of his more traditional wooden cask without the slightest hesitation.

The interrelated factors of demographic and economic growth in Zinacantan, which stem indirectly from a deeper involvement with the ladino world of modern Chiapas, have had more decisive effects on the ritual system than the mere presence of the ladino model of life or the direct pressures of ladinoization. Increased population has made land a scarce commodity, forcing Zinacantecos to range much farther afield in their search for Lowland tenancy rights (Cancian 1972) and to make more aggressive efforts to secure ejido land (Guarnaccia 1972). Land shortage has also led increasing numbers of Zinacantecos to seek alternative ways to support themselves, for example, as wage-workers on road construction projects, employees in Mexican government programs, or merchants reselling maize in the local markets. In addition, various government programs now involving most Zinacanteco hamlets—the purchase of trucks, the establishment of schools and clinics, installation of electricity (which has now reached Zinacantan Center and the three large hamlets of Nabencauk, Nacih, and Vo? Coh Vo?) and water lines (now found in Zinacantan Center and the hamlets of Paste? and Nacih)—have led to greater involvement of Zinacantecos in the Mexican economic system.

These trends have placed enormous pressures for change upon the traditional ritual system of Zinacantan. As Cancian correctly concludes, the rise in population and the increase in spending money have created crucial problems for the religious cargo systems in particular. For, while the number of positions in the cargo system has been increasing, the rate of increase is not keeping pace with the demographic explosion. The development of waiting lists has provided a temporary solution, but it is doubtful that a man will be willing to wait much more than twenty years for a cargo, especially since the average life span is still low by North American standards. Moreover, greater numbers of Zinacanteco entrepreneurs are growing large maize surpluses on rented lands in the Lowlands, and pressures are increasing to expand this wealth in other, more immediate, ways than for a cargo (Vogt 1969: 271). Cancian has predicted that the cargo system soon will be strained to the point where it will lose its importance as the social institution through which the municipio is integrated (1965: 193-194). Although this is still a definite possibility, indication of this change was not evident as of 1972.

Two other avenues should be considered. First, the number of cargo positions may expand markedly as hamlets build their own chapels and develop hierarchies of cargos to tend their saints. Second, a system might evolve in which the cargos are served by an elite group—families with more surplus wealth—as appears to have happened in Chamula and in Guatemalan communities such as Chichicastenango (Bunzel 1952), where the cargo systems maintain their essential integrating effects in the face of expanding populations and limited cargo positions.

The cargo and shamanistic rituals are, thus far, increasing in Zinacantan. Many are becoming more elaborate and complex, rather than losing their ritual and symbolic content. To what extent these processes stem from the pressures of demographic growth and economic change and to what extent they are temporary (or even long-run) nativistic reactions to the direct pressures of ladinoization is difficult to say. Both types of pressures seem inextricably involved in contemporary trends.

We are witnessing a marked increase in the number of cargos as new chapels are constructed and saints installed in the hamlets. This tendency to add new cargos can be traced through the colonial history of Zinacantan and has continued in the nineteenth and twentieth centuries. When the first Chapel of Esquipulas was constructed in 1899, the present positions of two Mayordomo Reyes were added to the cargo system; the two Mesoneros were added in 1938. The four Regidores, civil officials before the turn of the century, have been absorbed into the cargo system as the four REHIROLETIK, who, along with the Grand and Second Alcaldes, constitute the Elders. The second Alférez and the second Mayordomo of San Sebastián were added in the 1940s.

The construction of chapels in outlying hamlets began in the early 1900s when a small edifice for the Virgen de Rosario was erected in ?Az'am. Two cargo positions were established—a Mayor and a Mayordomo. In 1954 Nabencauk completed its chapel for the Virgen de Guadalupe, who is attended by two Mayordomos. The chapel in ?Apas, with Esquipulas as its patron, was constructed in 1962, necessitating four new cargo positions, two Mayordomo Reyes and two Mesoneros. Nacih finished its chapel in 1969 and installed an image of the Virgen de Fátima. The newest chapels, completed in 1971, are those of Paste? and Sekemtik, each with a Virgen de

Rosario as patron saint. These last three chapels will probably soon add two cargos each to the system.

Table 3 shows that while the rate of increase in cargo positions is not keeping pace with demographic growth, it has nevertheless been fairly consistent. Combined with the recent increase in civil cargo positions, it has relieved the pressures placed upon the cargo system by an expanding population. Although civil positions do not count for advancement in the more prestigious religious hierarchy, they do provide opportunities for an alternative mode of service to the community, offering the successful civil cargoholder a qualitatively different type of prestige. Examples include the six civil Regidores added to the cabildo, school committees (usually three positions for each school in the hamlets), and committees to manage fiestas.

Greater pressures still exist at the three highest levels of the hierarchy, where the traditional fourteen Alférez, four Regidor, and two Alcalde posts are maintained. Yet even within the highest ranks where pressures are especially intense, an interesting alternative has developed. Within the past two decades it has become common for a man to serve as either the Alférez of Santo Domingo or the Alférez of San Lorenzo in lieu of Grand or Second Alcalde, thereby making effectively four positions available in the topmost level. These two positions actually cost a cargoholder far more than either of the Alcalde posts, thus affording them equivalent prestige.

It can be argued that the construction of chapels in the hamlets adds a new dimension to the centrifugal tendencies in Zinacantan which are more fundamentally related to the construction of the Pan American Highway (Pellizzi, field notes 1969; Wasserstrom 1970: 265). This well-traveled road has provided easy access to markets in San Cristóbal and Tuxtla Gutiérrez for many Zinacantecos; it has lessened their economic dependence upon Zinacantan Center, through which the old road connecting San Cristóbal with the state capital passed. Zinacantecos in the affected hamlets now board buses or

Table 3 Growth in population and cargo positions, 1930-1970.

Year	Zinacanteco population[a]	Growth per decade (percentage)	Number of cargo positions	Growth per decade (percentage)
1930	2,129		55	
		111		3.6
1940	4,509		57	
		40		3.5
1950	6,312		59	
		21		3.3
1960	7,650		61	
		49		6.5
1970	11,428		65	
Increase	9,299	436	10	18

[a]Official Mexican census figures

trucks and reach San Cristóbal in less than a half-hour, Tuxtla Gutiérrez in two hours. Thus, there appears to be no need, other than political or religious, to journey to HTEK-LUM, and, with the establishment of hamlet chapels, even these justifications will be increasingly questioned. On the other hand, the proliferation of chapels has led to new cargo posts, which have served to ease the tensions inherent in increasing competition for ever more scarce municipio cargos. So, although Zinacantan continues to experience local differentiation, the establishment of hamlet chapels—outwardly acts of independence—may redirect competitive pressures and resulting frustrations away from the municipio system, thus contributing to its maintenance and security in the face of escalating demographic pressure.

Another notable trend in the cargo system in recent decades has been the proliferation and intensification of rituals. Instead of becoming truncated in a way common in North American Indian ceremonial life under pressure from the outside world, traditional Zinacanteco cargo rituals are being performed more frequently and are becoming more, rather than less, elaborate. An important example is the increased incidence of the ritual called BAL-TEʔ described in Chapter 8. When we first recorded the instances of Flower Renewal in the annual ceremonial round in the late 1950s and early 1960s, we discovered it was being performed at seven major cargo fiestas. By 1972 it was being performed in full-scale form (that is, flower renewal on house altars as well as in the three churches in the Center) at twenty-three fiestas each year—a more than threefold increase. Given that the BAL-TEʔ is a relatively complex rite with twelve ritual episodes for the house altars, to say nothing of the later changing of flowers in the three churches, this represents a fantastic jump in the investment of time, energy, and resources on the part of the twelve Mayordomos. A second example, in this case the intensification of a single rite, is provided by the ritual counting of the medallions for the saint images in the Chapel of Esquipulas, also described in Chapter 8. This case has been carefully documented by R. Rosaldo (field notes 1965), who noted that Esquipulas resided in the cabildo until 1899, when he was moved to a chapel constructed especially for him. The custom of having musicians play during a Sunday ceremony for the saint was added shortly thereafter. Initially, only a harp and a guitar were used; in 1910 the violin was added. For many years two Mayordomo Reyes were in charge of the entire ceremony; in 1938 the two Mesoneros were added. A weekly counting of the single necklace of medallions was instituted in 1944; by 1960 there were two necklaces; a third necklace, with new coins added each year, became part of the complex in 1966. In the meantime, the old chapel had been deemed small and inadequate, and a new and larger one was erected in 1962. What began as a single set of rituals for a single saint has developed into a complex cult which shows indications of becoming more elaborate each year without any direct influence, pressure, or intervention on the part of the local Catholic priest.

These elaborations in cargo ceremonies stem partly from an increase in Zinacanteco wealth and partly from a feeling of uneasiness about contemporary changes in Zinacanteco culture. Because of the fear of envy and consequent danger of witchcraft, Zinacantecos cannot conspicuously display increased wealth through fancy houses or ostentatious purchases of material goods. Hence, the most secure way of using increased wealth is to pour it into the cargo rituals, thereby gaining prestige through the generally approved service for the saints.

The trends we are witnessing in the cargo system are even exceeded in most respects in the shamanistic complex of Zinacantan. Here again we observe a significant increase in the number of practicing shamans. When we first counted them, hamlet by hamlet, in the early 1960s, we estimated the existence of about 160 practicing shamans; at that time informants reported there had recently been a notable increase in the numbers in most hamlets. In 1972, we estimated that approximately 250 shamans were officially performing ceremonies in Zinacantan, an increase which outstrips the rate of population growth. The example offered by ˀApas is dramatic: two shamans in 1940 increased to four in 1950, six in 1962, nine in 1965, and fifteen in 1968, not counting six who, for one reason or another, do not participate in the public K'IN KRUS ceremonies (Pellizzi, field notes 1968). The population of ˀApas was approximately 520 in 1940, 607 in 1950, 704 in 1960, and 860 in 1968, clearly demonstrating that the ratio of shamans to hamlet inhabitants is increasing.

Although we do not yet have sufficient data to determine whether or not there has been an overall per capita increase in the incidence of rituals of affliction, we do have evidence of their greater elaboration. Pellizzi reports on cases of Great Seeing ceremonies in the past three years in which four chickens were sacrificed, rather than the traditional two, and in which there was an increase in the number of shrines visited and candles offered. K'IN KRUS ceremonies occur more frequently than ever before in some hamlets. There is evidence that K'IN KRUS and Year Renewal ceremonies are becoming more elaborate in that each year new crosses are being added to the ceremonial circuits. The impetus for the erection of new crosses results from dreams of the shamans. The dream is communicated to the highest ranking shaman; if he is convinced it is true, he accompanies the dreamer to the Presidente, who must authorize a collection of money. A similar process takes place in the hamlets. If the Senior Shaman is convinced the dream is valid, the elders are asked to authorize the collection of funds from the heads of families within the hamlet. In ˀApas, Pellizzi discovered that the number of cross shrines had increased from eighteen to twenty-five within the past decade, thereby adding seven ritual stops to the ceremonial circuit for the Year Renewal rites.

The increase in wealth is an important factor in the proliferation of both shamanistic rites and cross shrines. However, the decisive factors in the increase in shamanistic dreaming, hence the rise in number of shamans, appear to be: (1) a compensatory, nativistic reaction to pressures Zinacantecos feel in the modern world and the consequent uneasy state of the system; and (2) the use of the shamanistic route to ritual power by increasing numbers of Zinacantecos who cannot hope to hold expensive cargos in a system in which there can never be enough positions to go around.

Nativistic Reactions in Contemporary Zinacantan

In a recent conference, the Catholic Bishop of San Cristóbal professed mystification as to why Indian municipios that are most accessible to the Pan American Highway and the ladino towns of San Cristóbal and Teopisca—Zinacantan, Chamula, and Amatenango—are those most resistant both to further proselytization by Catholic missionaries and to many of the modern improvements promoted by agencies of the Mexican government. For the anthropologist acquainted with nativist and revivalist movements around the world these reactions are not only understandable but predictable (Wallace 1956).

As external pressures for ladinoization increase with improved means of communication, and dramatic changes in demography and economics occur, the Indians are aware that their cultural cohesiveness and integrity are being threatened. The recent increase in tourists, who often disrupt ceremonies inside and outside churches by persistent efforts to approach and photograph the participants, has exacerbated the situation. In these three municipios we observe efforts not just to resist accelerated encroachment from outside but to define assertively new limits for outsiders. In Chamula, *all* ladinos (with the exception of schoolteachers and the secretary, who are granted temporary residence), including the merchants who formerly lived in the Center and the resident Catholic priest, have been forced to move out of the community. Further, there is each year more and more resistance to permitting outsiders to enter the churches or even look at, much less take photographs of, the sacred saint images.

Zinacantecos handle such threats to their integrity in another way, a boundary-establishing concept best described as "encapsulation." I have defined encapsulation as a process in which new elements imposed from the outside are conceptually and structurally incorporated into existing patterns of social and ritual behavior (Vogt 1969: 582-587). This phenomenon may be viewed as a special form of "syncretism" which Zinacantecos have evolved in order to cope with new elements injected into their way of life. Examples of how such cultural elements are encapsulated were provided by the National Indigenous Institute school and the Harvard field house in the hamlet of Paste?. Both were included in a special K'IN KRUS ritual, incorporated into a ceremonial circuit that featured visits to two cross shrines in a nearby cave and a KALVARYO established on a hill above the schoolhouse. In 1957 a man was struck by lightning and killed near the new school, an event attributed by Zinacantecos to anger of the Earth Lord and the ancestral gods because of the school's presence. The K'IN KRUS rite initiated that year was extended to include the field house in May 1960, a year after its construction. A similar process concerned the newly constructed Pan American Highway. Numerous speeding automobiles, never before witnessed by the inhabitants, passed daily through the center of Nacih. The inevitable happened: a child was struck and killed. Accordingly, cross shrines were erected on small hills at points where the highway enters and leaves the hamlet. K'IN KRUS ceremonies are now performed regularly, with ceremonial circuits encapsulating this section of the highway into the traditional ritual pattern, thereby offsetting its evil influence.

Other important instances of encapsulation are provided by the assimilation of civil offices, imposed by the ladinos, into the religious hierarchy of Zinacantan Center. The Alcaldes, Regidores, and Alféreces were assigned only civil duties at the time of their institution by the Spaniards in the colonial period; today the functions of these cargoholders are almost purely "religious." The *Alguaciles Indios* (Indian Constables), who acted as police in 1592, subsequently became both the Mayores, who although they have political duties are deeply involved in ritual activities, and the Mayordomo Reyes and Mesoneros, who now carry billy clubs but exercise important religious authority in the chapel of Esquipulas. Although the present cabildo officials continue to serve critical political functions, they have been given a number of ritual duties. The Presidente, for example, serves as a "godfather," placing the Christ children in the manger in the crèche on Christmas Eve.

Such historical and contemporary instances of encapsulation provide a basis for a series of speculations about how the society handled the imposition of new cultural patterns in the past. One of the major symbols of Catholicism, the cross, was probably adopted by the Zinacantecos early in the post-Conquest period. As has been mentioned, there is evidence that pinetree tops constitute the crucial symbols, since cross shrines can be constructed or expanded by the simple addition of one or more pine-tips. Moreover, Calnek (1962: 55) provides evidence of the sacrifice of various animals and birds to idols located outside the doors of houses, that is, at the present location of the house crosses. It is my hypothesis, therefore, that aboriginal altars were composed of pine trees and flowers strapped to some type of idol, and that the Christian cross may have been incorporated into the ritual system by the development of a set of procedures for covering the cross shrines with pine trees, red geraniums, and other plants to an extent that effectively obscures the cross. It is also probable that the Christian Calvary was encapsulated, in name if not in concept, by Zinacanteco ritual in the most important type of cross shrine, KALVARYO, a meeting place for ancestral deities who watch over a given lineage, waterhole, or hamlet, or over the entire municipio (Vogt 1969: 586).

The other important adoption from the Spanish are the saints, which probably replaced aboriginal idols of some type. According to the Zinacantecos, their saints were "found" in mythological times, and had "houses" built for them. They are now clothed in Zinacanteco clothes and ribbons, honored by having necklaces placed on them, are bathed, and have their clothes washed with the special care given to Zinacantecos treated in curing ceremonies.

Another example in which Catholic patterns conceivably were grafted onto aboriginal ones is in the case of talking idols, today referred to as talking saints (HK'OPOHEL RIOX). In form, these saints are usually cheap religious pictures or images of the type found throughout Mexico, although some, made of clay, were supposedly "found" in caves. They differ from ordinary saints in their alleged power to speak to those seeking their advice. Myths that explain how the saints of Zinacantan lost their ability to talk reinforces the hypothesis that at one time Zinacantecos believed that all saints spoke. A hypothesis corroborating the aboriginal nature of the talking saint is based on an extrapolation of the account of a talking idol encountered on the island of Cozumel written by Cortes' secretary, Gomarra (Thompson 1970: 189). This particular idol attracted the afflicted from far and near and communicated through a priestly figure who, in turn, gave advice and prescribed cures in exchange for offerings brought to him by the pilgrims.

In Zinacantan, the typical pattern of a consultation is as follows: a patient goes to the house of a talking-saint owner (YAHVAL RIOX) with standard payment of liquor, chickens, flowers, and so on, and places them in front of the box in which the saint is kept. Often, the owner covers his head and the box with his chamarra while he explains the patient's problem to the saint and waits for the response. Several informants who have witnessed consultations claim that a high-pitched, squeaky noise is emitted, construed to be the voice of the talking saint. Others claim that no sound is heard, that the owner acts as transmitter of the saint's message. One explanation of why talking saints are consulted as opposed to Zinacanteco shamans or San Cristóbal doctors is that they will diagnose special cases, such as those involving witchcraft. This may be why St. Michael, known for his power to protect the believer against his enemies, is the most commonly identified talking saint. The reputation of the talking-saint owner is extremely dubious in Zinacantan today. In several cases the diagnosis of a talking saint has resulted in the murder of a suspected witch, thus drawing the censure of Zinacanteco and ladino authorities. In other cases, the cure prescribed involved continued payments to the owner, with patients paying the sums out of fear for their lives. When the cures are unsuccessful the owners are accused of theft and become the objects of hostility and suspicion. Enough cases have been brought to court so that both Zinacanteco and ladino authorities have adopted a negative attitude. Their efforts to discredit talking saints apparently have been successful, and informants have noted a distinct decrease in the number of talking-saint owners in the last few years.

Encapsulation continues as an important

boundary-controlling mechanism. The most recent example involves the completion of a pipeline in 1969 which brought running water for the first time to Pasteˀ. The pipeline runs from a storage tank, fed by a spring on the south side of the volcanic mountain complex that includes Senior Large Mountain, to the hamlet some 5 kilometers away. The entire pipeline is now included in the K'IN KRUS ceremonial circuits, which include the offering of candles and prayers at the spring where the water emerges from the mountain and at the major tap on the pipeline in front of the school in Pasteˀ.

With regard to ritual, some of the nativistic reactions to the pressures of acculturation are more oblique. In 1969 a young Zinacanteco in Nabencauk dreamed about the bell inside BAYOCOB, a hill overlooking the lake southwest of the hamlet. The bell, said to have been placed inside the hill by the ancestral gods some one hundred years ago, used to be heard at noon. Nabencauk shamans have had various dreams about the hill—including one that there is a chapel of the Earth Lord inside it—and the year before various people had reported hearing the bell ring and seeing blue-green, red, yellow, or white lights hovering over the hill.

On July 1, Xun Peres Tanhol, aged about thirty, had three identical dreams concerning the bell on three consecutive nights. In the dream an assistant of the gods was sent to conduct Xun's innate soul back to KALVARYO. There, the six gods asked him to tell the people of Nabencauk that there was a bell in BAYOCOB. Standing on either side and grasping the top of the bell were San Rafael and a Virgen de Rosario (a younger sister of the three Virgin sisters found in HTEK-LUM, ˀAz'am, and Ixtapa). Xun's soul was then conducted back to Nabencauk and left on BAYOCOB with a representation of the Earth Lord in the form of an old man who told him that he wanted the bell taken out, pointed to the spot, and disappeared. Xun then awakened. He told a few trusted friends about his dream. He was unsure: so young, and not a shaman; perhaps his dreams would not be believed. His first helpers were a cousin and a neighbor. They started digging at night, afraid of what people might say, but after excavating a small hole on top of the hill, they gave up. Xun also told the local ejido commissioner about his dreams. The commissioner advised him to visit the municipal agent of Nabencauk, but Xun hesitated, afraid lest he be called a liar. Then he had a fourth dream in which his innate soul was in the earth, in the chapel of the Earth Lord, and was told to dig to one side of where he had started. Now more confident, he approached more people. He won the support of two shamans, one of whom suggested they consult a talking saint, and they visited a saint in Yaleb Taiv, a hamlet bordering Nabencauk. San Miguelito said, "yes, the bell is there," which was enough to launch official digging. The group made a pilgrimage to the sacred mountains and churches in the Ceremonial Center, offering candles and prayers and asking permission of the ancestral gods and saints to dig for the bell. Returning to Nabencauk, they reported to the municipal agent, had a ritual meal in the house of the commissioner, and set out for BAYOCOB. On top of the hill a green cross was erected and decorated, candles were lighted, and long prayers were said by the shamans to sanctify the tools. Digging began shortly after 2 A.M. The men were greatly excited when some rocks seemed to be giving off light, which was taken as a sign that they were digging in the right place. Ultimately over eighty Zinacantecos were engaged in digging into the solid limestone. As opposed to a secular project, such as digging rocks to build a road, this was a kind of "ritual operation," evidenced by the facts that the work never stopped, continuing day and night, and that women were prohibited from approaching the site. The hole was dug some 8 meters into the hill, during which time the shamans consulted the ancestral gods, talking saints, and even a spiritualist in Tuxtla Gutiérrez to divine more information about the bell's location. Among the messages received was one that the two saints holding onto the bell would not relinquish it. Meanwhile, Nabencauk was in a political uproar, with one faction believing the dream and another expressing total disbelief. The bell was never discovered, and the digging stopped (Rush 1969).

Three crucial aspects of this experience are relevant. First, the power of the dream to deflect so many Zinacanteco men from their maize-growing activities. The event occurred at the peak of the most intensive work period of the growing season—the first hoeing of the weeds. Yet some eighty men found the story sufficiently provocative to abandon, if temporarily, all agricultural responsibilities. Second, it was clear that memories were being evoked of a mythological event in which the Zinacanteco elders dug for a bell behind the cross shrine on the peak of MUXUL VIZ. After digging for days, they finally uncovered the top of the bell. Two versions of what ensued exist: in one, the foolish elders went home to eat and rest, and returned to find the bell gone; in the other, a Catholic priest had intercourse with a young Zinacanteco woman at the edge of the diggings, and the bell disappeared.* This myth explains why the Nabencauk diggers were adamant about keeping women away from their operations and why their work was continuous day and night. Finally, it seems clear that the power and credibility of the dream were related to the conviction that Zinacantecos are socially, economically, and culturally subordinate to ladinos in a bicultural world. Because the ladinos control the source supply of TAK'IN ("money" or "metal"), anything the Zinacantecos can do to increase their supply of TAK'IN—like finding another bell inside a mountain—will improve their position in the world.

*Today there is an immense hole on top of MUXUL VIZ and it is not known whether people actually dug there or whether it is a natural hole in the limestone.

From the start of our field research in Zinacantan in 1957 we realized that we were working with a classic example of a closed, corporate community. Outsiders of any kind were treated with deep suspicion, and it was only little by little over many years that we were able to make friends and establish rapport with Zinacanteco families. As our Tzotzil improved, and as Project members returned year after year, the Zinacantecos came to realize that we were not interested in taking away their lands, owning houses or stores in the municipio, or policing their activities (such as the illegal manufacture of POX) for the Mexican authorities. On the contrary, we offered a modest amount of employment to individuals as informants, provided rides in Project vehicles, and showed special hospitality and attention when they visited our San Cristóbal headquarters. We began to be invited to cargo and shamanistic rituals and soon were able to administer questionnaires, enter the churches and observe the saints, and even, after some time, take photographs and movies with their permission. Relations continued to be somewhat unsettled since any informant who worked for us was immediately subjected to gossip, and, indeed, suspected of witchcraft if he flaunted his newly earned wealth. On the whole, however, our work progressed very well—until December 29, 1969, when thieves broke into the Church of San Lorenzo in the middle of the night and stole the gold chalice from the altar and the ancient silver cross, called KRUS ʔAVANHEL (literally, "cross of the Evangelist," or "gospel cross"). The reaction was instantaneous. Word spread throughout the municipio that the sacred objects had been stolen by the anthropologists, that the sole purpose of our research over the years was to "steal the saints." Only with the astute work of two of our field workers—Francesco Pellizzi and John B. Haviland—and the active support of our informants, as well as the assistance of Mexican government authorities and the Catholic Bishop, were we able to ride out the tempest perpetrated by what probably was an organized ring of thieves of colonial art objects. (Thefts occurred the same week from churches in San Felipe, San Cristóbal, and Aguacatenango.) What made the reaction so violent was not only the loss of the objects per se but the fact that the Zinacantecos now faced a diminished supply and capacity for procuring TAK'IN: it was believed that the KRUS ʔAVANHEL had, in the mythological past, the power actually to "make money" and retained a related, if somewhat diminished, power to "attract money" to Zinacantan.

Zinacantecos have always been reluctant to allow photographs to be taken of themselves or of sacred objects; they believe a photograph, by creating an image, takes away a piece of the subject's innate soul. Since the theft of the cross and chalice, there has been a taboo on photographing sacred objects—whether saints' images or the T'EN-T'EN drum. There also is increasing resistance to the entrance of *any* outsider to the churches, even without cameras. As more and more people visit Zinacantan—in particular, tourists with cameras—it is possible that all the churches may become like southwestern Pueblo kivas: ceremonial chambers completely and forever closed to outsiders. Whether or not this nativistic trend will reach the point where the Catholic priest himself is excluded, except to perform weddings and baptisms, remains to be seen.

Contemporary Zinacantan displays a complex set of adjustments to the modern world: a measured acceptance of material goods for its households, a welcoming of improved modes of transport, an eagerness to be entertained by transistor radios; and, at the same time, a tightening of the internal lines and the external boundaries around its sacred ritual system—its conceptions, symbols, and ceremonies that carry on the essence of its traditional life. Whether this is a temporary episode or a long-term cycle in the cultural history of Zinacantan I will not be foolhardy enough to predict.

13

Symbols in Zinacanteco Culture

AT THE BEGINNING of this book I suggested that a culture may be conceptualized as a symbolic code programming systems of categorization, communication, and exchange. Though part of the orderly physical and biological processes of the universe, the human mind is not a videotape recording the complex stimuli in the natural and social world in which man lives. Rather, men have evolved ways of reducing complexity, of eliminating ambiguity, of certifying comprehensible order by categorizing and classifying into manageable form the information received. Through language and culturally conditioned processes of symbolic thought men learn, in the social world, to respond to categories of people—whether of age, sex, kinship, or occupation—and, in the natural world, to deal with classes of animals, plants, stars, units of time, and blocks of space. Man can communicate through verbal and nonverbal messages (gestures, clothing styles, types of food) which are segmented and patterned by the cultural code. Men in organized societies also exchange messages, goods and services, and energy with the natural environment. Such exchanges are programmed by the cultural code which provides continuous information on how, what, and why exchanges occur.

Although analysis of ritual symbols, the focus of this book, provides keys to the cultural code, viable alternative approaches to the understanding of the essence of Zinacanteco culture have been followed by many of my colleagues.*

*It is, for example, productive to focus on the economic system (Frank Cancian 1965, 1972); ecological adaptations (G. Collier 1975); law-ways (J. Collier 1973; Greenhouse 1971); language (L. Colby 1964; Laughlin 1975); family structure (Francesca Cancian 1964, 1965); myths (Laughlin 1963; Blaffer 1972; Wasserstrom 1970); patterns of shamanism (Fabrega and Silver 1973); cargo rituals (Early 1965); ceremonial humor (Bricker 1973); gossip (Haviland 1971); witchcraft (Pellizzi n.d.); and relations with the ladino world (B. Colby 1966).

But symbols are crucial in the Zinacanteco case, not only because the performance of ritual constitutes a focal concern of the society but also because it serves to store and transmit elements of the Zinacanteco prescriptions for a coherent and orderly society and to provide measured ways for the society to change over time.

Some Symbolic Themes

Recurring Zinacanteco ritual episodes, as exemplified by the drinking, eating, processional, and offering rituals, are "cells" that reveal the inner consistency of the action of the basic units—symbols which function like "molecules." A matrix of binary discriminations provides the principles by which the "molecular" symbols are organized into "cellular" episodes. As these episodes are compared, and viewed in the context of the longer ceremonial dramas, certain pervasive symbolic themes of cardinal importance can be isolated. Intricately involved in the flow of daily Zinacanteco life, they underline essential and distinctive qualities of the culture. The themes are focused around three actions, which I call "talking," "seeing," and "embracing," and two conditions or states, "heat" and "time." The actions are performed by Zinacantecos to affect or express two basic conditions: to provide for and symbolize the proper amount of "heat," and to place and symbolize the Zinacanteco and his activities within the flow of "time" in the universe.

Talking

Talking is a crucial way to affect directly one's life experience vis-à-vis other men and the gods. The Zinacantecos are a highly verbal people; the fact that many different terms describe and differentiate hierarchically the types of talking, ranging from LEKIL K'OP (ritual speech, a term which implies both what is "good" and "traditional") to ZAʔAL K'OP (deceitful speech), testifies to the importance of speech. A skilled talker is a highly valued member of the community, with the ability to convince a court, petition for a bride, pray to the gods. The very phrase BAZ'I K'OP, by which the Zinacantecos refer to their own language, means "the true language." The ability to speak BAZ'I K'OP well is a symbol of full humanity. (Our field workers who are still learning to speak Tzotzil are treated like babies who are not yet fully human.)

Types of supplicatory speech are similar. There is a startling structural resemblance between the petitions to the civil officials at the cabildo—whether to settle a courtship dispute, ask that a Zinacanteco be released from jail, or request that the MAYOLETIK be sent to arrest the thieves who stole some chickens—and the urgent prayers to the ancestral gods at the mountain shrines or the saints in the churches. This point is made very explicit when Zinacantecos describe the all-important shrine on top of KALVARYO as a supernatural cabildo, where the ancestral gods meet and discuss the affairs of their descendants just as the latter meet and discuss at the cabildo. It is made explicit in labeling the ritual advisers TOTIL MEʔILETIK. These Zinacantecos are not only repositories of complex ritual knowledge but also eloquent talkers and prayers; they can receive processions of ritualists at the doorways of houses in the same manner that the supernatural TOTIL MEʔILETIK, who possess vast knowledge, can respond eloquently when petitioned at their mountain homes.

K'OP means "dispute" as well as "word" and "language": -MELZAN K'OP means "to conduct a hearing"; -LAHES K'OP, to "beg pardon." A hearing is conducted by a HMELZANEH K'OP, a "mediator," whether he is the Presidente or other official at the cabildo or an elder in one of the hamlets (J. Collier 1973: 94). A plaintiff often brings along a kinsman or compadre known to be a good talker to help. Correspondingly, the Presidente must be an eloquent talker who can mediate and settle disputes. When Zinacantecos take disputes to ladino courts and other agencies in San Cristóbal, they take along a good talker to serve as a lawyer (HK'OPOHEL) to plead the case. Similarly, a young man will engage petitioners who are good talkers to plead his case with a prospective fiancée's father. (Unless her father is also a good talker, he may end up accepting an unfortunate proposition.) In pilgrimages to visit the mountain shrines and the saints in their churches, the Zinacantecos engage a shaman, often described as being "like a lawyer," who must be eloquent in the ritual prayers in order to present convincingly their cases before the gods.

A very high premium is placed on those with the ability to say the correct things at the right time. For without proper talking, communication among men, and between men and the gods, falters, and the whole social system creaks as it lacks effective intermediaries to mediate between the oppositions. This need for an intermediary further defines the separation of the gods from men, of authorities from ordinary people, incapable of pleading for themselves without the specialized assistance of a shaman or a good talker.

Seeing

Seeing is more than a metaphor for vision; it *is* knowing, insight in general. The shaman can look directly into the mountains. These powers are expressed by the very important word stem in Tzotzil, -IL, "to see"; HʔILOL means "seer." In the mythological past, all Zinacantecos could "see" into the mountains where the ancestral gods live; now only the shamans, via dreams, possess this special ability. The word BA means "face" when applied to gods or people; it means "top" when referring to mountains. When shamans are praying on top of the sacred mountains they are face-to-face with the gods.

The longest, most complicated ritual of affliction is called MUK'TA ʔILEL, the Great Seeing, which describes the lengthy circuit made as the patient visits the sacred mountains and "sees" the gods with the shaman as an intermediary. The ceremonial visits of cargoholders to each other's houses during the major fiestas are referred to as ʔIL-NA, implying that they are communicating through the greetings and prayers of ritual advisers, their TOTIL MEʔILETIK. NA means "house"; calling this ceremonial circuit ʔIL-NA draws an analogy between it and the ritual circuit which visits the houses of the supernatural TOTIL MEʔILETIK to seek advice and aid. To "see" the houses of other cargoholders or the gods means to communicate with them, in the ritual context.

ʔIL ʔOʔON (literally to "see one's heart") means to know a person intimately, and suggests that the heart is the seat of the C'ULEL. The same concept appears in the Zinacanteco view of socialization of the young. The long process of education is conceived as learning to see, that is, to learn about, understand, and interpret the world in which an adult Zinacanteco functions as a responsible member of his society (B. Colby 1967).

A shaman places multicolored candles in a row in front of a shrine to provide a shield so an evil witch cannot see into the ceremony being performed. In times of famine or epidemics shamans perform elaborate ceremonies at the cross shrines at the borders of the Ceremonial Center to "cut off the vision" of the evil agents causing the problem.

Embracing

The symbolic action of embracing pervades a vast range of ritual. The word stem -PET means "to embrace" or "to carry"; HPETOM means "embracer" or "carrier." One of the most important duties of the Zinacanteco father and mother, addressed as TOT and ME? (and referred to as TOTIL and ME?IL), is to embrace a child and care for it well so that it does not lose its C'ULEL. At baptism a child acquires a godfather and godmother, C'ULTOT and C'ULME? ("divine father" and "divine mother"), whose principal duty is to embrace their godchild during this important ceremony. At the wedding the ritual specialist called HPETOM introduces the bride into her new home. It is his duty to embrace or carry the souls of the bride and groom, to create a new and lasting relationship in which the bride will come to like and accept her new home.

During curing ceremonies a patient who has lost parts of his soul is embraced by the shaman, who helps him recover the misssing parts of his C'ULEL. The ancestral gods inside Senior Great Mountain take good care of the animal companions of the Zinacantecos; their assistants feed and water them and embrace them. But when a Zinacanteco becomes unruly, the gods stop embracing his animal companion, who, released from the supernatural corral, wanders lost in the woods. The animal companion is not embraced again until the patient is placed in the corral-bed during the Great Seeing ceremony.

In the socialization process within the family, in the rites of baptism, marriage, and affliction, and in the supernatural corral inside the mountain, fathers and mothers embrace their children in an amazingly consistent network of symbols replicated from one domain to another. But this symbolic action has deeper meanings. Frames are being drawn around the souls of people, around key relationships in society, around houses and fields, and around Zinacantan Center. They define boundaries within which order is continually generated and they shut out powerful symbols of disorder—the uncontrolled wild animals wandering loose in the woods, the unpredictable and terrifying demons who inhabit the wilderness, the baffling outsiders who impinge upon the Zinacanteco world. The cross shrines of Zinacantan are important symbols of this embracing action, for they enclose the arena of Culture and separate it from the domain of Nature, at the same time providing the means of communication across the boundaries between Culture and Nature, men and gods. The cross shrines stand between and belong to both domains; they face inward toward the center of the cultural domain, but are simultaneously the doorways to the homes of the gods, whose own culture is Nature itself. Nature is owned by the gods as a man might own a chicken or house. The order of the gods is seen as a threat to the order of man. To preserve these realms, they must be kept separate, although communication between them is equally necessary. The Zinacantecos recognize that what has been transformed into their own cultural domain is taken directly from Nature, and offerings are made in recompense for the loss to Nature. The belief in the animal companion renders a man inseparable from the natural world. It is as if his life were being lived in an exactly parallel fashion by an animal in the wild. The C'ULEL is the intermediate (and immortal) spirit uniting a mortal man with his equally mortal animal companion.

As Zinacanteco society is guarded within its "frame," so the universe is embraced by the paths traced by the Sun and the Moon, HC'UL TOTIK and HC'UL ME?TIK. As parents of the universe, they embrace their creation through ceaseless movements around it.

Heat

The symbolic state of "hotness," as opposed to "coldness," is one of the most seminal Zinacanteco concepts of opposition.* Although ultimately

*The Zinacanteco concepts of "hot" and "cold" clearly partake of widespread, if not universal,

this heat is derived from, or partakes of the Sun, it is measured not by degrees, but by conventional modes of Zinacanteco thought. Heat is a general quality of existence. It provides a language for describing the differences in power in the universe, whether this be the political power of an Indian leader, the ritual power of an expert shaman or competent cargoholder, the supernatural strength of the C'ULEL of a respected older man (and his associated animal), the curing power of a hot ritual plant, or the highly intoxicating potential of hot (strong) cane liquor.

Heat is a dynamic state, for people and things become hotter as power and age increase. An infant is born cold; its heat gradually increases as it grows up and its C'ULEL becomes stronger. Each year adds heat; each stage in the cycle (marriage, acquiring more political influence) adds strength; the hotness reaches a peak just before death, when the heat is again reduced to nothing. In the annual cycle of a cargoholder's ritual duties, the man becomes hotter and hotter, reaching maximum heat in the change of office ceremony at the end of his year in cargo. A young shaman, just after his debut, has a certain amount of heat, which increases with experience. The concept is governed, however, by a principle of balance, of an intermediate state of being which does not threaten life with either an excess or an insufficiency of heat. The process of gaining heat through ageing, serving cargos, or becoming a shaman, is limited by certain boundaries beyond which a Zinacanteco cannot pass without risking reprisal.

The symbolic importance of candles, in addition to their identification as tortillas and meat for the gods, comes into play here. As Pope points out, the candle has three properties: heat, light (symbolizing "sight"), and the faculty of transmuting from a solid into a gas—of "disappearing" or metaphorically crossing the threshold between the material and the spiritual worlds. "Thus, the candle flame symbolically combines the two forms of power Zinacantecos most respect—'heat' (health, strength, authority), and 'sight' (ability to communicate with the gods); it embodies their interrelation and demonstrates their possibility of linking man with the divine" (1969: 61).

As well as being "cigarettes" for the gods, another symbolic aspect to censing comes into play. Burning copal incense is used to heat newly born babies, patients suffering from soul-loss, candles before they are lighted, and so on. Incense, too, can change from a solid to a gas. Heat lends life force to the baby, to the sufferer from soul-loss, and to the candle.

Time

A preoccupation with time is often described as basic to Maya life, and the Zinacantecos are no exception. Whereas a Navaho asks, when meeting a person, "where are you going?" and "where have you come from?" a Zinacanteco asks, "when did you arrive in Chiapas?" and "when are you returning to your country?" A wristwatch is almost always the first acquisition from the industrial world. Zinacantecos insist on knowing (much more than their anthropological observers) what plans are scheduled for when. "When will the new student come to my house? When will he return to San Cristóbal?" Shamans are known to have appointments to perform ceremonies as far in advance as two weeks; cargo-

---

Mexican and Spanish-American concepts which most scholars believe are derived from Greek humoral pathology which was elaborated by the Arab world, brought to Spain as scientific medicine during the period of Moslem domination, and transmitted to America at the time of the Conquest (Foster 1953: 202-204; 1960; Currier 1966: 251-263). There are, however, some rather distinctive elements in the concepts developed by the Highland Chiapas Maya, as I have tried to show in this volume, and some of these elements, such as the relation of "heat" in persons to the Sun god, suggest that part of the conceptual system may have been pre-hispanic.

holders are on the waiting lists up to twenty-two years. Precise knowledge of the day of the week or month or of what fiesta is currently going on is emphasized.

I interpret this preoccupation as a manifestation of the general Zinacanteco emphasis upon the flow of time in the universe. Spatial concepts and dimensions are not ignored, but they are geared to temporal concepts and dimensions. This connection is built into the language: LOK'EB K'AK'AL and MALEB K'AK'AL mean both the time when and the place where the sun rises and sets. BANKILAL and ʔIZ'INAL mean not only older brother and younger brother, or even merely senior and junior, but also express (as the concepts are applied to such diverse phenomena as brothers, crosses, drums, and mountains) the time elapsed since a liminal threshold was crossed: the birth of a child, the erection of a cross, the construction of a drum, the establishment in the mythology of an ancestral god inside a mountain.

Zinacanteco society is a highly structured and articulated system whose dynamics depend on the functions of these symbolic clusters. If a Zinacanteco talks well, sees clearly, embraces others, has sufficient heat, then he is BANKILAL, and has achieved a valued status within his society. Those who are young, talk less well, see less clearly, are embraced, have less heat, are ʔIZ'INAL.

The Zinacantecos, like most other Maya groups, retain a strong, though imprecise, sense of the past. Most of the symbolic themes in the Zinacanteco world view contribute to a strong defensive posture with regard to the outside world and its threats to Zinacanteco society. The Zinacantecos know that their mythological times antedate the coming of the Spaniards. Their myths are suffused with a sense of a time when things were better: when all the land belonged to the Indians, the gods were more benevolent, there was less witchcraft and fewer shamans, and all Zinacantecos had the power to "see" into the mountains. But they are a shrewd people and have not retreated from the encroachment of ladino civilization. What is most valued and most vital to the culture has been reenforced, for the ritual life is, if anything, more intensified and elaborated than ever before. The Zinacantecos have been quick to take advantage of material objects and of economic opportunities which have benefited their lives without fundamentally distorting more crucial customs. Ladino elements have been encapsulated and incorporated, but that has not made full Mexican citizens nor "good Catholics" out of most Zinacantecos. They remain Indians and their value of what is traditional remains steadfast.

The culture of today's Zinacantecos is an intricate mixture of characteristics, many engendered by a fusion of elements. Although their society may appear vital and dynamic, threats from the outside world are ever stronger and the defensive measures they must take are ever more necessary to prevent disorder in their society and universe.

As the Zinacantecos offer "tortillas to the gods" at their mountain shrines, they pray that the centuries-old civilized Zinacanteco order will be regenerated as certainly as their ancestral gods receive the "tortillas" and reciprocate by "embracing" their animal companions and as certainly as the Sun travels his flowery path each day from sunrise to sunset.

Appendix I

Tzotzil Phonemes

THE FOLLOWING NOTES on Zinacanteco phonemes are drawn from Lore M. Colby (1964) and Robert M. Laughlin (1975). The letters used in this book for each Tzotzil phoneme are followed in parentheses by the equivalent phonemic symbols that are used in other publications on the Tzotzil cultures of Highland Chiapas.

a	low, central, open, occasionally closed vowel
e, o	mid, front, and back, opened, fluctuating between rounded and unrounded
i, u	high, front, and back, closed, unsounded
b	voiced bilabial stop; the phoneme "b" presents particular problems discussed by Weathers (1947)
c	(ch, č) voiceless, aspirated alveo-palatal affricate
c'	(ch', č') glottalized "c"
h	voiceless glottal spirant
k	voiceless aspirated stop more strongly aspirated in final position
ʔ	glottal stop
k'	glottalized "k"
l	voiced alveolar lateral with voiceless offglide in final position
m	voiced bilabial nasal
n	voiced alveolar nasal
p	voiceless, aspirated, bilabial stop, more strongly aspirated in final position
p'	glottalized "p"
r	voiced alveolar flap
s	voiceless alveolar spirant
x	(sh, š) voiceless alveopalatal spirant
t	voiceless, aspirated alveolar stop, more strongly aspirated in final position
t'	glottalized "t"
z	(ts, ¢) voiceless, aspirated alveolar affricate
z'	(ts', ¢') glottalized "z"
v	voiced labiodental spirant freely variable to bilabial w, with a voiceless offglide in final position
y	voiced alveopalatal spirant with voiceless offglide in final position

Appendix II

Harvard Chiapas Project Field Workers

1969-1975

(For a list of the field workers during the years 1957-1968 see Vogt 1969: 617-618).

Suzanne Abel
Ira Abrams
Judith L. Aissen
Samuel M. Anderson
Thor R. Anderson
Emily S. Apter
Jane B. Baird
Victoria Barber
Lauren Bardrick
Katherine Brazelton
T. Berry Brazelton
Victoria R. Bricker
John N. Burstein
Francesca M. Cancian
Frank A. Cancian
Kenneth L. Carson
Carla P. Childs
Jason W. Clay
George A. Collier
Jane F. Collier
Thomas Crump
Elizabeth M. Dodd
Susan E. Epstein
Horacio A. Fabrega, Jr.
Denise Z. Field
Rowena I. Frazer
William S. Freeman
Eliot M. Gelwan
Richard A. Gonzalez
Gary H. Gossen
Patricia M. Greenfield
Carol J. Greenhouse
Peter J. Guarnaccia
John B. Haviland
Leslie McC. Haviland
Peter L. Haviland
Jeffrey C. Howry
Kelly T. Jensen
Felisa M. Kazen
Sara J. Lacy
Miriam W. Laughlin
Robert M. Laughlin
Priscilla Rachun Linn
Patrice E. Lynch
Donald E. McVicker
Gilbert V. Marin
Benjamin S. Orlove
Thomas L. Paradise
Francesco Pellizzi
Philippa Pellizzi
Roger Reed
Marcy S. Richmond
Rachel Z. Ritvo
John S. Robey
Diane L. Rus
Jan Rus, III
Timothy N. Rush
Paul L. Saffo, III
Mary E. Scott
Daniel B. Silver
Suzanne E. Siskel
Joshua Smith
Lars C. F. Smith
Ricardo D. Sutton
Marta Turok
Catherine C. H. Vogt
Charles A. Vogt
Alaka Wali
Robert F. Wasserstrom
Elisabeth A. Werby
Lisa Wiesner
George Carter Wilson
Nancy A. Zweng

Glossary

Bibliography

Index

Glossary

ʔABTEL work

ʔABTEL TA HTEK-LUM "work in the ceremonial center," cargo service

ʔAC' HABIL New Year ceremony

ʔAC'EL POM "dripping incense" bush

ʔAHAN TOH "corn ear pine," yellow pine, *Pinus oaxacana* Mirov.

ʔAHA-TEʔES wild myrtle, *Gaultheria odorata* Willd.

ʔAK'OB KANTELA place of the candles at foot of cross shrine altar

ʔAK'OB K'EXOLIL place of the substitute, where chicken is left at cross shrine

ʔAK'OL above, over, upper

ʔAK'OL ʔOSIL the land above, Highlands

ʔAK'UBAL night

ʔALTAL (house) altar

ʔAMARA ʔUALETIK inner bags containing saints' necklaces

ʔANHELETIK "angels" (Spanish), also Earth Lord manifestations

BALAMIL earth, world, land

BAL-TEʔ flower renewal ceremony

BANKILAL senior, older

BANKILAL MUK'TA VIZ Senior Large (Great) Mountain

BAYOCOB hill in Nabencauk

BAZ'I right, true, genuine

BAZ'I ʔEC' "true bromeliad," *Tillandsia guatemalensis* L.B. Smith

BAZ'I K'OB the right hand

BAZ'I K'OP Tzotzil, the "true word"

BAZ'I POM "true incense," copal tree

BAZ'I TEʔ "true tree," oak, *Quercus crassifolia*

BAZ'I TOH "genuine pine"

BEK'TAL POM "flesh incense," from copal tree

BE TAIV "road of frost," Milky Way in dry season

BE VOʔ "road of water," Milky Way in wet season

BIK'IT VOʔ Little Waterhole

BIX shaman's bamboo staff of office

BOLOMETIK jaguars, any wild felines

BOLOM TEʔ Jaguar Tree, at fiesta of San Sebastián

BOLOM TON Jaguar Rock, at fiesta of San Sebastián

CAK XONOBIL high-backed sandals

CAMEL sickness, death

C'EN limestone sink, cave, waterhole

C'ENTIKAL VOʔ "water by a cliff," waterhole

C'IB mountain palm

CIKIN-IB live oak, *Quercus acatenangensis*, Trel.

CIKIN NA corner of a house

CILIL ceremonial poncho

C'IX TEʔ black cherry, *Prunus capuli* Cav.

C'IXAL VOʔ hawthorn waterhole

CKUX VAKAX revival of the bull, in drama of ritual aggression

COB (TIK) field(s)

CON animal

CUK-NICIM first day of a fiesta

CUʔIL POK'ETIK "breast bags" of the saints

C'ULEL innate soul

C'ULELAL NICIM "ghost flower," Mexican savory, *Satureja Mexicana* (Benth.) Brig.

C'UL KANTELA "holy candle," ceremony for completion of a new house

C'UL KRUS VIZ Holy Cross Mountain

C'UL MEʔ godmother

C'UL MOLETIK Holy Elders, ancestral elders

C'UL TOT godfather

C'UM cushaw, *Cucurbita moschata* Duch.

C'UPAK' soaproot

C'UT C'EN "stomach cave," shrine to Earth Lord

C'UT TEʔ "stomach tree," Spanish cedar, *Cedrela odorata* L.

C'UT TON "stomach rock," sacred rock

CUVAH madness

HABIL the year

HAX HK'OBTIK' "let's wash our hands," verbal signal in ritual meal

HC'OMILETIK ritual assistants

HC'UL MEʔTIK Our Holy Mother, the Moon, Virgin Mary

HC'UL TOTIK Our Holy Father, the Sun, God

HELOLILETIK substitutes, sacrificial chickens

HIC'IL ʔANAL TOH "thin foliage pine," yellow pine, *Pinus pseudostrobus* Lindl.

HʔIK'ALETIK blackmen (demons)

HʔILOL seer, shaman

HKAXLAN Castilians, anything ladino or foreign

HK'OPOHEL Zinacanteco "lawyer"

HK'OPOHEL RIOX "talking saints"

HKUCOMETIK assistants of the gods

HKUC'-KANTELA candle carrier, ritual role

HMANVANEH Christ (ritual speech), the buyer of souls

HMESETIK sweepers (ritual roles)

HOH "raven" ear of corn (split at top)

HOHOC' corn husk

HOL CUK house ritual (binding the head of the roof)

HPETOM embracer (ritual specialist)

HPINTOLETIK bull painters in drama of ritual aggression

HP'IS VOˀ drink pourer

HPWERSA force (Spanish *fuerza*), vital essence of a person

HTAK'AVEL ritual adviser, TOTIL MEˀIL

HTAM-HˀILOL escort of the shaman, in curing ceremonies

HTEK-LUM Zinacantan Center

HTOTIK K'AK'AL Our Father Heat, the Sun

HTOY-K'INETIK "lifters of the fiesta," ritual impersonators in fiesta of San Sebastián

HˀUK'UMAHELETIK laundresses (ritual assistants in curing ceremonies)

HXINULAN female HKAXLAN (ritual impersonator)

HZOB TAK'IN money collector, for fiestas

ˀIC'O "receive it," drinking response of offerer to receiver

ˀIK' black, also black-coated wax candle

ˀIK'OB BAIL ZU "summoner" gourds

ˀIL to see, observe

ˀIL ˀOˀON to "see one's heart"

ˀISAK'TIK sacred mountain

ˀISBON dogwood

ˀIZ'INAL junior, younger

KAˀBENAL Lacandon (ritual impersonator)

K'AK'AL day, heat

KALVARYO cross shrine, meetingplace of the gods

KAMARO hand-held cannon for fireworks

K'ANALETIK "The Yellow Ones," stars

K'ATIN-BAK placed warmed by bones, Hell

K'AT'IX hawthorn apples

K'EL-KANTELA candle inspection, by shaman

K'EXEL New Year's Day, change of office

K'EXOLIL (ETIK) substitute(s)

KIC'BAN "I receive," drinking response

KINH sun, day, time (general Maya)

K'IN fiesta

K'IN KRUS lineage and waterhole rituals

K'INUBAL winter storm from north

K'ISIN hot

K'OK' fire

KOKOˀON Mexican tea, an herb, *Chenopodium ambrosioides*

K'OLTIXYO Testing target, "heart" of San Sebastián

K'ON yellow-coated wax candle

K'OP talk, the word, language, dispute

KORAL corral bed

KORAL BURO "burro corral" waterhole

K'OS ritual plant, *Synardisia venosa* (Mast.) Lundell

K'OTEBAL the place of arrival (after death)

KRINSUPALETIK *principales*, officials

KRUS ˀAVANHEL sacred "evangel" cross

KRUS ˀEC' "cross bromeliad," see BAZ'I ˀEC'

KRUS TA HOL VIZ cross at the head of a mountain

KRUS TA TIˀ ˀEKLIXYA cross at the edge of the churchyard

KRUS TA TIˀ NA cross at the entrance to a house

KRUS TA TIˀ VOˀ cross at the edge of a waterhole

KRUS TA YOK VIZ cross at the foot of a mountain

K'UK' TOH white pine, *Pinus ayacahuite*

KUKULKAN Maya version of Aztec deity Quetzalcoatl

K'UK'UL CONETIK "plumed serpents," ritual impersonators at fiesta of San Sebastián

KUMPARE/KUMALE *compadre* and *comadre*, godparents

LA? CABOT "come," response of senior person to younger who approaches and bows

LA? HSUK'KETIK "come, let's rinse our mouths," verbal signal in ritual meal

LA? ME "come here," ritual calling of lost soul in curing ceremony

LA? YALANIK ME ?UN "come, fall to," verbal signal in ritual meal

LAC CIKIN sacred place

LANSA VIZ sacred mountain

LECOPAT crèche

LEKIL K'OP good speech

LOK'EB K'AK'AL rising sun

LOK'ESEH-VOB circuit made by Alféreces when they pick up their musicians

LOK'ESEL TA BALAMIL soul-calling ritual

MAHBENAL blows from the ancestral gods

MAHOBIL striker, used by shamans in curing ceremonies

MAK KANTELA shield of the candles (3 pine tips)

MAKOB CAMEL ceremony to prevent epidemics

MALEB K'AK'AL setting sun

MAMAL "grandfather," ritual role

MANTREX tablecloth (multiple usage pink-and-white stripped cloth)

MANTREX KAHVALTIK bag containing altar cloths and large tablecloth

MARTIR KAPITAN San Sebastián

MAYOL (ETIK) helper, assistant, messenger, errand boy, also an ear of corn which helps guard the fields

ME? mother

ME?CUN "grandmother," ritual role

ME? ZEB "mother of the girl," ritual parent surrogate

MEXA table

MIXATIK *posadas* (masses)

MIXIK' BALAMIL navel of the earth

MOLETIK elders

MORAL tooled leather shoulder bag

MUK'TA ?ILEL Great Seeing ceremony

MUK'TA K'ANAL Venus, "Large Star"

MUK'TA NICIM "Great Flower," alternate name for MUK'TA ?ILEL

MUK'TA P'IS large glass

MUK'TA TE? Great Tree

MUXUL VIZ sacred mountain

NA house, domestic group

NAETIK the houses (Culture)

NA HOH sacred mountain

NAKLEB ?OK' sacred mountain

NEKEB VIZ sacred mountain

NICIM flower, general term for ritual plants

NINAB CILO? sacred waterhole, "salty spring"

NIO? sacred mountain and waterhole

NINYO Christ Child

NOK alder tree

?OCEL TA NA house-entering ceremony

?O?LOL HABIL middle of the year ceremony

?OLON below, beneath

?OLON BALAMIL lower world

?OLON ?OSIL the land below, Lowlands

ˀORO gold (Spanish), a candle coated with alternating bands of red, yellow, and green

ˀOX YOKET "3 hearthstones," alternate name for Senior Great Mountain

PAT ˀOK "turtleback," ceremonial drums

PAT TOH "behind the pine," sacred water-hole

-PET to embrace (verb stem)

PIK C'IC' "touch blood," pulsing diagnosis

P'IS shot glass used in drinking ceremony; also, verb, to measure or serve (liquor, chicken)

POK' neckerchief

POK'EB sacred cave below Pasteˀ

POM incense

POP reed mat

POPOL TON "rock in the form of a reed mat," sacred waterhole

POSLOM soul of evil person in form of fire or shooting star; also, leg sickness, shooting star

POX sugar cane liquor

POXIL POX-like, medicinal

PUKUHETIK demons

PUS sweathouse

REHIROLETIK *regidores*, cargoholders

SAK C'EN "white cave," sacred mountain

SAK HOLETIK "white heads," ritual roles

SAN KIXTOVAL sacred mountain (San Cristóbal)

SANTOETIK saints, all sacred objects

SAT ˀIXIM grains of maize divination

SCANUL the animal of a person (animal companion)

SCIKIN its ear or corner (e.g. of houses, mountains)

SCUˀ MEˀTIK nipple nightshade, *Solanum mammosum* L.

SC'UT its stomach or middle, the midpoint in a mountainside or wall of a house

SERA white wax candle (Spanish)

SHOL its head (mountaintop or housetop)

SISIL VIZ sacred mountain

SKANTELAIL COBTIK field ritual ("candles for the maize fields")

SK'INAL K'IN-like

SKRUSAL C'EN cross for cave or limestone sink

SKRUSAL HOL ˀANIMA cross at the head of a grave

SKRUSAL HOL ˀEKLIXYA churchtop cross

SKRUSAL HOL NA rooftop cross

SKRUSAL ˀIXIM maize cross

SLAHEB HABIL end of year ceremony

SLIMUXNAIL COBTIK field ritual ("alms for the maize fields")

SMAKOBIL SAT ritual to "shut off the power of seeing" of foreigners

SMEˀ "mother" maize cob

SMEˀ ˀUNEN placenta

SNA localized lineage

SNA ˀUNEN umbilical cord

SNIˀ TOH pine tips

SNIC POK' "flower of the kerchief" (red tassles)

SNUP KANTELA veneration of the candles

SNUP HPETOM companion or consort of the embracer in wedding

SPIXOL KAHVALTIK ceremonial bundle containing saint's hat and mirrors

STEK'EL TOH pine tree tops

STOT "father" maize cob

SVOK' SMAIL SAKRAMENTU squash preparation ritual during MIXATIK

TAK'IN money, metal, bell

TAMBEIK ME LI SBATEBE "please take the chicken to make the flavor of the tortillas better," verbal signal in ritual meal

TA X?U?UNIBE "he incorporates"

TE?EL POM wood incense, from copal tree

T'ENT'EN ceremonial drum

TE?TIK the forest (Nature)

TILIL "flickering," wild highland tree, ritual plant, *Rapanea juergensenii* Mez.

TOT father

TOTIK "sir," father (term of reference and address to older man)

TOTIL ME?ILETIK "fathers and mothers," ancestral gods; also, ritual advisers

TON Z'IKIN sacred waterhole

TULAN oak

?UAL (ETIK) month, also necklace(s) hung on saints' images

?UAL KAHVALTIK bag containing saints' necklaces

?UC'BEIK ME LI YA?LELE' "drink the broth, please" verbal signal in ritual meal

VAKAX bull

VAXAK-MEN four corner gods, sky bearers

VE?EL TA MEXA ritual meal

VENTEXIL necklaces or rosaries worn by elders

VINAHEL heaven, sky

VIXOBTAKIL ritual plant, *Peperomia galioides* HBK.

VIZ mountain

VO? water

VO?-C'OH VO? "5 waterholes," sacred waterhole

VO? TA PASTE? Paste? waterhole

VO? ?EC'EL "five drinks," verbal signal in ritual meal

VOHTON ?EC' red bromeliad flower, *Tillandsia ponderosa* L. B. Smith

VOM C'EN waterhole group in Paste?

XAKITAIL ceremonial robe

XAK TOH pine needles

XAN palm frond

XCOLET ?EC'EL a ritual procession

XEMANA week (Spanish)

XEVU tallow candle

XI?EL *espanto,* fright leading to soul loss

XLOK' ?UAL ritual counting of saints' necklaces

XOHOBETIK "sun's rays," names of culture heros

XOKON VINAHEL the sides of the sky, i.e. north and south

XUL VO? waterhole group in Paste?

YA?AHVIL sacred waterhole

YA?AL ?UC sacred waterhole

YA?AM TON sacred mountain

YAHVAL BALAMIL Earth Lord

YAHVAL RIOX talking saint owner

YIHIL ?ANAL TOH ritual plant, *pinus montezumae* Lamb.

YOK its foot (of a mountain or house foundation)

(YOK) NIO? sacred waterhole (foot of the spring)

YOLON ?AHTE? shrine under *matasano* tree in Paste?

YOX blue-green, also blue or green-coated candle

YULO? KAHVALTIK "visits to the gods," offerings at cross shrines

YUT BALAMIL within the earth

ZA?AL K'OP deceitful speech

ZAHAL NICIM red geranium

ZAHAL POK' red turbans worn by elders

ZAKO ME AVAZ' AMIK "please take your salt," verbal signal in ritual meal

Z'ET K'OB left hand

ZIS ʔUC "fart of the opposum," ritual plant (bush laurel), *Litsea glaucescens* HBK

ZOH red, red-coated wax candle

ZONTEʔ Spanish moss

ZONTEʔETIK Spanish-moss wearers, ritual roles in fiesta of San Sebastián

ZONTEʔ AL BALAMIL lichens

ZU gourd

Z'UN Maya month name

Bibliography

(For a complete list of the publications of the Harvard Chiapas Project see Evon Z. Vogt, editor, Bibliography of the Harvard Chiapas Project, Peabody Museum, Harvard University, 1975.)

Abel, Suzanne. 1969. "Patterns of Political Influence—Zinacantan and Chamula," unpublished MS., Harvard Chiapas Project.

Adams, Robert M. 1961. "Changing Patterns of Territorial Organization in the Central Highland of Chiapas, Mexico," *American Antiquity*, 26: 341-360.

Aguirre Beltrán, Gonzalo. 1963. *Medicina y magia*. Colección de Antropología Social, vol. 1. Mexico: Instituto Nacional Indigenista.

Anschuetz, Mary H. 1966. "To be Born in Zinacantan," unpublished MS., Harvard Chiapas Project.

Apter, Emily S. 1973. "Talking Saints in Zinacantan," unpublished MS., Harvard Chiapas Project.

Baird, Jane. 1971. "Bankilal and ˀIz'inal," unpublished MS., Harvard Chiapas Project.

Bardrick, Lauren. 1970. "Face to Face with the Gods: A Study of Ritual Order and Holiness in Zinacantan," unpublished MS., Harvard Chiapas Project.

Baroco, John V. 1970. "Notas Sobre el Uso de Nombres Calendáricos durante el Siglo XVI," in Norman A. McQuown and Julian Pitt-Rivers, eds., *Ensayos de Antropología en la Zona Central de Chiapas*. Mexico: Instituto Nacional Indigenista, pp. 135-148.

Becerra, Marcos E. 1930. *Nombres Geográficos Indígenas del Estado de Chiapas*. Tuxtla Gutiérrez: Imprenta del Gobierno.

Berlin, Brent, Dennis E. Breedlove, and Peter H. Raven. 1974. *Principles of Tzeltal Plant Classification: An Introduction to the Botanical Ethnography of a Mayan Speaking People of Highland Chiapas*. New York: Academic Press.

Blaffer, Sarah C. 1972. *The Black-man of Zinacantan: A Central American Legend.* Austin: University of Texas Press.

Borhegyi, Stephan F. 1965. "Archaeological Synthesis of the Guatemalan Highlands," in Gordon R. Willey, ed., *Archaeology of Southern Mesoamerica;* vol. 2 of *Handbook of Middle American Indians,* ed. by Robert Wauchope. Austin: University of Texas Press, pp. 3-58.

Bricker, Victoria Reifler. 1966. "El Hombre, la Carga y el Camino: Antiguos Conceptos Mayas Sobre Tiempo y Espacio, y el Sistema Zinacanteco de Cargos," in Vogt, *Los Zinacantecos: Un Pueblo Tzotzil de Los Altos de Chiapas,* pp. 355-370.

______ 1968. "The Meaning of Laughter in Zinacantan: An Analysis of the Humor of a Highland Maya Community," unpublished diss., Harvard University.

______ 1972. "The Ethnographic Context of Some Traditional Mayan Speech Genres," paper prepared for the Conference on the Ethnography of Communication, Austin, Texas, April 1972.

______ 1973. *Ritual Humor in Highland Chiapas.* Austin: University of Texas Press.

Bunzel, Ruth. 1952. *Chichicastenango: A Guatemalan Village.* Seattle: University of Washington Press.

Calnek, Edward E. 1962. "Highland Chiapas Before the Spanish Conquest," unpublished diss., University of Chicago.

Cámara Barbachano, Fernando. 1943. "Aspectos de una Cultura Mayance en Chiapas," in Sol Tax, ed., *Notas Sobre Zinacantan, Chiapas.* Microfilm collection of manuscripts on Middle American Cultural Anthropology, no. 20, University of Chicago Library.

Cancian, Francesca M. 1964. "Interaction Patterns in Zinacanteco Families," *American Sociological Review,* 29: 540-550.

______ 1965. "The Effect of Patrilocal Households on Nuclear Family Interaction in Zinacantan," *Estudios de Cultura Maya,* 5: 299-315.

Cancian, Frank. 1964. "Some Aspects of the Social and Religious Organization of a Maya Society," *Actas y Memorias del XXXV Congreso Internacional de Americanistas,* 1:335-343.

______ 1965. *Economics and Prestige in a Maya Community: The Religious Cargo System in Zinacantan.* Stanford: Stanford University Press.

______ 1972. *Change and Uncertainty in a Peasant Economy: The Maya Corn Farmers of Zinacantan.* Stanford: Stanford University Press.

Cantor, Charles R. 1970. "An Analysis of the Principles of Ranking in Zinacanteco Ceremonies," unpublished MS., Harvard Chiapas Project.

Caso, Alfonso. 1971. "¿Religión o Religiones Mesoamericanas?" in *Verhandlungen des XXXVIII Internationalen Amerikanisten-kongresses.* Stuttgart-Munich, August 1968, band III, pp. 189-200.

Clay, Jason. 1971. "Final Report on the Pasteʔ Pipeline," unpublished MS., Harvard Chiapas Project.

Coe, Michael D. 1956. "The Funerary Temple among the Classic Maya," *Southwestern Journal of Anthropology,* 12: 387-394.

______ 1962. *Mexico.* New York: Frederick A. Praeger.

______ 1965. "A Model of Ancient Community Structure in the Maya Lowlands," *Southwestern Journal of Anthropology,* 21: 97-114.

Colby, Benjamin N. 1959. "A Field Sketch of Some Recurring Themes and Tendencies in Zinacantan Culture," unpublished MS., Harvard Chiapas Project.

______ 1966. *Ethnic Relations in the Chiapas Highlands.* Santa Fe: Museum of New Mexico Press.

______ 1967. "Psychological Orientations," in

Manning Nash, ed., *Social Anthropology of Middle America*, vol. 6 of *Handbook of Middle American Indians*, ed. by Robert Wauchope. Austin: University of Texas Press, pp. 416-431.

Colby, Lore M. 1964. "Zinacantan Tzotzil Sound and Word Structure," unpublished diss., Harvard University.

Collier, George A. 1966. "Categorias del Color en Zinacantan," in Vogt, *Los Zinacantecos: Un Pueblo Tzotzil de Los Altos de Chiapas*, pp. 414-432.

______ 1975. *Fields of the Tzotzil: The Ecological Bases of Tradition in Highland Chiapas*. Austin: University of Texas Press.

Collier, Jane Fishburne. 1968. *Courtship and Marriage in Zinacantan, Chiapas, Mexico*. Middle American Research Institute, publication 25. New Orleans: Tulane.

______ 1973. *Law and Social Change in Zinacantan*. Stanford: Stanford University Press.

Currier, Richard L. 1966. "The Hot-Cold Syndrome and Symbolic Balance in Mexican and Spanish-American Folk Medicine," *Ethnology*, 5: 251-263.

Douglas, Mary. 1966. *Purity and Danger*. London: Routledge and Kegan Paul.

Early, John D. 1965. "The Sons of San Lorenzo in Zinacantan," unpublished diss., Harvard University.

Edmonson, Munro S. 1971. *The Book of Counsel: The Popol Vuh of the Quiche Maya of Guatemala*. Middle American Research Institute, publication 35. New Orleans: Tulane.

Englander, Marilyn. 1970. "The Fiesta of San Sebastián," unpublished MS., Harvard Chiapas Project.

Fabrega, Horacio, Jr. 1970a. "On the Specificity of Folk Illnesses," *Southwestern Journal of Anthropology*, 26: 305-314.

______ 1970b. "Dynamics of Medical Practice in a Folk Community," *Milbank Memorial Fund Quarterly*, 48: 391-412.

______ and Daniel B. Silver. 1970. "Some Social and Psychological Properties of Zinacanteco Shamans," *Behavioral Science*, 15: 471-486.

______ 1973. *Illness and Shamanistic Curing in Zinacantan: An Ethnomedical Analysis*. Stanford: Stanford University Press.

Firth, Raymond. 1963. "Offering and Sacrifice: Problems of Organization," *Journal of the Royal Anthropological Institute*, 93: 12-24.

Fletcher, Christopher R. 1970. "The Drama of the Torito," unpublished MS., Harvard Chiapas Project.

Foster, George M. 1944. "Nagualism in Mexico and Guatemala," *Acta Americana*, 2: 85-103.

______ 1948. *Empire's Children: The People of Tzintzuntzan*. Washington: Smithsonian Institution, Institute of Social Anthropology, publication 6.

______ 1953. "Relationships Between Spanish and Spanish-American Folk Medicine," *Journal of American Folklore*, 66: 201-217.

______ 1960. *Culture and Conquest: America's Spanish Heritage*. Viking Fund Publications in Anthropology 27. Chicago: Quadrangle.

Frazer, James G. 1911-1915. *The Golden Bough: A Study in Magic and Religion*. 12 vols. London: Macmillan and Co.

Garcia de León, Antonio. 1971. *Los Elementos de Tzotzil Colonial y Moderno*. Mexico: Universidad Nacional Autonóma de México.

Gates, William. 1932. *The Dresden Codex Reproduced from Tracings of the Original Colorings and Finished by Hand*. Maya Society Publications, no. 2. Baltimore: Johns Hopkins University.

Geertz, Clifford. 1957. "Ritual and Social Change: A Javanese Example," *American Anthropologist*, 59: 32-54.

______ 1965. "Religion as a Cultural System," in Michael Banton, ed., *Anthropological Approaches to the Study of Religion*. New York: Frederick A. Praeger, pp. 1-46.

Gossen, Gary H. 1972. "Temporal and Spatial Equivalents in Chamula Ritual Symbolism," in

William A. Lessa and Evon Z. Vogt, eds., *Reader in Comparative Religion: An Anthropological Approach.* New York: Harper and Row, pp. 135-149.

______ 1974a. *Chamulas in the World of the Sun.* Cambridge, Mass.: Harvard University Press.

______ 1974b. "A Chamula Calendar Board from Chiapas, Mexico," in Norman Hammond, ed., *Meso-American Archaeology: New Approaches.* Austin: University of Texas Press, pp. 217-254.

Greene, Merle, Robert L. Rands, and John A. Graham. 1972. *Maya Sculpture.* Berkeley: Lederer, Street and Zeus.

Greenhouse, Carol J. 1971. "Litigant Choice: Secular and Non-Secular Options in Zinacanteco Conflict Resolution," unpublished thesis, Harvard College.

Guarnaccia, Peter J. 1972. "Land and Tortillas: Land Reform in a Maya Indian Village in Mexico," unpublished thesis, Harvard College.

Gudeman, Stephen. 1971. "The *Compadrazgo* as a Reflection of the Natural and Spiritual Person," *Proceedings of the Royal Anthropological Institute of Great Britain and Ireland,* 1971: 45-71.

Hamilton, Bruce. 1970. "The Change Rituals of the Zinacanteco Cargo System," unpublished MS., Harvard Chiapas Project.

Haviland, John B. 1966. "Vob: Traditional Music in Zinacantan," unpublished MS., Harvard Chiapas Project.

______ 1971. "Gossip, Gossips, and Gossiping in Zinacantan," unpublished diss., Harvard University.

Herskovits, Melville J. 1948. *Man and His Works.* New York: Alfred A. Knopf.

Hertz, Robert. 1960. *Death and the Right Hand.* London: Cohen and West.

Holland, William. 1963. *Medicina Maya en Los Altos de Chiapas: Un Estudio del Cambio Socio-Cultural.* Colección de Antropología Social, vol. 2. Mexico: Instituto Nacional Indigenista.

Hubert, Henri, and Marcel Mauss. 1964. *Sacrifice: Its Nature and Function.* Chicago: The University of Chicago Press.

Jakobson, Roman. 1966. "Grammatical Parallelism and Its Russian Facet," *Language,* 42: 398-429.

______ and Morris Halle. 1956. *Fundamentals of Language.* The Hague: Mouton and Co.

Kaufman, Terrence S. 1969. "Some Recent Hypotheses on Maya Diversification," working paper no. 26, Language-Behavior Research Laboratory, University of California, Berkeley.

______ 1971. "Materiales Lingüísticos para el Estudio de las Relaciones Internas y Externas de la Familia de Idiomas Mayanos," in Evon Z. Vogt and Alberto Ruz L., eds., *Desarrollo Cultural de los Mayas.* 2nd ed. Mexico: Universidad Nacional Autónoma de México, pp. 81-136.

Kelley, David H. 1962. "Glyphic Evidence for a Dynastic Sequence at Quiriguá, Guatemala," *American Antiquity,* 27: 323-335.

Köhler, Ulrich. n.d. "Reflections on Zinacantan's Role in Aztec Trade with Soconusco," in Thomas A. Lee, Jr., and Carlos Navarrete, eds., *Mesoamerican Routes of Communication and Cultural Contact.* Provo, Utah: New World Archaeological Foundation.

La Farge, Oliver, and Douglas Byers. 1931. *The Year Bearer's People.* Middle American Research Institute, publication 3. New Orleans: Tulane.

Langer, Suzanne. 1953. *Feeling and Form.* New York: Scribner's.

______ 1960. *Philosophy in a New Key.* Cambridge, Mass.: Harvard University Press.

Laughlin, Robert M. 1962a. "Through the Looking Glass: Reflections on Zinacantan Courtship and Marriage," unpublished diss., Harvard University.

______ 1962b. "El Símbolo de la Flor en la Religión de Zinacantan," *Estudios de Cultura Maya,* 2: 123-139.

______ 1975. *The Great Tzotzil Dictionary of San Lorenzo Zinacantán.* Washington: Smithsonian Institution, Smithsonian Contributions to Anthropology, no. 19.

______ in press. *Of Shoes and Ships and Sealing Wax: Sundries from Zinacantan.* Smithsonian Contributions to Anthropology.

Leach, Edmund. 1961. "Two Essays Concerning the Symbolic Representation of Time," in *Rethinking Anthropology.* London: The Athlone Press, pp. 124-136.

______ 1966. "Ritualization in Man in Relation to Conceptual and Social Development," *Philosophical Transactions of the Royal Society of London,* 251: 403-408.

______ 1967. "Brain-Twister," *New York Review of Books,* October 12, 1967, pp. 6-10.

______ 1970. *Claude Lévi-Strauss.* New York: The Viking Press.

Lee, Thomas A., Jr. 1972. "Jmetic Lubton: Some Modern and Pre-Hispanic Maya Ceremonial Customs in the Highlands of Chiapas, Mexico," *Papers of the New World Archaeological Foundation,* no. 29. Provo, Utah: New World Archaeological Foundation.

Lennihan, Marion. 1970. "The Great Vision: Symbolism of the MUK'TA ˀILEL," unpublished MS., Harvard Chiapas Project.

León-Portilla, Miguel. 1968. *Tiempo y Realidad en el Pensamiento Maya.* Mexico: Universidad Nacional Autónoma de México.

1973. *Time and Reality in the Thought of the Maya.* Boston: Beacon Press (English Translation of 1968).

Leslie, Charles M. 1960. *Now We Are Civilized: A Study of the World View of the Zapotec Indians of Mitla, Oaxaca.* Detroit: Wayne State University Press.

Lévi-Strauss, Claude. 1963. *Totemism.* Boston: Beacon Press.

______ 1966. *The Savage Mind.* Chicago: University of Chicago Press.

Lewis, Oscar. 1951. *Life in a Mexican Village: Tepoztlán Restudied.* Urbana: University of Illinois Press.

Lodge, Dorothy. 1971. "An Analysis of the Zinacantan Rituals from Birth to Marriage," unpublished MS., Harvard Chiapas Project.

Marcus, Joyce. 1970. "An Analysis of Color-Direction Symbolism among the Mayas," unpublished MS. for Anthropology 260, 1969-70, Peabody Museum, Harvard University.

Mauss, Marcel. 1954. *The Gift: Forms and Functions of Exchange in Archaic Societies.* Glencoe: The Free Press.

McQuown, Norman A. 1971. "Los Orígenes y la Diferenciación de los Mayas Según se Infiere del Estudio Comparativo de las Lenguas Mayanas," in Vogt and Ruz, *Desarrollo Cultural de los Mayas,* pp. 49-80.

Miller, Arthur G. 1974. "The Iconography of the Painting in the Temple of the Diving God, Tulum, Quintana Roo: The Twisted Cords," in Hammond, *Meso-American Archaeology.*

Mintz, Sidney W., and Eric R. Wolf. 1950. "An Analysis of Ritual Co-Parenthood (*Compadrazgo*)," *Southwestern Journal of Anthropology,* 6: 341-368.

Needham, Rodney. 1967. "Percussion and Transition," *Man,* II: 606-614.

Nicholson, Henry B. 1971. "Religion in Pre-Hispanic Central Mexico," in Gordon F. Ekholm and Ignacio Bernal, eds., *Archaeology of Northern Mesoamerica,* vol. 10 of *Handbook of Middle American Indians,* ed. by Robert Wauchope. Austin: University of Texas Press, pp. 395-446.

Opler, Morris E. 1936. "An Interpretation of Ambivalence of Two American Indian Tribes," *Journal of American Psychology,* 8: 82-115.

Pellizzi, Francesco. 1973. "Chickens and Other Bipeds: Miscellaneous Notes on the 'Great Vision' Healing Ceremonies and Related Practices of the Zinacantecos," unpublished MS., Harvard Chiapas Project.

______ n.d. "Witchcraft in Zinacantan," unpublished diss., Harvard University (in preparation).

Peñafiel, Antonio. 1885. *Nombres Geográficos de México: Católogo Alfabético de los Nombres de*

Lugar Pertenecientes al Idioma Nahuatl. Mexico: Secretaría de Fomento.

Phelps, Karin. 1970. "The T'ENT'EN Drum and Percussion in Zinacantan," unpublished MS., Harvard Chiapas Project.

Pope, Carolyn. 1969. "The Funeral Ceremony in Zinacantan," unpublished thesis, Radcliffe College.

Proskouriakoff, Tatiana. 1960. "Historical Implications of a Pattern of Dates at Piedras Negras, Guatemala," *American Antiquity*, 25: 454-475.

______ 1963-64. "Historical Data in the Inscriptions of Yaxchilán," in *Estudios de Cultura Maya*, 3: 149-167, and 4: 177-202.

Redfield, Robert. 1936. "The Coati and the Ceiba," *Maya Research*, 3: 231-243.

______ 1941. *The Folk Culture of Yucatan.* Chicago: University of Chicago Press.

______ and Alfonso Villa Rojas. 1934. *Chan Kom: A Maya Village.* Chicago: University of Chicago Press.

Reichel-Dolmatoff, Gerardo. 1971. *Amazonian Cosmos: The Sexual and Religious Symbolism of the Tukano Indians.* Chicago: University of Chicago Press.

Rosaldo, Michelle Zimbalist. 1972. "Metaphors and Folk Classification," *Southwestern Journal of Anthropology*, 28: 83-99.

Rosaldo, Renato I., Jr. 1968. "Metaphors of Hierarchy in a Mayan Ritual," *American Anthropologist*, 70: 524-536.

Roys, Ralph L. 1933. *The Book of Chilam Balam of Chumayel.* Washington: Carnegie Institution of Washington, publication 438. Norman: University of Oklahoma Press, 1967.

Rush, Timothy. 1969. "Digging for Bells in the Highlands of Chiapas," unpublished MS., Harvard Chiapas Project.

Saffo, Paul. 1973. "Evidence of Symbolic Celestial Movement in Zinacantan and Chamula," unpublished MS., Harvard Chiapas Project.

Sahagún, Bernardino de. 1950-69. *Florentine Codex: General History of the Things of New Spain.* 12 vols. Translation from the Aztec into English, with notes and illustrations, by A. J. O. Anderson and C. E. Dibble. Santa Fe: University of Utah and School of American Research.

Saville, Marshall H. 1925. *The Wood-Carver's Art in Ancient Mexico.* New York: Museum of the American Indian, Heye Foundation.

Scott, Mary E. 1971. "K'IN KRUS and Year Renewal Ceremonies in Zinacantan," unpublished MS., Harvard Chiapas Project.

Silver, Daniel B. 1966a. "Shamanism in Zinacantan," unpublished diss., Harvard University.

______ 1966b. "Enfermedad y Curación en Zinacantan: Esquema Provisional," in Vogt, *Los Zinacantecos: Un Pueblo Tzotzil de los Altos de Chiapas*, pp. 455-473.

Smith, A. Ledyard. 1962. "Residential and Associated Structures at Mayapán," in H. E. D. Pollock, R. L. Roys, Tatiana Proskouriakoff, and A. L. Smith, eds., *Mayapán, Yucatan, Mexico.* Washington: Carnegie Institution of Washington, publication 619.

Thompson, J. Eric S. 1934. *Sky Bearers, Colors and Directions in Maya and Mexican Religion.* Washington: Carnegie Institution of Washington, publication 436, pp. 209-242.

______ 1954. *The Rise and Fall of Maya Civilization.* Norman: University of Oklahoma Press.

______ 1959. "The Role of Caves in Maya Culture," *Mitterlungen aus dem Museum für völkerkunde.* Hamburg, Sonderdruck, 25: 122-129.

______ 1960. *Maya Hieroglyphic Writing.* Norman: University of Oklahoma Press.

______ 1970. *Maya History and Religion.* Norman: University of Oklahoma Press.

Thomsen, Evelyn R. 1966. "How to Handle an Earth Lord: An Analysis of Myths, Prayers, and Rituals which focus upon the Waterholes of Zinacantan," unpublished thesis, Vassar College.

Tozzer, Alfred M. 1941. *Landa's Relación de las Cosas de Yucatan.* Papers of the Peabody

Museum of American Archaeology and Ethnology, vol. 18. Cambridge, Mass.: Harvard University.

Townsend, Richard. (In preparation.) "Transformation and Continuity in Aztec Sculpture," unpublished diss., Harvard University.

Trosper, Ronald L. 1967. "Tradition and Economic Growth: Gradual Change in a Mexican Indian Community," unpublished thesis, Harvard College.

Turner, Victor. 1967. *The Forest of Symbols: Aspects of Ndembu Ritual.* Ithaca: Cornell University Press.

______ 1968. *The Drums of Affliction: A Study of Religious Processes among the Ndembu of Zambia.* Oxford: Oxford University Press.

______ 1969. *The Ritual Process: Structure and Anti-Structure.* Chicago: Aldine.

Tylor, Edward B. 1873. *Primitive Culture: Researches into the Development of Mythology, Philosophy, Religion, Language, Art and Custom.* 2nd ed., 2 vols. London: John Murray.

Uribe, Elena. 1966. "Algunas Consideraciones sobre el Compadrazgo en Mesoamerica," unpublished MS., Harvard Chiapas Project.

Van Gennep, Arnold L. 1909. *Les Rites de Passage.* Paris: E. Nourry.

Villa Rojas, Alfonso. 1963. "El nagualismo como recurso de control social entre los grupos mayances de Chiapas, Mexico," *Estudios de Cultura Maya,* 3: 243-260.

Villagutierre y Soto-Mayor, Juan de. 1933. *Historia de la conquista de la provincia de el Itzá reducción, y progresos de la de el Lacandon, y otras naciones de indios bárbaros, de la mediaciones de el reyno de Guatimala, a las provincias de Yucatán, en la América septentrional.* 2nd ed. Guatemala: Biblioteca "Goathemala" de la Sociedad de Geografía e Historia. (Originally published in 1701.)

Vogt, Evon Z. 1960. "On the Concepts of Structure and Process in Cultural Anthropology," *American Anthropologist,* 62: 18-33.

______ 1961. "Some Aspects of Zinacantan Settlement Patterns and Ceremonial Organization," *Estudios de Cultura Maya,* 1: 131-146.

______ 1964a. "Some Implications of Zinacantan Social Structure for the Study of the Ancient Maya," *Actas y Memorias del XXXV Congreso Internacional de Americanistas.* 1: 307-319.

______ 1964b. "Ancient Maya Concepts in Contemporary Zinacantan Religion," *VIe Congrés International des Sciences Anthropologiques et Ethnologiques.* Paris: Musée de l'Homme, 2: 497-502.

______ 1964c. "Ancient Maya and Contemporary Tzotzil Cosmology: A Comment on Some Methodological Problems," *American Antiquity,* 30: 192-195.

______ 1965a. "Zinacanteco 'Souls,' " *Man,* 29: 33-35.

______ 1965b. "Structural and Conceptual Replication in Zinacantan Culture," *American Anthropologist,* 67: 342-353.

______ 1965c. "Ceremonial Organization in Zinacantan," *Ethnology,* 4: 39-52.

______ 1966. (Editor) *Los Zinacantecos: Un Pueblo Tzotzil de los Altos de Chiapas.* Colección de Antropología Social, vol. 7. Mexico: Instituto Nacional Indigenista.

______ 1968. "Culture Change," in David L. Sills, ed., *International Encyclopedia of the Social Sciences.* vol. 3, pp. 554-558.

______ 1969. *Zinacantan: A Maya Community in the Highlands of Chiapas.* Cambridge, Mass.: The Belknap Press of Harvard University Press.

______ 1970a. "Human Souls and Animal Spirits in Zinacantan," *Échanges et communications: Mélanges offerts à Claude Lévi-Strauss à l'occasion de son 60eme anniversaire,* réunis par Jean Pouillon et Pierre Maranda. The Hague: Mouton, pp. 1148-1167.

______ 1970b. *The Zinacantecos of Mexico: A Modern Maya Way of Life.* New York: Holt, Rinehart and Winston.

______ 1971. "The Genetic Model and Maya Cultural Development," and "Summary and Appraisal," in Evon Z. Vogt and Alberto Ruz L., eds., *Desarrollo Cultural de los Mayas*, 2nd ed. Mexico: Universidad Nacional Autónoma de Mexico (first published in 1964), pp. 9-48, 409-447.

______ 1973. "Gods and Politics in Zinacantan and Chamula," *Ethnology*, 12: 99-113.

______ and Frank Cancian. 1970. "Social Integration and the Classic Maya: Some Problems in Haviland's Argument," *American Antiquity*, 35: 101-102.

______ and Catherine C. Vogt. 1970. "Lévi-Strauss among the Maya," *Man*, V: 379-392.

Wallace, Anthony F. C. 1956. "Revitalization Movements," *American Anthropologist*, 58: 264-281.

Wasserstrom, Robert F. 1970. "Our Lady of the Salt," unpublished thesis, Harvard College.

Weathers, Nadine. 1947. "Tzotzil Phonemes with Special Reference to Allophones of B," *International Journal of American Linguistics*, 13: 108-111.

Werby, Elisabeth. 1971. "Tzotzil Speech and Couplet Pair Formations in Zinacantan," unpublished MS., Harvard Chiapas Project.

Whelan, Frederick G., III. 1967. "The Passing of the Years," unpublished MS., Harvard Chiapas Project.

Willard, Theodore A. 1933. *The Codex Perez: An Ancient Mayan Hieroglyphic Book*. Glendale, Calif.

Ximénez, Francisco. 1929-31. *Historia de la Provincia de San Vicente de Chiapas y Guatemala de la Orden de Predicadores*. Guatemala: Biblioteca Goathemala, vols. I, II, III, LXXII.

Index

Book design by Marianne Perlak

Composed in Mallard on Compugraphic by
Stephen Daye Associates, Inc.

Display type/Roberta

Paper/Glatco Matte, Smooth, 70 pound;
supplied by Pratt Paper Company

Printed and bound by
Halliday Lithograph Corporation